HIGH COURT CASE SUMMARIES

CRIMINAL PROCEDURE

Keyed to Dressler and Thomas's Casebook on Criminal Procedure
4th Edition

Memory Graphics by Stu Rees (www.stus.com)

WEST®

A Thomson Reuters business

D1484605

Mat #41047882

© West, a Thomson business, 2005
© 2007 Thomson/West
© 2010 Thomson Reuters
    610 Opperman Drive
    St. Paul, MN 55123
    1–800–313–9378
Printed in the United States of America

ISBN: 978–0–314–26623–1

Table of Contents

Alphabetical Table of Cases

Teague v. Lane, 489 U.S. 288, 109 S.Ct. 1060, 103 L.Ed.2d 334 (1989), 341
Terry v. Ohio, 392 U.S. 1, 88 S.Ct. 1868, 20 L.Ed.2d 889 (1968), 77
Thomas, United States v., 116 F.3d 606 (2nd Cir.1997), 275, 297
Thompson v. City of Louisville, 362 U.S. 199, 80 S.Ct. 624, 4 L.Ed.2d 654 (1960), 337

United States v. _____ (see opposing party)

Vilardi, People v., 76 N.Y.2d 67, 556 N.Y.S.2d 518, 555 N.E.2d 915 (N.Y.1990), 217

Wade, United States v., 388 U.S. 218, 87 S.Ct. 1926, 18 L.Ed.2d 1149 (1967), 187
Wainwright v. Sykes, 433 U.S. 72, 97 S.Ct. 2497, 53 L.Ed.2d 594 (1977), 343
Warden, Md. Penitentiary v. Hayden, 387 U.S. 294, 87 S.Ct. 1642, 18 L.Ed.2d 782 (1967), 45

Watts, United States v., 519 U.S. 148, 117 S.Ct. 633, 136 L.Ed.2d 554 (1997), 306
Weeks v. United States, 232 U.S. 383, 34 S.Ct. 341, 58 L.Ed. 652 (1914), 11
White, United States v., 401 U.S. 745, 91 S.Ct. 1122, 28 L.Ed.2d 453 (1971), 21
Whren v. United States, 517 U.S. 806, 116 S.Ct. 1769, 135 L.Ed.2d 89 (1996), 57
Williams v. Florida, 399 U.S. 78, 90 S.Ct. 1893, 26 L.Ed.2d 446 (1970), 221
Williams v. People of State of N.Y., 337 U.S. 241, 69 S.Ct. 1079, 93 L.Ed. 1337 (1949), 305
Williams, United States v., 504 U.S. 36, 112 S.Ct. 1735, 118 L.Ed.2d 352 (1992), 211
Winship, In re, 397 U.S. 358, 90 S.Ct. 1068, 25 L.Ed.2d 368 (1970), 337
Wolf v. People of the State of Colo., 338 U.S. 25, 69 S.Ct. 1359, 93 L.Ed. 1782 (1949), 13
Wong Sun v. United States, 371 U.S. 471, 83 S.Ct. 407, 9 L.Ed.2d 441 (1963), 115

CHAPTER ONE

The Criminal Process: Failure and Legitimacy

Powell v. Alabama

Instant Facts: Nonresident black defendants accused of rape in Alabama state court received the death penalty after trial by jury.

Black Letter Rule: A criminal defendant in state court must be given ample opportunity to retain counsel before trial, and, if none is retained, an attorney must be appointed to represent him or her.

Brown v. Mississippi

Instant Facts: Three defendants found guilty of murder argued that their convictions were based on involuntary confessions obtained by physical violence and moved for a new trial, which the state supreme court denied.

Black Letter Rule: Confessions obtained through physical brutality and violence are inconsistent with the due process requirements of the Fourteenth Amendment to the U.S. Constitution and are inadmissible.

Duncan v. Louisiana

Instant Facts: Duncan (D) was denied his request for a jury trial on an assault charge because the Louisiana Constitution provided a right to jury trial only in felony cases.

Black Letter Rule: Under the Sixth Amendment, all criminal defendants have a constitutional right to trial by jury.

Powell v. Alabama

(*Convicted Rapist*) v. (*Prosecuting Government*)

287 U.S. 45, 53 S. Ct. 55, 77 L. Ed. 158 (1932)

CRIMINAL DEFENDANTS MUST BE AFFORDED AN OPPORTUNITY TO RETAIN COUNSEL

When you say the prosecution "must" turn over exculpatory evidence, is that a hard New York "must", or a squishy Supreme Court "must"?

stus.com

■ **INSTANT FACTS** Nonresident black defendants accused of rape in Alabama state court received the death penalty after trial by jury.

■ **BLACK LETTER RULE** A criminal defendant in state court must be given ample opportunity to retain counsel before trial, and, if none is retained, an attorney must be appointed to represent him or her.

■ **PROCEDURAL BASIS**

Certiorari to review decisions of the Alabama Supreme Court affirming judgments of a trial court convicting the defendants.

■ **FACTS**

Several non-resident black defendants were charged with rape in Alabama state court. The court appointed all the members of the state bar to represent the defendants for purposes of arraignment. Issuing no order appointing counsel after arraignment, the court assumed counsel would continue representing the defendants at trial. The defendants were arraigned and pleaded not guilty. The defendants did not personally retain counsel, and they were not given an opportunity to contact family and friends to arrange for counsel. Trial commenced six days later, and a Tennessee lawyer, Mr. Roddy, indicated to the court that he would like to participate in the defense with a member of the state bar appointed by the court. No local counsel was appointed, although on the morning of the trial, a local attorney, Mr. Moody, came forward to assist Mr. Roddy for purposes of that day's trials without reviewing the evidence or questioning witnesses. The defendants were convicted by a jury and given the death penalty. The Alabama Supreme Court affirmed the convictions.

■ **ISSUE**

Where illiterate non-resident criminal defendants are not appointed counsel prior to trial in a state court proceeding, are the defendants deprived of their Fourteenth Amendment right to counsel?

■ **DECISION AND RATIONALE**

(Sutherland, J.) Yes. State-court criminal defendants must be provided ample opportunity to retain counsel before trial and, if none is retained, an attorney must be appointed to represent them. A trial court bears the obligation to ensure that each defendant has had an opportunity to consult with an attorney. If a defendant has not chosen counsel, the trial court must appoint counsel if the defendant so chooses. By not appointing counsel following arraignment, the court deprived the defendants of their due process right to consult with an attorney and thoroughly prepare a defense for trial. The right to counsel is essential to a defendant's due process right to be heard. Without the assistance of counsel, defendants generally lack the skill and knowledge required to present their innocence, though their defense may be valid. This is especially true in this case. The defendants were young, illiterate, and ignorant of the laws and customs of the Alabama courts. Their friends and families resided in other states, making communication difficult. Under such circumstances, the court must afford a defendant in a capital case ample time and opportunity to retain counsel. If, after time is afforded, a defendant is unable to retain counsel, a court must promptly appoint counsel to assist with the defense. Reversed.

■ DISSENT

(Butler, J.) The defendants had representation at trial and were not deprived of their due process rights. If local counsel, who had come forward only on the morning of the trial, had insufficient opportunity to prepare for trial, counsel should have asked to postpone trial until he had time to prepare. Because both he and Mr. Roddy failed to so move, the defendants were afforded their due process rights at trial.

Analysis:

The Fourteenth Amendment does not explicitly afford defendants the right to counsel, as that constitutional protection is contained in the Sixth Amendment. The Court relied upon the Fourteenth Amendment in *Powell* because the issue was not whether the defendants had a Sixth Amendment right to counsel, which then applied only to federal criminal defendants, but whether state criminal defendants were deprived of their Fourteenth Amendment right to due process. While *Powell* laid the groundwork for right to counsel under other circumstances, its holding was specifically limited to indigent defendants in a state capital case. Fundamental to the Court's decision was the defendants' youth, ignorance, and illiteracy, requiring Fourteenth Amendment protections in a capital case.

■ CASE VOCABULARY

RIGHT TO COUNSEL: A criminal defendant's constitutional right, guaranteed by the Sixth Amendment, to representation by a court-appointed lawyer if the defendant cannot afford to hire one.

Brown v. Mississippi

(Murder Defendants) v. *(Prosecuting State)*

297 U.S. 278, 56 S. Ct. 461, 80 L. Ed. 682 (1936)

CONFESSIONS OBTAINED BY VIOLENCE AND THREATS VIOLATE DUE PROCESS

I'm a performance piece titled "Coerced Confession".

stus.com

■ **INSTANT FACTS** Three defendants found guilty of murder argued that their convictions were based on involuntary confessions obtained by physical violence and moved for a new trial, which the state supreme court denied.

■ **BLACK LETTER RULE** Confessions obtained through physical brutality and violence are inconsistent with the due process requirements of the Fourteenth Amendment to the U.S. Constitution and are inadmissible.

■ PROCEDURAL BASIS

Certiorari to review a decision of the Mississippi Supreme Court affirming conviction and denying the defendants' motion for a new trial.

■ FACTS

The Petitioners were indicted and charged with the murder of Raymond Stewart five days following his death. The only evidence sufficient to convict the defendants was their own confessions. The confessions were the result of continued physical coercion. One of the defendants (Ellington) was hanged by a rope by a sheriff's deputy (Dial). Each time Ellington was released, he was questioned about his role in the killing and each time he denied any participation in it. Ellington was eventually released, but within a few days, Dial returned to Ellington's home and arrested him. En route to the jail, Dial stopped, and this time Ellington was severely whipped. He was told the abuse would continue until he provided a confession acceptable to Dial. The other two defendants, Brown and Shields, were subsequently arrested and beaten with a leather strap and belt buckle. They also subsequently confessed to the terms Dial demanded in order to stop the beatings. The defendants entered pleas of not guilty and were given court-appointed counsel. At trial, each defendant showed evidenced of his earlier beating. Notwithstanding their physical appearance, the court received evidence of the defendants' confessions over the objections of defendants' counsel that the confessions were not free and voluntary. Each defendant testified at trial that his confession was false and had been given only to avoid infliction of further physical abuse. At the request of defendants' counsel, the jury was instructed that, should they determine the confessions were not voluntary and not true, the confessions should not be considered as evidence. By the end of the second day, the defendants had been found guilty and were sentenced to death. On appeal to the state supreme court, the judgment was affirmed and a motion for a new trial denied. The United States Supreme Court granted certiorari.

■ ISSUE

Does the due process requirement of the Fourteenth Amendment prohibit the use of confessions that were the result of brutality and violence committed by officers of the State?

■ DECISION AND RATIONALE

(Hughes, J.) Yes. Confessions obtained through physical brutality and violence are inconsistent with the due process requirements of the Fourteenth Amendment to the U.S. Constitution and are inadmissible.

A state is free to establish its own judicial procedures only within the confines of the Fourteenth Amendment. When a state policy violates the Due Process Clause, it is unconstitutional. The violence perpetrated on these three defendants was so severe that the physical evidence of their abuse had to be clear and apparent to all members of the court. Deputy Dial, who instigated the physical torture of the defendants, was present in the courtroom and testified freely about the whippings. The state argued that the defendants' counsel had not appropriately preserved this issue for appeal by (1) failing to renew his objection to the confessions after the circumstances surrounding the confessions had been established and (2) failing to move that the evidence be excluded. It would be impermissible to foreclose an avenue for appeal to the defendants, however, based on a trivial wrong committed by their counsel when the defendants had been so severely mistreated and denied due process. Fully aware of the torture and violence utilized to obtain the defendants' confessions, and recognizing that no other evidence supported the convictions, the court was required to exclude the confessions, even without objection from counsel, as contrary to fundamental notions in the Due Process Clause. Reversed.

Analysis:

The Fourteenth Amendment's due process requirement does not impose any specific set of rules on the state courts. The Court here went so far as to acknowledge that a state is free to regulate the procedures of its own courts, and may even eliminate trial by jury or the indictment process, but it recognized a limit on the state's power, explaining that a state cannot substitute a procedure that is offensive to the fundamental principles of justice. In reaching its decision, the Court appears to be quite upset by the fact that so many of the participants involved in the charade of a trial knew about the physical abuse of the defendants and turned a blind eye.

■ CASE VOCABULARY

CONFESSION: A criminal suspect's acknowledgement of guilt, usually in writing and often including details about the crime.

DUE PROCESS: The constitutional guarantee of notice and the opportunity to be heard and to defend in an orderly proceeding adapted to the nature of case; the guarantee of due process requires that every person have the protection of a day in court and the benefit of general law.

INTERROGATION: The formal or systematic questioning of a person, especially intensive questioning by the police, usually of a person arrested for or suspected of committing a crime.

Duncan v. Louisiana

(Defendant Convicted of Assault) v. *(State Government)*

391 U.S. 145, 88 S. Ct. 1444, 20 L. Ed. 2d 491 (1968)

THE SIXTH AMENDMENT AFFORDS DEFENDANTS A RIGHT TO A JURY TRIAL

■ **INSTANT FACTS** Duncan (D) was denied his request for a jury trial on an assault charge because the Louisiana Constitution provided a right to jury trial only in felony cases.

■ **BLACK LETTER RULE** Under the Sixth Amendment, all criminal defendants have a constitutional right to trial by jury.

■ **PROCEDURAL BASIS**

Certiorari to review the defendant's conviction.

■ **FACTS**

Duncan (D) was charged with simple assault in Louisiana state court. Duncan (D) requested a jury trial, which was denied because the Louisiana Constitution provided for jury trials only in felony cases. Duncan (D) was convicted and sentenced to sixty days in a local prison and a fine.

■ **ISSUE**

Is the Sixth Amendment's right to trial by jury incorporated in the Fourteenth Amendment?

■ **DECISION AND RATIONALE**

(White, J.) Yes. The Sixth Amendment guarantees all criminal defendants the constitutional right to a jury trial. The right to a trial by jury has long been considered "fundamental to the American scheme of justice." In the years leading up to the drafting of the Constitution, trial by jury had been a prominent right in England and carried forward to the state constitutions of the original thirteen colonies as a protection against oppression by the government. In light of this historical perspective, the right to trial by jury is afforded to all criminal defendants if such a right would be afforded in a federal court. Reversed.

■ **CONCURRENCE**

(Black, J.) Not only is the Sixth Amendment incorporated in the Fourteenth Amendment, but all provisions of the Bill of Rights are applicable to the states. The Fourteenth Amendment forbids a state from enacting or enforcing "any law which shall abridge the privileges and immunities of the citizens of the United States." The right to claim the protections afforded by the Bill of Rights is a fundamental privilege of American citizens. The dissent's view that the Due Process Clause provides no "permanent meaning" and is left to the subjective interpretation of the Court on a case-by-case basis strips the Fourteenth Amendment of the protections established to limit governmental power.

(Fortas, J.) While states are bound by the Sixth Amendment's right to a jury trial, the states need not follow federal procedures governing the operation of trial by jury. Federal notions of due process do not infringe upon the construction of that term by the states. Principles of federalism require that states be free to determine for themselves how due process can be achieved, because federal practices like unanimous verdicts and twelve-member juries, for example, should not be thrust upon the states as long as the states otherwise maintain practices furthering the fundamental fairness required by the Fourteenth Amendment.

■ DISSENT

(Harlan, J.) The majority's decision to incorporate the Sixth Amendment is without logical reason. If the goal of the Fourteenth Amendment is to achieve fundamental fairness in the judicial system, there is no justifiable reason to hold that the requirements of the Sixth Amendment are necessary in every case considered by a state court, as not every case presents such unfairness. The Court offers no reason to declare the rights afforded by the Sixth Amendment to be fundamental, while other rights in the Bill of Rights are not. While the Fourteenth Amendment was never intended to incorporate any of the rights afforded in the Bill of Rights, such total incorporation would at a minimum provide a logical reason to support the Court's conclusion. Instead, the Due Process Clause requires only that criminal trials in the states be fundamentally fair, and trial by jury is not necessarily a requirement for fairness. Without evidence of unfairness in the trial below, due process has not been offended, and the conviction should be sustained.

Analysis:

Justice Black's concurring opinion argues for "total incorporation" of the Bill of Rights by the Fourteenth Amendment. Under this approach, the Due Process Clause extends each right protected by the Bill of Rights to the states, but creates no other rights. Refusing to apply total incorporation, the majority employed "selective incorporation," the process of selecting those rights deemed fundamentally fair to the administration of justice to be encompassed by the Due Process Clause. Justice Harlan, on the other hand, argues in his dissenting opinion that the Fourteenth Amendment does not incorporate the Bill of Rights, but serves as a means to ensure that state procedures do not result in fundamental unfairness under the Due Process Clause. While Justice Black's "total incorporation" approach never gained support in the Supreme Court, many of the rights espoused in the Bill of Rights have been selectively incorporated over time.

■ CASE VOCABULARY

INCORPORATION: The process of applying the provisions of the Bill of Rights to the states by interpreting the Fourteenth Amendment's Due Process Clause as encompassing those provisions.

CHAPTER TWO

Fourth Amendment: An Overview

Weeks v. United States

Instant Facts: Weeks (D) was convicted for using the mail to transport illegal lottery tickets based on evidence obtained from his home without a warrant.

Black Letter Rule: The Fourth Amendment forbids federal officers from obtaining evidence through unreasonable searches and seizures.

Wolf v. Colorado

Instant Facts: Not provided.

Black Letter Rule: In a prosecution in a state court for a state crime, the Fourteenth Amendment does not forbid the admission of evidence obtained by an unreasonable search and seizure.

Mapp v. Ohio

Instant Facts: Mapp (D) was convicted of possession of obscene materials after police broke into her home and seized the materials without a warrant.

Black Letter Rule: All evidence obtained by unreasonable searches and seizures in violation of the Fourth Amendment is inadmissible in state court.

Weeks v. United States

(Gambler) v. *(Prosecuting Government)*

232 U.S. 383, 34 S. Ct. 341, 58 L. Ed. 652 (1914)

OBTAINING EVIDENCE WITHOUT A SEARCH WARRANT MAY VIOLATE THE FOURTH AMENDMENT

■ **INSTANT FACTS** Weeks (D) was convicted for using the mail to transport illegal lottery tickets based on evidence obtained from his home without a warrant.

■ **BLACK LETTER RULE** The Fourth Amendment forbids federal officers from obtaining evidence through unreasonable searches and seizures.

■ PROCEDURAL BASIS

In error to the District Court of the United States for the Western District of Missouri to review a conviction for the unlawful use of the mails.

■ FACTS

Weeks (D) was arrested without a warrant after police officers entered his home with a key found outside the premises. The officers searched Weeks's (D) bedroom and confiscated various papers and lottery tickets. After delivering the evidence to a federal marshal, the marshal also entered the home without a warrant, confiscating additional papers. An indictment was issued against Weeks (D), including a count of using the mails to transport illegal lottery tickets in violation of federal law. Weeks (D) objected to the search and requested return of the items. The objection was overruled, and Weeks (D) was subsequently convicted.

■ ISSUE

Were the defendant's Fourth Amendment rights violated by the search of his home and seizure of evidence found therein by the federal marshal without a proper warrant?

■ DECISION AND RATIONALE

(Day, J.) Yes. The Fourth Amendment forbids federal officers from employing unreasonable searches and seizures to obtain evidence. It protects all individuals from unreasonable searches and seizures of their homes and personal effects. The Fourth Amendment is designed to restrict the government from procuring convictions under inappropriate circumstances. The interests of the government in punishing those guilty of committing a crime must yield to the constitutional protections afforded by the Fourth Amendment. A court may not sanction the unconstitutional conduct of law enforcement officers in defiance of the Constitution. Here, the evidence obtained by the federal marshal may not be admitted against the defendant and must be returned upon his proper application. Reversed.

Analysis:

The Court addressed only the applicability of the Fourth Amendment to the federal marshal's search and seizure, not the state police officers. While the Fourth Amendment governs those acting under color of federal law, it did not apply to the states at that time. Under *Wolf v. Colorado*, it is likely that the Court would have held that the state police's actions violated the Fourth Amendment. However, based on *Wolf*'s holding that illegally seized evidence need not be excluded in a state court proceeding, the Court may have sustained the conviction nonetheless.

■ CASE VOCABULARY

SEARCH WARRANT: A judge's written order authorizing a law enforcement officer to conduct a search of a specified place to seize evidence.

EXCLUSIONARY RULE: A rule that excludes or suppresses evidence obtained in violation of an accused person's constitutional rights.

Wolf v. Colorado

(Criminal Defendant) v. *(Prosecuting State)*
338 U.S. 25, 69 S.Ct. 1359, 93 L.Ed. 1782 (1949)

EVIDENCE MAY BE ADMISSIBLE IN A STATE PROSECUTION THAT WOULD NOT BE ALLOWED IN A FEDERAL COURT

1949

For now, states should view the exclusionary "rule" as more of a suggestion.

stus.com

■ **INSTANT FACTS** Not provided.

■ **BLACK LETTER RULE** In a prosecution in a state court for a state crime, the Fourteenth Amendment does not forbid the admission of evidence obtained by an unreasonable search and seizure.

■ **PROCEDURAL BASIS**

United States Supreme Court review of the decision of the Colorado Supreme Court admitting the evidence and sustaining the convictions.

■ **FACTS**

Not provided.

■ **ISSUE**

Does a conviction by a state court for a state offense deny the due process of law required by the Fourteenth Amendment solely because evidence that was admitted at trial was obtained under circumstances that would have rendered it inadmissible in a prosecution for violation of a federal law, in a federal court, because there was deemed to be an infraction of the Fourth Amendment?

■ **DECISION AND RATIONALE**

(Frankfurter, J.) No. In a prosecution in a state court for a state crime, the Fourteenth Amendment does not forbid the admission of evidence obtained by an unreasonable search and seizure. Due process of law conveys neither formal, nor fixed, nor narrow requirements. The Due Process Clause simply exacts from the states all that is "implicit in the concept of ordered liberty." There is no tidy formula for enforcement. However, the security of one's privacy against arbitrary intrusion by the police, which is at the core of the Fourth Amendment, is basic to a free society. It is therefore implicit in the concept of ordered liberty, and as such enforceable against the states through the Due Process Clause. We therefore have no problem saying that were a state to affirmatively sanction police incursion into privacy, it would run counter to the guaranty of the Fourteenth Amendment. The *Weeks* decision, which held that, in a federal prosecution, the Fourth Amendment bars the introduction of evidence obtained through an illegal search and seizure, was not based on the Fourth Amendment, but on the judicially created exclusionary rule. After *Weeks*, only sixteen states considering the issue adopted the *Weeks* exclusionary rule. Although the exclusionary rule might be an effective way of deterring unreasonable searches, it is not for the Court to condemn as falling below the minimal standards assured by the Due Process Clause a state's reliance upon other methods that, if consistently enforced, would be equally effective.

Analysis:

Wolf generally provides that the Fourth Amendment right to be free from unreasonable searches and seizures is incorporated by the Fourteenth Amendment and applies to the states. But a distinction must be made between a state's use of an unreasonable search and seizure to obtain evidence and the exclusion of such evidence at trial. Here, the Court was willing to allow the state to use the evidence obtained by the police to convict Wolf (D). While the right to be free from unreasonable searches and seizures is fundamental to the concept of ordered liberty, the exclusion of relevant evidence obtained in violation of the Fourth Amendment "is not an essential ingredient of the right."

■ **CASE VOCABULARY**

SEIZURE: The act or an instance of taking possession of a person or property by legal right or process, especially, in constitutional law, a confiscation or arrest that may interfere with a person's reasonable expectation of privacy.

UNREASONABLE SEARCH: A search conducted without probable cause or other considerations that would make it legally permissible.

Mapp v. Ohio

(Defendant Convicted of Possessing Obscene Materials) v. *(Prosecuting Government)*

367 U.S. 643, 81 S. Ct. 1684, 6 L. Ed. 2d 1081 (1961)

SUPREME COURT OVERRULES *WOLF v. COLORADO*

■ **INSTANT FACTS** Mapp (D) was convicted of possession of obscene materials after police broke into her home and seized the materials without a warrant.

■ **BLACK LETTER RULE** All evidence obtained by unreasonable searches and seizures in violation of the Fourth Amendment is inadmissible in state court.

■ PROCEDURAL BASIS

Certiorari to review a decision of the Ohio Supreme Court sustaining the criminal defendant's conviction.

■ FACTS

Three state police officers approached Mapp's (D) apartment searching for a bombing suspect and illegal gambling paraphernalia. When the officers knocked, Mapp (D) refused to allow them into her home without a warrant. Three hours later, the officers again approached the home, broke through the door, and entered. When Mapp (D) demanded they produce their search warrant, one officer showed her a piece of paper, which Mapp (D) seized and concealed in her shirt. A struggle ensued in which the police physically recovered the paper from Mapp (D). After placing Mapp (D) in handcuffs, the police searched through her belongings, recovering four books alleged to contain obscene materials. No warrant was ever produced. Mapp (D) was convicted of possession of lewd and lascivious materials under state law. On appeal, the Ohio Supreme Court held that while the search and seizure may have violated the Fourth Amendment, the court was not obligated to exclude the evidence at trial.

■ ISSUE

Must evidence obtained as a result of an unreasonable search and seizure be excluded in a state proceeding?

■ DECISION AND RATIONALE

(Clark, J.) Yes. The evidence obtained through unreasonable searches and seizures that violate the Fourth Amendment is inadmissible in state court. In *Wolf v. Colorado*, the Court held that while the Fourth Amendment applies to the states through the Fourteenth Amendment, the exclusionary rule set forth in *Weeks v. United States* does not. The *Wolf* Court reasoned that the right to have relevant evidence excluded at trial is not an essential element of the right to be free from unreasonable searches and seizures. Without applying the *Weeks* exclusionary rule to state violations of the Fourth Amendment, *Wolf* leaves no remedy for the constitutional violation and states are free to violate the Fourth Amendment rights of its citizens without any meaningful consequences. *Wolf v. Colorado* is therefore overruled. Reversed and remanded.

■ CONCURRENCE

(Black, J.) Nothing in the Fourth Amendment specifically or implicitly requires that evidence obtained through unreasonable searches and seizures be excluded from trial. To reach that conclusion, the

Fourth Amendment and Fifth Amendment must be read together. Reading these two together, a state may not commit unreasonable searches and seizures under the Fourth Amendment, and the Fifth Amendment requires incriminating evidence obtained in violation of the Fourth Amendment to be excluded at trial. In a case such as this, there is no substantial difference between presenting evidence obtained in violation of the Fourth Amendment and requiring a defendant to testify against herself at trial.

■ **DISSENT**

(Harlan, J.) The majority has exceeded its authority in overruling *Wolf*. While the exclusionary rule was raised as a minor contention on appeal, the focus of the appeal was on the merits—whether the Ohio law criminalizing mere possession of obscene materials violates the First Amendment as applied by the Fourteenth Amendment to the States. In overruling *Wolf*, the majority avoided this primary issue, violating principles of *stare decisis*. Aside from this, the Fourth Amendment does not require exclusion of relevant evidence against a defendant in a state proceeding. The Fourteenth Amendment, through which the majority enforces the Fourth Amendment, requires that all defendants receive due process of the law. The exclusionary rule, which is primarily procedural in nature, is but one means of ensuring due process. Federalism requires that the states be free to utilize any procedural mechanism that preserves their citizens' due process rights in state court proceedings.

Analysis:

While several justifications have been offered for application of the exclusionary rule in state court proceedings, the reasoning that has continued to gain judicial approval is the deterrence against future Fourth Amendment violations. As stated by the majority, there is little value in holding that the Constitution requires the states to refrain from unreasonable searches and seizures if evidence obtained by those constitutional violations may nonetheless be used as if no violation occurred. The deterrence rationale serves to prevent future constitutional violations rather than remedy those that have already occurred.

■ **CASE VOCABULARY**

STARE DECISIS: The doctrine of precedent, under which it is necessary for a court to follow earlier judicial decisions when the same points arise again in litigation.

CHAPTER THREE

Passing the Threshold of the Fourth Amendment

Katz v. United States

Instant Facts: Katz (D) was convicted of transmitting gaming information via telephone based on evidence obtained by FBI agents who had attached a listening device to a public telephone.

Black Letter Rule: The Fourth Amendment protects all communications that a person does not knowingly expose to the public.

United States v. White

Instant Facts: White (D) was convicted of drug charges based on the testimony of government agents who overheard incriminating conversations between the defendant and an informant by way of a listening device carried by the informant.

Black Letter Rule: A defendant bears the risk that communications with another will be transmitted, electronically or otherwise, to government agents.

Smith v. Maryland

Instant Facts: Police installed a pen register at the telephone company to monitor calls made from Smith's (D) telephone without a warrant.

Black Letter Rule: An individual assumes the risk of disclosure of information knowingly conveyed to a third party.

Kyllo v. United States

Instant Facts: Federal agents used a thermal-imaging device from the street outside Kyllo's (D) residence to determine that the amount of heat emanating from the house was consistent with the presence of high-temperature lamps used to cultivate marijuana.

Black Letter Rule: The use of a device not used by the general public to obtain evidence emanating from the interior of a residence that cannot otherwise be obtained without physical intrusion constitutes a search.

United States v. Karo

Instant Facts: A federal agent installed a beeper in a container to be shipped to Karo (D) in order to track drug smuggling activity.

Black Letter Rule: Seizure of property requires a meaningful interference with a possessory interest.

Katz v. United States

(Gambler) v. *(Prosecuting Government)*
389 U.S. 347, 88 S. Ct. 507, 19 L. Ed. 2d 576 (1967)

A WIRETAP IN A PUBLIC PHONE BOOTH VIOLATES THE FOURTH AMENDMENT

I guess I should have known a <u>public</u> telephone booth wasn't "private".

stus.com

■ **INSTANT FACTS** Katz (D) was convicted of transmitting gaming information via telephone based on evidence obtained by FBI agents who had attached a listening device to a public telephone.

■ **BLACK LETTER RULE** The Fourth Amendment protects all communications that a person does not knowingly expose to the public.

■ **PROCEDURAL BASIS**

Certiorari to review a decision of a federal court of appeals sustaining the conviction.

■ **FACTS**

Katz (D) had been indicted for transmitting illegal wagering information over the telephone in violation of a federal statute. At trial, the prosecution introduced evidence of the defendant's conversations obtained by FBI agents through a listening device attached to a public telephone without a search warrant. Katz (D) objected to the use of the evidence as a violation of the Fourth Amendment. The trial court overruled the objection and the defendant was convicted. The court of appeals affirmed the conviction.

■ **ISSUE**

Does the use of a listening device to record conversations made in a public phone booth violate the Fourth Amendment?

■ **DECISION AND RATIONALE**

(Stewart, J.) Yes. The Fourth Amendment protects people—not places—against unreasonable searches and seizures. It affords protection to all communications that a person does not knowingly expose to the public. Because the defendant took precautions to ensure his conversations would not be overheard, he did not knowingly expose his conversations to the public. The fact that his conversations took place in a public place, as opposed to a home, office, or other private place, is constitutionally insignificant. An unreasonable search and seizure occurs even without any technical "trespass" into a space—public or private—in which a person has an expectation of privacy. Because the defendant had a reasonable expectation of privacy in the phone booth, it was a constitutionally protected area. Reversed.

■ **CONCURRENCE**

(Harlan, J.) A two-pronged analysis should determine what rights the Fourth Amendment affords. First, a person must have shown a subjective expectation of privacy. Second, that expectation must be objectively reasonable. Applied to the facts of this case, a telephone booth, isolated from the public at times of use, is a "temporarily private place" in which an expectation of privacy is reasonable. The Fourth Amendment protects such an expectation of privacy from unreasonable search and seizure.

■ DISSENT

(Black, J.) Recording a conversation by electronic means constitutes neither a search nor a seizure as the Fourth Amendment intended that those terms be applied. The plain language of the Fourth Amendment applies only to tangible objects and does not encompass conversations, which are capable of neither search nor seizure. Because eavesdropping existed at the time the Fourth Amendment was drafted, the framers' choice of language must be given effect and not applied to intangible objects.

Analysis:

Katz is widely accepted as the beginning of the "privacy approach" to Fourth Amendment analysis. As Justice Black's dissent highlights, the language of the Fourth Amendment applies literally only to tangible objects. Pre-*Katz* decisions held similarly by requiring a trespass to constitute a search and seizure. The majority departs from the trespass requirement, expanding the rights protected under the Fourth Amendment.

■ CASE VOCABULARY

RIGHT OF PRIVACY: The right to personal autonomy. The U.S. Constitution does not explicitly provide for a right of privacy, but the Supreme Court has repeatedly ruled that this right is implied in the "zones of privacy" created by specific constitutional guarantees.

United States v. White

(Prosecuting Government) v. *(Drug Dealer)*

401 U.S. 745, 91 S. Ct. 1122, 28 L. Ed. 2d 453 (1971)

ELECTRONIC SURVEILLANCE EVIDENCE OBTAINED WITH AN INFORMANT'S CONSENT IS ADMISSIBLE

■ **INSTANT FACTS** White (D) was convicted of drug charges based on the testimony of government agents who overheard incriminating conversations between the defendant and an informant by way of a listening device carried by the informant.

■ **BLACK LETTER RULE** A defendant bears the risk that communications with another will be transmitted, electronically or otherwise, to government agents.

■ PROCEDURAL BASIS

Certiorari to review a decision of the court of appeals setting aside the defendant's conviction.

■ FACTS

White (D) and a government informant, Jackson, discussed several illegal drug transactions in Jackson's home and car and in public. Government agents, through a listening device placed on Jackson's person with his permission, overheard the conversations. At trial, the prosecution was unable to locate Jackson and offered the testimony of the government agents to support the charges. Over objections, the court allowed the agents' testimony. White (D) was convicted. The court of appeals reversed, finding that *Katz* rendered evidence obtained through electronic surveillance inadmissible against the defendant.

■ ISSUE

Does the Fourth Amendment bar testimony from government agents who overheard conversations between a defendant and a government informant who was wearing a listening device on his person?

■ DECISION AND RATIONALE

(White, J.) No. Criminal defendants bear the risk that communications with others will be transmitted, electronically or otherwise, to government agents. Although *Katz* protects individuals from search and seizure when they maintain a justifiable expectation of privacy, White (D) had no such justifiable expectation. One who discusses criminal activities with another can have no justifiable expectation that the conversations will not be reported to the police. The fact that the police may overhear the conversations through a listening device carried by an informant does not affect this expectation. Whether the individual speaks directly to an undercover agent, the informant later reveals the conversation to the police, or the informant relays the conversation through a listening device, a defendant bears the risk that his or her privacy will be breached. This expectation of privacy is not justifiable. Reversed.

■ DISSENT

(Douglas, J.) Permitting the use of electronic surveillance as a means of eavesdropping endangers the fundamental privacy interests afforded by the Fourth Amendment. By allowing the government to listen

---

and record the conversations of an unknowing defendant, the majority empowers the government to "penetrate all the walls and doors which men need to shield them from the pressures of a turbulent life."

■ DISSENT

(Harlan, J.) The Court's holding affords law enforcement too much power and invades the fundamental protections of the Fourth Amendment. The admission of evidence obtained through electronic surveillance in every case overly burdens citizens' expectations of privacy under the Fourth Amendment. When, as here, the agents utilize a listening device solely with the consent of an informant, the free exchange of information underlying the liberties afforded by the Fourth Amendment is restricted. Courts should not rely exclusively on the self-restraint of law enforcement officers in deciding whether electronic surveillance will be used, but should first require a warrant so that the government must justify the need to employ such surveillance, rather than placing the risk on society.

Analysis:

The Court's opinion focuses on the defendant's risk that the person to whom he communicates is or may be betraying him to the government. In *Katz*, the government agents acted unilaterally in listening to the conversation, without assistance from the parties to the conversation. Here, however, the informant consented to the government's actions. While no warrant was obtained in either instance, the cooperation of one of the parties to the conversation relieves Fourth Amendment concerns. Note that the Court places some emphasis on the second prong of the analysis set forth in Justice Harlan's concurrence in *Katz*. While the defendant here had a subjective expectation of privacy, his expectation was considered objectively unreasonable.

■ CASE VOCABULARY

INFORMANT: One who informs against another; especially, one who confidentially supplies information to the police about a crime, sometimes in exchange for a reward or special treatment.

Smith v. Maryland

(Stalker) v. *(Prosecuting Government)*

442 U.S. 735, 99 S. Ct. 2577, 61 L. Ed. 2d 220 (1979)

RECOVERING TELEPHONE NUMBERS WITH A PEN REGISTER DOES NOT CONSTITUTE A SEARCH

■ **INSTANT FACTS** Police installed a pen register at the telephone company to monitor calls made from Smith's (D) telephone without a warrant.

■ **BLACK LETTER RULE** An individual assumes the risk of disclosure of information knowingly conveyed to a third party.

■ **PROCEDURAL BASIS**

Certiorari to review the defendant's conviction.

■ **FACTS**

After reporting a robbery to police, a woman began receiving threatening calls at her home. After stepping out onto her front porch at the request of the caller, she recognized a 1975 Monte Carlo she had identified at the scene of the robbery. Upon further investigation, police traced the vehicle's license plates to Smith (D). The police then, without a warrant, installed a pen register at the telephone company to determine if Smith (D) made any calls to the woman's house. After determining that a call was placed to the woman's house from Smith's (D) phone, the police obtained a search warrant and seized a phone book that was "turned down" to the woman's listing. At trial, Smith (D) sought to suppress the pen register record and the phone book, arguing that no warrant had been obtained to install the pen register. The request was denied and Smith (D) was convicted.

■ **ISSUE**

Does the use of a pen register to monitor numbers that are dialed from a private telephone constitute a search under the Fourth Amendment?

■ **DECISION AND RATIONALE**

(Blackmun, J.) No. Individuals assume the risk of disclosure of information they knowingly convey to a third party. Unlike electronic surveillance, which intercepts communications that may be subject to a reasonable expectation of privacy, a pen register merely records the numbers dialed, which are not subject to the same expectation. Under the first part of the test articulated by Justice Harlan's concurrence in *Katz*, the defendant here had no subjective expectation of privacy over the numbers he dialed. It is common knowledge that those numbers are conveyed to the telephone company, which maintains procedures for collecting and maintaining them. Second, if the defendant harbored such an expectation, it was unreasonable. Smith (D) voluntarily conveyed the numbers he dialed to the telephone company, assuming the risk that they would be turned over to the police. The use of a pen register was thus not a search under the Fourth Amendment.

■ **DISSENT**

(Stewart, J.) There is no difference between the numbers dialed on a telephone within one's own home and the communications that come about from the act of dialing. Disclosure of both threatens to "reveal the most intimate details of a person's life," falling within the Fourth Amendment's protections.

■ DISSENT

(Marshall, J.) One who conveys telephone numbers dialed from his home *does* maintain a subjective expectation of privacy. One may transfer such information for a limited purpose, but it does not follow that he reasonably expects such information to be revealed to the government or others. Further, one does not assume the risk of disclosure by transmitting dialed telephone numbers to the telephone company, for there is no alternative choice to the disclosure. In order to use a telephone, the user has no option to conceal the numbers dialed, unlike a personal conversation in which one may choose to speak or not. The risks involved for Fourth Amendment analysis should be those a person chooses to accept, not those thrust upon him. The use of pen registers threatens not only the privacy interests of a person who makes a call for an illegal purpose, but also those of the unsuspecting recipient of the call. A warrant should be required before the government is permitted to invade these interests.

Analysis:

In applying the subjective prong of the *Katz* test, the Court here indicated that the defendant could have no subjective expectation of privacy because they "doubt[ed] that people in general entertain any actual expectation of privacy in the numbers they dial." One may question whether the Court correctly applied the subjective standard. While the expectations of "people in general" may bear on the reasonableness of one's expectations, the subjective standard typically requires a look at the specific defendant's expectations. Nonetheless, the Court's analysis of the objective prong supports its conclusion.

■ CASE VOCABULARY

PEN REGISTER: A mechanical device that records the numbers dialed on a telephone, but not the oral communications, by monitoring the electrical impulses caused when the dial on the telephone is released.

Kyllo v. United States

(Drug Dealer) v. *(Prosecuting Government)*

533 U.S. 27, 121 S. Ct. 2038, 150 L. Ed. 2d 94 (2001)

USING THERMAL IMAGING TO OBTAIN EVIDENCE FROM A PRIVATE RESIDENCE CONSTITUTES A SEARCH

■ **INSTANT FACTS** Federal agents used a thermal-imaging device from the street outside Kyllo's (D) residence to determine that the amount of heat emanating from the house was consistent with the presence of high-temperature lamps used to cultivate marijuana.

■ **BLACK LETTER RULE** The use of a device not used by the general public to obtain evidence emanating from the interior of a residence that cannot otherwise be obtained without physical intrusion constitutes a search.

■ **PROCEDURAL BASIS**

Certiorari to review the defendant's conviction.

■ **FACTS**

A federal agent, suspecting Kyllo (D) was cultivating marijuana in his residence, used a thermal-imaging device to detect the relative amount of heat emanating from his residence as compared to those surrounding him. After reviewing the test results, the agent concluded that the heat disparity between Kyllo's (D) residence and those around him suggested the presence of high-temperature lamps used to grow marijuana. On the basis of the test results and other evidence, the agent obtained a warrant and seized over 100 marijuana plants. Kyllo (D) moved to suppress the evidence at trial, which motion was overruled.

■ **ISSUE**

Does the use of a non-intrusive technological device to obtain evidence from inside a person's home constitute a search under the Fourth Amendment?

■ **DECISION AND RATIONALE**

(Scalia, J.) Yes. The expectation of privacy safe-guarded by the Fourth Amendment protects one's actions within his own home. The use of technological devices not in use by the general public in order to obtain information regarding the interior of one's home, which could not otherwise be obtained without physical intrusion, thus constitutes a search. While technology has complicated questions concerning the Fourth Amendment, the privacy of one's home must be preserved to ensure that the Fourth Amendment maintains, at a minimum, the purpose for which it was adopted. Reversed and remanded.

■ **DISSENT**

(Stevens, J.) The information collected by the thermal-imaging device did not emanate from the interior of the house, but rather was only that exposed to the general public from the outside of the house. The device did not penetrate the walls into the house's interior, but measured heat disparity between that home's exterior walls as compared to its neighbors'. Heat differences can be determined from the exterior of the house by any member of the public using the senses. Once heat leaves the house, the occupant no longer maintains a subjective expectation of privacy. The Court's reliance on future advances in technology and the impact its decision will have on Fourth Amendment privacy rights is troubling. It is at once too broad and too narrow, in that it excepts technological advancements that come within the general use of the public and encompasses all "sense-enhancing technology," including dogs trained to sniff out narcotics, but it protects only the interior of a home, to the exclusion of other places where a reasonable expectation of privacy exists. Further, the Court's decision ignores the factual distinctions with *Katz*, in which the content of the communication was obtained through a listening device. Here, the device did not detect the source of the heat, but merely its presence outside the house.

Analysis:

Commentators suggest that the Court's decision will have only limited effect on Fourth Amendment cases. Generally siding with the dissent, they argue that the Court's holding leaves open to debate whether the device utilized in a given circumstance is generally used by the public. Even at the time of the decision in 2001, debate surfaced whether the device used by the officers in 1991 was in general use by the public.

United States v. Karo

(*Prosecuting Government*) v. (*Drug Smuggler*)

468 U.S. 705, 104 S. Ct. 3296, 82 L. Ed. 2d 530 (1984)

INSTALLING A BEEPER IN A CONTAINER BEFORE POSSESSION IS NOT A SEIZURE

■ **INSTANT FACTS** A federal agent installed a beeper in a container to be shipped to Karo (D) in order to track drug smuggling activity.

■ **BLACK LETTER RULE** Seizure of property requires a meaningful interference with a possessory interest.

■ **PROCEDURAL BASIS**

Certiorari to review decision of the court of appeals reversing the defendant's conviction.

■ **FACTS**

A federal agent learned from an informant that Karo (D) had ordered a large quantity of ether. After the informant told the agent the ether was to be used to extract cocaine from imported clothing, the informant consented to placement of a beeper inside a government-supplied container to be included in the shipment. Karo (D) was convicted after agents tracked the container. On appeal, the federal court of appeals reversed Karo's (D) conviction, holding that placement of the beeper constituted a seizure at the time the container was transferred.

■ **ISSUE**

Does the installation of a beeper in a container of chemicals with the consent of the original owner constitute a seizure under the Fourth Amendment when the container is delivered to a buyer with no knowledge of the presence of the beeper?

■ **DECISION AND RATIONALE**

(White, J.) No. A seizure occurs only when there is some meaningful interference with an individual's possessory interests in the subject property. While the container in which the beeper was placed in this case was the property of the government, the beeper could be placed therein without such interference. The government was also free to place the beeper in one of the informant's containers, since the agent had obtained the consent of the informant for placement of the beeper and the informant was free to do what he wanted with it prior to shipment. Upon transfer to the defendant, no seizure took place. Because the placement of the beeper did not infringe on the defendant's possessory interests in the container, no seizure occurred. Reversed.

■ **CONCURRENCE IN PART, DISSENT IN PART**

(Stevens, J.) A possessory interest in the container includes the right to exclude unwanted items and the right to use it exclusively. By attaching a beeper to a container, the government converted the property for its use, constituting a seizure.

Analysis:

This is the only case excerpt in the chapter that specifically relates to seizures as opposed to searches. In reality, however, the case is most often cited for its discussion of search-related issues. Nonetheless, the excerpted portions of the case highlight the issues that surround the constitutionality of seizures by government actors.

■ CASE VOCABULARY

SEIZURE: The act or an instance of taking possession of a person or property by legal right or process; especially, in constitutional law, a confiscation or arrest that may interfere with a person's reasonable expectation of privacy.

CHAPTER FOUR

The Substance of the Fourth Amendment

Spinelli v. United States

Instant Facts: Spinelli (D) was convicted of gambling offenses proscribed by Missouri law. Spinelli (D) challenged the constitutionality of the warrant authorizing the FBI search that uncovered the evidence supporting his conviction.

Black Letter Rule: In order for a search warrant based on an informant's tip to be valid, the informant must declare either that (1) he himself saw or perceived the fact or facts asserted; or (2) there is good reason for believing it, such as one of the usual grounds for crediting hearsay information.

Illinois v. Gates

Instant Facts: Lance and Susan Gates (D) were indicted for violation of state drug laws after police officers, executing a search warrant, discovered marijuana and other contraband in their automobile and home.

Black Letter Rule: So long as a substantial basis exists for concluding that a search would uncover evidence of wrongdoing, a warrant is valid under the Fourth Amendment.

Payton v. New York

Instant Facts: Payton (D) challenged the constitutionality of New York statutes that authorize police officers to enter a private residence without a warrant and with force, if necessary, to make a routine felony arrest.

Black Letter Rule: An arrest warrant is required to arrest a person in his or her home.

Lo-Ji Sales, Inc. v. New York

Instant Facts: The defendant was accused of violating state obscenity laws and argued that a warrant must describe with specificity each item to be seized during execution of the warrant.

Black Letter Rule: A warrant must particularly describe the things to be seized, and items not specifically listed on the search warrant may not be seized.

Richards v. Wisconsin

Instant Facts: Richards (D) was arrested for intent to deliver a controlled substance in violation of state law. Richards sought to have the evidence from his hotel room suppressed on the ground that the officers had failed to knock and announce their presence prior to forcing entry into the room.

Black Letter Rule: In order to dispense with the knock-and-announce requirement, police must show reasonable suspicion that it would be dangerous or futile or would result in destruction of evidence of the crime.

Warden v. Hayden

Instant Facts: Hayden (D) was charged with armed robbery. A shotgun, pistol, clothing matching the description of the robber, and ammunition for the pistol and shotgun were seized during a warrantless search of Hayden's home and were introduced as evidence against Hayden at his trial.

Black Letter Rule: Police may conduct a warrantless search of a dwelling the suspect has entered into if the police are in "hot pursuit" of the suspect.

Chimel v. California

Instant Facts: Chimel (D) was charged with two counts of burglary. He argued that items taken from his home and admitted into evidence against him had been unconstitutionally seized.

Black Letter Rule: Pursuant to a lawful arrest, the police may conduct a search of any area within the immediate reach of the accused criminal.

United States v. Robinson

Instant Facts: Robinson (D) was charged with possession of a controlled substance in violation of state law. Fourteen gelatin capsules of heroin obtained during a routine pat-down of the defendant pursuant to a lawful arrest were admitted into evidence against him.

Black Letter Rule: No matter how insignificant the arrest, the police have the right to search the suspect's person for potential weapons or evidence.

New York v. Belton

Instant Facts: Belton (D) was arrested for criminal possession of a controlled substance based on evidence found in the car he was in at the time of the arrest.

Black Letter Rule: When a suspect is arrested in his vehicle, the interior of the car and any containers in it can be searched pursuant to the lawful arrest.

Arizona v. Gant

Instant Facts: Police officers searched the passenger compartment of an arrestee's vehicle after the arrestee had been handcuffed and placed in the back of a locked squad car for traffic violations, and the arrestee objected to the introduction of drug-related evidence found during the search based on his Fourth Amendment rights.

Black Letter Rule: Police may search a vehicle incident to a recent occupant's arrest only if the arrestee is within reaching distance of the passenger compartment at the time of the search or it is reasonable to believe the vehicle contains evidence of the offense of arrest.

Whren v. United States

Instant Facts: Whren (D) was charged with violating various federal drug laws.

Black Letter Rule: The temporary detention of a motorist who the police have probable cause to believe has committed a civil traffic violation is consistent with the Fourth Amendment.

Chambers v. Maroney

Instant Facts: Chambers was charged with armed robbery. Articles taken from his vehicle during the search at the police station were admitted into evidence against him.

Black Letter Rule: If government agents have probable cause to believe an automobile contains articles that they may be entitled to seize, they may search the vehicle pursuant to a lawful arrest, without a warrant, or impound the vehicle into police custody to be searched at a later time.

California v. Carney

Instant Facts: Carney (D) was charged with possession of marijuana for sale after police discovered drugs in his motor home.

Black Letter Rule: The automobile exception to the warrant requirement includes protection for vehicles such as motor homes, vans, converted vans, minivans, and station wagons, which are capable of ready movement.

United States v. Chadwick

Instant Facts: Chadwick was indicted for possession of marijuana with intent to distribute it and for conspiracy after police seized and later, without a warrant, searched a foot locker that contained evidence.

Black Letter Rule: A search warrant is required to search personal property of an arrestee at the point where the property to be searched comes under the exclusive dominion of police authority.

California v. Acevedo

Instant Facts: Acevedo was charged with possession of marijuana. The charges were based on the search of a paper bag, which Acevedo had placed in the trunk of his car.

Black Letter Rule: Police can search an automobile and all containers in it when they have probable cause to believe contraband is contained somewhere within the automobile.

Horton v. California

Instant Facts: Horton was charged with armed robbery. Weapons seized during the search of his home pursuant to a valid warrant were admitted into evidence against him. The weapons seized were not listed on the search warrant.

Black Letter Rule: The warrantless seizure of evidence of a crime found in plain view should not be prohibited by the Fourth Amendment, even if the discovery of the evidence was not inadvertent.

Arizona v. Hicks

Instant Facts: Hicks (D) was charged with robbery based on stolen property found in Hicks's (D) apartment.

Black Letter Rule: The "plain view" doctrine may not be used to justify warrantless searches or seizures of a dwelling, which require probable cause.

Schneckloth v. Bustamonte

Instant Facts: Bustamonte (D) was charged with theft after three stolen checks were discovered during a search of the automobile in which Bustamonte (D) was a passenger. The driver consented to the search.

Black Letter Rule: An individual need not be informed that he has the right to refuse consent to a search before his consent to the search will be considered voluntary.

Georgia v. Randolph

Instant Facts: Randolph (D) was convicted of a drug offense based on evidence that resulted from a search of his home to which only his wife consented, over his objection.

Black Letter Rule: "[A] warrantless search of a shared dwelling for evidence over the express refusal of consent by a physically present resident cannot be justified as reasonable as to him on the basis of consent given to the police by another resident."

Illinois v. Rodriguez

Instant Facts: Rodriguez (D) was charged with possession of a controlled substance with intent to deliver after his girlfriend let the police into his apartment and they discovered evidence.

Black Letter Rule: If law enforcement officers have reason to believe the individual giving consent to a search has authority over the premises to be searched, then the entry will be validated even if it is later determined that the person did not have authority to consent.

Terry v. Ohio

Instant Facts: Evidence of a gun found on Terry during a protective frisk by a police officer was admitted into evidence. Terry (D) was convicted of carrying a concealed weapon.

Black Letter Rule: If the police have reasonable suspicion that a suspect has committed a crime or is about to commit a crime, they may stop the person, detain him briefly for questioning, and then frisk the suspect if they reasonably believe the suspect is carrying a dangerous weapon.

Dunaway v. New York

Instant Facts: Dunaway (D) was convicted of murder and attempted robbery based in part on statements he made during police questioning.

Black Letter Rule: Police may not subject a suspect to custodial interrogation unless they have probable cause to believe a crime has been committed.

United States v. Mendenhall

Instant Facts: Mendenhall (D) was arrested for possession of heroin. Evidence of heroin found on her person during a search conducted by DEA agents was admitted into evidence against her.

Black Letter Rule: A person is seized when, in light of the circumstances, a reasonable person would have believed that she was no longer free to leave.

United States v. Drayton

Instant Facts: Drayton (D) consented—involuntarily, he said—to being patted down as part of an all-passenger search of the Greyhound bus on which he was riding, and was convicted of a drug offense based on evidence discovered during the patdown.

Black Letter Rule: Police officers do not violate the Fourth Amendment prohibition on unreasonable seizures by approaching individuals in public places, questioning them, and requesting consent to search, if they do not induce cooperation by coercive means and a reasonable person would feel free to terminate the encounter.

California v. Hodari D.

Instant Facts: Hodari (D) was charged with possession of crack cocaine based on a rock of crack cocaine that he threw away while under police pursuit.

Black Letter Rule: An arrest requires either physical force or submission to the assertion of authority.

Alabama v. White

Instant Facts: White (D) was arrested for possession of cocaine and marijuana in violation of state law. The court held that the officers did not have the reasonable suspicion necessary under *Terry v. Ohio* to justify the investigatory stop of White's (D) car and that the marijuana and cocaine were fruits of the unconstitutional detention.

Black Letter Rule: An anonymous tip received by police and not completely corroborated can be used as the basis for a *Terry* stop as long as a significant portion of the tip is verified.

Illinois v. Wardlow

Instant Facts: Wardlow (D) was arrested for possession of a handgun in violation of state law. The handgun admitted into evidence was found on Wardlow's person during a protective frisk.

Black Letter Rule: Flight from police is not indicative of wrongdoing, but it is certainly suggestive of such.

Maryland v. Buie

Instant Facts: Buie (D) was arrested for armed robbery and convicted, based in part on evidence consisting of a running suit matching a witness's description that was found during a "sweep" of his home.

Black Letter Rule: The police can make a protective sweep of a dwelling during the course of an arrest if they have reasonable suspicion that there is some danger.

Michigan Department of State Police v. Sitz

Instant Facts: Sitz (R) filed complaint seeking injunctive relief or a declaratory judgment that a state program that set up sobriety checkpoints was unconstitutional.

Black Letter Rule: Police may set up temporary sobriety checkpoints and stop each car coming through to look for signs of intoxication.

City of Indianapolis v. Edmond

Instant Facts: Edmond (D) and others raised a Fourth Amendment challenge after being subjected to a highway checkpoint stop designed to detect illegal narcotics.

Black Letter Rule: Highway checkpoints designed to advance a general interest in ordinary crime control are unconstitutional.

Spinelli v. United States

(Convicted Criminal) v. *(Prosecuting Government)*
393 U.S. 410, 89 S. Ct. 584, 21 L. Ed. 2d 637 (1969)

AN INFORMANT MUST HAVE PERSONAL KNOWLEDGE OF THE SUBJECT MATTER OF HIS TIP

■ **INSTANT FACTS** Spinelli (D) was convicted of gambling offenses proscribed by Missouri law. Spinelli (D) challenged the constitutionality of the warrant authorizing the FBI search that uncovered the evidence supporting his conviction.

■ **BLACK LETTER RULE** In order for a search warrant based on an informant's tip to be valid, the informant must declare either that (1) he himself saw or perceived the fact or facts asserted; or (2) there is good reason for believing it, such as one of the usual grounds for crediting hearsay information.

■ **PROCEDURAL BASIS**

Certiorari to review the Eighth Circuit Court of Appeals' decision affirming the federal district court's conviction of the defendant for interstate travel in aid of racketeering.

■ **FACTS**

Spinelli (D) was convicted under 18 U.S.C. § 1952 of traveling to St. Louis, Missouri from Illinois with the intention of conducting gambling activities proscribed by Missouri law. The warrant police used to obtain the evidence necessary for Spinelli's (D) conviction was based on information from a confidential and reliable police informant. The informant indicated to police that Spinelli was accepting wagers and disseminating wagering information by means of two specific telephone numbers. The tip from the informant did not indicate whether the informant had personal knowledge of the alleged gambling activities.

■ **ISSUE**

Is a tip from an informant based on hearsay, even when part of it has been corroborated by independent police sources, as trustworthy as a tip from an informant who has seen or perceived the facts asserted, such that it supports the issuance of a search warrant?

■ **DECISION AND RATIONALE**

(Harlan, J.) No. An informant's report must first be measured against the standard set forth in *Aguilar v. Texas*, 378 U.S. 108 (1964), so that its probative value may be assessed. Under *Aguilar*, in order for a search warrant based on an informant's tip to be valid, the informant must declare either that (1) he himself saw or perceived the fact or facts asserted; or (2) there is good reason for believing it, such as one of the usual grounds for crediting hearsay information. Only if the tip is found inadequate under *Aguilar* may the other allegations that corroborate the information in the hearsay report be considered. However, even at this stage, the *Aguilar* standard must inform the magistrate's decision. *Aguilar* is the appropriate standard at this stage of the inquiry because the tests it establishes were designed to implement the long-standing principle that probable cause must be determined by someone "neutral and detached," and not by "the officer engaged in the often competitive enterprise of ferreting out crime." A magistrate cannot be said to have properly discharged his constitutional duties if he relies on an informant's tip that, even if partially corroborated, did not meet the *Aguilar* standard when standing alone. Reversed.

■ CONCURRENCE

(White, J.) Even if it may be inferred from an affidavit that the informant himself has observed the facts or has them from an actor in the event, no possible harm could come from requiring a statement to that effect, thereby removing the difficult and recurring questions that arise in such situations.

Analysis:

This decision affirmed the importance of the standards set forth by the Court in *Aguilar*. It is important to determine whether an informant has personal knowledge or observation of the events or circumstances referenced in the tip to authorities. Without evidence of such knowledge, further substantiation of the reasons for the informant's conclusions is required.

■ CASE VOCABULARY

PROBABLE CAUSE: A reasonable ground to suspect that a person has committed or is committing a crime or that a place contains specific items connected with a crime.

Illinois v. Gates

(Prosecuting State) v. *(Drug Offender)*

462 U.S. 213, 103 S. Ct. 2317, 76 L. Ed. 2d 527 (1983)

ANONYMOUS TIPS, STANDING ALONE, DO NOT GIVE RISE TO PROBABLE CAUSE

How do you define "probable cause"?

It's a "totality of the circumstances" test, which means getting the right judge.

stus.com

■ **INSTANT FACTS** Lance and Susan Gates (D) were indicted for violation of state drug laws after police officers, executing a search warrant, discovered marijuana and other contraband in their automobile and home.

■ **BLACK LETTER RULE** So long as a substantial basis exists for concluding that a search would uncover evidence of wrongdoing, a warrant is valid under the Fourth Amendment.

■ **PROCEDURAL BASIS**

Certiorari to review the decision of the Illinois Supreme Court affirming the trial court's decision granting the defendant's motion to suppress evidence seized pursuant to a search warrant.

■ **FACTS**

Respondents Lance and Susan Gates (D) were indicted for violation of state drug laws after police officers, executing a search warrant, discovered marijuana and other contraband in their automobile and home. The search was executed based on an anonymous handwritten letter that detailed how the couple traveled separately to Florida to buy drugs, with Susan Gates (D) driving the family car down to Florida and Lance Gates (D) flying down to Florida to meet her several days later before the couple would drive their automobile back to Illinois. The police verified driver's license information and flight information. Agents then followed Lance's flight to Florida and followed him to a hotel room rented by his wife. They observed the couple drive off in a car with Illinois plates on a freeway used to travel to Illinois. The couple returned to Illinois only thirty-six hours after Lance originally flew out of Illinois. A judge issued a search warrant for their residence based on this information.

■ **ISSUE**

In order for a warrant based on an informant's anonymous tip, even with police corroboration, to be valid, must the elements of ''veracity,'' ''reliability,'' and ''basis of knowledge'' exist separately and independently?

■ **DECISION AND RATIONALE**

(Harlan, J.) No. Rather, they should be understood simply as closely intertwined issues that may usefully illuminate the common-sense, practical question whether there is ''probable cause'' to believe that contraband or evidence is located in a particular place. This totality of the circumstances test is far more consistent with the Court's prior treatment of probable cause than any rigid demand that specific tests be satisfied by every tip. Such a high standard for probable cause may force magistrates to conduct full evidentiary hearings before issuing warrants or may force police to conduct warrantless searches in the hopes they will get consent. Reversed.

■ **CONCURRENCE**

(White, J.) The critical issue is not whether the activities observed by the police are innocent or suspicious. Rather, the proper focus should be whether the actions of the suspects, whatever their nature, give rise to an inference that the informant is credible and that he obtained his information in a reliable manner. Therefore, it was not necessary to overrule *Aguilar-Spinelli* in order to reverse the judgment of the Illinois Supreme Court.

■ **DISSENT**

(Brennan, J.) By requiring police to provide certain crucial information to magistrates and by structuring magistrates' probable cause inquiries, *Aguilar* and *Spinelli* assure the magistrate's role as an independent arbitrator of probable cause and insure greater accuracy in probable cause determinations.

Analysis:

This decision effectively overruled *Aguilar* and *Spinelli*, which required tips from informants to meet separate tests for "veracity" and "basis of knowledge," in favor a a "totality of the circumstances" test in which a deficiency in one element may be compensated for by the other in determining the overall reliability of the tip.

■ **CASE VOCABULARY**

VERACITY: Truthfulness.

CORROBORATION: Confirmation or support by additional evidence or authority.

Payton v. New York

(Accused Criminal) v. *(Prosecuting State)*

445 U.S. 573, 100 S. Ct. 1371, 63 L. Ed. 2d 639 (1980)

ARRESTS ARE SIMILAR TO SEARCHES FOR PURPOSES OF WARRANT REQUIREMENTS

■ **INSTANT FACTS** Payton (D) challenged the constitutionality of New York statutes that authorize police officers to enter a private residence without a warrant and with force, if necessary, to make a routine felony arrest.

■ **BLACK LETTER RULE** An arrest warrant is required to arrest a person in his or her home.

■ **PROCEDURAL BASIS**

Appeal to the Supreme Court from the state court decisions affirming the defendant's conviction.

■ **FACTS**

Police suspected that Theodore Payton (D) had murdered a gas station attendant. Police went to his apartment, without a warrant, with the intent to arrest Payton (D). Hearing music within the apartment, police knocked on the door but received no answer. Police then used crowbars to open the door to the apartment. No one was there, but police seized a shell casing that was found in plain view on the door opening. Payton (D) was indicted for murder and moved to suppress evidence of the shell casing found in his apartment.

■ **ISSUE**

Can police enter a private residence without a warrant to make a routine felony arrest?

■ **DECISION AND RATIONALE**

(Stevens, J.) No. It is a basic principle of Fourth Amendment law that searches and seizures inside a home without a warrant are presumptively unreasonable. The constitutional protection afforded to an individual's interest in privacy in is own home is equally applicable to a warrantless entry for the purpose of arresting a resident of the house, for it is inherent in such an entry that a search for the suspect may be required before he can be apprehended. Reversed and remanded.

■ **DISSENT**

(White, J.) The Fourth Amendment is concerned with protecting people, not places, and talismatic significance is given to the fact that an arrest occurs in the home rather than elsewhere. The requirements that police officers must knock and announce their presence for a felony arrest, do so only during daytime hours, and have reasonable grounds to believe that the arrestee has committed a crime and is in fact present in the home, should be sufficient protections of an individual's privacy interest in the home. It should not be necessary for the police to have an arrest warrant if it is guaranteed that the person's privacy interests in the home can be protected by a means less stringent to police.

Analysis:

The court emphasized that "the Fourth Amendment has drawn a firm line at the entrance to the house." The home has always been considered a sacred place. Requiring the police to obtain a warrant to arrest people in their homes does not place a significant burden on law enforcement. Police may, for instance, arrest the suspects when they leave their homes, or, if they know they are going to stay there, they can obtain a warrant.

Lo-Ji Sales, Inc. v. New York

(Accused Criminal) v. *(Prosecuting State)*

442 U.S. 319, 99 S. Ct. 2319, 60 L. Ed. 2d 920 (1979)

WARRANTS MUST INCLUDE SPECIFIC DETAILS

We have reports you rent obscene movies.

Al's Porn Shack

We guarantee it!

stus.com

■ **INSTANT FACTS** The defendant was accused of violating state obscenity laws and argued that a warrant must describe with specificity each item to be seized during execution of the warrant.

■ **BLACK LETTER RULE** A warrant must particularly describe the things to be seized, and items not specifically listed on the search warrant may not be seized.

■ **PROCEDURAL BASIS**

Certiorari to review the decisions of the lower courts denying the defendant's motion to suppress evidence.

■ **FACTS**

An investigator for the New York State police purchased two reels of film from an adult bookstore. The officer concluded the films violated the state's obscenity laws and took them to the Town Council for a determination of whether there was reasonable cause to believe the films violated the state obscenity laws so as to justify a search of the adult bookstore. A warrant was obtained to search the adult bookstore. The only items listed on the warrant were the copies of the two films the investigator had purchased. A search was conducted and many items not listed on the warrant were seized.

■ **ISSUE**

Can police seize items during a search pursuant to a valid search warrant if those items are not listed on the warrant?

■ **DECISION AND RATIONALE**

(Burger, C.J.) No. The warrant left it entirely to the discretion of the officials conducting the search to decide which items in the adult bookstore were likely to be obscene. The Fourth Amendment does not permit such action. This search warrant and what followed the entry on the defendant's premises were reminiscent of the general warrant or writ of assistance of the eighteenth century, against which the Fourth Amendment was intended to protect. Reversed and remanded.

Analysis:

This case set out the particularity requirement for warrants. Police cannot go on fishing expeditions during searches executed pursuant to a valid warrant. This rule is designed to require police to conduct a reasonable investigation prior to obtaining a warrant.

■ CASE VOCABULARY

OBSCENE: Extremely offensive under contemporary community standards or morality and decency; grossly repugnant to the generally accepted notions of what is appropriate.

Richards v. Wisconsin

(*Drug Offender*) v. (*Prosecuting State*)

520 U.S. 385, 117 S. Ct. 1416, 137 L. Ed. 2d 615 (1997)

POLICE USUALLY MUST KNOCK AND ANNOUNCE THEIR PRESENCE PRIOR TO EXECUTING A WARRANT

■ **INSTANT FACTS** Richards (D) was arrested for intent to deliver a controlled substance in violation of state law. Richards sought to have the evidence from his hotel room suppressed on the ground that the officers had failed to knock and announce their presence prior to forcing entry into the room.

■ **BLACK LETTER RULE** In order to dispense with the knock-and-announce requirement, police must show reasonable suspicion that it would be dangerous or futile or would result in destruction of evidence of the crime.

■ **PROCEDURAL BASIS**

Certiorari to review the Wisconsin Supreme Court's decision that officers are not required to knock and announce their presence when executing a search warrant during a felony drug investigation.

■ **FACTS**

Police went to Richard's motel room and knocked on the door. One officer was dressed as a maintenance man, two were in plain clothes, and one was a uniformed officer. They announced "Maintenance" when they knocked. The suspect opened door with the chain attached and slammed it shut when he saw officers. The officers waited two to three seconds before breaking the door open. The officers seized cash and cocaine found in the room.

■ **ISSUE**

Does the threat of physical violence or destruction of evidence during execution of a search warrant in felony drug cases justify dispensing with the knock-and-announce requirement in every such case?

■ **DECISION AND RATIONALE**

(Stevens, J.) No. The fact that felony drug investigations may frequently present circumstances warranting a no-knock entry cannot remove from the neutral scrutiny of the reviewing court the reasonableness of the police decision not to knock and announce in a particular case. In each case it is the duty of the court confronted with the question to determine whether the facts and circumstances of the particular entry justified dispensing with the knock-and-announce requirement. Creating a blanket exception to the knock-and-announce rule for a general category of criminal behavior creates concerns of overgeneralization and the possibility of the exception being applied to other categories of behavior that it was not intended to govern. Affirmed.

Analysis:

The Court affirmed the principles set out in *Wilson* and used them to preclude the *per se* rule set out by the Wisconsin Supreme Court. In *Wilson* the Court recognized that the knock-and-announce requirement could give way "under circumstances presenting a threat of physical violence," or "where police officers have reason to believe that evidence would likely be destroyed if advance notice were given." The Court here felt these dangers were not enough to warrant a blanket exception for all felony drug cases and that each case should be reviewed on an individual basis.

Warden v. Hayden

(*Prison Warden*) v. (*Armed Robbery Suspect*)

387 U.S. 294, 87 S. Ct. 1642, 18 L. Ed. 2d 782 (1967)

POLICE MAY CONDUCT A WARRANTLESS SEARCH WHEN IN HOT PURSUIT

I know I'm not supposed to follow the hamster into his cage, but I was in hot pursuit.

stus.com

■ **INSTANT FACTS** Hayden (D) was charged with armed robbery. A shotgun, pistol, clothing matching the description of the robber, and ammunition for the pistol and shotgun were seized during a warrantless search of Hayden's home and were introduced as evidence against Hayden at his trial.

■ **BLACK LETTER RULE** Police may conduct a warrantless search of a dwelling the suspect has entered into if the police are in "hot pursuit" of the suspect.

■ **PROCEDURAL BASIS**

Habeas Corpus proceeding brought by state prisoner.

■ **FACTS**

Hayden (D) was chased from the scene of a robbery to his home. He entered his home five minutes before the police arrived. The police entered the home, without a warrant, and began searching for the suspect and the weapon used in the crime. While searching the home for the weapon, they found suspicious clothes in the washing machine, in addition to two guns and the ammunition for those guns. Hayden (D) argued that the warrantless search of his home was invalid and that the evidence should not have been admitted.

■ **ISSUE**

Can police in hot pursuit of a criminal suspect enter a dwelling, without a warrant, to search for the suspect?

■ **DECISION AND RATIONALE**

(Brennan, J.) Yes. Police may conduct a warrantless search of a dwelling that a suspect has entered into if the police are in "hot pursuit" of the suspect. The Fourth Amendment does not require police officers to delay in the course of an investigation if to do so would gravely endanger their lives or the lives of others. There was exigency in these circumstances. Only a thorough search of the home for persons and weapons could have insured Hayden (D) was the only person in the home and that all weapons that could be used against the police were found. Reversed.

Analysis:

Searches conducted outside the judicial process, without a warrant issued by a detached magistrate or judge, are per se unreasonable, subject to a few exceptions. In this case, the warrantless search was deemed reasonable by the Court due to the hot pursuit of the suspect and the chance he would destroy or hide evidence. The hot pursuit doctrine is based on the premise that the suspect, knowing that he is being pursued, may try to escape, destroy evidence, or create a threat to public safety.

■ **CASE VOCABULARY**

EXIGENCY: A state of urgency; a situation requiring immediate action.

Chimel v. California

(Burglary Suspect) v. *(Prosecuting State)*

395 U.S. 752, 89 S. Ct. 2034, 23 L. Ed. 2d 685 (1969)

IMMEDIATE–REACH SEARCHES ARE ALLOWED WHEN AN ARREST IS MADE

■ **INSTANT FACTS** Chimel (D) was charged with two counts of burglary. He argued that items taken from his home and admitted into evidence against him had been unconstitutionally seized.

■ **BLACK LETTER RULE** Pursuant to a lawful arrest, the police may conduct a search of any area within the immediate reach of the accused criminal.

■ PROCEDURAL BASIS

Appeal to the Supreme Court to review the decisions of the state courts affirming the defendant's conviction.

■ FACTS

Police arrived at Chimel's (D) home with a warrant to arrest him for burglary. The officers knocked on the door and announced themselves to Chimel's (D) wife, who then let them into the home to wait for Chimel (D) to arrive. Chimel (D) arrived about fifteen minutes later and the police gave him the arrest warrant and asked for permission to search the house. Chimel (D) refused, but the police told him they were going to search the house anyway because they had the authority to do so incident to a lawful arrest. The police searched the entire house, including the attic and garage. The police also had Chimel's (D) wife open several drawers in the sewing room and move things aside so they could see clearly. Several items were seized, including coins, medals, tokens, and other objects.

■ ISSUE

Can the police search an accused criminal's entire home incident to a lawful arrest?

■ DECISION AND RATIONALE

(Stewart, J.) No. Pursuant to a lawful arrest, the police may conduct a search of any area within the immediate reach of the accused criminal. The purpose of this exception to the warrant requirement is to allow searches for weapons or anything the accused may use to harm police or conduct an escape. The search must be contained to any area where the police reasonably believe a weapon may be hidden and that the defendant may readily obtain access to. There is no comparable justification for routinely searching any room other than that in which an arrest occurs. Any such search may only be conducted pursuant to a valid search warrant or upon the existence or exigent circumstances. Reversed.

■ DISSENT

(White, J.) Where the existence of probable cause is independently established and would justify a warrant for a broader search for evidence, a search of the entire house should be permitted to be carried out without a warrant since the fact of arrest supplies an exigent circumstance justifying police action before evidence can be removed, and alerts the suspect to the search so that he can immediately seek judicial determination of probable cause.

Analysis:

The Court applied the "principle of particular justification," which provides that the police must, whenever practicable, obtain advance judicial approval of searches and seizures through the warrant procedure, and that the scope of a search must be strictly tied to and justified by the circumstances that rendered the initiation of the search permissible. In reaching this decision the Court overruled *Rabinowitz* and *Harris*, which permitted searches of an office and a four-room apartment incident to a lawful arrest. The Court believed that if police were allowed to search the entire dwelling where a suspect was arrested, the Fourth Amendment protection in this area would approach the evaporation point.

United States v. Robinson

(*Prosecuting Government*) v. (*Drug Offender*)

414 U.S. 218, 94 S. Ct. 467, 38 L. Ed. 2d 427 (1973)

POLICE MAY SEARCH ARRESTEES FOR EVIDENCE OR WEAPONS

■ **INSTANT FACTS** Robinson (D) was charged with possession of a controlled substance in violation of state law. Fourteen gelatin capsules of heroin obtained during a routine pat-down of the defendant pursuant to a lawful arrest were admitted into evidence against him.

■ **BLACK LETTER RULE** No matter how insignificant the arrest, the police have the right to search the suspect's person for potential weapons or evidence.

■ **PROCEDURAL BASIS**

Certiorari to review the decision of the court of appeals reversing the judgment of conviction.

■ **FACTS**

The police stopped Robinson (D) and arrested him on suspicion of driving without a license. They knew his license was revoked due to prior incidents with him. The police performed a protective frisk of Robinson (D) during the arrest and felt a hard object in his shirt pocket, which they removed. The police knew the object was not a weapon, but they did not know what it was. The object turned out to be a crumpled up cigarette pack that contained cocaine. The officer conducting the frisk said the object felt like a cigarette pack, but did not feel like it contained cigarettes. The defendant argued that the capsules of cocaine introduced as evidence against him were illegally obtained by the police.

■ **ISSUE**

Do government agents have the authority to conduct a full search of a person pursuant to a lawful custodial arrest?

■ **DECISION AND RATIONALE**

(Rehnquist, J.) Yes. It is the fact of the lawful arrest that establishes the authority to search, and, in the case of a lawful custodial arrest, a full search of the person is not only an exception to the warrant requirement of the Fourth Amendment, but is also a reasonable search under the Amendment. The arrest is the key triggering event. There does not need to be any independent justification for the search. Police should not be required to make subjective decisions in each case as to whether the suspect may be armed or in possession of valuable evidence in danger of destruction. Reversed.

■ **CONCURRENCE**

(Powell, J.) An individual lawfully subjected to a custodial arrest retains no significant Fourth Amendment interest in the privacy of his person. If the arrest is lawful, the privacy interest guarded by the Fourth Amendment is subordinated to a legitimate and overriding governmental concern.

■ **DISSENT**

(Marshall, J.) The search-incident-to-arrest exception to the warrant requirement was set out for the purpose of protecting officers from individuals who may be carrying weapons and thus pose a danger to police officers or the public, and to protect from destruction contraband or evidence of a crime that the arrestee may be carrying.

Analysis:

The Court here rejected the idea that the reason for searching a person incident to a lawful arrest must be litigated in each case. The Court set forth a bright-line rule that an arrest is a triggering event that entitles government agents to conduct a full search of the person, regardless of whether the police have reason to believe the suspect is armed or is carrying contraband.

■ CASE VOCABULARY

PROTECTIVE SEARCH: A search of a detained suspect and the area within the suspect's immediate control, conducted to protect the arresting officer's safety and often to preserve evidence.

AD HOC JUDGMENT: Formed for a particular purpose.

New York v. Belton

(*Prosecuting State*) v. (*Accused Criminal*)

453 U.S. 454, 101 S. Ct. 2860, 69 L. Ed. 2d 768 (1981)

ARRESTING OFFICERS MAY SEARCH THE INTERIOR OF A CAR AND ANY CONTAINERS THEREIN

If you didn't want an invasive search of your car and everything in it, you shouldn't have gotten yourself arrested.

stus.com

■ **INSTANT FACTS** Belton (D) was arrested for criminal possession of a controlled substance based on evidence found in the car he was in at the time of the arrest.

■ **BLACK LETTER RULE** When a suspect is arrested in his vehicle, the interior of the car and any containers in it can be searched pursuant to the lawful arrest.

■ PROCEDURAL BASIS

Certiorari to review decision of New York Court of Appeals reversing the decisions of the lower courts affirming the conviction of defendant.

■ FACTS

A New York state policeman saw an automobile traveling at an excessive rate of speed and ordered the driver over to the side of the road. Upon discovering that neither the driver, nor any of the passengers, owned the vehicle they were traveling in, the trooper ordered all four of the men out of the car. The officer then found a container he believed to contain marijuana laying on the floor by the passenger seat of the automobile. Upon opening the package, the officer discovered the package did indeed contain marijuana. The officer arrested all four men. The officer then searched the pockets of a jacket lying on the backseat of the automobile. The officer found cocaine in the pockets of the jacket.

■ ISSUE

When a suspect is arrested while driving operating a motor vehicle, can the vehicle and any containers within it be searched pursuant to the lawful arrest?

■ DECISION AND RATIONALE

(Stewart, J.) Yes. The Supreme Court decided in *Chimel* that a lawful custodial arrest creates a situation that justifies the contemporaneous search without a warrant of the person arrested and of the immediately surrounding area. Articles inside the relatively narrow compass of the passenger compartment of a vehicle are generally within the area into which an arrestee might reach in order to grab a weapon or evidentiary items. Under this rule, police may also examine the contents of any containers found within the passenger compartment, because if the passenger compartment is within reach of the arrestee, so will the containers be. Reversed.

■ DISSENT

(Brennan, J.) The purpose of the warrant exception set out in *Chimel* was to protect police officers from the danger that the arrestee might gain possession of a dangerous weapon or destructible evidence. When the arrest has been consummated and the arrestee safely taken into custody, the justifications underlying *Chimel's* limited exception to the warrant requirement cease to apply. At that point, there is no possibility that the arrestee could reach weapons or contraband. By approving the constitutionality of the warrantless search in this case, the Court carves out a dangerous precedent that is not justified by the concerns underlying *Chimel.*

Analysis:

The Court indicated the importance of setting a single familiar standard to guide police officers, who have only limited time and expertise to reflect on and balance the social and individual interests involved in specific circumstances they confront. The Court pointed out that when a person cannot know how a court will apply a settled principle to a recurring factual situation, that person cannot know the scope of his or her constitutional protection, nor can a police officer know the scope of his authority.

Arizona v. Gant

(*Prosecuting Authority*) v. (*Criminal Defendant*)
556 U.S. ___, 129 S. Ct. 1710, 173 L. Ed. 2d 485 (2009)

THE COURT DISAGREES ON THE SCOPE OF VEHICLE SEARCHES INCIDENT TO ARREST

■ **INSTANT FACTS** Police officers searched the passenger compartment of an arrestee's vehicle after the arrestee had been handcuffed and placed in the back of a locked squad car for traffic violations, and the arrestee objected to the introduction of drug-related evidence found during the search based on his Fourth Amendment rights.

■ **BLACK LETTER RULE** Police may search a vehicle incident to a recent occupant's arrest only if the arrestee is within reaching distance of the passenger compartment at the time of the search or it is reasonable to believe the vehicle contains evidence of the offense of arrest.

■ **PROCEDURAL BASIS**

Supreme Court review of a state appellate court decision in favor of the defendant.

■ **FACTS**

The police had reliable information that there was an outstanding arrest warrant for the arrest of Gant (D) for driving with a suspended license. The police came upon Gant (D) exiting his car in a driveway where they had just made a drug arrest. They handcuffed Gant (D) and put him in the back of a squad car, then they searched his vehicle and found cocaine in the pocket of a jacket on the backseat. Gant (D) was charged with two drug-related crimes, and he moved to suppress the evidence seized from his car on the ground that the warrantless search violated his Fourth Amendment rights. The trial court denied the motion, but the state supreme court held that the search did not fall within the parameters of the search-incident-to-arrest exception to the requirement of a warrant as defined in *Chimel v. California* and applied to vehicle searches in *New York v. Belton*. The case went to the United States Supreme Court.

■ **ISSUE**

Did the warrantless search of Gant's (D) vehicle after he was handcuffed and locked in the squad car violate Gant's (D) Fourth Amendment rights?

■ **DECISION AND RATIONALE**

(Stephens, J.) Yes. Police may search a vehicle incident to a recent occupant's arrest only if the arrestee is within reaching distance of the passenger compartment at the time of the search or it is reasonable to believe the vehicle contains evidence of the offense of arrest. The *Chimel* rationale authorizes police searches of a vehicle incident to a recent occupant's arrest only when the arrestee is unsecured and within reaching distance of the passenger compartment at the time of the search. Under *Chimel*, police may search incident to arrest only the space within an arrestee's immediate control, meaning the area within which he might gain possession of a weapon or destructible evidence. In *Belton*, we considered the application of *Chimel* in the automobile context. We held that when an officer lawfully arrests the occupant of a vehicle, he or she may, as a contemporaneous incident of that arrest, search the passenger compartment of the vehicle and any containers therein, based on our assumption that the articles within the relatively narrow compass of the passenger compartment of a car are in fact generally within the area into which an arrestee might reach. Lower courts have applied *Belton* overly broadly, using that decision to justify all vehicle searches incident to arrest, regardless of the confines of the *Chimel* decision. We reject this broad reading of *Belton*. We conclude that the circumstances unique to the vehicle context justify a search incident to a lawful arrest only when it is reasonable to believe that evidence relevant to the crime of arrest might be found in the vehicle. For many traffic-related crimes, there will be no such evidence.

The State seriously undervalues the privacy interests at stake here. At the same time, it exaggerates the scope of *Belton*. We also reject the State's contention that a broad application of *Belton* necessary to protect law enforcement officers. Construing *Belton* broadly to allow vehicle searches incident to *any* arrest would serve no purpose except to provide a police entitlement, and it is contrary to the Fourth Amendment to permit a warrantless search on that basis. Because in this case the arrestee was not within reaching distance of the passenger compartment at the time of the search, nor was it reasonable to believe the vehicle contained evidence of the offense of arrest (driving with a suspended license), the search was unconstitutional and the evidence inadmissible. Affirmed.

■ CONCURRENCE

(Scalia, J.) I believe that the application of *Chimel* in this context should be entirely abandoned. Justice Stevens's rule as announced today does not provide the certainty that is required in this field. But leaving the current understanding of *Belton* and the *Thornton* case in effect—always allowing arresting officers to search an arrestee's vehicle in order to protect themselves from hidden weapons—opens the field to searches that are plainly unconstitutional, and that is the greater evil. I therefore concur in the Court's judgment.

■ DISSENT

(Breyer, J.) *Belton* is best read as setting forth a bright-line rule that allows a warrantless search of the passenger compartment of automobiles incident to the lawful arrest of occupants, regardless of the danger the arrested individual poses. This rule can, however, produce results divorced from its Fourth Amendment rationale. I would look for a better rule, were the question before us one of first impression, but it is not. Principles or stare decisis must guide this Court.

■ DISSENT

(Alito, J.) The Court today overrules *Thornton* and *Belton*, although the defendant does not ask us to do so. *Belton* could not be clearer. The rule of that case is that when a police officer makes a lawful custodial arrest of the occupant of an automobile, the officer may, as a contemporaneous incident of that arrest, search the passenger compartment. The Court today adds the requirement that the passenger compartment be within the arrestee's reach. The *Belton* rule should be kept, without modification, because it has long been taught to police officers and relied on by them, nothing has changed to justify abandoning the rule, and it works. The Court does not, however, reexamine *Chimel*, and thus leaves the law relating to searches incident to arrest in a confused and unstable state. The new two-part rule, which permits an arresting officer to search the area within an arrestee's reach at the time of the search, applies only to vehicle occupants, but there is no logical reason why the same rule should not apply to all arrestees. The second part of the rule allows for an evidence-gathering search only when the officer has reason to believe—not the usual probable cause standard—that the vehicle contains evidence relevant to the crime of arrest. Why not any other crime? Nor is there reason to restrict the search to the passenger compartment. I would leave reexamination for our prior precedents for another day, if such a reexamination is to be undertaken at all. In this case, I would simply apply *Belton* and reverse the judgment below.

Analysis:

It is not hard to pick up on the tension between the Justices in this case. Justice Stevens, writing for the majority and joined by Justices Scalia, Souter, Thomas, and Ginsburg, the Court reasoned that warrantless searches are per se unreasonable and subject only to a few, very narrow exceptions not applicable here. Justice Alito, joined by Chief Justice Roberts and Justices Kennedy and Breyer, dissented, arguing that that the majority improperly overruled its precedent in *New York v. Belton*, which held that when an officer has made a lawful arrest, he or she may, as a contemporaneous incident of that arrest, search the passenger compartment of that automobile. Justice Breyer's separate dissenting opinion laments that the Court should not use this case to create a new governing rule.

■ CASE VOCABULARY

STARE DECISIS: [Latin "to stand by things decided."] The doctrine of precedent, under which it is necessary for a court to follow earlier judicial decisions when the same points arise again in litigation.

Whren v. United States

(Drug Offender) v. *(Prosecuting Government)*

517 U.S. 806, 116 S. Ct. 1769, 135 L. Ed. 2d 89 (1996)

POLICE STOPS NEED ONLY BE SUPPORTED BY PROBABLE CAUSE

I used to feel naughty following suspects until they committed minor traffic violations, then using that pretext to stop them. But, it turns out under *Whren* that I've been on the cutting edge of law enforcement.

stus.com

■ **INSTANT FACTS** Whren (D) was charged with violating various federal drug laws.

■ **BLACK LETTER RULE** The temporary detention of a motorist who the police have probable cause to believe has committed a civil traffic violation is consistent with the Fourth Amendment.

■ PROCEDURAL BASIS

Certiorari to determine whether the temporary detention of a motorist who the police have probable cause to believe has committed a civil traffic violation is inconsistent with the Fourth Amendment's prohibition against unreasonable seizures, unless a reasonable officer would have been motivated to stop the car by a desire to enforce the traffic laws.

■ FACTS

Plainclothes officers saw a vehicle stopped in a suspicious manner in high crime area. When they turned to pull up next to the vehicle, the vehicle turned without signaling and sped off. The officers chased the vehicle and stopped it. When the officer's went to the window of the vehicle, they saw bags of drugs laying on the defendant passenger's lap.

■ ISSUE

Is the temporary detention of a motorist who the police have probable cause to believe has committed a civil traffic violation inconsistent with the Fourth Amendment's prohibition against unreasonable seizures, unless a reasonable officer would have been motivated to stop the car by a desire to enforce the traffic laws?

■ DECISION AND RATIONALE

(Scalia, J.) No. The balance of all relevant factors in a reasonableness determination under the Fourth Amendment is not in doubt when the search or seizure is based on probable cause. The traditional common-law rule is that probable cause justifies a search and seizure. Thus, the temporary detention of a motorist who the police have probable cause to believe has committed a civil traffic violation is not inconsistent with the Fourth Amendment's prohibition against unreasonable seizures. Affirmed.

Analysis:

This decision has been criticized as overlooking an important issue regarding a pervasive law enforcement practice. Critics have alleged that pretextual traffic stops have increased markedly since the *Whren* decision. Critics also believe that the *Whren* decision has led to increased racial profiling in traffic stops.

Chambers v. Maroney

(*Armed Robber*) v. (*Prosecutor*)

399 U.S. 42, 90 S. Ct. 1975, 26 L. Ed. 2d 419 (1970)

ARRESTING OFFICERS MAY SEARCH A CAR WITHOUT A WARRANT IF THEY HAVE PROBABLE CAUSE TO BELIEVE IT CONTAINS ARTICLES THEY ARE ENTITLED TO SEIZE

Taking your car to search at the station would be a huge invasion of your privacy rights, if you had any.

stus.com

■ **INSTANT FACTS** Chambers was charged with armed robbery. Articles taken from his vehicle during the search at the police station were admitted into evidence against him.

■ **BLACK LETTER RULE** If government agents have probable cause to believe an automobile contains articles that they may be entitled to seize, they may search the vehicle pursuant to a lawful arrest, without a warrant, or impound the vehicle into police custody to be searched at a later time.

■ **PROCEDURAL BASIS**

Habeas corpus proceeding. Certiorari was granted to review the decision of the Third Circuit Court of Appeals affirming the lower court's conviction of the defendant for armed robbery.

■ **FACTS**

A convenience store was held up by two men and the stolen money was placed in a glove. Two witnesses reported a vehicle speeding away from the store. The witnesses gave police a description of the vehicle and the clothing the two men were wearing. Two hours later the police apprehended a vehicle matching the description given by the witnesses. The petitioner was one of the men riding in the car and his clothing matched the description given by the witnesses. The police arrested all four men. The police also impounded the car and the vehicle was searched later at the police station. The search of the car revealed two handguns, a glove containing small change, and cards bearing the name of the convenience store attendant who was robbed.

■ **ISSUE**

If police have the right to search an automobile at the time of a lawful arrest, may they instead choose to impound the vehicle into police custody and conduct a search at a later time?

■ **DECISION AND RATIONALE**

(White, J.) Yes. Automobiles may be searched without a warrant in circumstances that would not justify the search without a warrant in a home, or when there is probable cause to believe that the automobile contains articles the police are entitled to seize. The opportunity to search an automobile is fleeting because automobiles are readily moveable. If an effective search is to be made at any time, either the search must be made immediately without a warrant or the car itself must be seized. Affirmed.

■ **CONCURRENCE IN PART, DISSENT IN PART**

(Harlan, J.) It is clear from the decision in *Carroll* that police have the authority to conduct a warrantless search of an automobile on the side of the roadway, pursuant to a lawful arrest. This step is necessary

---

to preserve evidence. However, in circumstances in which a search at the time of arrest is impracticable and the automobile must be seized for a later search, it is less intrusive on privacy, and indeed not unreasonable, to require the automobile to remain seized while a valid warrant is obtained.

Analysis:

The police in this case were allowed to search the car later at the station, without a warrant, because there is a lesser expectation of privacy in cars than relates to houses under the Fourth Amendment. In reaching this conclusion, the Court relied heavily on its previous decision in *Carroll v. United States,* in which it ruled that the invasion of privacy in an automobile is not as significant as a warrantless entry into the sanctity of one's home.

■ **CASE VOCABULARY**

FRUITS OF THE CRIME: The proceeds acquired through criminal acts.

California v. Carney

(*Prosecuting State*) v. (*Accused Criminal*)

471 U.S. 386, 105 S. Ct. 2066, 85 L. Ed. 2d 406 (1985)

THE AUTOMOBILE EXCEPTION TO THE WARRANT REQUIREMENT ALSO APPLIES TO LIVE–IN VEHICLES

■ **INSTANT FACTS** Carney (D) was charged with possession of marijuana for sale after police discovered drugs in his motor home.

■ **BLACK LETTER RULE** The automobile exception to the warrant requirement includes protection for vehicles such as motor homes, vans, converted vans, minivans, and station wagons, which are capable of ready movement.

■ **PROCEDURAL BASIS**

Certiorari to decide whether law enforcement agents violated the Fourth Amendment when they conducted a warrantless search, based on probable cause, of a fully mobile "motor home" located in a public place.

■ **FACTS**

Police received information that a motor home occupied by Carney (D) was being used to exchange marijuana for sex. Government agents then accompanied a youth to the motor home and the youth entered the motor home and remained inside for one and one-quarter hours. When the youth emerged from the motor home, he informed a drug enforcement agent that he had received marijuana in exchange for allowing Carney to engage in sexual contact with him. The agent then accompanied the youth to the motor home, where the youth knocked on the door. When Carney stepped out, the agents identified themselves as law enforcement officers and entered the motor home without a warrant or consent. Inside the motor home, the agents observed marijuana, plastic bags, and a scale of the kind used to measure drugs. Carney was taken into custody and the agents took possession of the motor home. During a later search of the motor home, they discovered additional marijuana in the cupboards and refrigerator.

■ **ISSUE**

Does the automobile exception to the warrant requirement apply to vehicles such as a motor home, which individuals may be using as their home?

■ **DECISION AND RATIONALE**

(Burger, C.J.) Yes. If a vehicle is being used on the highways or if it is readily capable of such use and is found stationary in a place not regularly used for residential purposes, temporary or otherwise, the two justifications for the vehicle exception come into play. The vehicle is readily mobile and there is a reduced expectation of privacy stemming from its use as a licensed motor vehicle subject to a range of police regulation inapplicable to a fixed dwelling. In these circumstances, the overriding societal interests in effective law enforcement justify an immediate search before the vehicle and its occupants become unavailable. Reversed.

■ DISSENT

(Stevens, J.) Motor homes, by their common use and construction, afford their owners a substantial and legitimate expectancy of privacy when they dwell within. When a motor home is parked in a location that is removed from the public highway, society should be prepared to recognize that the expectations of privacy within are not unlike the expectations one has in a fixed dwelling.

Analysis:

Critics have argued the decision in this case goes too far. The Court's decision was based partly on the fact that automobiles are subject to a variety of government regulations. The critics of this decision have questioned whether it opened the door for warrantless searches of individual dwellings that are subject to building, health, and safety codes.

■ CASE VOCABULARY

NOLO CONTENDERE: No contest.

United States v. Chadwick

(*Prosecuting Government*) v. (*Drug Offender*)

433 U.S. 1, 97 S. Ct. 2476, 53 L. Ed. 2d 538 (1977)

A WARRANT IS REQUIRED TO SEARCH A CLOSED CONTAINER AFTER IT IS TAKEN INTO POLICE CUSTODY

■ **INSTANT FACTS** Chadwick was indicted for possession of marijuana with intent to distribute it and for conspiracy after police seized and later, without a warrant, searched a foot locker that contained evidence.

■ **BLACK LETTER RULE** A search warrant is required to search personal property of an arrestee at the point where the property to be searched comes under the exclusive dominion of police authority.

■ **PROCEDURAL BASIS**

Appeal to the Supreme Court from the lower court's decision to grant the defendant's motion to suppress evidence.

■ **FACTS**

Railroad officials in San Diego observed two men boarding a train bound for Boston with a footlocker, which they believed, because of their training, contained drugs. They reported this information to their counterparts in Boston, who had police-trained drug-detecting dogs on hand when the train arrived. The officials confiscated the footlocker and detained the suspects. The dogs signaled the presence of drugs in the footlocker. The men were arrested and the footlocker kept in law enforcement custody. An hour and a half after the suspects were arrested, the law enforcement officials searched their luggage and the footlocker without obtaining consent and without a warrant.

■ **ISSUE**

Can warrantless searches of luggage or other property seized at the time of an arrest be justified as incident to that arrest if the search is remote in time or place from the arrest or if no exigency exists?

■ **DECISION AND RATIONALE**

(Burger, C.J.) No. Once law enforcement officers have reduced luggage or other personal property not immediately associated with the person of the arrestee to their exclusive to their control, and there is no longer any danger that the arrestee might gain access to the property to seize a weapon or destroy evidence, a search of that property is no longer incident to the arrest. If there is no danger that evidence will be destroyed or that the arrestee might gain access to the property, there is no great burden placed on the government by requiring that they wait and obtain a search warrant before opening the closed container. Affirmed.

■ **CONCURRENCE**

(Brennan, J.) I agree with the dissent that it is unfortunate that the government in this case sought to vindicate an extreme view of the Fourth Amendment. However, the dissent cites no decisions of this Court to support the constitutionality of any of the possible alternative courses of action it suggests the agents could have followed without violating the Constitution.

■ DISSENT

(Blackmun, J.) It is likely that a warrant would be routinely forthcoming in the vast majority of situations in which the property has been seized in conjunction with the valid arrest of a person in a public place. It is doubtful that requiring the authorities to go through the formality of obtaining a warrant in this situation would have much practical effect in protecting Fourth Amendment values.

Analysis:

This decision has been criticized as being an extreme interpretation of the protections afforded by the Fourth Amendment. The Court determined that an individual who locks his belongings in a container has no less an expectation of privacy than one who locks the doors of his home against intruders. One who safeguards his personal possessions in this manner is due the protection of the Fourth Amendment Warrant Clause. The decision in this case was further expanded upon by the Court in *Arkansas v. Sanders*, in which the Court ruled that the automobile exception to the warrant requirement did not apply to a closed suitcase placed in the trunk of an automobile, but later removed and placed in police custody.

■ CASE VOCABULARY

INHERENTLY DANGEROUS: Requiring special precautions at all times to avoid injury.

California v. Acevedo

(Prosecuting State) v. *(Drug Offender)*
500 U.S. 565, 111 S. Ct. 1982, 114 L. Ed. 2d 619 (1991)

CONTAINERS IN AUTOMOBILES MAY BE SEARCHED IF THERE IS PROBABLE CAUSE TO BELIEVE THERE IS CONTRABAND IN THE AUTOMOBILE

When I asked permission to search the package in your trunk, I was just being polite. Actually, you have no choice.

stus.com

■ **INSTANT FACTS** Acevedo was charged with possession of marijuana. The charges were based on the search of a paper bag, which Acevedo had placed in the trunk of his car.

■ **BLACK LETTER RULE** Police can search an automobile and all containers in it when they have probable cause to believe contraband is contained somewhere within the automobile.

■ **PROCEDURAL BASIS**

Certiorari to review the decision of the California Court of Appeals affirming the defendant's conviction.

■ **FACTS**

The police were monitoring one Daza's apartment, because they had observed him take a package, which they knew from prior inspection contained marijuana, into his home. Some officers kept the home under surveillance while another officer went to obtain a warrant to search the home. Before the warrant could be obtained, the officers observed Acevedo (D) enter Daza's apartment and emerge ten minutes later carrying a brown paper bag. The officers noted that the bag looked to be the size of one of the marijuana packages Daza had entered his home with. Acevedo (D) placed the bag in the trunk of his car and drove away. Police then stopped his car, opened the trunk, and found the bag of marijuana, which they then opened.

■ **ISSUE**

Does the Fourth Amendment require police to obtain a warrant to open a container placed in an automobile, which they have probable cause to believe contains contraband, simply because they lack probable cause to search the entire car?

■ **DECISION AND RATIONALE**

(Blackmun, J.) No. The interpretation of the *Carroll* doctrine set forth in *Ross* now applies to all searches of containers found in an automobile. In other words, the police may search without a warrant if their search is supported by probable cause. Until today, this Court has drawn a curious line between the search of an automobile that coincidentally turns up a container and the search of a container that coincidentally turns up in an automobile. The protections of the Court must not turn on such coincidences. Therefore, *Carroll* must provide the one rule to govern all automobile searches. The police may search an automobile and the containers within it when they have probable cause to believe contraband or evidence is contained therein. Affirmed.

■ **CONCURRENCE**

(Scalia, J.) The standard for automobile searches should be the "reasonableness" requirements of the Fourth Amendment, which affords the same protection the common law afforded. The judgment in the present case should be reversed not because a closed container carried inside a car becomes subject to the "automobile" exception to the general warrant requirement, but because the search of a closed container, outside a privately owned building, with probable cause to believe that the container contains contraband, and when it does in fact contain contraband, is not one of those searches whose Fourth Amendment reasonableness depends upon a warrant.

■ DISSENT

(Stevens, J.) A person carrying a bag or a briefcase down the street may not be subject to a warrantless search, yet here the Court has decided that once that same container is placed in a car, those protections disappear. One's privacy interest in one's personal belongings can certainly not be diminished by one's removing it from a public thoroughfare and placing it, out of sight, in a privately owned vehicle. Nor is the danger that evidence will escape increased if the personal belongings are placed in a car rather than on the street. In either location, if the police have probable cause, they are authorized to seize the property and detain it until they obtain judicial approval for a search. Any line demarking an exception to the warrant requirement will appear blurred at the edges, but the Court has certainly erred if it believes that, by erasing one line and drawing another, it has drawn a clearer boundary.

Analysis:

The law applicable to a closed container in an automobile has troubled courts and law enforcement since it was first considered in *Chadwick*. The Court here attempted to set out a bright-line rule that would govern all searches of automobiles, including any containers contained within an automobile. This decision has been critiqued by many as merely muddying the confusion surrounding the "automobile" exception to the general warrant requirement even more.

■ CASE VOCABULARY

STARE DECISIS: The doctrine of precedent, under which it is necessary for a court to follow earlier judicial decisions when the same points arise again in litigation.

Horton v. California

(Armed Robber) v. *(Prosecuting State)*

496 U.S. 128, 110 S. Ct. 2301, 110 L. Ed. 2d 112 (1990)

POLICE MAY SEIZE EVIDENCE FOUND IN PLAIN VIEW

Of course I ate the fish. He was in "plain view". You, of all people, should understand how irresistible that is.

stus.com

■ **INSTANT FACTS** Horton was charged with armed robbery. Weapons seized during the search of his home pursuant to a valid warrant were admitted into evidence against him. The weapons seized were not listed on the search warrant.

■ **BLACK LETTER RULE** The warrantless seizure of evidence of a crime found in plain view should not be prohibited by the Fourth Amendment, even if the discovery of the evidence was not inadvertent.

■ PROCEDURAL BASIS

Appeal to the Supreme Court for a determination of whether the warrantless seizure of evidence in plain view is prohibited by the Fourth Amendment if the discovery of the evidence was not inadvertent.

■ FACTS

Police suspected Horton (D) of armed robbery. They requested a warrant to search his home for weapons used in the crime and the fruits of the robbery. The warrant they received failed to mention the weapons. The police searched the home and did not find the stolen merchandise the warrant specified, but did find the guns used in the robbery and other evidence linking Horton (D) to the robbery. The officers conducting the search indicated that while they were searching for the items listed on the search warrant, they were interested in finding other evidence connecting Horton (D) to the robbery.

■ ISSUE

Should the warrantless seizure of evidence of a crime in plain view be prohibited by the Fourth Amendment if the discovery of the evidence was not inadvertent?

■ DECISION AND RATIONALE

(Stevens, J.) No. The warrantless seizure of evidence of a crime, found in plain, view should not be prohibited by the Fourth Amendment, even if the discovery of the evidence was not inadvertent. The suggestion that the inadvertence requirement is necessary to prevent the police from conducting general searches, or from converting specific warrants into general warrants, is not persuasive because that interest is already served by the requirements that no warrant issue unless it particularly describes the place to be searched and the persons or things to be seized, and that a warrantless search be circumscribed by the exigencies that justify its initiation. Affirmed.

■ DISSENT

(Brennan, J.) The inadvertent discovery requirement is essential if we are to take seriously the Fourth Amendment's protection of possessory interests as well as privacy interests. The rationale behind the inadvertent discovery requirements is simply that we will not excuse officers from the general requirement of a warrant to seize if the officers know the location of evidence, have probable cause to seize it, intend to seize it, and yet do not bother to obtain a warrant particularly describing that evidence. When an officer with probable cause to seize an item fails to mention that item in his application for a search warrant, for whatever reason, and then seizes the item anyway, his conduct is per se unreasonable.

Analysis:

The "plain view" doctrine is often considered an exception to the general rule that warrantless searches are presumptively unreasonable, but this characterization overlooks the important difference between searches and seizures. If an article is in plain view, neither its observation not its seizure would involve any invasion of privacy. A seizure of the article, however, would obviously invade the owner's possessory interest. The Court set out in *Horton* to clarify the application of the "plain view" rule on seizures that was set out in *Coolidge v. New Hampshire.*

■ CASE VOCABULARY

"PLAIN VIEW" DOCTRINE: The rule permitting a police officer's warrantless seizure and use as evidence of an item seen in plain view from a lawful position or during a legal search when the officer has probable cause to believe that the item is evidence of a crime.

Arizona v. Hicks

(Prosecuting State) v. *(Robbery Suspect)*

480 U.S. 321, 107 S. Ct. 1149, 94 L. Ed. 2d 347 (1987)

PROBABLE CAUSE IS REQUIRED TO INVOKE THE PLAIN VIEW DOCTRINE

■ **INSTANT FACTS** Hicks (D) was charged with robbery based on stolen property found in Hicks's (D) apartment.

■ **BLACK LETTER RULE** The "plain view" doctrine may not be used to justify warrantless searches or seizures of a dwelling, which require probable cause.

■ **PROCEDURAL BASIS**

Certiorari to review the decision of the Arizona Court of Appeals affirming the lower court's decision to grant the defendant's motion to suppress evidence.

■ **FACTS**

A bullet went through the floor of Hicks's (D) apartment and injured a man in the apartment below. Police entered Hicks's (D) apartment to search for the shooter, other victims, and weapons. While searching the apartment, one of the police officers noticed expensive stereo equipment that he thought looked out of place in the apartment and suspected was stolen. The officer read the serial numbers on the equipment by moving some of the components. He reported these numbers to headquarters and determined the items were in fact stolen. The officer seized the components.

■ **ISSUE**

Is probable cause required to invoke the "plain view" doctrine?

■ **DECISION AND RATIONALE**

(Scalia, J.) Yes. Searches and seizures involving a dwelling require probable cause. The "plain view" doctrine alone may not justify warrantless searches or seizures of a dwelling. To say that probable cause is not required to invoke the "plain view" doctrine would be to cut the "plain view" doctrine loose from its theoretical and practical moorings. The "plain view" doctrine simply extends, to nonpublic places such as the home, where searches and seizures are presumptively unreasonable, the state's longstanding authority to make warrantless seizures of weapons and contraband. The practical justification for this extension is the desire to spare police, whose viewing of the object in the course of a lawful arrest is as legitimate as it would have been in a public place, the inconvenience and risk of going to obtain a warrant. Dispensing with the need for a warrant is worlds apart from permitting a lesser standard of cause for the seizure than a warrant would require. Affirmed.

■ **DISSENT**

(Powell, J.) The distinction between "looking" at a suspicious object in plain view and "moving" it even a few inches trivializes the Fourth Amendment. The Court's new rule will cause uncertainty and could deter conscientious police officers from lawfully obtaining evidence necessary to convict guilty persons.

■ DISSENT:

(O'Connor, J.) The Court today gives the right answer to the wrong question. The question this case presents is whether police must have probable cause before conducting a cursory inspection of an item in plain view or whether reasonable suspicion is enough. The purpose of the probable cause requirement is to prevent "general, exploratory rummaging" in a person's belongings. When a police officer makes a cursory inspection of a suspicious item, there is no "exploratory rummaging." Only those items that the police officer "reasonably suspects" are evidence of a crime may be inspected. The balance of the governmental and privacy interests strongly supports a reasonable-suspicion standard for the cursory examination of items in plain view.

Analysis:

The Court pointed out that there is nothing new in the realization that the Constitution sometimes insulates the criminality of a few in order to protect the privacy of many. In reaching its decision the Court declined to distinguish between searches of dwellings and seizures involving dwellings. The Court pointed out that while the interest protected by the Fourth Amendment injunction against unreasonable searches is quite different from that protected by its injunction against unreasonable seizures, neither one nor the other is inferior or necessarily requires lesser protection.

Schneckloth v. Bustamonte

(Prosecutor) v. *(Thief)*

412 U.S. 218, 93 S. Ct. 2041, 36 L. Ed. 2d 854 (1973)

CONSENT TO A SEARCH IS VALID EVEN IF THE CONSENTER DID NOT KNOW HE COULD REFUSE

■ **INSTANT FACTS** Bustamonte (D) was charged with theft after three stolen checks were discovered during a search of the automobile in which Bustamonte (D) was a passenger. The driver consented to the search.

■ **BLACK LETTER RULE** An individual need not be informed that he has the right to refuse consent to a search before his consent to the search will be considered voluntary.

■ PROCEDURAL BASIS

Certiorari to review the decision of the Ninth Circuit Court of Appeals vacating the judgment of the lower court.

■ FACTS

A police officer stopped a car because one of its headlights and the car's license plate light were burned out. The driver of the car could not produce a license, so the officer asked the driver, Alcala, who claimed his brother owned the car, for permission to search the vehicle. Alcala said, "Sure, go ahead." Alcala actually opened the trunk and the glove compartment for the officer. The search uncovered three stolen checks that were later linked to Bustamonte (D), one of the passengers in the car.

■ ISSUE

In order for consent to a search to be considered voluntary, must the individual consenting be informed that he has the right to refuse consent?

■ DECISION AND RATIONALE

(Stewart, J.) No. An individual need not be informed that he has the right to refuse consent to a search before his consent to such a search will be considered voluntary. Whether consent to a search was in fact "voluntary" and not the product of duress or coercion is a question of fact to be determined from the totality of the circumstances. The problem of reconciling the recognized legitimacy of consent searches with the requirement that they be free from any aspect of official coercion cannot be resolved by any infallible touchstone. In examining all the surrounding circumstances to determine if in fact the consent to the search was coerced, account must be taken of subtly coercive police questions, as well as the possibly vulnerable subjective state of the person who consents. Neither this Court's prior cases, nor the traditional definition of "voluntariness," requires proof of knowledge of a right to refuse as the *sine qua non* of an effective consent to a search. Reversed.

■ DISSENT

(Marshall, J.) Consent should be viewed as a relinquishment of Fourth Amendment rights and should be taken literally to mean a "knowing" choice. If consent to search means that a person has chosen to forgo his right to exclude the police from the place they seek to search, it follows that his consent cannot be considered a meaningful choice unless he knew that he could not in fact exclude the police.

Analysis:

In situations in which the police have some evidence of illicit activity, but lack probable cause to arrest or search, a search authorized by a valid consent may be the only means of obtaining important and reliable evidence. Even in those cases in which there is probable cause to arrest or search, but the police lack a warrant, a consent search may still be valuable. If the search is conducted and proves fruitless, that in itself may convince police that an arrest with its possible stigma and embarrassment is unnecessary, or that a far more extensive search pursuant to a warrant is not justified. A search pursuant to consent may result in significantly less inconvenience for the subject of the search, and, properly conducted, is a constitutionally permissible and wholly legitimate aspect of effective police activity.

■ CASE VOCABULARY

CONSENT: Agreement, approval, or permission as to some act or purpose, especially if given voluntarily by a competent person.

VOLUNTARY: Done by design or intention.

SINE QUA NON: An indispensable condition or thing; something on which something else necessarily depends.

Georgia v. Randolph

(Prosecuting State) v. *(Convicted Criminal)*
547 U.S. 103, 126 S. Ct. 1515, 164 L. Ed. 2d 208 (2006)

POLICE MAY NOT SEARCH A DWELLING IF ONE CO–OCCUPANT REFUSES TO CONSENT

I aksed Daddy. He said "no", so tonight I'll ask Mom.

■ **INSTANT FACTS** Randolph (D) was convicted of a drug offense based on evidence that resulted from a search of his home to which only his wife consented, over his objection.

■ **BLACK LETTER RULE** "[A] warrantless search of a shared dwelling for evidence over the express refusal of consent by a physically present resident cannot be justified as reasonable as to him on the basis of consent given to the police by another resident."

■ **PROCEDURAL BASIS**

Certiorari to review a state court decision on the admissibility of evidence.

■ **FACTS**

When the police responded to a domestic disturbance, the wife told the officers that there were items of drug evidence in the house, but Randolph (D), the husband, refused to let the officers search. They turned back to the wife for consent, which she readily granted, leading the officers to the evidence. When one of the officers went outside to get an evidence bag, he called the district attorney's office and was advised to get a warrant. Then, when the officer re-entered the house, the wife withdrew her consent. Nonetheless, the officers took what evidence they already had, along with the Randolphs (D), to the police station; they later returned to the house, pursuant to a search warrant, to gather more evidence. Randolph (D) was indicted for possession of cocaine, and at his trial he moved to suppress the evidence obtained at his home as the fruit of a warrantless search. He argued that his wife could not consent to the search over his refusal. The trial court disagreed, ruling that Randolph's (D) wife had common authority to consent, and Randolph (D) was convicted. He appealed, and the court of appeals reversed, holding that the evidence was not admissible, and the state supreme court affirmed. The Supreme Court granted certiorari to resolve a split of authority on the issue of co-occupant consent to searches.

■ **ISSUE**

Can one co-occupant of a dwelling consent to a search of the premises over the other co-occupant's refusal?

■ **DECISION AND RATIONALE**

(Souter, J.) No. Although a fellow occupant who shares common authority over a premises may consent to a search of that premises in the absence of the suspect, the same is not true if the suspect is present and refuses. "[A] warrantless search of a shared dwelling for evidence over the express refusal of consent by a physically present resident cannot be justified as reasonable as to him on the basis of consent given to the police by another resident." It is true that one co-tenant may have an interest in bringing his or her criminal co-tenant to justice, but this result can be accomplished by means other than allowing a warrantless search of the home in the presence of the suspect's outright refusal.

Based on common-sense concepts of co-tenants' rights and ordinary principles of joint residency, it follows that the police may assume that one who jointly resides in a home may consent to its search if the other tenant is not present. But customary social understanding does not accord the consenting tenant authority powerful enough to prevail over a physically present co-tenant's objections. In the *Matlock* case, the suspect was not available to consent, although he was nearby in a squad car; and in the *Rodriguez* case, the suspect was unavailable, although asleep in the apartment. This is admittedly a very fine line, but it is the one the Court chooses to draw. If the co-tenant is at the door refusing entry, a search cannot be conducted even if a co-tenant consents. Affirmed.

■ CONCURRENCE

(Stevens, J.) Even the most dedicated adherent to a constitutional-interpretation approach that relies primarily on a search for original understanding would recognize the relevance of societal changes. In today's world, males and females are equal partners. Neither one is a master possessing the power to override the other's constitutional right to deny entry to their shared dwelling.

■ CONCURRENCE

(Breyer, J.) Because the Court's holding is case-specific, I concur. The totality of the circumstances here does not justify abandoning Fourth Amendment proscriptions on police entry into a home without a warrant. This decision will not adversely affect law enforcement practices, because the fact that an abuse victim invites police officers into the home and consents to a search may itself provide the proof sought.

■ DISSENT

(Roberts, J.) The majority's analogy to the social situation of declining to enter a home if one of the occupants shouts "stay out" does not support its conclusion, because there are many situations in which a social caller would enter despite such hostility from one co-tenant. Moreover, according to the majority's random rule, a co-tenant is not present for purposes of refusing to consent to a search if he or she is merely in the backyard, or listening to music through headphones so that he doesn't hear the police at the door. This rule could have particularly adverse consequences in domestic abuse situations, such as this case. The majority's decision would apparently prevent the police from entering the victim's home in a domestic disturbance call if the abuser stands at the door telling them they cannot come inside. The majority attempts to brush this concern aside by saying the police can respond differently in exigent circumstances, but why craft such a rule in the first place? Law enforcement and trial courts alike are left with no guidance as a result of this decision.

■ DISSENT

(Scalia, J.) This is not just a case about property rights, but even if it were, we can be cognizant of recent alterations in property rights in regard to married women, without altering the Fourth Amendment itself. Moreover, I'm not sure that today's decision champions women's rights; in fact, it may put them at greater risk if they are unable to consent to police entry into their homes in the face of an abuser's resistance.

Analysis:

The Court admits to drawing a fine line here, but as Justice Roberts's dissenting opinion points out, that line could result in random law-enforcement application. The majority opinion suggests that the only time a co-tenant's refusal to consent bars a search is when he or she is physically present, virtually in the doorway, and proactively asserts the refusal. In other words, the police do not need to seek out the occupant and ask for permission to search, even if he or she is a short distance away, or even within view but asleep or listening to his iPod. It is apparent why the dissenting Justices had concerns with the majority's viewpoint in this case.

■ CASE VOCABULARY

CONSENT: Agreement, approval, or permission as to some act or purpose, especially given voluntarily by a competent person; legally effective assent.

Illinois v. Rodriguez

(Prosecuting State) v. *(Drug Offender)*
497 U.S. 177, 110 S. Ct. 2793, 111 L. Ed. 2d 148 (1990)

CONSENT THAT APPEARS VALID WILL BE DEEMED VALID

■ **INSTANT FACTS** Rodriguez (D) was charged with possession of a controlled substance with intent to deliver after his girlfriend let the police into his apartment and they discovered evidence.

■ **BLACK LETTER RULE** If law enforcement officers have reason to believe the individual giving consent to a search has authority over the premises to be searched, then the entry will be validated even if it is later determined that the person did not have authority to consent.

■ PROCEDURAL BASIS

Appeal to the Supreme Court from lower court decisions affirming the granting of the defendant's motion to suppress evidence.

■ FACTS

Police officers were summoned to a home, where they were met by Gail Fischer, who showed signs of a severe beating. Fischer told police she had been assaulted by Rodriguez (D) earlier that day in an apartment on South California Avenue. Fischer told police that Rodriguez (D) was asleep in the apartment and she would take them there and unlock the door with her key to let them in. She repeatedly referred to the apartment as "our" apartment. She also told police she had clothes and furniture at the apartment. Fischer unlocked the door to the apartment and gave police permission to enter. The police did not obtain an arrest warrant for Rodriguez or a search warrant for the apartment. Once police entered the apartment, they discovered drug paraphernalia and containers filled with what they believed to be cocaine, in plain view. They seized these containers and two other containers found in cases in the bedroom where Rodriguez (D) was sleeping.

■ ISSUE

Even if a person does not, in fact, have authority to give consent to a search, can the entry be validated if the law enforcement officers reasonably believed she did?

■ DECISION AND RATIONALE

(Scalia, J.) Yes. If a person does not have authority to consent to a search of the premises, an entry by law enforcement officers will be validated if the officers reasonably believed at the time of their entry that the individual possessed the authority to consent. In order to satisfy the Fourth Amendment, what is generally demanded of the many factual determinations that must regularly be made by agents of the government—whether the magistrate issuing a warrant, the police officer executing a warrant, or the police officer conducting a search or seizure under one of the exceptions to the warrant requirement—is not that they always be correct, but that they always be reasonable. As with other factual determinations bearing upon search and seizure, determination of consent to enter must be judged against an objective standard: would the facts available to the officer at the moment of the search warrant that a man of "reasonable caution" believe that the consenting party had authority over the premises? Reversed and remanded.

■ DISSENT

(Marshall, J.) The validity of third-party consent searches rests not on the premise that they are "reasonable" under the Fourth Amendment, but on the premise that a person may voluntarily limit his expectation of privacy by allowing others to exercise authority over his possessions. If an individual has not so limited his expectation of privacy, the police may not dispense with the safeguards established by the Fourth Amendment.

Analysis:

The Fourth Amendment merely insures that no "unreasonable" searches of an individual's home will occur. To require that all consent searches must, in fact, be based on valid consent, not merely on reasonable belief of consent, would require that the government agent's judgment not only be responsible, but correct—a higher standard than the Court generally imposes in this arena. Such a requirement would greatly impede government agents and would essentially destroy the consent exception to the general warrant requirement.

■ CASE VOCABULARY

RESIDENT: A person who lives in a particular place, or has a home in a particular place.

Terry v. Ohio

(Weapons Violator) v. *(Prosecuting State)*

392 U.S. 1, 88 S. Ct. 1868, 20 L. Ed. 2d 889 (1968)

POLICE MAY STOP AND SEARCH SOMEONE REASONABLY BELIEVED TO HAVE COMMITTED A CRIME

■ **INSTANT FACTS** Evidence of a gun found on Terry during a protective frisk by a police officer was admitted into evidence. Terry (D) was convicted of carrying a concealed weapon.

■ **BLACK LETTER RULE** If the police have reasonable suspicion that a suspect has committed a crime or is about to commit a crime, they may stop the person, detain him briefly for questioning, and then frisk the suspect if they reasonably believe the suspect is carrying a dangerous weapon.

■ **PROCEDURAL BASIS**

Certiorari to review the decision of the Eighth Circuit Court of Appeals affirming the lower court's conviction of the defendant for carrying a concealed weapon.

■ **FACTS**

A police officer observed two men standing on a corner for a long time. They then walked down the street, peered into a store window, and turned around to walk back to the corner again. This series of events happened several times. At one point, another man approached the two men and spoke with them and then walked in the other direction. He then came back and they followed him. The officer suspected the men were casing the store before committing a robbery. He stopped them to ask for their names. When the men failed to answer audibly, the officer spun Terry (D) around and patted down the outside of his overcoat for a weapon. Upon feeling a gun, the officer ordered the men into a store, where he removed Terry's (D) overcoat and retrieved the gun. After finding a gun on another man, the men were arrested.

■ **ISSUE**

If the police have reason to believe a suspect has committed a crime or is about to commit a crime, may they conduct a stop on less than probable cause?

■ **DECISION AND RATIONALE**

(Warren, C.J.) Yes. If the police have reasonable suspicion that a suspect has committed a crime or is about to commit a crime, they may stop the person and detain him briefly for questioning, on less than probable cause. An officer may then frisk the suspect if the officer reasonably believes the suspect is carrying a dangerous weapon. In order for crime prevention and detection to be effective, an officer must be able to, in appropriate circumstances and in an appropriate manner, approach a person for purposes of investigating possible criminal behavior even though there is no probable cause to make an arrest. Law enforcement officers must be able to protect themselves and other prospective victims of violence in situations in which they are investigating suspicious behavior of suspected criminals at close range. Affirmed.

■ CONCURRENCE

(Harlan, J.) In order for a frisk to protect an officer to be justified, the officer must first have constitutional grounds to insist on an encounter and make a forcible stop. When the reason for the stop is an articulable suspicion of a crime of violence, however, the right to frisk must be immediate and automatic.

■ DISSENT

(Douglas, J.) By holding that a police officer may stop a person based only upon reasonable suspicion that a crime has been committed, the Court gives the police greater authority to make a seizure and conduct a search than a judge has to authorize such actions. To give the police greater power than a magistrate is to take a long step down a totalitarian path. Even if this is a desirable step, it should be taken by the people through a constitutional amendment.

Analysis:

The result of the *Terry* decision has been a significant diminution in the role of the Warrant Clause in Fourth Amendment jurisprudence. *Terry* provided the impetus for the Supreme Court to move away from the proposition that warrantless searches are per se unreasonable, to the competing view that the appropriate test of police conduct is not whether it was reasonable for police to have secured a search warrant, but whether the search was reasonable. After *Terry*, warrantless searches became much more justifiable. Also, the Court now takes into consideration the level of intrusiveness of each search, instead of treating all searches and seizures alike.

■ CASE VOCABULARY

FRISK: A pat-down search to discover a concealed weapon.

PER SE: Of, in, or by itself; standing alone, without reference to additional facts.

REASONABLE SUSPICION: A particularized and objective basis, supported by specific and articulable facts, for suspecting a person of criminal activity.

Dunaway v. New York

(*Accused Criminal*) v. (*Prosecuting State*)
442 U.S. 200, 99 S. Ct. 2248, 60 L. Ed. 2d 824 (1979)

PROBABLE CAUSE MUST PRECEDE CUSTODIAL INTERROGATION

■ **INSTANT FACTS** Dunaway (D) was convicted of murder and attempted robbery based in part on statements he made during police questioning.

■ **BLACK LETTER RULE** Police may not subject a suspect to custodial interrogation unless they have probable cause to believe a crime has been committed.

■ PROCEDURAL BASIS

Certiorari to review the decision of the New York appellate court reversing the lower court's granting of the defendant's motion to suppress the defendant's confession.

■ FACTS

Police received a tip from an informant that implicated Dunaway (D) in a murder that occurred during an attempted robbery. Police did not have enough information from the tip to obtain a warrant for Dunaway's (D) arrest. Nevertheless, police took Dunaway (D) into custody. Dunaway (D) was not told he was under arrest, but he would have been restrained had he attempted to leave. Dunaway (D) was taken to the police station and given *Miranda* warnings before the police questioned him. Dunaway (D) made statements and drew sketches that implicated him in the crime.

■ ISSUE

May seizures for purposes of custodial interrogation be justified by mere "reasonable suspicion"?

■ DECISION AND RATIONALE

(Brennan, J.) No. Police may not subject a suspect to custodial interrogation unless they have probable cause to believe a crime has been committed. Any "exception" that could cover a seizure as intrusive as a custodial interrogation would threaten to swallow the general rule that Fourth Amendment seizures are "reasonable" only if based on probable cause. Reversed.

■ CONCURRENCE

(White, J.) The key principle of the Fourth Amendment is reasonableness, which is judged by the balancing of competing interests. But if courts and law enforcement are to have workable rules, this balancing must in large part be done on a categorical basis, not in a case-by-case fashion by individual police officers.

■ DISSENT

(Rehnquist, J.) This is a case in which the defendant voluntarily accompanied police to the station to answer questions, not where the defendant was seized. Just because a request to come to the station can be an "awesome experience" does not mean that in every instance in which a person assents to such a request there has been a "seizure" within the meaning of the Fourth Amendment. The question turns on whether the officer's conduct is objectively coercive or physically threatening, not on the mere fact that a person might in some measure feel cowed by a request from a police officer.

Analysis:

If the transportation of an individual to police headquarters for questioning cannot be considered a "seizure" of an individual for Fourth Amendment purposes, what could be? However, if the Court had ruled that the police can seize a person for purposes of custodial interrogation based merely on "reasonable suspicion," the protection provided for the Fourth Amendment against seizure of an individual would essentially have been destroyed. "Reasonable suspicion" is a very low standard for review of police actions.

■ CASE VOCABULARY

CUSTODIAL INTERROGATION: Police questioning of a detained person about the crime that he or she is suspected of committing.

United States v. Mendenhall

(*Prosecuting Government*) v. (*Drug Offender*)

446 U.S. 544, 100 S. Ct. 1870, 64 L. Ed. 2d 497 (1980)

IF A REASONABLE PERSON WOULD BELIEVE SHE WAS FREE TO LEAVE, THERE WAS NO SEIZURE

■ **INSTANT FACTS** Mendenhall (D) was arrested for possession of heroin. Evidence of heroin found on her person during a search conducted by DEA agents was admitted into evidence against her.

■ **BLACK LETTER RULE** A person is seized when, in light of the circumstances, a reasonable person would have believed that she was no longer free to leave.

■ PROCEDURAL BASIS

Certiorari to review the decision of the Sixth Circuit Court of Appeals reversing the defendant's conviction for drug offenses.

■ FACTS

DEA agents observed Mendenhall (D) disembarking from a flight from Los Angeles. After observing her behavior, they determined it to be characteristic of person unlawfully carrying narcotics. DEA agents identified themselves and stopped Mendenhall (D), asking for her identification and ticket. Her ticket was not in her name. They asked Mendenhall (D) to come to office and she did so without protest. Mendenhall (D) consented to a search of her person and bag.

■ ISSUE

Is being detained by police for questioning without being placed under arrest always an unlawful seizure in violation of the Fourth Amendment?

■ DECISION AND RATIONALE

(Stewart, J.) No. A person has been "seized" within the meaning of the Fourth Amendment only if, in view of all of the circumstances surrounding the incident, a reasonable person would have believed that she was not free to leave. Examples of circumstances that might indicate a seizure, even when the person did not attempt to leave, include the threatening presence of several officers, the display of a weapon by an officer, some physical touching of the person, and the use of language or tone of voice indicating that compliance with the officer's request might be compelled. In the absence of such evidence, otherwise offensive contact between a member of the public and the police cannot, as a matter of law, amount to a seizure of that person. Reversed and remanded.

■ CONCURRENCE

(Powell, J.) If federal agents have reasonable suspicion that a suspect was engaging in criminal activity, they will not violate the Fourth Amendment by stopping him or her for routine questioning. The reasonableness of a stop depends on the facts and circumstances of each case. The Court should look to (1) the public interest served by the seizure, (2) the nature and scope of the intrusion, and (3) the objective facts upon which law enforcement officers relied in light of their knowledge and expertise.

■ DISSENT

(White, J.) Throughout the lower court proceedings in this case, the prosecution never questioned that the initial stop of Mendenhall (D) was a "seizure" that required reasonable suspicion. Having failed to convince the court of appeals that the DEA agents had reasonable suspicion for the stop, the government seeks reversal here by arguing for the first time that no "seizure" occurred. Even if one believes the prosecution should be permitted to raise the "seizure" question in this Court, the proper course would be to direct a remand to the district court, rather than to decide it in the first instance in this Court.

Analysis:

The test put forth here is an objective test. The standard is that of a reasonable person in the same situation. Determinations in these types of seizure cases have always been, and continue to be, very fact specific. This approach has been criticized as a hindrance on law enforcement because police must guess at whether the detainees understand they are free to leave or risk being held accountable for an unlawful seizure.

■ CASE VOCABULARY

SEIZURE: The act or an instance of taking possession of a person or property by legal right or process.

United States v. Drayton

(Prosecuting Authority) v. *(Convicted Drug Offender)*

536 U.S. 194, 122 S. Ct. 2105, 153 L. Ed. 2d 242 (2002)

SUSPICIONLESS SEARCHES OF BUS PASSENGERS ARE LEGAL

■ **INSTANT FACTS** Drayton (D) consented—involuntarily, he said—to being patted down as part of an all-passenger search of the Greyhound bus on which he was riding, and was convicted of a drug offense based on evidence discovered during the patdown.

■ **BLACK LETTER RULE** Police officers do not violate the Fourth Amendment prohibition on unreasonable seizures by approaching individuals in public places, questioning them, and requesting consent to search, if they do not induce cooperation by coercive means and a reasonable person would feel free to terminate the encounter.

■ PROCEDURAL BASIS

Certiorari to review a reversal of the defendant's conviction.

■ FACTS

When the Greyhound bus on which Drayton (D) was a passenger made a routine stop, three police officers, not in uniform but displaying badges, boarded the bus and began questioning the passengers and searching their luggage as part of a drug and weapons interdiction effort. One of the officers, Lang, displayed his badge to Drayton (D) and asked him if he had any bags. Drayton (D) and Brown, his traveling companion, directed the officers toward a green bag in the overhead rack. The officers found no contraband, but they noticed that Drayton (D) and Brown were inappropriately dressed for the warm weather, wearing heavy jackets and baggy pants. Officer Lang became suspicious that they were hiding weapons or drugs, so he asked Brown if he could check his person. Brown consented, upon which Lang patted him down and discovered objects that felt like drugs. Brown was handcuffed, arrested, and led off of the bus. Lang then asked Drayton (D) if he could check him, and Drayton (D) responded by lifting his hands about eight inches from his legs. Officer Lang found similar drug-like objects during his patdown of Drayton (D), who was also arrested and escorted from the bus. Further searches revealed that the hard objects detected during the patdowns were powder cocaine in plastic bundles, duct-taped to the suspects' boxer shorts.

Drayton (D) and Lang moved to suppress the drugs, arguing that their consent to the patdown was invalid. The district court allowed the evidence, reasoning that the consent was entirely voluntary, there was nothing coercive about the officers' conduct, and everyone on the bus would have understood that they were free to leave at any time. The court of appeals reversed, remanding with instructions to grant the suppression motion. The court held that bus passengers do not feel free to disregard police officers' requests, absent some positive indication that consent could be refused. The Supreme Court granted certiorari.

■ ISSUE

Did the bus passengers voluntarily consent to the patdowns by the police officer, such that the searches of their person were constitutional and the evidence therefrom was admissible?

■ DECISION AND RATIONALE

(Kennedy, J.) Yes. Police officers do not violate the Fourth Amendment prohibition on unreasonable seizures by approaching individuals in public places, questioning them, and requesting consent to search, if they do not induce cooperation by coercive means and a reasonable person would feel free to terminate the encounter. The relevant inquiry is whether a reasonable person would feel free to decline the police officer's request, which depends on the surrounding circumstances; there is no generally applicable per se rule in the Fourth Amendment context. Thus, in *Florida v. Bostick*, where the police had found contraband in the defendant bus-rider's luggage, we identified two key factors for consideration on remand in determining whether the search was constitutional: (1) although the officer was armed, he did not remove the gun from its pouch or use it in a threatening way; and (2) the officer advised the passenger that he could refuse consent to the search.

Here, Officer Lang did not brandish a weapon or make threatening moves. There was no show of force or blocking of exits. Although Officer Lang showed his badge, this factor was held to be benign in *INS v. Delgado*. And although Officer Hoover stood at the front of the bus, he did nothing to intimidate the passengers. In *Delgado*, we held that the presence of officers by exists poses no reasonable threat. Moreover, the fact that Brown had already been arrested did not mean that Drayton (D) was seized; the arrest of one person does not invoke the seizure of all others around him. In fact, to the contrary, it should put a person on notice as to the possible consequences of consenting to a search.

Not only was there no unconstitutional seizure, there was also no unreasonable search. Although Officer Lang did not advise Drayton (D) that he could refuse, he did obtain Drayton's (D) permission before he patted him down. Under a totality of the circumstances approach, this was all that was required here. Consent has a dignity of its own, and police officers act in full accord with the law when they ask citizens for consent. Reversed and remanded.

■ DISSENT

(Souter, J.) Under the *Bostick* totality of the circumstances test, there is no way that the defendant here would have reasonably believed he could have refused consent in this case. Just the presence of three officers in the confined space of the bus tips the balance of power and is intimidating. Although I will not go so far as to say the officers must have explicitly told the bus passengers that they could refuse consent, I do believe that more than a quiet tone of voice was required of them. "A police officer who is certain to get his way has no need to shout."

Analysis:

In *Bostick*, the Court held that police officers could enter a bus, approach passengers at random, and request their consent to engage in a search of their luggage or persons if no compulsion was involved in obtaining that consent. Here, the Court applies the same principles, but stops short of requiring police officers to inform citizens of their right to refuse consent to a warrantless consent search. If the passengers had been told they could withhold consent in this case, there would be no debate about whether their acquiescence was voluntary. Note the distinction between searches and seizures under the Fourth Amendment and interrogations under the Fifth Amendment. *Miranda* requires warnings about the right to remain silent and the right to the assistance of a lawyer before custodial interrogation may begin, but no such warning requirement attaches to Fourth Amendment rights.

■ CASE VOCABULARY

INTERDICTION: **The interception and seizure of something, especially contraband.**

PER SE: Of, in, or by itself; standing alone, without reference to additional facts.

California v. Hodari D.

(Prosecuting State) v. *(Drug Offender)*

499 U.S. 621, 111 S. Ct. 1547, 113 L. Ed. 2d 690 (1991)

POLICE CHASES ARE NOT SEIZURES

No, chasing you was not a "seizure". You'd know it if you'd been seized.

stus.com

■ **INSTANT FACTS** Hodari (D) was charged with possession of crack cocaine based on a rock of crack cocaine that he threw away while under police pursuit.

■ **BLACK LETTER RULE** An arrest requires either physical force or submission to the assertion of authority.

■ **PROCEDURAL BASIS**

Certiorari to review the decision of the Ninth Circuit Court of Appeals reversing the defendant's conviction for possession of cocaine.

■ **FACTS**

The police came upon a group of kids hovered around a car. When the youths saw the police approaching, they fled and the car sped off. Hodari (D) was one of the youths who ran in the direction in which the car disappeared. The police gave chase in that direction. One of the officers caught up to Hodari (D), who tossed away what appeared to be a small rock, before he was tackled and handcuffed by the officer. The rock Hodari (D) discarded turned out to be crack cocaine.

■ **ISSUE**

When police engage in a show of authority as to the application of physical force, can a seizure occur even if the suspect does not yield?

■ **DECISION AND RATIONALE**

(Scalia, J.) No. An arrest requires either physical force or, where that is absent, submission to the assertion of authority. The word "seizure" requires a laying on of hands or application of physical force to restrain movement, even when it is untimely unsuccessful. It does not remotely apply, however, to a police officer yelling, "Stop, in the name of the law!" at a fleeing form that continues to flee. Reversed and remanded.

■ **DISSENT**

(Stevens, J.) The Court concludes that the timing of the seizure is governed by the citizen's reaction, rather than by the officer's conduct. One consequence of this conclusion is that the point at which the interaction between citizen and police officer becomes a seizure occurs not when a reasonable citizen believes he or she is no longer free to go, but rather only after the officer exercises control over the citizen. Our interests in effective law enforcement would be better served by adhering to a standard that allows the police to determine in advance whether the conduct contemplated will implicate the Fourth Amendment.

Analysis:

Street pursuits often place the public at some risk, and the pervasive view is that compliance with police orders to stop should therefore be encouraged. This view makes the assumption that police will not abuse their authority and will only order suspects to stop if they have suspicion of criminal activity. The rule allows police to question suspicious behavior on a standard less than reasonable suspicion. The overwhelming interest in public law enforcement outweighs the minimal irritation to persons who are stopped by police for brief questioning.

■ CASE VOCABULARY

YIELD: To give up, relinquish, or surrender

SUBMISSION: A yielding to the authority or will of another.

Alabama v. White

(Prosecuting State) v. *(Drug Offender)*

496 U.S. 325, 110 S. Ct. 2412, 110 L. Ed. 2d 301 (1990)

AN ANONYMOUS BUT PARTIALLY VERIFIED TIP CAN BE USED AS THE BASIS FOR A *TERRY* STOP

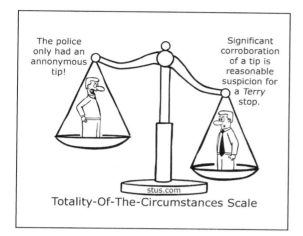

The police only had an annonymous tip!

Significant corroboration of a tip is reasonable suspicion for a *Terry* stop.

stus.com

Totality-Of-The-Circumstances Scale

■ **INSTANT FACTS** White (D) was arrested for possession of cocaine and marijuana in violation of state law. The court held that the officers did not have the reasonable suspicion necessary under *Terry v. Ohio* to justify the investigatory stop of White's (D) car and that the marijuana and cocaine were fruits of the unconstitutional detention.

■ **BLACK LETTER RULE** An anonymous tip received by police and not completely corroborated can be used as the basis for a *Terry* stop as long as a significant portion of the tip is verified.

■ PROCEDURAL BASIS

Certiorari to review the decision of the Alabama Court of Appeals reversing the defendant's conviction for possession of marijuana and cocaine.

■ FACTS

Police received an anonymous tip that a woman would be leaving a certain room in an apartment complex, getting into a brown car with a broken taillight, and driving toward Dobey's Hotel with an ounce of cocaine inside a brown briefcase. The police set up surveillance and observed White (D) leaving the room in the apartment complex and getting into a car matching the given description. The police pulled White's (D) car over just before she reached Dobey's Hotel. They asked permission to search the car and White (D) consented. The police found a briefcase containing marijuana in the car. The police placed White (D) under arrest. During processing, police found cocaine in her purse.

■ ISSUE

Can an anonymous tip, received by police and not completely corroborated, be used as the basis for a *Terry* stop as long as a significant portion of the tip is verified?

■ DECISION AND RATIONALE

(White, J.) Yes. An anonymous tip received by police and not completely corroborated can be used as the basis for a *Terry* stop as long as a significant portion of the tip is verified before the stop. Reasonable suspicion, like probable cause, is dependent on both the content of the information possessed by police and its reliability. Both of these factors are considered in the "totality of the circumstances" test, which must be used in evaluating whether reasonable suspicion exists. Thus, if a tip has a low degree of reliability, more information will be required to establish the requisite quantum of suspicion than would be required than if the tip were more reliable. Reversed and remanded.

■ DISSENT

(Stevens, J.) Anybody with enough knowledge about a given person to make her the target of a prank, or to harbor a grudge against her, will certainly be able to formulate a tip about her like the one

---

predicting Vanessa White's (D) excursion. In addition, under the Court's holding, every citizen is subject to being seized and questioned by any officer who is prepared to testify that the warrantless stop was based on an anonymous tip predicting whatever conduct the officer just observed.

Analysis:

Critics have noted that the ability to predict someone's future behavior may not always be indicative of inside information. Many people are familiar with the routines of their neighbors. Neighbors are generally aware of the sort of information included in the tip given about White (D) in this case, such as the time a person usually leaves home, what kind of car they drive, and the places they go. It has been argued that this information is hardly indicative of criminal behavior and "tips" could sometimes arise out of a personal vendetta.

Illinois v. Wardlow

(Prosecuting State) v. *(Weapons Violator)*

528 U.S. 119, 120 S. Ct. 673, 145 L. Ed. 2d 570 (2000)

FLIGHT ALONE IS NOT INDICATIVE OF WRONGDOING

■ **INSTANT FACTS** Wardlow (D) was arrested for possession of a handgun in violation of state law. The handgun admitted into evidence was found on Wardlow's person during a protective frisk.

■ **BLACK LETTER RULE** Flight from police is not indicative of wrongdoing, but it is certainly suggestive of such.

■ PROCEDURAL BASIS

Certiorari to review the decision of the Illinois Supreme Court reversing the defendant's conviction for unlawful use of a weapon by a felon.

■ FACTS

A police caravan was driving through an area known for heavy narcotics trafficking in order to investigate drug transactions, when officers observed Wardlow (D) flee after he spotted them. Two police officers gave chase and eventually cornered Wardlow (D). One officer conducted a protective frisk of Wardlow (D) and looked in the bag Wardlow (D) was carrying. They found a handgun in the bag.

■ ISSUE

Is flight from police in a high crime area indicative of criminal wrongdoing?

■ DECISION AND RATIONALE

(Rehnquist, C.J.) No. Flight from police is not indicative of wrongdoing, although it is certainly suggestive of such. An individual's presence in an area of expected criminal activity, standing alone, is not enough to support a reasonable, particularized suspicion that the person is committing a crime. But, on the other hand, officers are not required to ignore the relevant characteristics of a location in determining whether the circumstances are sufficiently suspicious to warrant further investigation. The fact that a stop occurred in a high crime area is a relevant contextual consideration in a *Terry* analysis. Reversed and remanded.

■ CONCURRENCE AND DISSENT

(Stevens, J.) The Court was right to reject the per se rules preferred by the parties. A pedestrian may break into a run for a variety of reasons, many of them innocent and having no relation to flight from police. There are unquestionably circumstances in which a person's flight is suspicious, and undeniably instances in which a person runs for entirely different reasons. Given the diversity of possible motivations for flight, it would be profoundly unwise to adopt a per se rule that flight alone gives rise to reasonable suspicion.

Analysis:

The Court has held in previous cases that nervous, evasive behavior is a pertinent factor in determining reasonable suspicion. Although the Court stated that flight is the consummate act of evasion, it declined to adopt a bright-line rule that flight equals reasonable suspicion. There is concern that if such a bright-line rule were adopted, it could be subject to police abuse, particularly in high-crime areas.

Maryland v. Buie

(Prosecuting State) v. *(Robbery Defendant)*

494 U.S. 325, 110 S. Ct. 1093, 108 L. Ed. 2d 276 (1990)

PROTECTIVE SWEEPS OF DWELLINGS ARE VALID PURSUANT TO A LAWFUL ARREST

Sarge, we need a warrant to search for hair evidence.

Well, I say this is just a "protective sweep".

stus.com

■ **INSTANT FACTS** Buie (D) was arrested for armed robbery and convicted, based in part on evidence consisting of a running suit matching a witness's description that was found during a "sweep" of his home.

■ **BLACK LETTER RULE** The police can make a protective sweep of a dwelling during the course of an arrest if they have reasonable suspicion that there is some danger.

■ PROCEDURAL BASIS

Certiorari to review the decision of the Maryland Court of Appeals reversing the conviction of the defendant for robbery with a deadly weapon and use of a handgun in the commission of a felony.

■ FACTS

Police executed an arrest warrant for Buie (D) at his home as part of a robbery investigation. Officers fanned throughout the house and one officer stationed himself at the top of the stairs so that no one could surprise the police from the basement. Buie (D) emerged from the basement with his hands up. An officer then entered the basement to make sure there was no one else down there. While in the basement, the officer noticed a red running suit matching the description of the one worn by one of the robbers, lying in plain view. The running suit was seized.

■ ISSUE

May the police conduct a sweep of a home pursuant to a lawful arrest?

■ DECISION AND RATIONALE

(White, J.) Yes. Police can make a protective sweep of a dwelling during the course of an arrest if the police have reasonable suspicion that there is some danger. The officers may, as a precautionary measure, and without probable cause or even reasonable suspicion, look in other rooms, closets, or any other space immediately adjoining the place of an arrest from which an attack could be launched. In order to search beyond the immediate area of the arrest, there must be articulable facts that, taken together with the rational inferences from those facts, would warrant a reasonably prudent officer's belief that the area to be swept harbors an individual posing a danger to those on the arrest scene. Police may not, as part of a protective sweep, search dresser drawers, file cabinets, or other items not capable of hiding a would-be assailant. Vacated and remanded.

■ CONCURRENCE

(Stevens, J.) It is important to emphasize that this exception applies only to *protective* sweeps. Officers conducting such a sweep must have a reasonable basis for believing their search will reduce the danger of harm to themselves or of violent interference with their mission.

■ DISSENT

(Brennan, J.) The Court's implicit judgment that a protective sweep constitutes a "minimally intrusive" search akin to that involved in *Terry* markedly undervalues the nature and scope of the privacy interests involved. While perhaps not a "full-blown" or "top-to-bottom" search, a protective sweep is much closer to it than a "limited patdown for weapons" or a "frisk."

Analysis:

The Court noted that the intrusion on privacy involved here is slight when weighed against the safety of the officers. The Court compared the situation in this case to that in *Terry* and *Long* and found that the officers in this case had an analogous interest in taking steps to assure themselves that the house in which a suspect is being, or just has been, arrested is not harboring other persons who are dangerous and who could launch an attack. The risk of danger in the context of an arrest in the home is as great as, if not greater than, it is in an on-the-street or roadside investigatory encounter.

Michigan Department of State Police v. Sitz

(*State Police*) v. (*Sobriety Checkpoint Detainee*)
496 U.S. 444, 110 S. Ct. 2481, 110 L. Ed. 2d 412 (1990)

SOBRIETY CHECKPOINTS ON STATE HIGHWAYS ARE CONSTITUTIONAL

I totally dishagree wish da Subreme Curt on da Constitooty of sobrity checkpointies.

stus.com

■ **INSTANT FACTS** Sitz (R) filed complaint seeking injunctive relief or a declaratory judgment that a state program that set up sobriety checkpoints was unconstitutional.

■ **BLACK LETTER RULE** Police may set up temporary sobriety checkpoints and stop each car coming through to look for signs of intoxication.

■ **PROCEDURAL BASIS**

Certiorari to review the decision of the Michigan Court of Appeals affirming the decision of the lower court invalidating the highway sobriety checkpoint program.

■ **FACTS**

The Michigan Department of State Police developed a pilot program for sobriety checkpoints. Under the guidelines, checkpoints would be set up at selected sites along state roads. All vehicles passing through a checkpoint would be stopped and their drivers briefly examined for signs of intoxication. In cases in which a checkpoint officer detected signs of intoxication, the motorist would be directed to a location out of traffic flow where an officer would check the motorist's driver's license and car registration and, if warranted, conduct further sobriety tests.

■ **ISSUE**

Are sobriety checkpoints set up by state police constitutional?

■ **DECISION AND RATIONALE**

(Rehnquist, C.J.) Yes. The balance of the state's interest in preventing drunken driving, the extent to which this system can reasonably be said to advance that interest, and the degree of intrusion upon individual motorists who are briefly stopped weigh in favor of the state program. The Court reached a similar conclusion in *United States v. Martines–Fuerte*, in which it allowed brief stops of motorists at a highway checkpoint looking for illegal aliens. There is virtually no difference between the levels of intrusion on law-abiding motorists for brief stops necessary to the effectuation of these two types of checkpoints, which to the average person would seem identical save for the nature of questions the checkpoint officer might ask. Reversed and remanded.

■ **DISSENT**

(Brennan, J.) By holding that no level of suspicion is necessary before the police may stop a car for the purpose of preventing drunk driving, the Court potentially subjects the general public to arbitrary and harassing conduct by the police. The idea that stopping every car might make it easier to prevent drunken driving is an insufficient justification for abandoning the requirement of individualized suspicion.

■ **DISSENT**

(Stevens, J.) The Court overvalues the law enforcement interest in using sobriety checkpoints, undervalues the citizen's interest in freedom from random unannounced seizures, and mistakenly assumes that there is "virtually no difference" between a routine stop at a permanent, fixed checkpoint and a surprise stop at a sobriety checkpoint. Unannounced investigatory seizures are the hallmark of regimes far different from ours; the surprise intrusion upon individual liberty is not minimal.

Analysis:

At this time of the decision, only one checkpoint had been operated under the program and it was only operational for seventy-five minutes, during which 126 vehicles passed through and were stopped. Only one driver was arrested for drunken driving. However, there are several other states that operate such programs, and between 0.4% and 2.0% of drivers stopped have been arrested for drunken driving as a result of such checkpoints. The Court determined that this percentage gives rise to a strong enough interest in public safety to justify the minimal intrusion on privacy that it causes.

■ CASE VOCABULARY

SOBRIETY CHECKPOINT: A part of a roadway at which police officers maintain a roadblock to stop motorists and ascertain whether drivers are intoxicated.

City of Indianapolis v. Edmond

(Prosecuting Authority) v. *(Highway Checkpoint Challenger)*
531 U.S. 32, 121 S. Ct. 447, 148 L. Ed. 2d 333 (2000)

CHECKPOINTS CANNOT BE USED FOR ORDINARY LAW ENFORCEMENT PURPOSES

■ **INSTANT FACTS** Edmond (D) and others raised a Fourth Amendment challenge after being subjected to a highway checkpoint stop designed to detect illegal narcotics.

■ **BLACK LETTER RULE** Highway checkpoints designed to advance a general interest in ordinary crime control are unconstitutional.

■ PROCEDURAL BASIS

Undisclosed.

■ FACTS

The City of Indianapolis set up vehicle checkpoints in an effort to interdict illegal drugs. At each checkpoint location, police officers stopped a predetermined number of vehicles, checked licenses and registration, looked for signs of impairment, and conducted an open-view examination of the vehicle from the outside. A drug-sniffing dog also walked around the outside of each vehicle. The officers had no discretion to stop any vehicles out of sequence and could conduct a search only by consent or based on reasonable suspicion. Edmond (D) and others claimed that the roadblocks violated the Fourth Amendment.

■ ISSUE

Are highway checkpoints for the discovery and interdiction of illegal narcotics constitutional?

■ DECISION AND RATIONALE

(O'Connor, J.) No. Highway checkpoints designed to advance a general interest in ordinary crime control are unconstitutional. The Fourth Amendment requires searches and seizures to be reasonable, and we have recognized only certain circumstances in which individualized suspicion of wrongdoing is not a component of reasonableness. In other words, suspicionless searches may be warranted to serve special needs, beyond routine law enforcement, or for administrative purposes, if they are appropriately limited. In *United States v. Martinez–Fuerte*, for example, we upheld brief, suspicionless searches at fixed border checkpoints to detect illegal aliens, based on considerations specifically applicable to the need to police our borders. And in *Michigan Department of State Police v. Sitz*, we approved sobriety checkpoints to detect drunk driving, where the magnitude of the drunk driving problem and the state's interest in getting drunk drivers off the road weighed heavily in favor of a finding of constitutionality. But when the primary purpose of a roadblock or checkpoint is a general interest in deterring or detecting crime, the program contravenes the Fourth Amendment.

Here, the purpose of the checkpoints was to advance a general interest in crime control. We decline to suspend the requirement of individualized suspicion to this context. Although there are specific circumstances that may justify a checkpoint where the purpose seems to relate to ordinary crime control—such as to thwart terrorist activity or prevent a fleeing felon—this is not a case presenting such exigencies. The constitutionality of a checkpoint program depends on a balancing of the competing interests at stake and the effectiveness of the program. The checkpoints here violate the Fourth Amendment.

■ DISSENT

(Rehnquist, C.J.) The use of roadblocks to look for signs of impairment was approved in *Sitz*, and the use of roadblocks to check licenses and registration was recognized in *Delaware v. Prouse*. These purposes were served here as well, and the fact that forty-nine of the resulting arrests were non-drug-related is further evidence of the state's legitimate interests. Because the stops were neutral, regularized, and only minimally intrusive, they were constitutional.

■ DISSENT

(Thomas, J.) Although I believe that *Sitz* and *Martinez-Fuerte* may have been wrongly decided, we are not asked to overrule them, so those decisions compel the upholding of the checkpoints in this case.

Analysis:

Martinez-Fuerte and *Sitz* established that roadblocks are constitutional in appropriate circumstances. Some may argue that the roadblocks at issue in this case are not sufficiently distinguishable to warrant a different outcome. Had the Court applied the principles set forth in earlier cases, it could be argued, it would have upheld the drug interdiction checkpoints as constitutional. But instead, the majority created a confusing distinction and, as a result, roadblock case law became confusing. States can circumvent the Court's decision and establish roadblocks found to be constitutional by articulating a purpose that the Court has deemed acceptable.

■ CASE VOCABULARY

CHECKPOINT SEARCH: A search in which police officers set up roadblocks and stop motorists to ascertain whether the drivers are intoxicated [or engaged in other illegal activity].

CHAPTER FIVE

Remedies for Fourth Amendment Violations

Rakas v. Illinois

Instant Facts: Rakas (D) and another were convicted based on evidence seized from a locked glove compartment and from under the front passenger seat in an automobile in which they were riding as passengers.

Black Letter Rule: To sustain a Fourth Amendment challenge, a defendant must establish a legitimate expectation of privacy in the areas searched or in the items seized.

Minnesota v. Carter

Instant Facts: Carter (D) and another were at a third party's apartment for approximately two and one-half hours solely to package cocaine.

Black Letter Rule: Residential visitors, who are on the premises for only a short time and who claim no connection to the host other than to transact business, have no legitimate expectation of privacy in the premises under the Fourth Amendment.

Mapp v. Ohio

Instant Facts: Police forcefully entered Mapp's (D) home without justification and seized documents that were later used to convict Mapp (D) of a crime.

Black Letter Rule: The exclusionary rule, which prohibits introduction of unconstitutionally seized evidence, applies to state court criminal proceedings by virtue of the Fourteenth Amendment.

United States v. Leon

Instant Facts: Acting on a search warrant ultimately determined to be unsupported by probable cause, police seized evidence that was used against Leon (D) in the prosecution's direct case.

Black Letter Rule: The exclusionary rule does not bar use by the prosecution in its case-in-chief of evidence seized by law enforcement acting in reasonable reliance on a search warrant issued by a detached and neutral magistrate, subsequently found to be unsupported by probable cause.

Silverthorne Lumber Company v. United States

Instant Facts: Silverthorne Lumber Company (D) was convicted based on the contents of books, papers, and documents illegally obtained from its place of business while the individual defendants were detained at their homes.

Black Letter Rule: The Fourth Amendment prohibits not only use of evidence obtained by an illegal search and seizure, but also evidence that is obtained as a result of that constitutional violation unless an independent source for the evidence is shown.

Murray v. United States

Instant Facts: Murray (D) was convicted based on evidence seized under a search warrant obtained after law enforcement initially entered the premises illegally and saw the evidence in plain view.

Black Letter Rule: The independent source doctrine applies to both evidence obtained for the first time during an independent lawful search, and also to evidence initially discovered during, or as a consequence of, an unlawful search, but later discovered independently from activities untainted by the initial illegality.

Hudson v. Michigan

Instant Facts: Police entered Hudson's (D) home just seconds after knocking and announcing their presence, and Hudson (D) moved to suppress the evidence discovered in the resulting search.

Black Letter Rule: The exclusionary rule does not apply to suppress evidence obtained through a violation of the knock-and-announce rule.

Herring v. United States

Instant Facts: Herring (D) was arrested based on a mistaken belief that he had an outstanding warrant, and evidence obtained in the search incident to that arrest was used to support drug and weapons charges against him.

Black Letter Rule: The exclusionary rule is not an individual right and applies only where it results in appreciable deterrence.

Wong Sun v. United States

Instant Facts: Wong Sun (D) was convicted based on evidence that flowed from evidence initially obtained as the result of an unlawful search.

Black Letter Rule: Evidence (verbal or physical) that derives so immediately from an unlawful search or seizure is inadmissible as "fruit of the poisonous tree" unless the evidence was obtained from an independent source or the connection between the lawless conduct and the discovery of the challenged evidence has become so attenuated as to dissipate the taint.

Rakas v. Illinois

(*Criminal Defendant*) v. (*Prosecuting State*)

439 U.S. 128, 99 S. Ct. 421, 58 L. Ed. 2d 387 (1978)

THE STANDING REQUIREMENT IS NO LONGER AN ELEMENT OF FOURTH AMENDMENT ANALYSIS

■ **INSTANT FACTS** Rakas (D) and another were convicted based on evidence seized from a locked glove compartment and from under the front passenger seat in an automobile in which they were riding as passengers.

■ **BLACK LETTER RULE** To sustain a Fourth Amendment challenge, a defendant must establish a legitimate expectation of privacy in the areas searched or in the items seized.

■ **PROCEDURAL BASIS**

Certiorari to review affirmance by the Illinois appellate court of the trial court's refusal to suppress evidence seized in an automobile in which the petitioner-defendants were passengers.

■ **FACTS**

Rakas (D) and another were convicted based on evidence seized from an automobile that was stopped on suspicion that it was a getaway car used in a robbery. The police ordered the owner, who was driving the vehicle, and the defendants from the car, and conducted a search that uncovered a box of rifle shells in a locked glove compartment and a sawed-off rifle under the front passenger seat, where one of the defendants was sitting. The defendants moved to suppress the evidence, claiming that their Fourth Amendment rights were violated because they were the targets of the search and because they were lawfully in the automobile with the owner's permission. The defendants conceded that they were simply passengers in the vehicle, and that they owned neither the incriminating evidence nor the automobile. Invoking *Jones v. United States*, 362 U.S. 257 (1960), the defendants argued that, because they were "legitimately on [the] premises," i.e., lawfully in the car, they could challenge the validity of the search.

■ **ISSUE**

May defendants who were passengers in an automobile owned by another raise a Fourth Amendment challenge to the seizure of items from the vehicle's locked glove compartment and from under the front passenger seat?

■ **DECISION AND RATIONALE**

(Rehnquist, J.) No. Fourth Amendment rights are personal to a particular individual, and may not be raised on behalf of another. The defendants, as mere passengers in the vehicle, failed to establish any legitimate expectation of privacy in the contents of the locked glove compartment or in the area beneath the front passenger seat. The defendant argues that his situation is similar to *Jones*, in which the Court stated that "anyone legitimately on premises where a search occurs may challenge its validity." The defendants' reliance on *Jones* is, however, misplaced. The defendant in that case was in exclusive possession of a friend's apartment, he had keys to the apartment, he stayed there at least one night, and he stored several personal items in the home. Here, the defendants did not assert either a property or possessory interest in the automobile or in its contents, and the fact that they were "legitimately on

---

[the] premises," i.e., in the car with the owner's permission, was not determinative of whether they had a legitimate expectation of privacy in the particular areas of the automobile that were searched. Unlike the defendants in *Jones* and in *Katz* (in which the defendant had a legitimate expectation of privacy in the contents of a call placed from a public telephone booth, the door to which could be closed to exclude all others), the defendants herein did not have complete dominion and control to the extent that they could exclude others from the vehicle. Affirmed.

■ CONCURRENCE

(Powell, J.) There is a distinction between a person's minimal expectation of privacy in an automobile and the greater expectation in other locations, such as a residence, and a distinction between the Fourth Amendment rights of a passenger and an individual who has exclusive control of the vehicle and its locked compartments. When passengers allege exclusive control and retain the keys to a vehicle owned by another, Fourth Amendment rights might be implicated under similar circumstances.

■ DISSENT

(White, J.) By tying application of the Fourth Amendment and the exclusionary rule to property law concepts, *Rakas* effectively rules that the Fourth Amendment protects property, not people. The holding prevents a legitimate occupant of a vehicle from invoking the exclusionary rule to challenge a search of that vehicle unless the occupant owns or has a possessory interest in it. Contrary to the majority's ruling, the Fourth Amendment protects not property, but privacy, which the defendants alleged, and the issue is whether the premises searched fell within "a protected zone of privacy." Because the defendants were in a private place with the permission of the owner, they were protected under the Fourth Amendment. The facts in *Jones* are similar to the ones here. The majority undermines the force of the exclusionary rule and invites police to engage in patently unreasonable searches every time an automobile contains more than one occupant. As a result of the ruling, only the owner of a vehicle, or of the item, will be protected under the Fourth Amendment; other occupants against whom the evidence will presumably be usable are prohibited from asserting their Fourth Amendment rights.

Analysis:

Rakas supercedes the Court's ruling in *Alderman* by eradicating the standing requirement as an element of Fourth Amendment analysis. The analysis under *Rakas* is: (1) whether the challenged search and seizure violated the Fourth Amendment rights of a criminal defendant who seeks to exclude the evidence; and (2) whether the disputed search and seizure has infringed an interest of the defendant which the Fourth Amendment was designed to protect. Note that the Court also restricted the holding in *Jones* to the facts of that case, holding that to allow all who are "legitimately on [the] premises" to invoke Fourth Amendment protections would extend the law too far.

■ CASE VOCABULARY

SEIZURE: The act or an instance of taking possession of a person or property by legal right or process; especially, in constitutional law, a confiscation or arrest that may interfere with a person's reasonable expectation of privacy.

STANDING: A party's right to make a legal claim or seek judicial enforcement of a duty or right. To have standing in federal court, a plaintiff must show (1) that the challenged conduct has caused the plaintiff actual injury, and (2) that the interest sought to be protected is within the zone of interests meant to be regulated by the statutory or constitutional guarantee in question.

Minnesota v. Carter

(*Prosecuting State*) v. (*Drug Offender*)

525 U.S. 83, 119 S. Ct. 469, 142 L. Ed. 2d 373 (1998)

SHORT–TERM VISITORS DO NOT HAVE THE SAME EXPECTATION OF PRIVACY

Guests! Welcome! I'd like to extend my hospitality, though not my Fourth Amendment protection.

stus.com

■ **INSTANT FACTS** Carter (D) and another were at a third party's apartment for approximately two and one-half hours solely to package cocaine.

■ **BLACK LETTER RULE** Residential visitors, who are on the premises for only a short time and who claim no connection to the host other than to transact business, have no legitimate expectation of privacy in the premises under the Fourth Amendment.

■ PROCEDURAL BASIS

Certiorari to review the decision of the Minnesota Supreme Court reversing the court of appeals' affirmance of the defendants convictions.

■ FACTS

Carter (D) and his partner, Johns, were in the apartment of one Thompson (the lessee), packaging cocaine into baggies. A police officer, acting on a confidential tip, peeked through a gap in a window blind and observed the operations. After securing a warrant, police searched the apartment and found cocaine residue and plastic baggies on the kitchen table. Carter (D) and Johns were arrested. In order to suppress the evidence, Carter (D) attempted to establish that he possessed a legitimate expectation of privacy in the lessee's apartment. The trial court held that Carter (D) was not an overnight social guest, but rather a temporary out-of-state visitor not entitled to claim the protection of the Fourth Amendment. The court of appeals affirmed but the Minnesota Supreme Court reversed, holding that Carter (D) had "standing" to invoke the Fourth Amendment because he had a legitimate expectation of privacy in the premises.

■ ISSUE

Does a person who was only on the premises for a short period and only to transact business, and who had no previous relationship with the lessee, have a legitimate expectation of privacy in the premises under the Fourth Amendment?

■ DECISION AND RATIONALE

(Rehnquist, J.) No. In view of the purely commercial nature of the transaction, the relatively short period of time on the premises, and the lack of any previous connection between the defendants and the lessee, the defendants had no legitimate expectation of privacy in the apartment and, therefore, could not invoke Fourth Amendment protections. The defendants were not overnight guests, and while the residence was a "home" to the lessee, it was for the defendants merely a place to do business. The defendants were "simply permitted on the premises." Reversed and remanded.

■ CONCURRENCE

(Scalia, J.) The obvious meaning of the Fourth Amendment is that "*each* person has the right to be secure against unreasonable searches and seizures in *his own* person house, papers and effects." The key to a determination whether a person has protected Fourth Amendment rights in a home is whether a person actually lives there, even if temporarily. The *Olsen* case (in which Fourth Amendment protections were afforded an overnight guest) is the "absolute limit of what text and tradition permit in an unreasonable search of a host's apartment."

■ CONCURRENCE

(Kennedy, J.) Almost all social guests have a legitimate expectation of privacy in the homes of their host. Most social guests expect that the homeowner will exercise discretion to include or exclude others for the guest's benefit. Where such social expectations exist, they create a legitimate expectation of privacy even though the guest does not personally have a property right to exclude others. The defendants established only a fleeting and insubstantial connection with the lessee's home. In the absence of a meaningful tie or connection to the owner, to the owner's home, or to the owner's expectation of privacy, the defendants were not entitled to invoke the protection of the Fourth Amendment.

■ CONCURRENCE

(Breyer, J.) The defendants could claim the Fourth Amendment's protections, but the police officer's observation made through the window, in a public area outside the residence, did not constitute an unreasonable search.

■ DISSENT

(Ginsburg, J.) *Carter* undermines the security of both short-term guests and home residents. When a lessor or home owner invites a guest into the home to share in a common endeavor (whatever it may be, licit or illicit), the guest shares the host's shelter against unreasonable searches and seizures; i.e., under *Katz*, both host and guest "have exhibited an actual (subjective) expectation of privacy, and that 'expectation [is] one [our] society is prepared to recognize as "reasonable." ' " An individual has the right to associate with persons of his or her choosing, and Fourth Amendment decisions should reflect the complementary prerogatives to include or exclude others. Finally, *Carter* "veers sharply from the path marked in *Katz*." A person who places a business call to a person's home from a public telephone booth has no more reasonable expectation of privacy than one who actually enters that person's premises to transact business.

Analysis:

For Fourth Amendment purposes, an individual has a lesser expectation of privacy in commercial premises than in a person's home. While a worker may sometimes claim Fourth Amendment protection in the workplace, such was not the case here where there was no significant business connection to the lessee's apartment. The Court regarded the overnight guest in *Olsen* as typifying those who may claim Fourth Amendment protection in the home of another. However, it stated that one merely "legitimately on the premises" typifies those who may not claim such protection. Thus, we see the erosion of the "legitimately on premises" standard, which, in *Jones*, was initially sufficient to invoke Fourth Amendment protections; was reconfigured in *Rakas*, wherein the Court interpreted the phrase to mean a "legitimate expectation of privacy"; and diluted in *Carter*, which describes the standard as befitting individuals who may not rely at all on the protection of the Fourth Amendment.

■ CASE VOCABULARY

CURTILAGE: The land or yard adjoining a house, usually within an enclosure. Under the Fourth Amendment, the curtilage is an area usually protected from warrantless searches.

EXPECTATION OF PRIVACY: A belief in the existence of the right to be free of governmental intrusion in regard to a particular place or thing. To suppress a search on privacy grounds, a defendant must show the existence of the expectation and that the expectation was reasonable.

Mapp v. Ohio

(Accused Criminal) v. *(Prosecuting State)*

367 U.S. 643, 81 S. Ct. 1684, 6 L. Ed. 2d 1081 (1961)

STATES ARE SUBJECT TO THE EXCLUSIONARY RULE

■ **INSTANT FACTS** Police forcefully entered Mapp's (D) home without justification and seized documents that were later used to convict Mapp (D) of a crime.

■ **BLACK LETTER RULE** The exclusionary rule, which prohibits introduction of unconstitutionally seized evidence, applies to state court criminal proceedings by virtue of the Fourteenth Amendment.

■ **PROCEDURAL BASIS**

Certiorari to review the Ohio Supreme Court's decision affirming the trial court's refusal to suppress evidence seized from the defendant's home.

■ **FACTS**

Three police officers arrived at Mapp's (D) home after being informed that a suspect wanted for questioning in a recent bombing was hiding there and that the house contained a large amount of paraphernalia related to the bombing. After speaking with her attorney, Mapp (D), who occupied the second level of a two-family house, refused to allow the officers entry without a search warrant. About three hours later, after four or more police officers had arrived on the scene, the officers again sought entrance, this time successfully by forcing open one of the several doors to the house. Mapp's (D) attorney had arrived on the scene, but police refused to let him see his client or enter the house. After the officers broke open the door, Mapp (D) demanded to see the search warrant. An officer held up a paper that he claimed was a search warrant, and Mapp (D) grabbed the paper and placed it down the front of her blouse. After struggling with Mapp (D), the officers recovered the paper, handcuffed Mapp (D) (because she had been "belligerent"), and otherwise "ran roughshod" over Mapp (D), grabbing and twisting her hand. Still in handcuffs, Mapp (D) was forcibly taken upstairs to her bedroom, where police searched a dresser, a chest of drawers, a closet, and some suitcases. They also looked through Mapp's (D's) photo album and personal papers. A second bedroom, the living room, and the kitchen and dinette were also searched. The officers continued the search in the basement and a trunk found therein. During this widespread search, police uncovered the obscene materials of which Mapp (D) was charged with possession under Ohio law.

■ **ISSUE**

Does the exclusionary rule, which prohibits introduction of unconstitutionally seized evidence, apply to state court criminal proceedings by virtue of the Fourteenth Amendment?

■ **DECISION AND RATIONALE**

(Clark, J.) Yes. All evidence obtained by searches and seizures in violation of the Constitution is inadmissible in a state court. While the exclusionary rule announced in *Weeks* is a judicially created rule, it is of constitutional origin in the sense that it is necessary to give effect to the provisions of the Fourth

Amendment against unreasonable searches and seizures, which are applicable to the states through the Fourteenth Amendment. Reversed and Remanded.

■ CONCURRENCE

(Black, J.) Imposition of the exclusionary rule upon the states is justified by a combination of the Fourth and Fifth Amendments, not just the Fourth Amendment, which does not contain any provision excluding use of evidence seized in violation of its provisions. "When the Fourth Amendment's ban against unreasonable searches and seizures is considered together with the Fifth Amendment's ban against compelled self-incrimination, a constitutional basis emerges which not only justifies but actually requires the exclusionary rule."

■ CONCURRENCE

(Douglas, J.) A discrepancy in the admissibility of illegally seized evidence in the state and federal courts leads to a double standard, which breeds forum shopping and leads to working arrangements that undercut federal policy and reduce some aspects of law enforcement to "shabby business."

■ DISSENT

(Harlan, J.) The central issue is not whether illegally state-seized evidence is constitutionally admissible in a state prosecution, but rather whether the Ohio statute making criminal the mere knowing possession or control over obscene material, and under which Mapp (D) was convicted, is consistent with the rights of free thought and expression assured against state action by the Fourteenth Amendment. This was the principal issue before the Oregon Supreme Court. Moreover, a trial does not become unfair simply because a state determines that evidence may be considered by the trier of fact, regardless of how it was obtained, if it is relevant to the one issue with which the trial is concerned—the guilt or innocence of the accused.

Analysis:

Prior to the holding in Mapp, state courts were not subject to the exclusionary rule. So long as the states recognized that a particular search and seizure was unreasonable and illegal, the prosecution could admit evidence obtained as a result of that search. The exclusionary rule applied to federal criminal court proceedings since its inception.

■ CASE VOCABULARY

FEDERALISM: The legal relationship and distribution of power between the national and regional governments within a federal system of government.

STARE DECISIS: The doctrine of precedent, under which it is necessary for a court to follow earlier judicial decisions when the same points arise again in litigation.

United States v. Leon

(Prosecuting Government) v. *(Drug Offender)*

468 U.S. 897, 104 S. Ct. 3405, 82 L. Ed. 2d 677 (1984)

THE EXCLUSIONARY RULE IS LIMITED BY THE GOOD–FAITH EXCEPTION

Defense attorneys should be able to challenge every judge's good faith probable cause determination for search warrants.

Get real.

stus.com

■ **INSTANT FACTS** Acting on a search warrant ultimately determined to be unsupported by probable cause, police seized evidence that was used against Leon (D) in the prosecution's direct case.

■ **BLACK LETTER RULE** The exclusionary rule does not bar use by the prosecution in its case-in-chief of evidence seized by law enforcement acting in reasonable reliance on a search warrant issued by a detached and neutral magistrate, subsequently found to be unsupported by probable cause.

■ **PROCEDURAL BASIS**

Certiorari to review the lower courts' determination that the exclusionary rule prohibits the introduction of evidence seized in reasonable, good-faith reliance on a search warrant subsequently held to be defective.

■ **FACTS**

Police initiated an investigation after a confidential informant (of unproven reliability) told them that two persons were selling large quantities of cocaine and methaqualone from their residence at a specified address. Based on observations, an officer, who was an experienced and well-trained narcotics investigator, prepared an application for a warrant to search three residences and automobiles registered to each of the defendants for an extensive list of items believed to be related to their drug-trafficking. Several Deputy District Attorneys reviewed the application, and a facially valid search warrant was issued by a state superior court judge. The District Court suppressed the evidence on the ground that the affidavit accompanying the warrant application was insufficient to establish probable cause.

■ **ISSUE**

May the prosecution use in its case-in-chief evidence obtained by officers acting in reasonable reliance on a search warrant issued by a detached and neutral magistrate but ultimately found to be unsupported by probable cause?

■ **DECISION AND RATIONALE**

(White, J.) Yes. The exclusionary rule is designed to safeguard Fourth Amendment rights through its deterrent effect. Whether it should be applied in a particular case is determined by weighing the costs and benefits of excluding the evidence. The rule should be restricted to those cases in which its remedial objectives are most effectively served. In the instant case, suppression of the evidence seized pursuant to a warrant does not further the deterrent effect of the rule. First, exclusion of the evidence will not have a significant deterrent effect on the issuing judge or magistrate, who unlike members of law enforcement, are neutral judicial officers with no stake in the outcome of particular criminal prosecutions. Moreover, the exclusionary rule cannot deter offending officers who acted on the objective reasonable belief that their conduct was lawful, because there is nothing to deter. But, the officers' reliance on the magistrate's probable cause determination and on the technical sufficiency of the warrant must be objectively reasonable. Therefore, suppression remains an appropriate remedy if (1) the magistrate or judge issuing the warrant was misled by information in an affidavit that the affiant knew was false or would have known was false except for his reckless disregard of the truth; (2) the issuing magistrate wholly abandons his judicial role, such that no reasonably well-trained officer should rely on the warrant; (3) an affidavit is "so lacking in indicia of probable cause as to render official belief in its existence entirely unreasonable"; or (4) a warrant is so facially deficient, e.g., in failing to particularize the place to be searched or the items to be seized, that the executing officers cannot reasonably presume its validity. In the case at bar, the officers' application for a warrant clearly was supported by much more than a "bare bones" affidavit. It related the results of an extensive investigation, and reviewing judges disagreed as to whether it was sufficient enough to give rise to probable cause. Under these circumstances, the officers' reliance on the magistrate's determination of probable cause was objectively reasonable, and the evidence should have been admitted. Reversed.

■ CONCURRENCE

(Blackmun, J.) The good-faith exception to the exclusionary rule must be tested in the real world of state and federal law enforcement. If its application materially changes police compliance with the Fourth Amendment, the Court will have to reconsider the exception.

■ DISSENT

(Brennan, J.) *Leon* sanctions conduct that has been forbidden in the past, i.e., the use by the prosecution in their case in chief of illegally obtained evidence against the individual whose rights have been violated. *Mapp* put to rest what *Leon* revives today, i.e., that the exclusionary rule is merely a judicially created prophylactic rule designed to safeguard Fourth Amendment rights through its deterrent effect, rather than a personal constitutional right. However, the Fourth Amendment condemns not only the initial unconstitutional invasion of privacy, but also the subsequent use of any evidence so obtained. Its provisions are not directed solely at government agents who actually invade an individual's constitutionally protected privacy, but also to the courts, who are under a direct constitutional duty to exclude illegally obtained evidence. When a court admits illegally obtained evidence, the same constitutional concerns as apply to the initial seizure are implicated. The judiciary thereby becomes part of what is in fact "a single governmental action" prohibited by the terms of the Amendments.

Furthermore, as applied in *Leon*, the deterrence theory is misguided and unworkable. It is not the exclusionary rule, but the Fourth Amendment itself, that imposes the "cost" of excluding reliable evidence. In performing the cost/benefit analysis, *Leon* mistakenly weighs the aggregated costs of exclusion in *all* cases against the potential benefits associated in the narrow range of cases in which law enforcement has mistakenly, but reasonably, relied on a search warrant. Moreover, the deterrent effect of the exclusionary rule does operate in those situations that fall under the good-faith exception. The chief deterrent function of the rule is its tendency to promote institutional law enforcement compliance with the Fourth Amendment, not to "punish" individual officers who violate its strictures. As to situations that fall within the exception, the exclusionary rule has a long-term deterrent effect. If, for example, evidence is consistently excluded in such cases, police departments will instruct their officers to devote greater care and attention to providing sufficient information to establish probable cause in the warrant application, and to review attentively the form of the warrant issued, rather than automatically assuming that whatever document the magistrate has signed will necessarily comport with Fourth Amendment requirements. Additionally, *Leon* insulates the magistrate's decisions to issue warrants from subsequent judicial review. Because any mistakes made by a magistrate will have virtually no consequence, their standard of care in reviewing warrant applications will significantly decrease.

Taken in conjunction with *Illinois v. Gates* (holding that magistrates must have a substantial basis for concluding that probable cause existed), *Leon* makes it virtually inconceivable that a reviewing court, when faced with a defendant's motion to suppress, could first find that a warrant was invalid under the *Gates* standard, but then at the same time, find that a police officer's reliance on such an invalid warrant was nevertheless "objectively reasonable" under the test announced today.

■ DISSENT

(Stevens, J.) The precise problem that the Fourth Amendment was intended to address was the unreasonable issuance of warrants. The Amendment was actually motivated by the practice of issuing general warrants, warrants that did not satisfy the particularity and probable cause requirements.

Analysis:

The government's burden of demonstrating that officers acted in objective good faith is not a difficult one. Therefore, in order to suppress evidence when a warrant is involved, one of the four situations enunciated in *Leon* must be shown to have existed. In most cases in which the good-faith exception is argued, successful counterarguments emphasize that the rule's deterrent purpose would not be furthered by the exception's application.

■ CASE VOCABULARY

EMPIRICAL: Of, relating to, or based on experience, experiment, or observation.

EXCLUSIONARY RULE: A rule that excludes or suppresses evidence obtained in violation of an accused person's constitutional rights.

GOOD–FAITH EXCEPTION: An exception to the exclusionary rule whereby evidence obtained under a warrant later found to be invalid (especially because it is not supported by probable cause) is nonetheless admissible if the police reasonably relied on the notion that the warrant was valid.

Silverthorne Lumber Company v. United States

(*Criminal Defendants*) v. (*Prosecuting Government*)
251 U.S. 385, 40 S.Ct. 182, 64 L.Ed. 319 (1919)

INFORMATION OBTAINED AS THE RESULT OF AN UNLAWFUL SEARCH AND SEIZURE IS INADMISSIBLE UNLESS IT HAS AN INDEPENDENT SOURCE

■ **INSTANT FACTS** Silverthorne Lumber Company (D) was convicted based on the contents of books, papers, and documents illegally obtained from its place of business while the individual defendants were detained at their homes.

■ **BLACK LETTER RULE** The Fourth Amendment prohibits not only use of evidence obtained by an illegal search and seizure, but also evidence that is obtained as a result of that constitutional violation unless an independent source for the evidence is shown.

■ PROCEDURAL BASIS

Certiorari to review the lower courts' determination that the prosecution could not make use of illegally seized evidence.

■ FACTS

Representatives of Silverthorne Lumber Company (D), indicted on a single specific charge, were arrested and detained at their homes for several hours while law enforcement officials entered the defendants' business office without a warrant and seized all the books, papers, and documents found there. The defendants applied to the court for return of the items that were taken unlawfully.

■ ISSUE

May the prosecution avail itself of the information contained in the books, documents, and papers obtained by an illegal search and seizure?

■ DECISION AND RATIONALE

(Holmes, J.) No. The Fourth Amendment prohibits not only use of evidence obtained by an illegal search and seizure, but also information that is indirectly obtained as a result of that constitutional violation, unless an independent source for the secondary evidence is shown. In other words, the Fourth Amendment prohibits both the direct and indirect use of all illegally acquired evidence. However, if the prosecution can show that the indirectly obtained information is gained from an independent source, such evidence may be offered like any other. Affirmed.

Analysis:

The independent-source exception contemplates the existence of an actual independent source, not merely the possibility that one existed. It is based on the policy that the government, while not permitted to benefit from unlawful conduct, should not be placed in a worse position than it would otherwise have occupied absent any error or violation.

■ CASE VOCABULARY

FRUIT–OF–THE–POISONOUS–TREE DOCTRINE: The rule that evidence derived from an illegal search, arrest, or interrogation is inadmissible because the evidence (the "fruit") was tainted by the illegality (the "poisonous tree"). Under this doctrine, for example, a murder weapon is inadmissible if the map showing its location and used to find it was seized during an illegal search.

INDEPENDENT–SOURCE RULE: The rule providing—as an exception to the fruit-of-the-poisonous-tree doctrine—that evidence obtained by illegal means may nonetheless be admissible if that evidence is also obtained by legal means unrelated to the original illegal conduct.

Murray v. United States

(Drug Offender) v. *(Prosecuting Government)*

487 U.S. 533, 108 S. Ct. 2529, 101 L. Ed. 2d 472 (1988)

EVIDENCE INITIALLY OBTAINED AS FROM AN UNLAWFUL SEARCH BUT LATER OBTAINED AGAIN FROM UNTAINTED ACTIVITIES IS ADMISSIBLE

■ **INSTANT FACTS** Murray (D) was convicted based on evidence seized under a search warrant obtained after law enforcement initially entered the premises illegally and saw the evidence in plain view.

■ **BLACK LETTER RULE** The independent source doctrine applies to both evidence obtained for the first time during an independent lawful search, and also to evidence initially discovered during, or as a consequence of, an unlawful search, but later discovered independently from activities untainted by the initial illegality.

■ **PROCEDURAL BASIS**

Certiorari to review the First Circuit's affirmance of the district court's refusal to suppress evidence on the ground that the warrant was invalid.

■ **FACTS**

Federal agents had been surveilling Murray (D) and others based on information provided by an informant. They observed Murray (D) drive a truck and Carter drive a green camper into a warehouse in South Boston. As the vehicles emerged about twenty minutes later, officers observed through the open doors two individuals and a tractor-trailer rig bearing a long, dark container. Agents followed Murray (D) and Carter, who eventually turned the vehicles over to two other individuals. These individuals were ultimately arrested and the vehicles, which were lawfully seized, were found to contain marijuana. When other agents learned of the arrest, they converged on the warehouse and forced entry. The building was unoccupied, but agents observed in plain view numerous burlap-wrapped bales (that were later found to contain marijuana). The bales were left undisturbed, and surveillance of the warehouse was maintained. The agents immediately sought to secure a search warrant. In their application, the agents did not mention the prior entry, nor did they rely on observations made through the open doors of the warehouse. The warrant was issued about eight hours after the initial entry and agents reentered the warehouse. Two hundred and seventy bales of marijuana (along with notebooks listing the customers for the bales) were seized. Murray (D), Carter, and others were convicted for conspiracy to possess and distribute illegal drugs.

■ **ISSUE**

Does the independent source doctrine apply to both evidence obtained for the first time during an independent lawful search and also to evidence initially discovered during, or as a consequence of, an unlawful search, but later discovered independently from activities untainted by the initial illegality?

■ **DECISION AND RATIONALE**

(Scalia, J.) Yes. In its more specific sense, the concept of "independent source" refers to that particular category of evidence acquired by an untainted source that is identical to the evidence unlawfully acquired. For example, if police make an illegal entry and learn facts x and y, and if they also discover those same facts from an independent source, the facts are admissible. Contrary to petitioners' argument, exclusion of evidence that is initially discovered during an illegal search will not hinder deterrence and encourage unlawful police searches. The fear that law enforcement will no longer obtain a warrant until and unless a previous unlawful search is undertaken is alleviated by the fact that no information gained from the illegal entry may affect law enforcements' decision to seek a warrant or the magistrate's decision to grant it. In other words, an officer without probable cause to obtain a search warrant has no added incentive to conduct an unlawful entry, since whatever he finds cannot be used to establish probable cause before a magistrate. Here, knowledge that the marijuana was in the warehouse was acquired at the time of the unlawful entry. But it was also acquired at the time of entry pursuant to the warrant, and if that later acquisition was not the result of the earlier entry there is no reason why the independent source doctrine should not apply. The officers did not mention the prior entry in their warrant application, nor did they rely on observations made through the open doors of the warehouse. The ultimate question, therefore, is whether the search pursuant to warrant was in fact a genuinely independent source of the information and tangible evidence at issue here. Judgment vacated and remanded for a determination of whether the warrant-authorized search of the warehouse was an independent source of the challenged evidence in the sense described.

■ DISSENT

(Marshall, J.) The decision loses sight of the "practical moorings" of the independent source exception and creates an affirmative incentive for unconstitutional searches. Admission of the evidence "reseized" during the second search severely undermines the deterrence function of the exclusionary rule and encourages illegal searches. Obtaining a warrant is inconvenient and time-consuming. Therefore, officials may be tempted to search the premises (i.e., to conduct "confirmatory" searches) to determine whether they should spend the time required to obtain a warrant. However, if contraband is discovered, the officers may seek a warrant to "shield the evidence from the taint of the illegal search." Another problem with the ruling is that officers committing the illegal search are the ones with the knowledge and control of the factors central to the trial court's determination. As was seen in this case, it is a simple matter to exclude from the warrant application any information gained from the initial entry so that the magistrate's determination of probable cause is not influenced by the prior illegal search. Also, application of the independent source exception should not turn entirely on an evaluation of the officers' intent. How does a trial court verify, or the defendant rebut, an assertion by officers that they always intended to obtain a warrant regardless of the results of the illegal search? The officers' testimony is the only direct evidence of intent and the defendant is relegated simply to arguing that the officer should not be believed.

To ensure that the source of the evidence is genuinely independent, the basis for a finding that a search was untainted by a prior illegal search must focus on "demonstrated historical facts capable of ready verification or impeachment," none of which appear in the case at bar. No such facts support a finding that the subsequent warrant search was wholly unaffected by the prior illegal search. The same team of investigators was involved in both searches, and no effort was made to obtain a warrant prior to the discovery of the marijuana during the illegal search. The only evidence available for which the warrant search was a wholly independent source is the testimony of the agents who conducted the illegal search. Under these circumstances, the threat that the subsequent search was tainted by the illegal search is too great to allow for the application of the independent source exception.

Analysis:

A court that is trying to determine whether a warrant was independent of an illegal entry must ask whether officers would have sought the warrant even if what actually happened had not occurred. In other words, did the actual illegal search have any effect in producing the warrant, or was there a genuinely independent source for the evidence at issue? There is an important distinction between cases in which the agents' decision to seek the warrant was motivated by what was revealed during the initial entry, but such revelations are not disclosed, and those in which information obtained during the initial entry is presented in the application and affects the magistrate's decision to issue the warrant.

■ CASE VOCABULARY

INDEPENDENT–SOURCE RULE: The rule providing—as an exception to the fruit-of-the-poisonous-tree doctrine—that evidence obtained by illegal means may nonetheless be admissible if that evidence is also obtained by legal means unrelated to the original illegal conduct.

INEVITABLE–DISCOVERY RULE: The rule providing—as an exception to the fruit-of-the-poisonous-tree doctrine—that evidence obtained by illegal means may nonetheless be admissible if the prosecution can show that the evidence would eventually have been legally obtained anyway.

Wong Sun v. United States

(Drug Offender) v. *(Prosecuting Government)*

371 U.S. 471, 83 S. Ct. 407, 9 L. Ed. 2d 441 (1963)

EVIDENCE THAT IS SO ATTENUATED FROM THE ORIGINAL UNLAWFUL CONDUCT AS TO DISSIPATE THE TAINT IS ADMISSIBLE

Twelve feet. Is that sufficiently attenuated?

stus.com

■ **INSTANT FACTS** Wong Sun (D) was convicted based on evidence that flowed from evidence initially obtained as the result of an unlawful search.

■ **BLACK LETTER RULE** Evidence (verbal or physical) that derives so immediately from an unlawful search or seizure is inadmissible as "fruit of the poisonous tree" unless the evidence was obtained from an independent source or the connection between the lawless conduct and the discovery of the challenged evidence has become so attenuated as to dissipate the taint.

■ PROCEDURAL BASIS

Certiorari to review the trial court's admission of verbal statements and physical evidence that were the byproduct of an illegal search.

■ FACTS

At 2:00 a.m., police arrested Hom Way, who was found with heroin in his possession. Hom Way told police that he had purchased an ounce of heroin the night before from someone known to him only as "Blackie Toy," who owned a laundry on Leavenworth Street. About 6:00 a.m. that same day, six or seven federal agents arrived at Oye's Laundry, which was operated by James Wah Toy (D). While the other officers remained out of sight, Agent Alton Wong, of Chinese ancestry, rang the bell, and requested laundry and dry cleaning service. Toy (D) opened the door and informed the agent to return at 8:00 a.m., when the store was open. As Toy (D) started to close the door, Agent Wong showed Toy (D) his badge, and introduced himself as a federal narcotics agent. Toy (D) slammed the door and ran down the hallway through the laundry to his living quarters at the back, where his wife and child were asleep in a bedroom. Accompanied by other officers, Agent Wong broke open the door to the laundry and followed Toy (D) into the bedroom. Toy reached into a nightstand drawer, and Agent Wong drew his pistol, removed Toy's (D) hand from the drawer, and arrested and handcuffed Toy (D). Officers found nothing in the drawer; nor did a search of the premises uncover any narcotics. Toy (D) denied selling any narcotics, but indicated that a person, whom he knew only as "Johnny," was selling drugs.

Acting on information provided by Toy (D), the officers located and entered Johnny's residence, where they found Johnny Yee in the bedroom. Yee eventually surrendered several tubes (containing in total less than one ounce of heroin) to the agents. Within the hour, Yee and Toy (D) were taken into custody, where Yee stated that the heroin had been brought to him about four days earlier by petitioner Toy (D) and another Chinese man known only to him as "Sea Dog." Toy (D), when questioned, revealed the identity of "Sea Dog" to be defendant Wong Sun (D). Again, based on information provided by Toy (D), police located Wong Sun's (D) residence, where Agent Wong ran a downstairs bell and was buzzed into the building. He met a woman on the stairway and introduced himself as a narcotics agent who was looking for Mr. Wong. The woman, who turned out to be Wong Sun's wife, told the officer that

Wong Sun (D) was in the back room sleeping. Officer Wong and several other agents entered the apartment and Wong Sun (D) was escorted from the back bedroom in handcuffs. A thorough search of the apartment did not uncover any narcotics. All three men—Toy (D), Yee and Wong Sun (D)—were arraigned and released on their own recognizance.

A few days later, the three men were interrogated at the office of the Narcotics Bureau by Agent William Wong (also of Chinese descent). All were given *Miranda* warnings and were questioned separately. Each made statements that were reduced to writing. After making several corrections to his written statement, Toy (D) refused to sign it. Wong Sun (D), who had considerable difficulty understanding the statement in English, was read it in Chinese, and refused to sign the statement although he admitted the accuracy of its contents.

Hom Way did not testify at Toy's (D) or Wong Sun's (D) trials. Yee, at first offered as the prosecution's principal witness, was excused after he invoked the privilege against self-incrimination and flatly repudiated the statement he had given to Agent William Wong. That statement was not offered in evidence, nor was any testimony elicited from him identifying either of the other defendants as the source of the heroin in his possession or otherwise tending to support the charges against the petitioners.

The prosecution offered four items of evidence tending to prove Toy's (D) and Wong Sun's (D) possession of heroin: (1) the statements made orally by Toy (D) in his bedroom at the time of his arrest; (2) the heroin surrendered to the agents by Johnny Yee; (3) petitioner Toy's (D) pretrial unsigned statement; and (4) petitioner Wong Sun's (D) similar statement. The trial court admitted these items into evidence.

■ ISSUE 1

Should the statements made by Toy (D) in his bedroom be excluded as "fruits" of the agents' unlawful action?

■ DECISION AND RATIONALE

(Brennan, J.) Yes. Toy (D) was arrested without reasonable or probable cause. As is the case with more traditional physical evidence, verbal evidence that derives so immediately from an unlawful entry and unauthorized arrest like the officers' action in the present case is the "fruit" of official illegality. Moreover, Toy's (D) statements were not, as the prosecution contends, "an intervening act of free will." Six or seven officers had broken down the door and pursued Toy (D) into the bedroom, where his wife and child were sleeping. Toy (D) was almost immediately handcuffed and arrested. Under these circumstances, it is unreasonable to infer that Toy's (D) response was sufficiently an action of free will to purge the primary taint of the unlawful invasion. Reversed.

■ ISSUE 2

Does the exclusion of Toy's (D) declaration make the narcotics taken from Yee, to whom those declarations led the police, inadmissible against Toy (D)?

■ DECISION AND RATIONALE

(Brennan, J.) Yes. The prosecution would not have found the narcotics without Toy's (D) statements. Hence, the prosecution did not learn of the evidence "from an independent source." Nor was the connection between the lawless conduct of the police and the discovery of the challenged evidence "so attenuated as to dissipate the taint." Not all evidence is "fruit of the poisonous tree" simply because it would not have come to light but for the illegal actions of the police. Rather, the issue is "whether, granting establishment of the primary illegality, the evidence to which the instant objection is made has been come at by exploitation of that illegality or instead by means sufficiently distinguishable to be purged of the primary taint." Here, the narcotics were "come at by exploitation of the illegality" and are, therefore, inadmissible against Toy (D). Reversed.

■ ISSUE 3

Was the unsigned confession of Wong Sun (D) the fruit of the unlawful arrest and therefore inadmissible against Wong Sun (D) at trial?

■ DECISION AND RATIONALE

(Brennan, J.) No. Wong Sun had been released on his own recognizance after a lawful arraignment and returned voluntarily several days later to make the statement. Therefore, the connection between his initially unlawful arrest and the statement had "become so attenuated as to dissipate the taint." The fact that the statement was unsigned does not affect its admissibility. Wong Sun understood and adopted its substance, and has not suggested any impropriety in the interrogation itself that would require the exclusion of this statement. Affirmed.

■ ISSUE 4

Were the narcotics surrendered by Yee admissible against Wong Sun (D)?

■ DECISION AND RATIONALE

(Brennan, J.) Yes. The exclusion of the drugs as to Toy (D) was required solely by their tainted relationship to information unlawfully obtained from Toy (D), and not by any impropriety connected with their surrender by Yee. The seizure of the heroin invaded no right of privacy of person or premises that would entitle Wong Sun (D) to object to its use at his trial. Affirmed.

Analysis:

The "fruit of the poisonous tree" doctrine prohibits the admissibility of evidence illegally seized and any evidence obtained as the result of an illegal seizure. Where, however, intervening circumstances or a sufficient amount of time has elapsed between the illegality, the evidence may be introduced on the ground that the taint of illegality has "dissipated." Note, however, that the passage of time means little when the illegality involves an unlawful detention; a long detention, like a short one, may compound the taint of an illegal arrest.

■ CASE VOCABULARY

FRUIT–OF–THE–POISONOUS–TREE DOCTRINE: The rule that evidence derived from an illegal search, arrest, or interrogation is inadmissible because the evidence (the "fruit") was tainted by the illegality (the "poisonous tree"). Under this doctrine, for example, a murder weapon is inadmissible if the map showing its location and used to find it was seized during an illegal search.

INDEPENDENT–SOURCE RULE: The rule providing—as an exception to the fruit-of-the-poisonous-tree doctrine—that evidence obtained by illegal means may nonetheless be admissible if that evidence is also obtained by legal means unrelated to the original illegal conduct.

PROPHYLACTIC: Formulated to prevent something.

Hudson v. Michigan

(Convicted Criminal) v. *(Prosecuting State)*

547 U.S. 586, 126 S. Ct. 2159, 165 L. Ed. 2d 56 (2006)

POLICE ANNOUNCING THEIR PRESENCE AT A HOME MUST WAIT AN APPROPRIATE AMOUNT OF TIME BEFORE ENTERING

I hate having to "knock and announce".

Relax, these days it's over with really, really fast.

stus.com

■ **INSTANT FACTS** Police entered Hudson's (D) home just seconds after knocking and announcing their presence, and Hudson (D) moved to suppress the evidence discovered in the resulting search.

■ **BLACK LETTER RULE** The exclusionary rule does not apply to suppress evidence obtained through a violation of the knock-and-announce rule.

■ PROCEDURAL BASIS

Certiorari to review a state appellate court decision refusing to suppress the evidence.

■ FACTS

Police executing a search warrant at Hudson's (D) home waited only three to five seconds after knocking and announcing their presence before they entered. Hudson (D) moved to suppress the drugs and weapons found as a result of the search. The trial court held that the premature entry violated Hudson's (D) Fourth Amendment rights and that the evidence was inadmissible, but the appellate court reversed, holding that suppression is an inappropriate remedy when entry is made, pursuant to a warrant, after a "knock and announce."

■ ISSUE

If the police violate the knock-and-announce rule, must the evidence they obtain through the subsequent entry and search be excluded?

■ DECISION AND RATIONALE

(Scalia, J.) No. The exclusionary rule does not apply to suppress evidence obtained through a violation of the knock-and-announce rule. The knock-and-announce rule is ancient, and is also commanded by the Fourth Amendment. There are, however, exceptional circumstances when the rule does not apply. If the police have a reasonable suspicion that evidence may be destroyed, for instance, or if a threat of physical harm exists, officers do not need to knock and announce their presence. When the rule does apply, just how long must the officers wait? The reasonable wait time depends on how long it would take to destroy or conceal the evidence, but that question is not at issue here. In this case, the knock-and-announce rule was violated, as all the lower courts agreed. The question here is what sanction should be imposed for that violation.

The exclusionary rule has a high cost and should not be applied indiscriminately. Exclusion is not appropriate in every case in which the defendant's Fourth Amendment rights have been violated, because not all evidence resulting from an unconstitutional search is the "fruit of the poisonous tree," particularly where the causal connection is remote. The knock-and-announce rule is meant to protect various rights, including the protection of one's dwelling from forcible entry and one's person from possible harm, but it was not meant to prevent the government from taking evidence described in a warrant.

If an officer has to be concerned that too short a wait will result in the exclusion of seized evidence, he or she may err on the side of waiting too long, thereby potentially jeopardizing a case and subjecting the public to a risk of harm. And it cannot be assumed that exclusion of the evidence would even serve a deterrent function. Moreover, the victim of a knock-and-announce violation has the option of redressing his injury through a civil action. This potential civil liability of the violating officers, as well as the prospect of discipline within the police department itself, serves a sufficient deterrent function, without the need to exclude the evidence obtained. For all of these reasons, when the knock-and-announce rule is violated, resort to suppressing evidence of guilt is unjustified. Affirmed.

CONCURRENCE

(Kennedy, J.) The majority's decision should not be read as stating that knock-and-announce violations are trivial, nor is application of the exclusionary rule in doubt. Rather, the holding here is simply that a violation of the knock-and-announce rule is not sufficiently related to the later discovery of evidence to justify suppression.

■ DISSENT

(Breyer, J.) The exclusionary rule *should* apply to knock-and-announce violations. The use of evidence secured through illegal, unconstitutional searches and seizures is barred at criminal trials, and the deterrent effect of that suppression cannot be ignored. What reason is there to think the police will be deterred by the threat of civil litigation? That threat was not held sufficient in the *Mapp* case, nor should it be here.

Prior to this decision, the Court has declined to apply the exclusionary rule only when it would not result in appreciable deterrence to do so, and when admissibility in contexts other than criminal trials was at issue. Neither of those exceptions exists here. Nor does the majority's "inevitable discovery" argument work. The government could not show in this case that the evidence sought to be suppressed would have inevitably been discovered through lawful means. In this case, had the illegal entry not occurred, the police simply would not have discovered the guns and drugs. And the fact that the officers had a warrant does not change that conclusion, because it was *not* a no-knock warrant. The inevitable discovery rule requires a showing that the evidence would have been discovered anyhow through legal means, such as in *Nix*, where a search party would have discovered the victim's body, irrespective of the defendant's unconstitutional admission as to where the body was, after he had invoked his right to counsel. In *Segura* and *Murray*, the evidence was independently obtained pursuant to a valid warrant, well after the initial, illegal search. Here, by contrast, without the unlawful entry, the police would not have discovered the incriminating evidence at all; the majority has wrongfully construed and applied the inevitable discovery rule.

The majority also argues that the exclusionary rule does not apply if the causal connection between the unlawful search and the evidence is attenuated, but then it goes on to give "attenuated" an entirely new meaning. The majority argues that attenuation occurs when the constitutional interest that has been violated would not be served by suppressing the evidence. But that argument ignores the fact that the knock-and-announce rule serves not only the interests listed by the majority, but also to protect the important privacy rights of the occupants. But even this is not really the point in this case. When evidence results from an unlawful search, it should be suppressed, despite what interests are served or violated. Moreover, the argument that compliance with the knock-and-announce rule may subject police officers to danger is an argument against the rule itself, not against the exclusion of evidence obtained by its violation.

The knock-and-announce rule is a subsidiary of the Fourth Amendment, and the majority could not, therefore, simply conclude that it is not important enough to warrant a suppression remedy. The knock-and-announce rule *is* important, as established precedent confirms. Common sense dictates that without suppression, there is little to deter violations of the knock-and-announce rule. The departures from Fourth Amendment principles in this case are simply not justified.

Analysis:

There is significant tension between the majority and dissenting opinions in this case, with the majority coming down on the side of the prosecution and the dissent favoring the protection of criminal defendants' constitutional rights. Lower courts had grappled with this conflict, with the Seventh Circuit Court of Appeals and the Michigan Supreme Court holding that the inevitable discovery doctrine creates a per se exception to the exclusionary rule for evidence seized after a Fourth Amendment knock-and-announce violation, and the Sixth and Eighth Circuits, the Arkansas Supreme Court, and the Maryland Court of Appeals holding that evidence is subject to suppression after such violations. The Supreme Court resolved that conflict in this case, and now all lower courts must follow suit.

■ CASE VOCABULARY

EXCLUSIONARY RULE: A rule that excludes or suppresses evidence obtained in violation of an accused person's constitutional rights.

FRUIT–OF–THE–POISONOUS–TREE DOCTRINE: The rule that evidence derived from an illegal search, arrest, or interrogation is inadmissible because the evidence (the "fruit") was tainted by the illegality (the "poisonous tree"). Under this doctrine, for example, a murder weapon is inadmissible if the map showing its location and used to find it was seized during an illegal search.

INEVITABLE DISCOVERY RULE: The rule providing—as an exception to the fruit-of-the-poisonous-tree doctrine—that evidence obtained by illegal means may nonetheless be admissible if the prosecution can show that the evidence would eventually have been legally obtained anyway.

KNOCK–AND–ANNOUNCE RULE: The requirement that the police knock at the door and announce their identity, authority, and purpose before entering a residence to execute an arrest or search warrant.

NO–KNOCK SEARCH WARRANT: A search warrant that authorizes the police to enter premises without knocking and announcing their presence and purpose before entry because a prior announcement would lead to the destruction of the objects searched for or would endanger the safety of the police or another person.

SEARCH WARRANT: A judge's written order authorizing a law-enforcement officer to conduct a search of a specified place and to seize evidence.

Herring v. United States

(Criminal Defendant) v. *(Prosecuting Authority)*

555 U.S. ___, 129 S. Ct. 695, 172 L. Ed. 2d 496 (2009)

SEARCHES INCIDENT TO ARREST ARE VALID EVEN IF THE ARREST WAS BASED ON A MISTAKE

Why do they want me to update this? Shouldn't we leave recalled warrants in the system so we can "mistakenly" arrest and search people?

■ **INSTANT FACTS** Herring (D) was arrested based on a mistaken belief that he had an outstanding warrant, and evidence obtained in the search incident to that arrest was used to support drug and weapons charges against him.

■ **BLACK LETTER RULE** The exclusionary rule is not an individual right and applies only where it results in appreciable deterrence.

■ PROCEDURAL BASIS

Certiorari to review a decision by the Eleventh Circuit Court of Appeals affirming the trial court's admission of the evidence against the defendant.

■ FACTS

Herring (D) got a ride to the Sheriff's Department to retrieve something from his impounded truck. Herring was no stranger to the officers there, so upon learning that he was present they checked to see if Herring (D) had any outstanding arrest warrants. Their computers showed nothing, so they checked with a neighboring county, and the warrant clerk in that county reported back that there was an active arrest warrant for Herring's (D) failure to appear on a felony charge. Based on this information, a deputy followed Herring (D) as he left the impound lot and arrested him. A search incident to the arrest revealed methamphetamine in Herring's (D) pocket and a pistol in his vehicle. The information about the warrant was, however, mistaken. The warrant had actually been recalled five months earlier, but the information about the recall was not in the database. The correct information was discovered and relayed within ten or fifteen minutes, but Herring (D) had already been arrested by that time. Herring (D) was indicted for the illegal gun and drug possession, and he moved to suppress the evidence from his initial arrest because the arrest was illegal, having been based on the rescinded warrant. The court refused to suppress the evidence, however, finding that the arresting officers had acted on a good faith belief that the warrant was outstanding, so there was no reason to believe the application of the exclusionary rule would deter the occurrence of any future similar mistakes. The Eleventh Circuit Court of Appeals affirmed, concluding that the benefit of suppressing the evidence would be marginal at best, and that it was therefore admissible under the good faith rule of *United States v. Leon.* Because other courts had required the exclusion of evidence obtained through similar police errors, the Supreme Court granted certiorari.

■ ISSUE

Did the court properly admit evidence obtained from a search incident to Herring's (D) arrest, even though it was based on a mistaken belief that there was an outstanding warrant for his arrest?

■ DECISION AND RATIONALE

(Roberts, C.J.) Yes. The exclusionary rule is not an individual right and applies only where it results in appreciable deterrence. The suppression of evidence is not an automatic consequence of a Fourth Amendment violation. The exclusionary rule, which prohibits the use of improperly obtained evidence at

---

trial, is designed to safeguard Fourth Amendment rights through its deterrent effect. The *Leon* case admonished that we must consider the actions of all police officers involved when analyzing the applicability of the rule. Here, the officers did nothing improper—indeed, the error was caught quickly because they required a faxed confirmation of the warrant. Although the Eleventh Circuit concluded that someone should have updated the computer to indicate the recall of the arrest warrant, the court also concluded that the error was negligent, not reckless or deliberate. Based on that fact, we conclude that the error was not enough by itself to require the extreme sanction of exclusion.

In *Leon* we held that when police act under a warrant that is invalid for lack of probable cause, the exclusionary rule does not apply if the police acted in objectively reasonable reliance on the subsequently invalidated search warrant. An assessment of the flagrancy of the police misconduct is an important step in the analysis. To trigger the exclusionary rule, police conduct must be sufficiently deliberate that exclusion can meaningfully deter it and sufficiently culpable that such deterrence is worth the price paid by the justice system. The rule serves to deter deliberate, reckless, or grossly negligent conduct, or in some cases recurring or systemic negligence. The error in this case does not rise to that level. The criminal should not "go free because the constable has blundered." Affirmed.

■ DISSENT

(Ginsburg, J.) The exclusionary rule is a remedy necessary to ensure that the Fourth Amendment's prohibitions are observed in fact. Beyond doubt, a main objective is deterrence. But exclusion is also often the only remedy available to redress a Fourth Amendment violation. Civil remedies, or administrative or criminal penalties, are rarely available to defendants whose rights have been violated. Moreover, contrary to the majority's assertion, application of the exclusionary rule in this case would have more than a scant deterrent effect. Just because the error here was a negligent failure to make a computer entry does not mean application of the rule would have minimal value. As tort law recognizes, even negligent conduct can lead to liability, and the doctrine of respondeat superior encourages supervisors to more closely monitor their employees' conduct. Electronic databases form the nervous system of contemporary criminal justice operations. The risk of error arising from these databases is not slim. Inaccuracies in electronic information raise grave concerns for individual liberty. In summary, negligent recordkeeping errors by law enforcement personnel threaten individual liberty, are susceptible to deterrence by the exclusionary rule, and cannot be remedied effectively through other means. The rule is needed to make the Fourth Amendment something real. Suppression should have attended the unconstitutional search in this case.

Analysis:

Once again the dissent raises some strong points, illustrating the sharply differing viewpoints of the Justices when it comes to the admission or exclusion of evidence. As dissenting Justice Ginsburg, joined by Justices Stevens, Souter, and Breyer, notes, computer programs are the central nervous system of police and sheriff's departments throughout the country, and information is often shared among them. Data are frequently stored in national databases by federal departments and agencies. A minor typographical error, or a failure to enter information, could have dire consequences for individual rights. Perhaps the majority's viewpoint is couched more in principal than in practicality, but the dissenting Justices refuse to ignore the realities of how present day law enforcement works.

■ CASE VOCABULARY

RESPONDEAT SUPERIOR: [Law, Latin, "let the superior make answer."] *Torts*. The doctrine holding an employer or principal liable for the employee's or agent's wrongful acts committed within the scope of the employment or agency.

CHAPTER SIX

Confessions: The Voluntariness Requirement

Hector (A Slave) v. State

Instant Facts: A slave was discovered in the area of a burglary and, after hours of beating by an angry mob, confessed to the crime.

Black Letter Rule: Coerced confessions, offered under the influence of pain as a way of seeking respite from that pain, are not admissible in evidence.

Lisenba v. California

Instant Facts: Lisenba (D), referred to in the opinion as "James," and a co-defendant, Hope, were indicted for the murder of James's wife. Hope pleaded guilty. James was tried and found guilty.

Black Letter Rule: A voluntary confession does not violate due process when used to convict a defendant of a capital crime.

Spano v. New York

Instant Facts: Spano, convicted on the basis of his confession of murdering the decedent, sought to have his confession excluded.

Black Letter Rule: A confession provided by a defendant suffering from fatigue and emotional distress brought on by police pressure is not voluntary.

Hector (A Slave) v. State

(*Confessing Criminal Defendant*) v. (*Prosecuting Authority*)

2 Mo. 166 (1829)

THE COURT MUST DECIDE WHETHER A CONFESSION WAS VOLUNTARY

■ **INSTANT FACTS** A slave was discovered in the area of a burglary and, after hours of beating by an angry mob, confessed to the crime.

■ **BLACK LETTER RULE** Coerced confessions, offered under the influence of pain as a way of seeking respite from that pain, are not admissible in evidence.

■ **PROCEDURAL BASIS**

On appeal from a verdict of guilty.

■ **FACTS**

At about 10:30 one night, a burglary was discovered and Hector (D), a slave, was caught in the area. The angry mob that caught him began to flog Hector (D) to make him confess. After hours of flogging, Hector (D) said that if his abusers would let him go, he would show them the stolen money. McKinney, a witness at Hector's (D) trial, testified that he heard some screaming near his home at about daybreak, and discovered the mob flogging Hector (D), who was calling out for assistance. McKinney got out of bed and went to Hector (D), telling him that if he had taken the money, he should confess. Hector (D) told McKinney that if he took him to his master's house, he would show McKinney the money. They all went there together, but there was no money. McKinney thought Hector (D) had tricked him, so he whipped him some more.

Hector's (D) counsel attempted to exclude McKinney's testimony, arguing that any confession Hector (D) made to McKinney was not free and voluntary, but extorted by pain. Hector's (D) counsel also sought to exclude the evidence of Hector's (D) confession to his abusers. The court allowed the evidence, but instructed the jury to disregard any confession they thought arose from duress. Any confession the jury thought was freely given, however, could be considered as evidence of Hector's (D) guilt. Hector's (D) counsel objected to the instruction.

■ **ISSUE**

Were the so-called confessions of Hector (D) admissible in evidence?

■ **DECISION AND RATIONALE**

(M'Girk, J.) No. Coerced confessions, offered under the influence of pain as a way of seeking respite from that pain, are not admissible in evidence. Hector (D) had been abused for most of the night, which in itself may have subdued him into confessing. When he saw McKinney, Hector (D) probably hoped for some relief, so his words to McKinney were a way of seeking respite, which is further evidenced by the fact that no money was found at Hector's (D) master's house. And the court erred in instructing the jury that free and voluntary confessions were evidence, because whether a confession is voluntary is a matter of law to be decided by the court, not the jury. The court should have decided that the confession to the angry mob was also made under the influence of pain, and it should have removed that evidence from the jury's consideration as well.

Analysis:

A confession is one of the most powerful forms of evidence against a criminal defendant. As this case shows, however, not all confessions are true; that is, innocent persons confess to crimes they did not commit. Because confessions have such authoritative weight, care must be taken to ensure a confession's truthfulness before presenting it to a jury. Although not all coerced confessions are false, confessions that are not freely and voluntarily given, and that are offered up as a way of escaping intolerable treatment that has gone on for hours, are inherently unreliable. Unreliable evidence is inadmissible.

■ CASE VOCABULARY

COERCED CONFESSION: A confession that is obtained by threats or force.

Lisenba v. California

(Convicted Murderer) v. *(Prosecuting Government)*

314 U.S. 219, 62 S. Ct. 280, 86 L. Ed. 166 (1941)

THE USE OF A VOLUNTARY CONFESSION DOES NOT VIOLATE DUE PROCESS

They used my confession against me. I totally didn't see that coming.

stus.com

■ **INSTANT FACTS** Lisenba (D), referred to in the opinion as "James," and a co-defendant, Hope, were indicted for the murder of James's wife. Hope pleaded guilty. James was tried and found guilty.

■ **BLACK LETTER RULE** A voluntary confession does not violate due process when used to convict a defendant of a capital crime.

■ PROCEDURAL BASIS

Review by the U.S. Supreme Court, based on the existence of a constitutional question, of the decision of the California Supreme Court affirming the trial court's finding that James's (D) confession was voluntary.

■ FACTS

James (D) married Mary E. Busch. Prior to the marriage, James (D) had purchased life insurance on Mary. The policies were valid even though Mary was not his legal wife when purchased. James (D) enlisted Hope to help him kill Mary. When Mary's death was reported, an investigation took place, but no charges resulted. When James (D) attempted to collect on the insurance policies, another investigation occurred and payment was denied. As a result of the insurance investigation, James (D) was arrested on the charge of incest. After his arrest, police took James (D) to nearby house and then to the District Attorney's office, but did not question him. He was asked to comment about the incest charge but refused. James (D) was held in the DA's office until late afternoon and then taken back to the house near his home, where he was questioned throughout the night about Mary's death. He was not permitted to sleep. The next morning (Monday) James (D) was taken from the house but returned later for further interrogation. The questioning continued until approximately 3:00 a.m. on Tuesday. At that time, James (D) claimed he collapsed. The others present claimed he fell asleep. When he awoke, James (D) was arrested and taken to jail. James (D) insisted that while being questioned, he was physically assaulted, but witnesses denied the beatings. Notwithstanding the alleged physical mistreatment, James (D) made no incriminating statements. Following James's (D) arrest, Hope was arrested and he made a statement about his role in Mary's death. James (D) declined to respond to Hope's statement. James (D) requested that his lawyer be summoned and was told that his attorney was unavailable. James (D) requested that another attorney be provided, but none was. Questioning continued into the night based on Hope's confession, and eventually James made a statement to the police, confessing his role in Mary's murder. At trial, James (D) insisted that he only tried to please his interrogators after hours of questioning by telling them a story that was similar in fact to the one they told him they had received from Hope. James (D) claimed that, in reality, Mary's murder was Hope's idea and that Hope had killed Mary during James' (D) absence by drowning her in the bathtub. He explained all of the other evidence in a way that deflected his guilt.

■ ISSUE

Does the use of a voluntary confession to convict a defendant of a capital crime violate due process?

■ DECISION AND RATIONALE

(Roberts, J.) No. A confession does not always violate due process when used to convict a defendant of a capital crime, particularly when the confession is voluntary. In this case, the illegal acts of the police in detaining James (D) for each of the extended periods before James (D) confessed to Mary's murder were, taken alone, insufficient to determine whether the confession was admissible. Where evidence as to whether the confession was voluntary is contradicted, the Court is required to rely on the decision of the trier of fact, so long as sufficient evidence exists to support that finding. While the actions of the investigators in this case came dangerously close to the edge of the law, the conditions of the interrogations were not sufficient to render to James's (D) confession involuntary. This conclusion is reinforced by James's (D) own statement that he would not have confessed had his co-conspirator, Hope, not made a confession. Thus, James's (D) confession was admissible. Affirmed.

■ DISSENT

(Black, J.) Questioning the defendant for hours on end and denying him access to his attorney when he requested it did, in fact, constitute sufficient coercion and compulsion to violate due process.

Analysis:

Unlike the beatings and physical abuse in *Brown v. Mississippi* that were not denied, the existence of physical abuse of the defendant here was not admitted. The Court is advancing a subjective standard for these close cases. The Court specifically noted that while the defendant in this case was not a highly educated individual, he did appear to have ample intelligence and business experience.

Spano v. New York

(Convicted Murderer) v. *(Prosecuting Government)*
360 U.S. 315, 79 S. Ct. 1202, 3 L. Ed. 2d 1265 (1959)

CONFESSIONS OBTAINED BY RELENTLESS QUESTIONING AND PLAYS FOR SYMPATHY VIOLATE DUE PROCESS

■ **INSTANT FACTS** Spano, convicted on the basis of his confession of murdering the decedent, sought to have his confession excluded.

■ **BLACK LETTER RULE** A confession provided by a defendant suffering from fatigue and emotional distress brought on by police pressure is not voluntary.

■ PROCEDURAL BASIS

Certiorari to review a decision of the New York Court of Appeals affirming the defendant's conviction.

■ FACTS

Spano (D) was in a bar with the decedent when Spano (D) concluded the decedent had taken some money belonging to him. When Spano (D) followed him out of the bar to recover the money, the two fought and Spano (D) was severely beaten by the decedent, who had been a professional boxer. Spano (D) later obtained a gun and went to a candy store where he expected to find the decedent. He entered the store and fired five shots, two of which struck the decedent and killed him. Of the people in the store at the time of the shooting, only one, a boy, saw Spano (D) shoot the decedent. Spano (D) was subsequently indicted for first-degree murder. On learning of the indictment, Spano (D) phoned a long-time friend, Bruno, who was attending the police academy. Spano (D) told Bruno that after the decedent beat him, he was not thinking clearly, but he knew he had shot the decedent. He also told Bruno that he intended to get a lawyer and surrender to the police. Before Spano's (D) surrender, Bruno told his superiors about the phone call. After Spano's (D's) surrender, Bruno was repeatedly asked about the murder but, on the advice of his attorney, he refused to answer despite long hours of questioning. The police made use of Bruno's relationship with Spano (D). Bruno told Spano a fabricated story that his job was in jeopardy because of Spano's (D's) unwillingness to talk. After four attempts to get Spano (D) to confess to Bruno, Spano finally agreed to make a statement. The confession was introduced at trial.

■ ISSUE

Does a confession comply with due process when it is given after relentless questioning and based on emotional distress?

■ DECISION AND RATIONALE

(Warren, J.) No. A confession given by a defendant suffering from fatigue and emotional distress brought on by police pressure is not voluntary. Unreliability is not the only reason to avoid using such a coerced confession. Another reason for insisting on truly voluntary confessions is the thought that law enforcement officials should be required to obey the law when doing their jobs. Spano (D) had a history of mental instability and had only attended a year and a half of high school. He had been questioned for eight hours straight and was suffering from fatigue. Despite repeated requests from Spano (D) to consult with his attorney, the questioners persisted. The use of a close, personal friend of Spano's (D's) to participate in the questioning was key in overcoming Spano's (D's) resistance to questioning. Given that the only goal the police had in questioning Spano (D) was to obtain a confession, the confession should be closely examined. Reversed.

■ CONCURRENCE

(Douglas, J.) Spano (D) should not have been denied his request to meet with counsel.

■ CONCURRENCE

(Stewart, J.) The failure of the police to comply with Spano's (D's) request to confer with counsel should be sufficient to render his confession inadmissible. Spano (D) had already been indicted and surrendered. At this stage, his right to counsel was absolute.

Analysis:

The concurring justices believed that the failure to provide Spano (D) with the benefit of counsel would have, by itself, served to exclude his confession. The majority, on the other hand, made the decision based on a totality of the circumstances, and the denial of counsel was but one of the factors to be reviewed, together with, among other things, the attempts to play on Spano's (D's) emotions. By placing their emphasis on the police misconduct in obtaining the confession, the majority is sending a message that, even if all other rights are respected, police misconduct can destroy an investigation.

CHAPTER SEVEN

Police Interrogation: Self–Incrimination Clause

Chavez v. Martinez

Instant Facts: Police questioned a suspect while he received emergency medical treatment for serious injuries, despite his pleas to stop, and the suspect, whose statements were never used at trial, sued for violations of the Fifth and Fourteenth Amendments.

Black Letter Rule: A violation of the constitutional right against self-incrimination occurs only when one is compelled to be a witness against himself in a criminal case.

Bram v. United States

Instant Facts: Bram (D) was convicted of murder on the high seas based on an involuntary confession Bram (D) made to police while he was in custody.

Black Letter Rule: An involuntary confession is not admissible as evidence against the accused by virtue of the Fifth Amendment privilege against self-incrimination.

Miranda v. Arizona

Instant Facts: While in custody, Miranda (D) signed a written confession after being questioned by two police officers who did not advise Miranda (D) that he had a right to have an attorney present.

Black Letter Rule: No statements obtained during a custodial interrogation, whether exculpatory or inculpatory, may be used against the defendant at trial unless the prosecution proves that the accused was advised (1) of the right to remain silent, (2) that any statements made can and will be used against the accused at trial, and (3) that the accused has the right to an attorney prior to and during questioning.

New York v. Quarles

Instant Facts: Quarles (D) was arrested in a supermarket where he had discarded a gun allegedly used to commit a recent crime and responded to police questions regarding the location of the weapon, without being advised of his *Miranda* rights.

Black Letter Rule: *Miranda* warnings are not required before police question a suspect in custody about imminent matters related to public safety.

Oregon v. Elstad

Instant Facts: Elstad's (D) conviction for burglary was reversed because his signed confession, although voluntary, was rendered inadmissible by a prior confession he made in response to police questioning without the benefit of *Miranda* warnings.

Black Letter Rule: Although *Miranda* requires the suppression of an un-warned admission, the admissibility of any subsequent statement turns solely on whether it was knowingly and voluntarily made.

Dickerson v. United States

Instant Facts: Dickerson (D) was convicted based on statements admitted against him pursuant to a federal statute under which, contrary to the *Miranda* decision, admissibility was based on voluntariness.

Black Letter Rule: Congress may not legislatively supersede Court decisions interpreting and applying the Constitution.

Missouri v. Seibert

Instant Facts: Police adopted a protocol for custodial interrogation that called for giving no warnings of the rights to silence and counsel until the interrogation had produced a confession, after which the police would provide *Miranda* warnings and further interrogate the suspect so he would repeat the earlier confession.

Black Letter Rule: The midstream recitation of *Miranda* warnings after interrogation elicits an unwarned confession does not effectively comply with *Miranda*'s constitutional requirements, and a confession repeated after such a warning is inadmissible.

Oregon v. Mathiason

Instant Facts: Mathiason (D), a parolee who was suspected of burglary, voluntarily appeared at the police station in response to an officer's request, was informed that he was not under arrest, and confessed after being questioned, without being given *Miranda* warnings.

Black Letter Rule: An individual who appears voluntarily at the police station for questioning, and who is not placed under arrest, is not in a custodial setting such that *Miranda* warnings must be given.

Berkemer v. McCarty

Instant Facts: McCarty (D) was initially stopped for a traffic infraction but became suspected of driving under the influence (a misdemeanor traffic offense in Ohio) shortly after the stop. McCarty (D), who was never advised of his rights under *Miranda*, made several incriminating statements both before and after he was formally arrested.

Black Letter Rule: All suspects in custody must be given *Miranda* warnings prior to questioning, regardless of the nature or severity of the crime, but an ordinary traffic stop does not render the detainee(s) "in custody" for purposes of *Miranda*.

Rhode Island v. Innis

Instant Facts: Innis (D) was arrested for murder and was given *Miranda* warnings on several different occasions. After Innis (D) requested to speak with a lawyer, he made incriminating statements in response to a conversation between police while riding in the back of the patrol vehicle.

Black Letter Rule: For purposes of *Miranda*, an "interrogation" occurs when police either expressly question a suspect in custody or engage in any actions or dialogue that the police should know is reasonably likely to elicit an incriminating response from the suspect.

North Carolina v. Butler

Instant Facts: After Butler (D) was arrested and given his *Miranda* warnings, he refused to sign a written waiver of his rights but agreed to speak with FBI agents.

Black Letter Rule: An express statement is not indispensable to a finding of waiver of the right to counsel; waiver may also be inferred by the words or conduct of the suspect.

Edwards v. Arizona

Instant Facts: Edwards (D) invoked his right to counsel and his right to remain silent on the night of his arrest; on the following day, while he was still incarcerated and still without counsel, police repeated the *Miranda* warnings and re-questioned Edwards (D), who made incriminating statements.

Black Letter Rule: An accused who expresses a desire to deal with police only through counsel does not waive that right merely by responding to further police-initiated questioning, even though he has been re-advised of his rights, and may not be subjected to further interrogation until counsel has been made available to him, unless the accused himself initiates further communication, exchanges, or conversations with the police.

Chavez v. Martinez

(*Interrogator*) v. (*Suspect*)

538 U.S. 760, 123 S. Ct. 1994, 155 L. Ed. 2d 984 (2003)

WHERE THERE IS NO CRIMINAL TRIAL TESTIMONY THERE IS NO SELF–INCRIMINATION

It's time for your interrogation. But don't worry, it's not a Fifth Amendment violation unless we prosecute you.

stus.com

■ **INSTANT FACTS** Police questioned a suspect while he received emergency medical treatment for serious injuries, despite his pleas to stop, and the suspect, whose statements were never used at trial, sued for violations of the Fifth and Fourteenth Amendments.

■ **BLACK LETTER RULE** A violation of the constitutional right against self-incrimination occurs only when one is compelled to be a witness against himself in a criminal case.

■ PROCEDURAL BASIS

Supreme Court review of a court of appeals holding in favor of Martinez (P).

■ FACTS

As two police officers investigated possible narcotics activity in a vacant lot, they heard a bicycle approaching, spotted Martinez (P), asked him to dismount, and patted him down, finding a weapon on his person. An altercation ensued. One of the officers yelled, "He's got my gun," although Martinez (P) initially denied having taken it from the officer's holster. The other officer shot Martinez (P) several times, resulting in partial blindness and paralysis. The officers arrested Martinez (P) at the scene.

Chavez (D), a patrol supervisor, arrived at the scene with paramedics a few minutes later. He accompanied Martinez (P) to the hospital and questioned him while he was being treated. Chavez (D) left the room a number of times to allow medical personnel to do their work. The questioning totaled about ten minutes over a forty-five-minute period. Most of Martinez's (P) answers were limited to "I don't know," "I'm dying," "I'm choking," and the like, although he did ultimately admit to having removed the officer's gun from the holster and pointing it at the police officer, and that he regularly used heroin.

Chavez (D) never gave Martinez (P) *Miranda* warnings, but no charges were ever brought, and Martinez's (P) responses were never used against him in any criminal proceeding. Nonetheless, Martinez (P) sued under 42 U.S.C. § 1983, alleging a violation of the Fifth Amendment's right to be free from compelled testimony against oneself in a criminal proceeding, and of the Fourteenth Amendment substantive due process right to be free from coercive questioning. The Ninth Circuit found in favor of Martinez (P), holding that Chavez (D) was not entitled to qualified immunity because he violated Martinez's (P) clearly established constitutional rights. Chavez (D) sought review in the Supreme Court.

■ ISSUE

Did the interrogating officer who questioned a seriously injured Martinez (P) while he received emergency medical treatment, even after Martinez (P) asked him to stop, violate Martinez's (P) Fifth Amendment right against self-incrimination?

■ DECISION AND RATIONALE

(Thomas, J.) No. A violation of the constitutional right against self-incrimination occurs only when one is compelled to be a witness against himself in a criminal case. The Ninth Circuit concluded that no reasonable officer would have thought it permissible to interrogate Martinez (P) under these circumstances, in view of his injuries and his repeated requests to stop. But the Fifth Amendment, made applicable to the states through the Fourteenth, provides that no person may be compelled *in any criminal case* to be a witness against himself. Based on this clear language, Martinez (P) has not alleged a violation of a clearly established right, because he was never prosecuted, let alone compelled to be a witness against himself. "Criminal case" requires at the very least the initiation of criminal proceedings; police interrogation is not a "case." And Martinez (P) was never forced to be a witness, because his statements were never admitted as testimony against him. The text of the Self–Incrimination Clause simply does not support the Ninth Circuit's view.

Moreover, witnesses can constitutionally be compelled to testify at trial, and in certain other contexts, as long as the case is not about them and the statements will not be used in another criminal case against the speaker. The threat of contempt can be levied in order to ensure cooperation. Martinez (P) was no more compelled to be a witness against himself than is an immunized witness forced to testify on pain of contempt, even though Martinez (P), unlike such a witness, did not know that his statements could not be used against him.

Although the Fifth Amendment may be invoked in contexts outside the criminal trial, such as at grand jury, civil, and administrative proceedings, a violation of the constitutional *right* occurs only if one is compelled to be a witness against himself at a criminal trial. This does not mean that a confession can be obtained through torturous means without violating the confessor's rights as long as the confession is not used against the confessor at his criminal trial; it simply means that the Fourteenth, rather than the Fifth, Amendment is the source of the constitutional right at stake in such cases.

■ CONCURRENCE

(Souter, J.) I concur in the judgment, but the privilege against self-incrimination should not be extended to allow a claim for money damages such as the plaintiff attempts to make here.

■ CONCURRENCE IN PART, DISSENT IN PART

(Kennedy, J.) Justices Thomas and Souter are wrong in their opinion that a Fifth Amendment violation cannot occur outside the context of a criminal trial, no matter how egregious the conduct at issue. The Self–Incrimination Clause is intended to deter police abuse, and the holding in this case fails to serve that purpose. Pursuant to the Court's holding here, torture that exacts a confession does not violate the Self–Incrimination clause. This conclusion "damages the law."

■ CONCURRENCE IN PART, DISSENT IN PART

(Ginsburg, J.) Martinez's (P) Fifth Amendment rights were violated. The Self–Incrimination Clause applies whenever police use severe compulsion to extract a statement from a suspect. Like the Due Process Clause, the Self–Incrimination Clause is intended to protect individual interests by discouraging abuses by those in power; "the privilege should instruct and control all officialdom."

Analysis:

In the previous chapter, we looked at the Fourteenth Amendment analysis in the Court's various opinions in this case. On that basis, too, the Court held that the plaintiff's constitutional rights were not violated. As noted in the earlier discussion, the number of concurring and dissenting opinions in *Chavez* illustrates the tension that exists in self-incrimination and due-process jurisprudence. Justices Kennedy and Ginsburg would prefer to create a broad remedy against coercive interrogation practices, but Justices Thomas would define the relevant cause of action so narrowly as to make it virtually unavailable.

Bram v. United States

(Accused Murderer) v. (Prosecuting Government)

168 U.S. 532, 18 S. Ct. 183, 42 L. Ed. 568 (1897)

THE ADMISSIBILITY OF CONFESSIONS IS DETERMINED USING FIFTH AMENDMENT PRINCIPLES

1897

The confession is inadmissable. I don't care if it *is* "the naked truth".

stus.com

■ **INSTANT FACTS** Bram (D) was convicted of murder on the high seas based on an involuntary confession Bram (D) made to police while he was in custody.

■ **BLACK LETTER RULE** An involuntary confession is not admissible as evidence against the accused by virtue of the Fifth Amendment privilege against self-incrimination.

■ PROCEDURAL BASIS

Certiorari to review a murder conviction based on the admission of an involuntary statement.

■ FACTS

Bram (D), the first officer of a ship, was convicted of murdering the captain of the vessel, who was found dead in his room shortly after 2:00. The evidence was entirely circumstantial, and no particular individual was initially suspected. A few days after the crime, Brown, who was stationed at the wheel of the ship until 2:00 on the day of the murder, was suspected of committing the crime and was seized on board the ship. Brown informed shipmates that he saw Bram (D) commit the murder from a window into the captain's cabin, and Bram (D) too, was seized. Upon the ship's arrival in Halifax, and while Bram (D) was in custody, he was brought into the private office of a detective, stripped of his clothing, and questioned. The official informed Bram (D) that Brown made a statement that he saw Bram (D) commit the murder. Bram (D) responded thus: "He could not have seen me. Where was he?" When the detective informed him that Brown stated that he was at the wheel, Bram (D) replied, "Well, he could not see me from there." Near the close of the interrogation, the detective also stated to Bram (D) that he was "satisfied that [Bram (D)] killed the captain," but he further intimated that Bram (D) worked with an accomplice whom he should turn in so as "not to have the blame of this horrible crime [three people were actually murdered] on your own shoulders." These statements were admitted into evidence against Bram (D) at trial. Bram (D) was convicted of murdering the captain and sentenced to death.

■ ISSUE

Did the statements elicited from the defendant by the detective constitute an involuntary confession, which was erroneously admitted into evidence?

■ DECISION AND RATIONALE

(White, J.) Yes. In order to be admissible, a confession must be free and voluntary, i.e., not extracted by threats or violence, or obtained by direct or implied promises (however slight), or by improper influence. Confessions resulting from such conduct must be excluded because it is impossible to measure the force of the influence used, or to determine its effect upon the defendant's mind. A court must consider all the circumstances surrounding the interrogation to determine whether a confession is voluntarily made. Here, the defendant was stripped of his clothing, isolated in a private office—and in a foreign land—when the conversation occurred. Given this situation and the nature of the communication, the defendant's reply to the detective was not the result of a purely voluntary mental action; it was impelled by "either hope or fear, or both, operating on the mind"—fear, because if the defendant had remained silent, it would be considered an admission of guilt; and hope, because the defendant might perceive the denial as removing suspicion from his person. Moreover, the detective's express intimation that the defendant might benefit from implicating another further rendered the confession involuntary. Since the confession was compelled and thus involuntary, its introduction into evidence against the accused is prohibited under the Fifth Amendment privilege against self-incrimination. Reversed.

■ DISSENT

(Brewer, J.) The statements made by the defendant were voluntary. The interrogator's remarks, intending to elicit from the defendant information to alleviate the entire blame, did not suggest to the defendant a benefit, i.e., "the holding out of a hope that a full disclosure might somehow inure to his advantage" if he were to speak. However, even if the latter comment did contain an improper suggestion, it was made near the close of the conversation and did not retroactively transform the previous voluntary statements into statements made under the influence of fear or hope.

Analysis:

Under early common law, confessions were admissible at trial without restriction. Later, the common law rule evolved to afford protection against involuntary confessions by identifying certain inducements that made a confession unreliable (e.g., actual or threatened physical harm, a promise of leniency in exchange for cooperation, etc.). The *Bram* case is important because it adopted a new, radical approach to determining the admissibility of confessions in federal courts based on violation of the Fifth Amendment privilege against self-incrimination, and considering whether, based on all the factors surrounding the interrogation, the confession "was, in fact voluntarily made."

■ CASE VOCABULARY

INVOLUNTARY CONFESSION: A confession induced by the police or other law-enforcement authorities who make promises to, coerce, or deceive the suspect.

RIGHT AGAINST SELF–INCRIMINATION: A criminal defendant's or a witness's constitutional right under the Fifth Amendment, guaranteeing that a person cannot be compelled by the government to testify if the testimony might result in the person's being criminally prosecuted. Although this right is most often asserted during a criminal prosecution, a person can also "plead the Fifth" in a civil, legislative, administrative, or grand-jury proceeding.

Miranda v. Arizona

(*Convicted Rapist and Kidnapper*) v. (*Prosecuting State*)
384 U.S. 436, 86 S. Ct. 1602, 16 L. Ed. 2d 694 (1966)

DEFENDANTS MUST BE INFORMED OF THEIR RIGHTS PRIOR TO INTERROGATION

Yes, you're in my "legal custody". No, that doesn't entitle you to *Miranda* warnings before I question you about your report card.

stus.com

■ **INSTANT FACTS** While in custody, Miranda (D) signed a written confession after being questioned by two police officers who did not advise Miranda (D) that he had a right to have an attorney present.

■ **BLACK LETTER RULE** No statements obtained during a custodial interrogation, whether exculpatory or inculpatory, may be used against the defendant at trial unless the prosecution proves that the accused was advised (1) of the right to remain silent, (2) that any statements made can and will be used against the accused at trial, and (3) that the accused has the right to an attorney prior to and during questioning.

■ **PROCEDURAL BASIS**

Certiorari to review the Arizona Supreme Court's decision affirming the lower court's determination that police did not unlawfully obtain a confession from the defendant.

■ **FACTS**

Miranda (D), a psychologically disturbed indigent Mexican, was arrested in Arizona and taken into police custody. After the complaining witness identified him, Miranda (D) was taken into an interrogation room and questioned by two police officers. The officers did not advise Miranda (D) that he had the right to have an attorney present during questioning. After two hours, the police secured a written confession signed by Miranda (D). The confession, which contained a paragraph to the effect that the confession was made voluntarily, without threats or promises of immunity and "with full knowledge of my legal rights, understanding that any statement I may make may be used against me," was admitted as evidence against Miranda (D) at trial. Miranda (D) was convicted of rape and kidnapping and sentenced to concurrent terms of twenty to thirty years' imprisonment on each count. Emphasizing that Miranda (D) did not specifically request counsel, the Supreme Court of Arizona affirmed the conviction, finding that police did not obtain the confession in violation of Miranda's (D) constitutional rights.

■ **ISSUE**

In order for statements to be admissible at trial, must a defendant subject to custodial interrogation be advised of his Fifth Amendment privilege against self-incrimination prior to questioning?

■ **DECISION AND RATIONALE**

(Warren, C.J.) Yes. The privilege against self-incrimination protects persons from compulsion in all settings in which the "freedom of action is curtailed in any significant way." A person interrogated in police custody is confronted with an extremely intimidating, unfamiliar, and psychologically coercive environment. Therefore, before an individual in custody may be interrogated, states must ensure that the following safeguards (or equally effective procedures) are observed:

(1) The accused must first be informed in clear and unequivocal terms that he or she has the right to remain silent.

---

(2) The interrogators must explain to the accused that anything said can and will be used against him or her in court.

(3) The accused must be clearly informed that he or she has the right to consult with a lawyer prior to questioning and to have the lawyer present during interrogation, and, in the case of indigent defendants, that a lawyer will be appointed to represent him or her.

Because Miranda was not advised in any way that he had the right to consult with an attorney and to have an attorney present during questioning, and because his right against self-incrimination was not otherwise protected, the statements were inadmissible. Moreover, the signed statement that contained the paragraph asserting that Miranda had "full knowledge" of his "legal rights" did not constitute a knowing and intelligent waiver of his constitutional rights. Reversed.

■ DISSENT

(Harlan, J.) The new rules frustrate an effective law enforcement tool, i.e., the confession. The rules do not guard against police brutality or other egregious forms of coercion, but rather negate all pressures and ultimately discourage any confession at all.

■ DISSENT

(White, J.) There is no adequate factual basis for the conclusion that all confessions obtained during custodial interrogation are the product of compulsion. It is illogical to distinguish between a spontaneous product of the coercion (e.g., a blurted out confession), which the decision views as "voluntary" despite the absence of warnings or knowledge of the rights, and the answer to an express question posed by law enforcement, which is "compelled" even if the accused has been clearly warned of his right to remain silent. In the latter instance, the response may be "involuntary" in the sense that it was provoked by an inquiry, but it is "patently unsound" to assert that the response is compelled. But, even assuming the existence of a factual basis for the aforementioned conclusion, the *Miranda* rule is "irrational" because it is only if the accused is also warned of the right to counsel, and waives both that right and the right against self-incrimination, that the inherent compulsiveness of the interrogation disappears. It is impossible to foreclose questioning without the necessary warnings yet at the same time permit the accused to waive his right to consult with an attorney, for in the latter instance, would not the answer also be compelled? The decision undermines the most basic governmental function to provide for the security of the individual and his property.

Analysis:

Another important aspect of *Miranda* deals with the issue of waiver. The case makes clear that any statements introduced into evidence against the accused must be shown to have been obtained after the accused knowingly and intelligently waived his privilege against self-incrimination and his right to retained or appointed counsel. Waiver is not presumed from the silence of an accused, or from the fact that a confession was eventually obtained. Nor is the privilege waived by an accused who begins to speak, but then decides it is better to invoke the privilege. Note that a lengthy interrogation or incommunicado incarceration before a statement is made is strong evidence that the accused did not validly waive his rights.

■ CASE VOCABULARY

CUSTODIAL INTERROGATION: Police questioning of a detained person about the crime that he or she is suspected of having committed.

DURESS: Strictly, the physical confinement of a person or the detention of a contracting party's property.

EXCULPATORY EVIDENCE: Evidence tending to establish a criminal defendant's innocence.

INCULPATORY EVIDENCE: Evidence showing or tending to show one's involvement in a crime or wrong.

New York v. Quarles

(Prosecuting State) v. *(Convicted Criminal)*
467 U.S. 649, 104 S. Ct. 2626, 81 L. Ed. 2d 550 (1984)

PUBLIC EXIGENCIES OUTWEIGH *MIRANDA* REQUIREMENTS

If you need to get around *Miranda*, claim you were "protecting public safety". Judges like the public even more than they like criminals.

stus.com

■ **INSTANT FACTS**: Quarles (D) was arrested in a supermarket where he had discarded a gun allegedly used to commit a recent crime and responded to police questions regarding the location of the weapon, without being advised of his *Miranda* rights.

■ **BLACK LETTER RULE** *Miranda* warnings are not required before police question a suspect in custody about imminent matters related to public safety.

■ **PROCEDURAL BASIS**

Certiorari to review a decision of the New York Court of Appeals affirming the trial court's suppression of evidence.

■ **FACTS**

Two officers on patrol were approached by a woman who told them that she had just been raped. The woman specifically described the alleged rapist and told the officers that he had just entered an A & P supermarket located nearby and was carrying a gun. Quarles (D), who fit the exact description given by the woman, was quickly spotted by the officer who entered the supermarket. Upon seeing the officer, Quarles (D) turned and ran toward the rear of the store. The officer pursued Quarles (D) with his gun drawn and ordered Quarles (D) to stop and put his hands over his head. Three other officers arrived at the scene. The officer who had given pursuit frisked Quarles (D) and found that Quarles (D) was wearing an empty shoulder holster. The officer handcuffed Quarles (D) and asked him where the gun was. Quarles (D) nodded in the direction of some empty cartons and replied, "[T]he gun is over there." The officer retrieved a loaded .38–caliber revolver from one of the cartons, formally placed Quarles (D) under arrest, and read him his *Miranda* rights from a printed card. Quarles (D) indicated that he was willing to answer questions without an attorney present. The officer then asked Quarles (D) if he owned the gun and where it was purchased. Quarles (D) admitted that the gun was his and that it was purchased in Miami, Florida. The trial court excluded the statement "the gun is over there" because it was obtained in violation of *Miranda*. The other statements were likewise excluded as "evidence tainted by the prior *Miranda* violation." The New York Court of Appeals affirmed, rejecting the prosecution's argument that the exigencies of the situation justified the failure to read Quarles (D) his *Miranda* rights until after the gun was located, and refusing to carve an exigency exception to the usual *Miranda* requirements because the police officer's testimony did not establish that his conduct was motivated by a concern for self protection or for public safety.

■ **ISSUE**

Where public safety is at risk, may law enforcement officials lawfully interrogate an individual in custody without first administering the *Miranda* warnings?

■ **DECISION AND RATIONALE**

(Rehnquist, J.) Yes. The concern for public safety takes precedence over adherence to the literal language of the "prophylactic rules" enunciated in *Miranda*. Contrary to the lower court's holding, the availability of this "public safety" exception does not depend on the subjective motivation of the officers involved. Here, the officers had every reason to believe that the suspect was armed and had discarded the weapon in a public place. In this locale, the weapon posed several dangers to the public safety, e.g., it could be used by an accomplice, or found by a customer or employee. If, under circumstances like these, police are required to administer *Miranda* warnings before posing questions geared toward securing public safety, the suspect might be deterred from responding. The cost of deterrence in public safety situations would far exceed the mere failure of obtaining evidence useful in convicting the suspect. The *Miranda* warnings are "not themselves rights protected by the Constitution but [are] instead measures to insure that the right against compulsory self-incrimination [is] protected." Here, the defendant does not claim that his statements were the product of police compulsion. Rather, the issue is whether the officer justifiably withheld procedural safeguards associated with the Fifth Amendment privilege. The court of appeals erred in excluding the statement regarding the gun, the gun itself, and the subsequent statements as illegal fruits of a Miranda violation. Reversed and remanded.

CONCURRENCE IN PART, DISSENT IN PART

(O'Connor, J.) [Concurred that gun was admissible.] There is no need to depart from the clear strictures of *Miranda*, which has never prohibited police from interrogating suspects about matters of public safety. The critical question is whether the State or the suspect should bear the cost of securing pubic safety when questions are asked and answered in violation of the suspect's Fifth Amendment rights. *Miranda* correctly holds that the State bears the burden. Moreover, the creation of a "public safety" exception unnecessarily blurs *Miranda* and makes it more difficult to understand. What one court views as a particularly exigent circumstance, another clearly will not. "The end result will be a finespun new doctrine on public safety exigencies incident to custodial interrogation, complete with the hair-splitting distinctions that currently plague . . . Fourth Amendment jurisprudence."

■ DISSENT

(Marshall, J.) There is no factual basis to conclude that the public safety was in danger; no customers or employees were wandering about the store at the time of the occurrence, and although the store was open to the public, the defendant's arrest took place during the middle of the night when the store was apparently deserted except for the clerks at the checkout counter. The police, aware that the gun was discarded somewhere near the scene of the arrest, could easily have cordoned off the store and searched for the missing weapon. The rationale of the decision is based on a "serious misunderstanding" of *Miranda* and the Fifth Amendment. *Miranda* never adopted a cost-benefit analysis over the issue of public safety versus individual rights against compelled self-incrimination, because the first factor was never part of the problem. Rather, *Miranda* was concerned with whether, under the Fifth Amendment, government officials could prosecute individuals based on statements made during custodial interrogations, which were presumed to be compelled. The public safety exception makes no reference to this problem. There is no basis for the determination that questioning a suspect in custody about public safety matters is any less coercive than interrogations into other matters. Moreover, the reasoning that *Miranda* warnings will deter responses from suspects in like circumstances is unpersuasive and clearly at odds with *Miranda*, which, unlike the case today, prohibits police officers from coercing criminal defendants into making involuntary statements. As a result of the opinion, the government is now free to use coerced statements in its case-in-chief in violation of the Fifth Amendment privilege against self-incrimination. The government may always question suspects without administering *Miranda* warnings. It simply may not use those statements against the accused in a court of law.

Analysis:

In addition to situations like *Quarles*, several lower courts have recognized the public safety exception (1) after warnings are given and the accused invokes the right to counsel, (2) when questions concern the location and condition of a kidnap victim, and (3) when questions are asked to protect the health of the accused. Note that the Court's repeated reference to the *Miranda* warnings as "prophylactic rules" becomes extremely relevant in the case of *Dickerson v. United States*, 530 U.S. 428, 120 S. Ct. 2326, 147 L. Ed. 2d 405 (2000).

■ CASE VOCABULARY

EXIGENCY: A state of urgency; a situation requiring immediate action.

MIRANDA RULE: The doctrine that a criminal suspect in police custody must be informed of certain constitutional rights before being interrogated. The suspect must be advised of the right to remain silent, the right to have an attorney present during questioning, and the right to have an attorney appointed if the suspect cannot afford one. If the suspect is not advised of these rights or does not validly waive them, any evidence obtained during the interrogation cannot be used against the suspect at trial (except for impeachment purposes).

SUB SILENTIO: Under silence; without notice being taken; without being expressly mentioned.

Oregon v. Elstad

(Prosecuting Authority) v. *(Convicted Burglar)*

470 U.S. 298, 105 S. Ct. 1285, 84 L. Ed. 2d 222 (1985)

THE FRUIT OF THE POISONOUS TREE DOCTRINE APPLIES TO FOURTH—NOT FIFTH—AMENDMENT VIOLATIONS

■ **INSTANT FACTS** Elstad's (D) conviction for burglary was reversed because his signed confession, although voluntary, was rendered inadmissible by a prior confession he made in response to police questioning without the benefit of *Miranda* warnings.

■ **BLACK LETTER RULE** Although *Miranda* requires the suppression of an un-warned admission, the admissibility of any subsequent statement turns solely on whether it was knowingly and voluntarily made.

■ **PROCEDURAL BASIS**

Supreme Court review of the state appellate court's reversal of the defendant's conviction.

■ **FACTS**

After the burglary of the Gross's home, a witness implicated Elstad (D), an eighteen-year-old neighbor and friend of the Gross's son. Officers went to Elstad's (D) home with an arrest warrant and began questioning him after speaking briefly with his mother. The officers asked Elstad (D) if he knew the Grosses, and he said he did and had heard about the burglary. The officers suggested that Elstad (D) was involved, and he responded, "Yes, I was there." They then took him to the station and, after an hour or so, resumed questioning, at which time the officers first read Elstad (D) his Miranda rights. Elstad (D) stated that he understood his rights but wanted to talk to the officers, and he thereafter made a complete written confession, even adding additional incriminating details. Elstad (D) was convicted, but appealed.

On appeal, the prosecution admitted that Elstad (D) was in custody when he made the statement, "I was there," and that the statement was therefore inadmissible for failure to provide *Miranda* warnings. But the state argued that any "taint" had dissipated prior to Elstad's (D) written confession, given after the requisite warnings had been provided. The Oregon Court of Appeals reversed, and the Supreme Court granted review.

■ **ISSUE**

Does an initial failure of law enforcement officers to administer *Miranda* warnings taint subsequent admissions made after a suspect has been fully advised of and waived his rights?

■ **DECISION AND RATIONALE**

(O'Connor, J.) No. Although *Miranda* requires the suppression of an un-warned admission, the admissibility of any subsequent statement turns solely on whether it was knowingly and voluntarily made.

There are two oft-used metaphors that confuse the real issue here. One is "the fruit of the poisonous tree," which applies in the Fourth Amendment search-and-seizure context, but not to Fifth Amendment protections. The other is "the cat is out of the bag," urged by Elstad (D) as a way of saying that once he admitted his involvement, the subsequent warnings made no difference and his statements were not really voluntary.

A *Miranda* violation differs significantly from a Fourth Amendment violation, to which the fruit of the poisonous tree doctrine applies. In fact, the *Miranda* exclusionary rule sweeps even more broadly than the Fifth Amendment itself. The Fifth Amendment prohibits only *compelled* testimony, but under the *Miranda* rule, even voluntary statements are inadmissible if given without the benefit of *Miranda* warnings, because the rule creates a *presumption* of compulsion. But the rule and its presumption, though irrebuttable in the prosecutor's case in chief, do not prohibit all evidence of the statements. For instance, voluntary statements provided without benefit of *Miranda* warnings may be introduced on cross-examination for impeachment purposes. In such instances, the primary criterion for admissibility is the old due-process voluntariness test.

When, unlike in this case, the original, un-warned statement results from coercion, the time that passes between the confessions, as well as other changes in circumstances, bear on whether the coercion carried over to the second statement. But when it is just the un-warned *presumption* of—and not *actual*—coercion that taints the original confession, the later provision of the *Miranda* warnings, in itself, cures the condition that renders the prior statement inadmissible. Although it is true that once "the cat is out of the bag," the cat can never to back in the bag, it does not necessarily follow that a suspect is thereafter perpetually disabled from making a usable confession. A subsequent administration of *Miranda* warnings should usually suffice to remove the conditions that preclude the admission of the original confession, and the finder of fact may reasonably conclude, under appropriate circumstances, that the suspect made a rational and intelligent choice whether to waive or invoke his rights.

Here, though belated, the *Miranda* warnings were complete. Elstad (D) argues, however, that his waiver was not really informed, because he was unaware that his earlier confession could not be used against him, and the officers should have told him as much. But police officers are not substitutes for counsel and cannot be expected to address all the murky areas and potential questions. And we have never held that the *sine qua non* for a knowing and voluntary waiver of the right to remain silent is a complete appreciation of all the consequences flowing from the nature and quality of the evidence in the case. Reversed.

■ DISSENT

(Brennan, J.) Yet again the Court delivers a crippling blow to *Miranda*. The Court rejects the "cat out of the bag" presumption entirely, adopting a new rule that " 'the psychological impact of *voluntary* disclosure of a guilty secret' neither 'qualifies as state compulsion' nor 'compromises the voluntariness' of subsequent confessions." The Court's marble-palace psychoanalysis flies in the face of our own precedents and demonstrates a startling unawareness of the realities of police interrogation.

Analysis:

Justice Brennan's dissent may have been prescient. The holding in this case led to a deliberate police tactic of delaying *Miranda* warnings in order to get suspects to confess, a charge the Court took up nearly two decades later in *Missouri v. Seibert*. In that case, the Supreme Court again considered whether the answers from the second phase of questioning could be used in court, but this time the Court answered "no." Justice Souter wrote that the facts of *Seibert* "by any objective measure reveal a police strategy adapted to undermine the *Miranda* warnings," and that the police had created a situation "in which it would have been unnatural to refuse to repeat at the second stage what had been said before." In her dissent, however, Justice O'Connor stated that the decision in *Seibert* "devours *Oregon v. Elstad*."

■ CASE VOCABULARY

SINE QUA NON: An indispensable condition or thing; something on which something else necessarily depends.

Dickerson v. United States

(*Convicted Bank Robber*) v. (*Prosecuting Government*)
530 U.S. 428, 120 S. Ct. 2326, 147 L. Ed. 2d 405 (2000)

MIRANDA CANNOT BE SUPERCEDED BY ACTS OF CONGRESS

■ **INSTANT FACTS** Dickerson (D) was convicted based on statements admitted against him pursuant to a federal statute under which, contrary to the *Miranda* decision, admissibility was based on voluntariness.

■ **BLACK LETTER RULE** Congress may not legislatively supersede Court decisions interpreting and applying the Constitution.

■ **PROCEDURAL BASIS**

Certiorari to review reversal by Fourth Circuit Court of Appeals of a suppression order entered by district court.

■ **FACTS**

Congress enacted 18 U.S.C. § 3501, which made statements obtained during a custodial interrogation admissible against the accused if the statements were voluntarily made. Dickerson (D), who never received the *Miranda* warnings prior to interrogation, was convicted on evidence admitted under the statute. The United States Court of Appeals for the Fourth Circuit held that the decision in *Miranda* was not a constitutional holding and that, therefore, Congress could by statute have the final say on the question of admissibility.

■ **ISSUE**

Is *Miranda* a constitutional holding that cannot be effectively overruled by an act of Congress?

■ **DECISION AND RATIONALE**

(Rehnquist, C.J.) Yes. Even though several exceptions exist to *Miranda's* warning requirements and *Miranda* has repeatedly been referred to as "prophylactic," the protections announced in *Miranda* are constitutionally required. The following factors establish *Miranda* as a constitutional holding: (1) it has been consistently applied in state courts over which the Court has power only concerning constitutional issues, (2) certiorari was granted "to give concrete constitutional guidelines for law enforcement and agencies to follow," and (3) it invites legislative bodies to create procedures to protect the constitutional rights against coerced self-incrimination. That Congress intended to overrule *Miranda* by enactment of § 3501 is clear from the following: (1) the statute expressly designates voluntariness as the foundation of admissibility; (2) the statute omits any warning requirement; and (3) the trial court is instructed to consider a nonexclusive list of factors relevant to the circumstances of a confession (a test previously found to risk overlooking involuntary custodial confessions and therefore, not a legislative alternative to *Miranda* "equally effective in preventing coerced confessions"). But, only the court may overrule a constitutional decision. Therefore, following the rule of *stare decisis*, which weighs heavily against overruling a decision whose "doctrinal underpinnings" remain strong, *Miranda* and its progeny will continue to govern the admissibility of statements made during custodial interrogation in both state and federal courts. Reversed.

■ DISSENT

(Scalia, J.) Section 3501 is not unconstitutional; it forbids the same use of the evidence that is forbidden by the Constitution—a compelled confession. By disregarding a statute that is constitutional but contradictory to a decision that "announced a constitutional rule," the Court not only applies the Constitution (a valid power), but *expands* it by imposing upon Congress and the states what are, in the Court's view, useful "prophylactic" restrictions. "That is an immense and frightening antidemocratic power, and it does not exist. By denying effect to this Act of Congress, the Court acts in plain violation of the Constitution." Moreover, the *Miranda* decision is "preposterous" if read in terms of what the Constitution requires. There is no basis for concluding that a suspect, aware of all the rights described in *Miranda,* who responds to police questioning, is acting anyway but volitional. And why is the right to counsel included among the *Miranda* rights, if not for any reason other than to prevent a suspect from incriminating himself *foolishly* rather than simply from incriminating himself. The former is not required by the Constitution. *Dickerson* establishes that a decision is "constitutional" if the Constitution "requires the result that the decision announces and the statute ignores."

Analysis:

Commentators, while agreeing with most of the "prophylactic rules," criticize their use, because the Court has failed to adequately explain its authority to prescribe such rules. The most often-noted criticisms are: (1) the Court's failure to fully explain any difference between prophylactic and administratively based per se rules, (2) the Court's failure to provide clear guidelines as to when use of a prophylactic rule is justified, (3) the Court's inconsistency in using the "prophylactic" characterization to describe seeming functionally similar standards, and (4) the Court's failure to establish any significant guidelines for determining when legislative safeguards are sufficient to replace prophylactic standards.

■ CASE VOCABULARY

PROPHYLACTIC: Formulated to prevent something.

STARE DECISIS: The doctrine of precedent, under which it is necessary for a court to follow earlier judicial decisions when the same points arise again in litigation.

Missouri v. Seibert

(Prosecuting Authority) v. *(Murder Suspect)*
542 U.S. 600, 124 S. Ct. 2601, 159 L. Ed. 2d 643 (2004)

THE COURT PUTS A STOP TO A PLOY SPAWNED BY *ELSTAD*

■ **INSTANT FACTS** Police adopted a protocol for custodial interrogation that called for giving no warnings of the rights to silence and counsel until the interrogation had produced a confession, after which the police would provide *Miranda* warnings and further interrogate the suspect so he would repeat the earlier confession.

■ **BLACK LETTER RULE** The midstream recitation of *Miranda* warnings after interrogation elicits an unwarned confession does not effectively comply with *Miranda*'s constitutional requirements, and a confession repeated after such a warning is inadmissible.

■ **PROCEDURAL BASIS**

Certiorari to review the state supreme court's finding of inadmissibility.

■ **FACTS**

Seibert's (D) son, who suffered from cerebral palsy, died in his sleep. Seibert (D) feared charges of neglect due to bed sores on her son's body, so she and her other sons, plus two of their friends, devised a plan to burn down their mobile home while the dead son was in it. To make it appear that she had not left the twelve-year old deceased son unattended, they planned to also leave a mentally ill teenager who lived with the family in the home while it burned. Seibert's (D) son and a friend set the fire, and the teenager died. The son who set the fire also suffered burn injuries and was hospitalized.

Five days later, the police awakened Seibert (D) at the hospital where her son was being treated. The police arrested Seibert (D), took her to the station, and, after about an hour, interrogated her without providing *Miranda* warnings. After intense questioning, Seibert (D) admitted that the mentally ill teen was meant to die in the fire. She was then allowed a short coffee and cigarette break, after which the police turned on a tape recorder, provided *Miranda* warnings, and resumed questioning. The interrogator goaded Seibert (D) into repeating what she had already said. She was charged with murder.

Seibert's (D) counsel moved to suppress the statements made in the second phase of questioning. At the suppression hearing, the interrogating officer admitted that he had been taught the interrogation technique of deliberately withholding *Miranda* warnings, eliciting a confession, giving the warnings, and then getting the suspect to repeat what he or she had already said. Based on the *Elstad* case, the trial court held that the second confession was nonetheless admissible. The state supreme court reversed, holding that *Elstad* was distinguishable, because in that case there had been no intentional withholding of *Miranda* warnings. In this case, by contrast, the officer's intentional omission was designed to deprive Seibert (D) of the opportunity to knowingly and intelligently waive her rights, which tactic encourages constitutional violations and diminishes *Miranda*'s role. The Supreme Court granted certiorari to resolve a split in the circuits.

■ **ISSUE**

If a police officer intentionally withholds *Miranda* warnings and elicits a confession, then provides the warnings and gets the suspect to repeat the confession, is the second confession admissible?

■ DECISION AND RATIONALE

(Souter, J.) No. The technique of interrogating in successive unwarned and warned phases raises new challenges to *Miranda*. Yet this methodology has been heralded by both local police departments and national training organizations. We hold today that the midstream recitation of *Miranda* warnings after interrogation elicits an unwarned confession does not effectively comply with *Miranda*'s constitutional requirements, and a confession repeated after such a warning is inadmissible.

The threshold inquiry in cases like this is whether the warning was truly effective when given. Did the warnings really convey that the suspect had the right not to speak, when he had already spoken? Would the suspect think, if everything I say can be used against me, and I've already said everything there is to say, what point is there in being silent now? Thus, when *Miranda* warnings are inserted in the midst of continuing interrogation, they are actually more likely to mislead and confuse a suspect than to inform him.

Elstad does not control the outcome here, because in that case the unwarned confession resulted from a good-faith mistake by the police officer, not a deliberate attempt to trick the suspect. Moreover, In *Elstad* there were distinct differences in the extensiveness of questioning, time, and setting of the two periods of interrogation. A reasonable person in the suspect's shoes could have understood the station-house questioning in *Elstad* to be a new and distinct experience. Here, however, the unwarned interrogation was exhaustive, and there was little left unsaid. The second phase followed after only a brief pause, in the same place as the unwarned segment. The police officer gave the impression that the second phase was merely a continuation of the first, by repeatedly referencing statements made during the initial interrogation. These circumstances challenge the efficacy of the *Miranda* warnings to the point that a reasonable person in the suspect's shoes would not have understood a message that she retained a choice about whether to keep talking.

Because the question-first tactic employed here effectively threatens to thwart *Miranda*'s purpose of reducing the risk of admitting coerced confessions into evidence, and because the facts here do not support a conclusion that the warnings given could have served that purpose, Seibert's (D) post-warning statements are inadmissible. Affirmed.

■ CONCURRENCE

(Breyer, J.) The "fruit of the poisonous tree" doctrine applied in other criminal contexts should apply in cases like this to determine whether the second confession is sufficiently removed from the first to have eliminated the taint.

■ CONCURRENCE

(Kennedy, J.) The principles announced in *Elstad* should continue to govern the admissibility of post-warning subsequent confessions, unless the deliberate two-phase approach used here was involved. In the latter case, the second confession will be inadmissible unless curative steps—such as a substantial break in time, or more detailed warnings—are taken between the two periods of interrogation. Because no curative steps were taken here, the confession was inadmissible and the conviction cannot stand.

■ DISSENT

(O'Connor, J.) The plurality gives insufficient deference to *Elstad*, and Justice Kennedy puts improper emphasis on the police officer's subjective intent, so I dissent. The interrogator's intent has no bearing on the voluntariness of a suspect's waiver. Thus, basing admissibility on whether the officer's delay in providing *Miranda* warnings was deliberate or calculated is ill advised. Instead, the two-step interrogation procedure must be analyzed using the same principles applied in other Fifth Amendment contexts. Accordingly, the court must consider whether the taint affecting the first confession has adequately dissipated through the passage of time, a change of location, or a change in the identity of the interrogator, for example. I would leave this analysis for the state court on remand, but also point out the fact that the officer's references to the unwarned statement during the subsequent questioning in this case may bear on the voluntariness inquiry here.

Analysis:

In light of the contradictory approaches taken by the plurality and Justice Kennedy, who provided the crucial fifth vote in the judgment, it could be argued that *Seibert* offered no real guidance to state courts. The dispute between Justice Kennedy and the plurality turned on whether *Miranda*'s exclusionary rule required an effect-based analysis or an intent-based test. The plurality focused on the *effect* of two-step interrogation, and would suppress second confessions whenever the two-step procedure was reasonably likely to undermine the voluntariness of the subsequent confession. The plurality would conduct the inquiry from the perspective of a reasonable person in the suspect's shoes. Justice Kennedy, by contrast, would focus not on the state of mind of the suspect, but on the motives of the interrogating officers. Under this approach, suppression of post-warning statements would be appropriate only when the interrogator employed the two-step interrogation technique purposely to undermine the *Miranda* warning.

Oregon v. Mathiason

(Prosecuting State) v. *(Convicted Burglar)*

429 U.S. 492, 97 S. Ct. 711, 50 L. Ed. 2d 714 (1977)

MIRANDA WARNINGS ARE NOT REQUIRED IN NONCUSTODIAL INTERROGATIONS

■ **INSTANT FACTS** Mathiason (D), a parolee who was suspected of burglary, voluntarily appeared at the police station in response to an officer's request, was informed that he was not under arrest, and confessed after being questioned, without being given *Miranda* warnings.

■ **BLACK LETTER RULE** An individual who appears voluntarily at the police station for questioning, and who is not placed under arrest, is not in a custodial setting such that *Miranda* warnings must be given.

■ **PROCEDURAL BASIS**

Certiorari to review the decision of the Oregon Supreme Court that held that, because defendant was in a "coercive setting," he was entitled to *Miranda* warnings.

■ **FACTS**

Mathiason (D), a parolee, was suspected of burglarizing a residence. An officer investigating the crime attempted unsuccessfully to contact Mathiason (D) on three or four occasions. Approximately twenty-five days after the burglary, the officer left a card at Mathiason's (D) apartment with a note requesting that he contact the officer "to discuss something." Mathiason (D) called the officer the next day, and as Mathiason (D) expressed no preference as to where the two should meet, the officer suggested the patrol office, located about two blocks from Mathiason's (D) apartment. At the station, the officer informed Mathiason (D) that he was not under arrest and took him into an office. Behind closed doors, the officer informed Mathiason (D) that he wanted to speak with him about the burglary, and that if Mathiason was truthful, the district attorney or the judge might show some leniency. The officer further expressed his personal belief that Mathiason (D) was involved in the burglary, and falsely stated that Mathiason's (D) fingerprints were found at the scene. After a few minutes, Mathiason (D) admitted that he took the property. After Mathiason (D) made the admission, the officer advised Mathiason (D) of his *Miranda* rights and taped a confession. The officer then told Mathiason (D) that he was not being placed under arrest at that time, and that he was free to go. Mathiason (D) was eventually arrested for the crime and convicted of first-degree burglary based on his confession.

■ **ISSUE**

Is an individual who voluntarily appears at the police station for questioning but is not placed under arrest "in custody" within the meaning of *Miranda*?

■ **DECISION AND RATIONALE**

(Per curiam.) No. The defendant was in a noncustodial setting, i.e., he was not "taken into custody or otherwise deprived of his freedom of action in any significant way." The defendant appeared voluntarily and was immediately informed that he was not under arrest. Thus, he was free to leave the police station and abandon the interview any time. While any interview of a suspect by a police officer has coercive aspects, a noncustodial setting is not transformed into one in which *Miranda* applies simply because it is a "coercive environment." *Miranda* warnings are not required simply because the questioning takes place at the police station, or because the one being questioned is a suspect, but only when there has been such a restriction on a person's freedom as to render him "in custody." Moreover, the officer's false statement about finding the respondent's fingerprints at the crime scene (found by the Oregon Supreme Court to be a factor contributing to the coercive environment) has "nothing to do with whether [the defendant] was in custody for purposes of the *Miranda* rule." Reversed and remanded.

■ DISSENT

(Marshall, J.) The defendant was in a custodial setting when he was questioned by the police officer. He was behind closed doors, at police headquarters, being questioned as a suspect in a burglary. The fact that the defendant was not placed under arrest is not controlling. Rather, if the defendant had "an objectively reasonable belief" that he was not free to leave during the questioning, he was "deprived of his freedom of action in a significant way." The defendant could quite feasibly have believed that he was not free to leave: he was told by the police that he was a suspect in a burglary, and that his fingerprints had been found at the scene. Moreover, the rationale of *Miranda* should not be limited to custodial interrogations, but should apply where, as here, the coercive elements were so persuasive as to require *Miranda*-type warnings. The defendant was interrogated in "privacy" and in "unfamiliar surroundings"—the very factors on which *Miranda* placed great stress—and "deceptive stratagems" were used.

Analysis:

The *Mathiason* Court uses a subjective approach (from the perspective of law enforcement) to determine the issue of "custody." The fact that the officer had not placed the defendant under arrest was pivotal to the decision. That the defendant's state of mind had no relevance to the determination is clear from the Court's assertion that the officer's false statement regarding the defendant's fingerprints had "nothing to do with" determining the custody issue. Note that the dissent's recommendation that the Court employ an objective test, which focused on whether the defendant had an objective, reasonable belief that he was not free to leave during the questioning, was later adopted by the Court in *Berkemer v. McCarty*, 468 U.S. 420, 104 S. Ct. 3138, 82 L. Ed. 2d 317 (1984).

■ CASE VOCABULARY

CUSTODIAL INTERROGATION: Police questioning of a detained person about the crime that he or she is suspected of having committed.

NONCUSTODIAL INTERROGATION: Police questioning of a suspect who has not been detained and can leave at will.

Berkemer v. McCarty

(*County Sheriff*) v. (*Convicted Criminal*)

468 U.S. 420, 104 S. Ct. 3138, 82 L. Ed. 2d 317 (1984)

ORDINARY TRAFFIC STOPS DO NOT GIVE RISE TO A NEED FOR *MIRANDA* WARNINGS

Miranda warning? No, this is just a routine traffic stop. You don't get *Mirandized* until after you finish incriminating yourself.

stus.com

■ **INSTANT FACTS** McCarty (D) was initially stopped for a traffic infraction but became suspected of driving under the influence (a misdemeanor traffic offense in Ohio) shortly after the stop. McCarty (D), who was never advised of his rights under *Miranda*, made several incriminating statements both before and after he was formally arrested.

■ **BLACK LETTER RULE** All suspects in custody must be given *Miranda* warnings prior to questioning, regardless of the nature or severity of the crime, but an ordinary traffic stop does not render the detainee(s) "in custody" for purposes of *Miranda*.

■ **PROCEDURAL BASIS**

Certiorari to review the court of appeals' reversal of the trial court's denial of the defendant's petition for a writ of habeas corpus.

■ **FACTS**

McCarty (D) was driving on an interstate highway when he was stopped by a police officer, who observed McCarty (D) weaving in and out of a lane. The officer directed McCarty (D) to exit the car and noticed that McCarty (D) had difficulty standing. The officer determined immediately that McCarty (D) would be charged with a traffic offense, but he did not inform McCarty (D) that he would be taken into custody. McCarty (D) also failed the field sobriety test. During the traffic stop, the officer asked McCarty (D) whether he had been using intoxicants, and McCarty (D) (whom the officer found difficult to understand due to his slurred speech) replied that he had "consumed two beers and had smoked several joints of marijuana a short time before." McCarty (D) was formally placed under arrest and transported to jail. An intoxilyzer test indicated that no alcohol was present in McCarty's (D) system. The officer then resumed questioning McCarty (D), who admitted that he had been drinking, and who, when asked whether he was under the influence of alcohol, replied, "I guess, barely." McCarty (D) indicated on an Alcohol Influence Report form on which he signed his name that the marijuana had not been treated with any chemicals, by writing "No ang[el] dust or PCP in the pot." McCarty (D) was never advised of his *Miranda* rights. McCarty (D) was charged with operating a motor vehicle while under the influence of alcohol and/or drugs (at that time misdemeanor offense in Ohio), and moved to suppress the various incriminating statements on the ground that their admissibility would violate his Fifth Amendment rights, of which he had not been informed prior to interrogation.

Issue 1: Is a motorist, who is detained pursuant to a traffic stop for roadside questioning, "in custody" for purposes of *Miranda*?

■ **DECISION AND RATIONALE**

(Marshall, J.) No. The atmosphere surrounding an ordinary traffic stop is substantially less "police-dominated" than that of a police interrogation, as in *Miranda*. A traffic stop significantly curtails the "freedom of action" of its occupants, but it does not exert pressures such that an individual is

---

compelled to answer questions he would not otherwise address. This conclusion is based on (1) the presumptively temporary and brief detention of the motorist and (2) the public nature of the traffic stop. A motorist expects that a traffic stop will last only a few minutes, and that after brief questioning, he or she will be free to leave, even if a citation is eventually issued. The public nature of the stop alleviates the pressure associated with stationhouse interrogations; the person(s) detained are less likely to fear that police will question them unlawfully, or that uncooperative behavior will result in abuse. The presence of only one or two officers further "mutes" the detainee's sense of vulnerability. In the instant case, the defendant was unaware that his detention would be anything but temporary. Although the officer knew at the moment McCarty (D) stepped from his car that he would place him under arrest, McCarty (D) was not made aware of the officer's intention. A policeman's "unarticulated plan" is irrelevant when deciding whether a suspect was "in custody" at a particular time. Rather, "the only relevant inquiry is how a reasonable man in the suspect's position would have understood his situation." Therefore, the statements respondent made prior to his formal arrest were admissible against him. Affirmed.

Issue 2: Does *Miranda v. Arizona* govern the admissibility of statements made during custodial interrogation by a suspect accused of a misdemeanor traffic offense?

■ DECISION AND RATIONALE

(Marshall, J.) Yes. Under *Miranda*, *all* suspects must be given warnings before custodial interrogation, regardless of the nature or severity of the crime. Therefore, the statements made by McCarty (D) after he was formally arrested were inadmissible against him at trial. To except misdemeanor traffic offenses from application of *Miranda* would undermine the simplicity and clarity of the rule. Moreover, it is difficult for police to know with any certainty whether, at the time of arrest, an individual has committed a misdemeanor or felony, and unreasonable to expect police to speculate as to the nature of the criminal conduct before deciding how to properly interrogate the suspect. Affirmed.

Analysis:

Berkemer signals a shift from the subjective standard previously used to determine questions of custody, to an objective, "reasonable person" standard. The inquiry is no longer what the police intended, but rather "how a reasonable man in the suspect's position would have understood his situation."

■ CASE VOCABULARY

CUSTODIAL INTERROGATION: Police questioning of a detained person about the crime that he or she is suspected of having committed.

NONCUSTODIAL INTERROGATION: Police questioning of a suspect who has not been detained and can leave at will.

Rhode Island v. Innis

(Prosecuting State) v. *(Convicted Murderer)*
446 U.S. 291, 100 S. Ct. 1682, 64 L. Ed. 2d 297 (1980)

"INTERROGATION" INCLUDES THE "FUNCTIONAL EQUIVALENT" OF EXPRESS QUESTIONING

■ **INSTANT FACTS** Innis (D) was arrested for murder and was given *Miranda* warnings on several different occasions. After Innis (D) requested to speak with a lawyer, he made incriminating statements in response to a conversation between police while riding in the back of the patrol vehicle.

■ **BLACK LETTER RULE** For purposes of *Miranda*, an "interrogation" occurs when police either expressly question a suspect in custody or engage in any actions or dialogue that the police should know is reasonably likely to elicit an incriminating response from the suspect.

■ **PROCEDURAL BASIS**

Certiorari to review reversal by the Rhode Island Supreme Court of the defendant's conviction.

■ **FACTS**

Innis (D) was arrested for murdering a taxicab driver with a sawed-off shotgun. At the time of his arrest, Innis (D) was unarmed. The police read Innis (D) his *Miranda* rights on three separate occasions, and Innis (D) stated that he understood those rights and that he wanted to speak with an attorney. On the way to the stationhouse, the officers spoke between themselves, indicating that a school for handicapped children was in the vicinity where Innis (D) was arrested, and that it would be unfortunate if an innocent handicapped child found and hurt herself with the missing weapon. Innis (D) interrupted the conversation from the backseat of the car, telling the officers to return to the arrest scene so that he could show them where the gun was located. When they arrived back at the scene, Innis (D) was again given *Miranda* warnings. Innis (D) once more indicated that he understood those rights, but that he "wanted to get the gun out of the way because of the kids in the area in the school." Innis (D) then showed the officers where the gun was located. He was charged with kidnapping, robbery, and murder.

■ **ISSUE**

Was the police officers' conversation in the defendant's presence an "interrogation" that violated the defendant's right to remain silent until he had consulted with a lawyer?

■ **DECISION AND RATIONALE**

(Stewart, J.) No. For purposes of *Miranda*, "interrogation" means express questioning or its functional equivalent, i.e., "any words or actions on the part of police officers that they *should have known* were reasonably likely to elicit an incriminating response." In the present case, two officers merely had a dialogue with each other and invited no response from the defendant. Nor was the conversation the "functional equivalent" of questioning. The record does not reflect that the officers knew that the defendant was susceptible to an appeal to conscience concerning the safety of handicapped children, and nothing showed him to be unusually disoriented or upset at the time of arrest. Vacated and remanded.

■ CONCURRENCE

(Burger, C.J.) The meaning of *Miranda* is clear and law enforcement has adjusted to it; there is no need to overrule, disparage, or extend *Miranda*.

■ DISSENT

(Marshall, J.) Applying an objective inquiry into the likely effect of police conduct on a typical individual (taking into account any special susceptibility of the suspect to certain kinds of pressure of which the police know or have reason to know), the facts of this case warrant the conclusion that an interrogation occurred. There is a strong appeal to *any* suspect that if a weapon is not found, an innocent individual (especially a handicapped child) will be hurt or killed. The appeal to a suspect to confess for the sake of others is a classic interrogation technique.

■ DISSENT

(Stevens, J.) There is a vast difference between a "faithful adherence" to *Miranda*, and the "stinted test" enunciated in *Innis*, under which the form of the question is critical. The new test requires that any express question be labeled an "interrogation," whether or not the police have reason to believe that the defendant was susceptible to a particular appeal. Correspondingly, statements not in the form of a question but that, as in *Innis*, are just as likely to elicit a response, are not considered "interrogation." Police now have an incentive to ignore a suspect's invocation of his right in order to make incessant attempts at extracting information from him. A suspect who does not appear susceptible to a particular psychological pressure is an easy target to police who "are apparently free to exert that pressure on him despite [his] request for counsel, so long as they are careful not to punctuate their statements with question marks."

Analysis:

Innis suggests that an "interrogation" might occur other than by police-initiated questioning in situations such as (1) a line-up in which a coached witness picks the defendant as the perpetrator, which is designed to establish the fact of the defendant's guilt as a predicate for further interrogation; (2) the "reverse line-up," in which a defendant is identified by coached witnesses as having committed a fictitious crime to induce him to confess to the actual crime of which he was suspected; and (3) the use of psychological play, such as to "posi[t]" "the guilt of the subject," to "minimize the moral seriousness of the offense," and "to cast blame on the victim or on society." Such techniques of persuasion, in a custodial setting, amount to interrogation. Note that if police carry on a lengthy "harangue" in the presence of the suspect, or if their comments are particularly "evocative," an interrogation may have occurred.

■ CASE VOCABULARY

INTERROGATION: The formal or systematic questioning of a person; especially intensive questioning by the police, usually of a person arrested for or suspected of committing a crime. The Supreme Court has held that, for purposes of the Fifth Amendment right against self-incrimination, interrogation includes not only express questioning but also words or actions that the police should know are reasonably likely to elicit an incriminating response.

North Carolina v. Butler

(*Prosecuting State*) v. (*Criminal Defendant*)

441 U.S. 369, 99 S. Ct. 1755, 60 L. Ed. 2d 286 (1979)

WAIVER OF THE RIGHT TO COUNSEL MAY BE EXPRESS OR IMPLIED

■ **INSTANT FACTS** After Butler (D) was arrested and given his *Miranda* warnings, he refused to sign a written waiver of his rights but agreed to speak with FBI agents.

■ **BLACK LETTER RULE**: An express statement is not indispensable to a finding of waiver of the right to counsel; waiver may also be inferred by the words or conduct of the suspect.

■ **PROCEDURAL BASIS**

Certiorari to review reversal by North Carolina Supreme Court of conviction on the ground that statements had been admitted in violation of *Miranda* where defendant-respondent did not specifically and orally waive his right to counsel.

■ **FACTS**

Butler (D) was arrested and was given *Miranda* warnings. Butler (D) also received the FBI's "Advice of Rights" form, which he read. When asked whether he understood his rights, Butler (D) stated that he did, but he refused to sign the waiver at the bottom of the form. The agents told Butler (D) that he need not speak nor sign the form, but that they would like to speak with him. Butler (D) replied: "I will talk to you but I am not signing any form." Butler (D) thereafter made incriminating statements. At no time did Butler (D) request counsel or attempt to terminate the agents' questioning.

■ **ISSUE**

May an individual intelligently and knowingly waive the right to the assistance of counsel even though the individual refuses to sign a written waiver and does not specifically waive the right orally?

■ **DECISION AND RATIONALE**

(Stewart, J.) Yes. An express statement is not indispensable to a finding of waiver. The question is not one of form, but rather whether the defendant in fact knowingly and voluntarily waived the *Miranda* rights. While mere silence is not enough, the defendant's silence, coupled with an understanding of his rights and a course of conduct indicating waiver, may support a conclusion that a defendant has waived his rights. In other words, waiver may be based upon "infer[ence] from the actions and words of the person interrogated." The question of waiver is determined on a case-by-case basis, taking into consideration the background, experience, and conduct of the accused. By creating an inflexible *per se* rule, i.e., that no implicit waiver can ever suffice, the North Carolina Supreme Court went beyond the requirements of federal law. Vacated and remanded.

■ **DISSENT**

(Brennan, J.) Only the most explicit waivers of rights can be considered knowingly and freely given. Permissible waivers based on inference from the actions and words of the person interrogated will result in erroneous inferences constructed from ambiguous words and gestures. A rule requiring police to

---

obtain an express waiver of the right to counsel before proceeding with interrogation would eliminate these types of problems.

Analysis:

Drawing on language in *Miranda*, the *Butler* Court clearly established that an express waiver is not necessary to a finding that a defendant has waived his right to counsel. There are three necessary components to a waiver by implication: (1) silence, (2) an understanding of the rights, and (3) a course of conduct indicating waiver. In practice, the test is not so easily applied, and, as subsequent conflicting cases make clear, it raises more questions than it answers. Factors considered by the courts on the matter of waiver by implication include whether the forewarned defendant initiated the conversation and whether his contact with law enforcement was an act of cooperation.

■ CASE VOCABULARY

EXPRESS WAIVER: A voluntary and intentional waiver.

IMPLIED WAIVER: A waiver evidenced by a party's decisive, unequivocal conduct reasonably inferring the intent to waive.

WAIVER: The voluntary relinquishment or abandonment—express or implied—of a legal right or advantage. The party alleged to have waived a right must have had both knowledge of the existing right and the intention of forgoing it.

WAIVER OF COUNSEL: A criminal defendant's intentional relinquishment of the right to legal representation. To be valid, a waiver of counsel must be made voluntarily, knowingly, and intelligently.

Edwards v. Arizona

(Convicted Criminal) v. *(Prosecuting State)*

451 U.S. 477, 101 S. Ct. 1880, 68 L. Ed. 2d 378 (1981)

INVOKING THE RIGHTS TO COUNSEL AND TO REMAIN SILENT STOPS POLICE ACTION

When it comes to *Miranda* waivers, I say "try, try, and try again".

stus.com

■ **INSTANT FACTS** Edwards (D) invoked his right to counsel and his right to remain silent on the night of his arrest; on the following day, while he was still incarcerated and still without counsel, police repeated the *Miranda* warnings and re-questioned Edwards (D), who made incriminating statements.

■ **BLACK LETTER RULE** An accused who expresses a desire to deal with police only through counsel does not waive that right merely by responding to further police-initiated questioning, even though he has been re-advised of his rights, and may not be subjected to further interrogation until counsel has been made available to him, unless the accused himself initiates further communication, exchanges, or conversations with the police.

■ PROCEDURAL BASIS

Certiorari to review the Arizona Supreme Court's decision affirming the defendant's conviction.

■ FACTS

Edwards (D) was arrested pursuant to a warrant. After receiving the *Miranda* warnings at the police station, Edwards (D) stated the he understood the rights and that he was willing to submit to questioning. During the interrogation, Edwards (D) indicated that he wanted to "make a deal." The interrogating officer told Edwards (D) that any "deal" would have to be negotiated with the county attorney. Edwards (D) called the county attorney at the telephone number provided by the interrogating officer, but hung up after a few minutes. At that point, Edwards (D) told the interrogating officer that he "want[ed] an attorney before making a deal." Questioning ceased and Edwards (D) was incarcerated. The next morning, two detectives, colleagues of the interrogating officer, arrived at the jail and asked to see Edwards (D). When he learned that the detectives wanted to speak with him, Edwards (D) told the guard that he did not want to talk to anyone. The guard said that Edwards (D) "had to" talk to the detectives and escorted him to meet with them. The officers gave Edwards (D) the *Miranda* warnings. After hearing a taped conversation from another suspect who implicated him in the crime, Edwards (D) eventually agreed to speak with the officers, stating that he would "tell [them] anything [they] wanted to know, but I don't want it on tape." Edwards (D) then implicated himself in the crime. The Arizona Supreme Court affirmed Edwards' (D) conviction on the ground that Edwards (D) waived the right to remain silent and the right to counsel at the second meeting when he voluntarily gave his statement to the detectives after again being warned under *Miranda*.

■ ISSUE

When an accused invokes his right to have counsel present during custodial interrogation, does his response to further police-initiated custodial questioning, after being re-advised of his rights, constitute a valid waiver of that right?

■ DECISION AND RATIONALE

(White, J.) No. Once an accused has invoked the right to counsel, the issue is not only whether the waiver was voluntary, but whether the defendant understood that right and knowingly and intelligently relinquished it. Waiver is determined on a case-by-case basis, with consideration given to the particular facts, including the background, experience, and conduct of the accused. By failing to consider the facts relevant to this issue, the Arizona Supreme Court conducted an erroneous review of the case. *Miranda* and its progeny forbid authorities, at their instance, to reinterrogate an accused in custody if he has clearly asserted his right to counsel. An exception exists where the accused himself initiates further communication, exchanges, or conversations with the police because neither the Fifth nor Fourteenth Amendments prohibit police from listening to volunteered statements, or from using them against the accused at trial. Given the circumstances of this case, the defendant's statement to the police, made after he invoked counsel and at the instance of law enforcement, did not constitute a valid waiver, and was therefore inadmissible. Reversed.

■ CONCURRENCE

(Powell, J.) Whether an accused has waived his right to counsel should not be determined solely on the basis of who "initiated" a conversation between an accused and police officials. Rather, when the accused has received the warnings and has invoked the right to counsel, the relevant inquiry, i.e., whether the suspect *now* desires to speak to the police in the absence of counsel, is a question of fact to which "initiation" is surely relevant, but that must be determined in light of all the circumstances. The ultimate question is whether the accused freely and knowingly waived counsel before interrogation commenced.

Analysis:

It is no wonder that Justice Powell expresses confusion over the Court's holding. In determining the issue of whether response to further custodial interrogation constitutes a waiver of the accused's right to counsel, the Court states that waiver is determined on a case-by-case basis, considering the particular factors of the case, including the background, experience, and conduct of the accused. In the same breath, the Court holds that waiver can be established by one factor, i.e., who initiated the conversation, communication, or exchange. The concurrence makes clear that a totality of the circumstances (not the single factor of "initiation") should determine whether an accused voluntarily, knowingly, and intelligently waived the right to counsel.

■ CASE VOCABULARY

RIGHT AGAINST SELF–INCRIMINATION: A criminal defendant's or a witness's constitutional right under the Fifth Amendment, guaranteeing that a person cannot be compelled by the government to testify if the testimony might result in the person's being criminally prosecuted. Although this right is most often asserted during a criminal prosecution, a person can also "plead the Fifth" in a civil, legislative, administrative, or grand-jury proceeding.

RIGHT TO COUNSEL: A criminal defendant's constitutional right, guaranteed by the Sixth Amendment, to representation by a court-appointed lawyer if the defendant cannot afford to hire one.

SINE QUA NON: An indispensable condition or thing; something on which something else necessarily depends.

CHAPTER EIGHT

Police Interrogation: The Sixth Amendment Right to Counsel

Massiah v. United States

Instant Facts: Massiah (D) was convicted of drug violations on the basis of incriminating statements overheard on a listening device by federal agents after indictment.

Black Letter Rule: The Sixth Amendment prohibits government interrogation of a defendant after indictment outside the presence of counsel.

Brewer v. Williams

Instant Facts: Williams (D) confessed to murder during a long car trip with a police officer after the officer persuaded him to reveal the location of the victim's body outside the presence of his attorney.

Black Letter Rule: The right to the assistance of counsel can be waived only by the knowing relinquishment of that right.

Patterson v. Illinois

Instant Facts: A Vice Lord gang member voluntarily and without counsel confessed to his role in a murder, and then argued that his confessions could not be used against him because, although he was given *Miranda* warnings, those warnings sufficed for Fifth Amendment purposes, but not to protect his Sixth Amendment right to counsel at post-indictment questioning.

Black Letter Rule: Whatever warnings suffice for *Miranda*'s purposes will also be sufficient to safeguard the right to counsel in the context of post-indictment questioning.

McNeil v. Wisconsin

Instant Facts: After charged with armed robbery and requesting counsel, McNeil (D) waived his *Miranda* rights and confessed to committing a murder unrelated to the robbery charges.

Black Letter Rule: The Sixth Amendment right to counsel is offense-specific, and invocation of such right does not also invoke the right to counsel under the Fifth Amendment, which is not offense-specific.

Kansas v. Ventris

Instant Facts: A criminal defendant in jail awaiting trial confessed to an informant planted there by the state, but at trial he blamed the crime on another, and the state sought to introduce the testimony of the informant to impeach the defendant's statements.

Black Letter Rule: An informant's testimony, elicited in violation of the Sixth Amendment, is admissible to challenge the defendant's inconsistent testimony at trial.

Massiah v. United States

(Drug Dealer) v. *(Prosecuting Government)*

377 U.S. 201, 84 S. Ct. 1199, 12 L. Ed. 2d 246 (1964)

POST–INDICTMENT INCRIMINATING STATEMENTS MADE TO A CO–DEFENDANT ARE INADMISSIBLE

I'm excluding the post-indictment statements made to the co-defendant. I don't want to undermine the trusting relationship between two criminals.

stus.com

■ **INSTANT FACTS** Massiah (D) was convicted of drug violations on the basis of incriminating statements overheard on a listening device by federal agents after indictment.

■ **BLACK LETTER RULE** The Sixth Amendment prohibits government interrogation of a defendant after indictment outside the presence of counsel.

■ PROCEDURAL BASIS

Certiorari to review a decision of the court of appeals affirming the conviction.

■ FACTS

Massiah (D) was indicted on drug charges. After retaining counsel and pleading not guilty, he was released on bail. Several days later, a co-defendant, Colson, agreed to cooperate with government agents, who installed a listening device in Colson's car. Through the listening device, an agent overheard Massiah (D) make incriminating statements concerning the crimes with which he was charged. Over the objection of defense counsel, the statements were offered to the jury, which convicted Massiah (D) on the drug charges. The court of appeals affirmed.

■ ISSUE

Is the Sixth Amendment violated when the government deliberately elicits incriminating statements from an accused after indictment, outside the presence of counsel?

■ DECISION AND RATIONALE

(Stewart, J.) Yes. After indictment, a criminal defendant in a federal proceeding has a right to counsel under the Sixth Amendment. This right is undermined when the government, outside the presence of counsel, deliberately elicits a confession or other incriminating statements and those statements are offered into evidence against the defendant. This is especially true when, as here, the defendant is unaware that he is being interrogated by government agents through a cooperative co-defendant. While the government's actions are an appropriate function of its duty to further investigate the matter, the incriminating statements may not be used as evidence to convict the defendant.

■ DISSENT

(White, J.) The exclusion of the defendant's incriminating statements, which are highly relevant, reliable, and probative, threatens the pursuit of truth and justice in that crucial evidence of the commission of the crime will not be considered. Unlike the exclusion of evidence obtained through an illegal search, in which the evidence seized violates the Fourth Amendment, the incriminating statements elicited from Massiah (D) do not require the same constitutional protection. Defendant had retained counsel and was free to consult with him as often as needed. The agent did not interfere with this right nor defendant's ability to properly prepare for trial. Similarly, the statements were not made in the coercive environment of a police station or under intimidation of federal agents. The defendant voluntarily chose to make the incriminating statements outside the presence of counsel. The fact that the statements were deliberately elicited through Colson should not require exclusion when the statements would be otherwise admissible had Colson agreed to cooperate with the agents only after the statements were made. Massiah (D) assumed the risk that his statements would be passed along to the agents. Like a voluntary confession, the statements should be admissible.

Analysis:

Massiah demonstrates the scope of the right to counsel under the Sixth Amendment. Once a person is indicted, his status changes from merely a "suspect" to an "accused," resulting in the commencement of an adversary proceeding. Once an adversary proceeding is commenced, the Sixth Amendment right to counsel attaches and police interrogation outside the presence of counsel is prohibited.

■ CASE VOCABULARY

INDICTMENT: The formal written accusation of a crime, made by a grand jury and presented to a court for prosecution against the accused person.

SIXTH AMENDMENT: The constitutional amendment guaranteeing in criminal cases the right to a speedy and public trial by jury, the right to be informed of the nature of the accusation, the right to confront witnesses, the right to counsel, and the right to compulsory process for obtaining favorable witnesses.

Brewer v. Williams

(Prosecuting Authority) v. *(Convicted Murderer)*

430 U.S. 387, 97 S. Ct. 1232, 51 L. Ed. 2d 424 (1977)

ABSENT WAIVER, A CONFESSION CANNOT BE OBTAINED OUTSIDE COUNSEL'S PRESENCE AFTER COUNSEL IS SECURED

You think it would be un-Christian for me to not locate the body so she can have a proper burial? Gosh, you must <u>really</u> disapprove of me killing her.

stus.com

■ **INSTANT FACTS** Williams (D) confessed to murder during a long car trip with a police officer after the officer persuaded him to reveal the location of the victim's body outside the presence of his attorney.

■ **BLACK LETTER RULE** The right to the assistance of counsel can be waived only by the knowing relinquishment of that right.

■ **PROCEDURAL BASIS**

Certiorari to review a decision of the Eighth Circuit Court of Appeals affirming in part a federal district court decision reversing the conviction on a writ of habeas corpus.

■ **FACTS**

On Christmas Eve, ten-year-old Pamela Powers went with her family to the YMCA in Des Moines to watch a wrestling tournament and disappeared. That same day, Robert Williams (D), a YMCA resident who had recently escaped from a mental hospital, was seen carrying a large bundle wrapped in a blanket. A teenage boy assisting Williams (D) with the door to his vehicle saw two white legs extending from the blanket as it was placed in the car. Williams (D) drove away before he could be questioned. After his abandoned vehicle was found 160 miles away in Davenport, Iowa, a warrant was issued for his arrest on abduction charges. The day after Christmas, a Des Moines lawyer, McKnight, received a call from Williams (D), who wished to surrender. Williams (D) surrendered to the Davenport police and was booked. McKnight requested that Williams (D) be returned to Des Moines, and he asked the police officers to cease their questioning of Williams (D) until he had an opportunity to consult with McKnight. After agreeing not to interrogate Williams (D), a Des Moines police officer, Leaming, drove to Davenport to transport Williams (D) back to Des Moines. In the meantime, Williams (D) was arraigned in Davenport and represented by a Davenport attorney, Kelly. Kelly advised Williams (D) not to speak with Leaming during the trip to Des Moines. Kelly similarly advised Leaming that he was not to interrogate Williams (D) until he had an opportunity to meet with McKnight in Des Moines. During the ride, and knowing that Williams (D) was a former mental patient and deeply religious man, Leaming broached the subject of religion. Leaming played on Williams' (D) religious beliefs by requesting that he inform them where Powers was located as her body would be lost under the snow and she would not receive a proper Christian burial. Leaming similarly told Williams (D) that they knew where the body was located, though he in fact had no such knowledge. Leaming asked for no answer, but requested that Williams (D) think about his statements. Williams then volunteered the location of Powers' shoes and the blanket, though neither was recovered. As the car approached the location of Powers' body, Williams (D) took Leaming to the scene, and the body was recovered. At trial, the defense moved to suppress all evidence relating to the statements made during the car ride. While acknowledging the validity of the agreement between McKnight and Leaming not to interrogate Williams (D) in the absence of counsel, as the ride represented a critical stage of the litigation, the judge denied the motion because Williams (D) had waived his right to an attorney by giving the information. The defendant was convicted, and the Iowa

Supreme Court affirmed. The federal district court granted a petition for a writ of habeas corpus and reversed the conviction, finding that the evidence was improperly admitted and that Williams (D) did not waive his right to counsel. The Eighth Circuit Court of Appeals affirmed in part.

■ ISSUE

Was the defendant denied the right to the assistance of counsel when he was persuaded by police to confess outside the presence of his attorney after arraignment?

■ DECISION AND RATIONALE

(Stewart, J.) Yes. While the scope of the Sixth Amendment right to counsel may be debated, at a minimum it provides a defendant the right to the assistance of counsel during interrogation after judicial proceedings have begun. Judicial proceedings were clearly instituted here as a warrant had been issued for Williams's (D) arrest and he was arraigned in Davenport on that warrant. Leaming clearly sought to deliberately elicit incriminating information without the presence of counsel, though he knew the defendant was represented and wished to confer with counsel prior to questioning. Though the trial court conceded that Williams's (D) Sixth Amendment rights were violated, its conclusion that Williams (D) waived these rights under the totality of the circumstances by failing to expressly invoke his right to counsel at the time the statements were made conflicts with federal law. Under federal law, which governs the issue of waiver, the State must prove an intentional relinquishment or abandonment of a known right or privilege, and all reasonable presumptions must be indulged against waiver. Applying these standards, it is clear that Williams (D) had invoked his right to counsel by consulting with both Kelly and McKnight before the trip and securing an agreement from Leaming not to engage in questioning outside the presence of counsel. Nonetheless, Leaming proceeded with his questioning without first reminding the defendant of his right to counsel and securing a voluntary waiver of that right. While the need for swift, energetic law enforcement is recognized, such a clear violation of the defendant's Sixth Amendment rights cannot support his conviction. Affirmed.

■ CONCURRENCE

(Marshall, J.) There can be no doubt that Leaming set out to knowingly violate the defendant's Fifth and Sixth Amendment rights by isolating him from counsel and intentionally persuading the defendant to provide incriminating statements. If the defendant is to be freed, it is not because he deserves to be free, but because Leaming knowingly risked reversal when he chose to violate the defendant's constitutional rights. Good police work requires not only that the crime be solved, but that a defendant's constitutional rights be upheld in the process.

■ CONCURRENCE

(Powell, J.) The law permits a waiver of the right to counsel without notice to counsel and may be obtained through a confession free of coercion and interrogation. The defendant's actions in this case may be sufficient in other settings to constitute a valid waiver, but Leaming's coercive conduct here leads to the conclusion that no such a waiver was made.

■ CONCURRENCE

(Stevens, J.) Despite the emotional aspects of a case such as this, the function of the Court must be to look beyond those emotions and toward the impact the law will have on this case and in the future. The defendant here voluntarily surrendered in reliance upon the advice of his attorney, who trusted the police would honor an agreement not to engage in interrogation outside of his presence. In order to encourage the apprehension of dangerous persons, the State must be held to honor those commitments it assumes to a defendant and his counsel.

■ DISSENT

(Burger, C.J.) The Court's decision punishes society for the wrongdoing of one individual officer by excluding relevant and reliable evidence of the defendant's guilt and setting a guilty defendant free. Williams (D) had been informed of his right to counsel on five different occasions and chose to confess to Leaming voluntarily, free from any coercion or threats. The Court's decision stretches the exclusionary rule too far by depriving a jury of the circumstances under which police found a murder victim's body, resulting in a game of "hide and seek" that threatens our criminal justice system. The evidence establishes that Williams (D) waived his Sixth Amendment right to counsel. He had been fully advised of his rights and it was not suggested that he failed to understand their import. The elements of voluntary waiver are established. A defendant who has initially asserted the right to counsel need not be permitted to consult with counsel before voluntarily waiving that right, for constitutional rights are personal and a suspect cannot be legally presumed incompetent to change his mind unless an attorney is present.

■ DISSENT

(White, J.) The majority fashions no new law respecting the waiver of one's constitutional rights, relying instead on well-founded principles contained in prior cases and holding merely that no waiver was proved in this case. A waiver requires the intentional relinquishment or abandonment of a known right or privilege. That defendant knew of his right is unquestioned, as he had been informed of this right on numerous occasions by the police and two attorneys representing him. Similarly, the defendant's choice to reveal where he had hidden the evidence resulted from his own free will as the car approached each location without prodding or questioning from Leaming. Even if Leaming's earlier statements influenced his disclosures, those statements were not coercive or threatening and, in fact, were accompanied by a request not to respond. The defendant was not compelled to answer without the presence of counsel, but he chose to do so nonetheless. His waiver was knowing and intentional. The fact that Williams (D) had previously asserted his right to counsel does not make the waiver unintentional, but rather strengthens the grounds for finding it intentional as he was better informed of the rights he possessed. Waiver need not be express, but can arise out of events that demonstrate the defendant knew of his rights and chose to relinquish them. Furthermore the right to counsel protects an accused from giving incriminating answers, not from being asked questions pertinent to the case. When no evidence of coercion exists, such as here, a rule requiring waiver at the time of the answer, rather than on the advice of counsel, adequately serves these purposes.

Analysis:

While the Court held that Williams (D) did not waive his Sixth Amendment right to counsel, it did not hold that such a waiver is impossible in the absence of counsel, as emphasized by Justice Powell's concurrence. Pointing to Williams's (D) express assertion of his Sixth Amendment rights both before the long trip and during his conversation with Leaming, the Court held that no voluntary waiver was given. If, however, the facts indicate that such a confession was voluntary, even in the absence of counsel, a waiver may be valid.

■ CASE VOCABULARY

WAIVER: The voluntary relinquishment or abandonment—express or implied—of a legal right or advantage.

EXPRESS WAIVER: A voluntary and intentional waiver.

IMPLIED WAIVER: A waiver evidenced by a party's decisive, unequivocal conduct reasonably inferring the intent to waive.

HABEAS CORPUS: A writ employed to bring a person before a court, most frequently to ensure that the party's imprisonment or detention is not illegal.

Patterson v. Illinois

(*Criminal Defendant*) v. (*Prosecuting State*)

487 U.S. 285, 108 S. Ct. 2389, 101 L. Ed. 2d 261 (1988)

THE RIGHT TO COUNSEL CAN BE WAIVED EVEN POST–INDICTMENT IF THE PROSECUTOR EXPLAINS THE RIGHT AND THE CONSEQUENCES OF WAIVER

I accidentally confessed to Mom, so I'm trying to figure out the difference between my 5th and 6th Amendment rights.

■ **INSTANT FACTS** A Vice Lord gang member voluntarily and without counsel confessed to his role in a murder, and then argued that his confessions could not be used against him because, although he was given *Miranda* warnings, those warnings sufficed for Fifth Amendment purposes, but not to protect his Sixth Amendment right to counsel at post-indictment questioning.

■ **BLACK LETTER RULE** Whatever warnings suffice for *Miranda*'s purposes will also be sufficient to safeguard the right to counsel in the context of post-indictment questioning.

■ **PROCEDURAL BASIS**

On certiorari to the United States Supreme Court.

■ **FACTS**

Patterson (D) and fellow members of the Vice Lords street gang got into a fight with members of a rival gang, the Black Mobsters. After the fight, the Vice Lords fled to a nearby house. Jackson, a Black Mobster, went to the house where the Vice Lords were, and a second fight ensued. The Vice Lords beat Jackson severely, and then drove him to the end of a nearby street, where they left him face down in a puddle. The police later found Jackson dead, where he had been left. Patterson (D) and two other Vice Lords were indicted for the murder of Jackson. When he was in jail, Patterson (D) asked a police officer which other Vice Lords had been indicted. When the officer told him, Patterson (D) inquired as to why another particular member of the gang had not been indicted, because "he did everything," Patterson (D) said, and other witnesses could corroborate his story. The officer interrupted Patterson (D) at that point and handed him a *Miranda* waiver form. The form included the standard *Miranda* warnings, and the officer read them aloud to Patterson (D) as Patterson (D) read along. Patterson (D) initialed each of the warnings and signed the waiver, and then gave a lengthy statement about the murder, describing in detail each Vice Lord's role in the crime, including his own. Later that same day, Assistant State's Attorney Smith went through the waiver procedure with Patterson (D) for a second time, and then Patterson (D) again confessed to his role in Jackson's murder. Before trial, however, Patterson (D) moved to suppress his statements, arguing that they were unconstitutionally obtained. The court denied the motions and the statements were used against Patterson (D) at trial. The jury found him guilty of murder and sentenced him to twenty-four years in prison. Patterson (D) appealed, arguing that he did not knowingly or intelligently waive his Sixth Amendment right to counsel before he gave his confessions. Although the warnings adequately protected his Fifth Amendment rights, he said, they failed to protect the Sixth Amendment right to counsel. The Illinois Supreme Court rejected his argument. The United States Supreme Court granted certiorari to resolve a split in authority among the lower courts and answer an unresolved question on the issue of whether *Miranda* warnings adequately safeguard the Sixth Amendment right to counsel.

■ ISSUE

Do *Miranda* warnings given post-indictment adequately safeguard a criminal defendant's right to counsel?

■ DECISION AND RATIONALE

(White, J.) Yes. Whatever warnings suffice for *Miranda*'s purposes will also be sufficient to safeguard the right to counsel in the context of post-indictment questioning. A waiver of the Sixth Amendment right to counsel is valid when it reflects an intentional relinquishment or abandonment of a known right or privilege. That is, the accused must know what he is doing so that his choice is made with eyes open. In the *Edwards* case, we held that once an accused has expressed his desire to deal with the police only through counsel, he should not be subject to further interrogation until counsel has been made available to him, or until he himself initiates further communication. But the essence of *Edwards* is preserving the accused's choice to deal with the police only through counsel, not barring an accused from making an initial election as to whether he will face the state's officers with or without the aid of counsel. Patterson's (D) more substantial claim is that questioning him without counsel present violated the Sixth Amendment because he did not validly waive his right to have counsel present during the interviews—he did not, he says, knowingly and intelligently waive his right to counsel. The key inquiry in cases like this is, was the accused, who waived his Sixth Amendment rights during post-indictment questioning, made sufficiently aware of his right to have counsel present during the questioning, and of the possible consequences of a decision to forgo the aid of counsel? In this case, by admonishing Patterson (D) with the *Miranda* warnings, this burden was met, and the petitioner's questioning was valid. The warnings made him aware of the right to have counsel present, and served to make him aware of the consequences of deciding not to. Affirmed.

■ DISSENT

(Blackmun, J.) After formal adversary proceedings have been commenced, the Sixth Amendment mandates that the defendant not be subject to further interrogation by the authorities until counsel has been made available to him, unless the accused himself initiations further communication with the police.

■ DISSENT

(Stevens, J.) Without a careful discussion of the pitfalls of proceeding without counsel, the Sixth Amendment right cannot be waived. An adversary party simply cannot adequately provide such advice. Accordingly, once the right to counsel attaches and the adversary relationship between the state and the accused solidifies, a prosecutor cannot conduct a private interview with an accused without diluting the protection afforded by the right to counsel. The Court's single-minded focus on the interest in effective law enforcement could lead to the toleration of similar practices at any stage of the trial. It is clear that such private communications are intolerable at any point after adversary proceedings have commenced.

Analysis:

The Court made clear that it had never adopted Patterson's (D) suggestion that the Sixth Amendment right to counsel is somehow "superior" to or "more difficult" to waive than its Fifth Amendment counterpart. Rather, in Sixth Amendment cases, the Court has defined the scope of the right to counsel by an assessment of the usefulness of counsel to the accused at the particular stage of the proceedings in question, and the dangers to the accused of proceeding without counsel at that stage. According to the Court, *Miranda* warnings are sufficient in the post-indictment questioning context because, at that stage, the role of counsel is relatively simple and limited, and the dangers and disadvantages of self-representation are less substantial and more obvious to an accused than they are at trial.

■ CASE VOCABULARY

INDICT: To charge (a person) with a crime by formal legal process, especially by grand-jury presentation.

INDICTMENT: The formal written accusation of a crime, made by a grand jury and presented to a court for prosecution against the accused person.

SIXTH AMENDMENT: The constitutional amendment, ratified with the Bill of Rights in 1791, guaranteeing in criminal cases the right to a speedy and public trial by jury, the right to be informed of the nature of the accusation, the right to confront witnesses, the right to counsel, and the right to compulsory process for obtaining favorable witnesses.

McNeil v. Wisconsin

(Convicted Armed Robber) v. *(Prosecuting State)*
501 U.S. 171, 111 S. Ct. 2204, 115 L. Ed. 2d 158 (1991)

INVOKING THE SIXTH AMENDMENT RIGHT TO COUNSEL DOES NOT INVOKE THE *MIRANDA* RIGHT TO COUNSEL

I found out the Fifth and Sixth Amendment rights to counsel are totally different. I never realized living a life of crime would be so complicated.

stus.com

■ **INSTANT FACTS** After charged with armed robbery and requesting counsel, McNeil (D) waived his *Miranda* rights and confessed to committing a murder unrelated to the robbery charges.

■ **BLACK LETTER RULE** The Sixth Amendment right to counsel is offense-specific, and invocation of such right does not also invoke the right to counsel under the Fifth Amendment, which is not offense-specific.

■ **PROCEDURAL BASIS**

Certiorari to review the defendant's conviction.

■ **FACTS**

McNeil (D) was arrested in Nebraska on a warrant for armed robbery committed in West Allis, Wisconsin. Two Wisconsin police officers arrived shortly thereafter to transport McNeil (D) to Wisconsin. After reading McNeil (D) his *Miranda* rights, the officers began to question him. When the defendant refused to answer but did not request counsel, the officers ceased their questioning. Back in Wisconsin, a public defender represented McNeil (D) before a county commissioner, who charged McNeil (D), set bail, and scheduled a preliminary examination. That evening, a detective from a neighboring county visited McNeil (D) in jail to investigate a murder and armed robbery the defendant was suspected of committing in Caledonia, Wisconsin. After the defendant signed a written waiver of his *Miranda* rights, he denied participation in the crimes, but not knowledge of them. Two days later, the detective returned with two other detectives and McNeil (D) again waived his *Miranda* rights by initialing the waiver form and attaching his signature. This time, the defendant admitted his involvement in the crimes and identified two other individuals involved with him. He reviewed the detective's typed statement, again initialing and signing the statement. The detectives returned again two days later after investigating one of the individuals identified by McNeil (D) and finding he was not involved in the crimes. Again waiving his *Miranda* rights, McNeil (D) admitted he had lied to minimize his role in the crimes. He was later convicted.

■ **ISSUE**

Does an accused's invocation of his Sixth Amendment right to counsel during a judicial proceeding constitute an invocation of his *Miranda* right to counsel?

■ **DECISION AND RATIONALE**

(Scalia, J.) No. The Sixth Amendment right to counsel is offense specific. It does not attach until adversary proceedings are brought against an accused and does not apply to other crimes with which the accused has not yet been charged. An accused's right to counsel in the latter instance arises out of his *Miranda* rights under the Fifth Amendment. Because the Sixth Amendment right to counsel is specific only to the West Allis crime, it cannot affect McNeil's (D) waiver of his right to counsel with respect to the Caledonia crimes. The right to counsel on which McNeil (D) relies comes from the Fifth Amendment. Accordingly, under *Edwards v. Arizona*, once McNeil (D) asserted his Fifth Amendment right to counsel, the police had to cease all interrogation of the defendant until counsel has been made available to him. The *Edwards* rule is not offense-specific. It applies to all police interrogation regardless of the offense. The Sixth Amendment and the Fifth Amendment, however, cannot be combined to render a voluntary waiver of one's *Miranda* rights as to the Caledonia crimes ineffective because McNeil (D) invoked his Sixth Amendment right to counsel as to the West Allis crimes. The purpose of the Sixth Amendment right to counsel is to protect the defendant from critical confrontations arising after adversary proceedings are commenced, while the Fifth Amendment right to counsel serves to honor a suspect's desire to deal with police only in the presence of counsel. The invocation of a Sixth Amendment right is not the same as an invocation of the Fifth Amendment right. A defendant may be willing to discuss certain matters unrelated to the crime with which he is charged, but not matters related to the charged crime. An implication of invocation of the Fifth Amendment simultaneously with exercising one's Sixth Amendment rights is not sound policy. It would seriously impede law enforcement on unrelated crimes if an unwilling defendant need only assert his *Miranda* rights in order to request counsel during interrogation of those unrelated crimes. A clear waiver of those rights is not ineffective because of a prior invocation of Sixth Amendment rights. Affirmed.

■ DISSENT

(Stevens, J.) The Court's opinion demeans the importance of the right to counsel. As a practical matter, the opinion will have little effect on the majority of cases. As a theoretical matter, the development of an offense-specific limitation on the attorney-client relationship undermines the protections afforded by the adversarial system. As a symbolic matter, the opinion reflects the Court's view of defense counsel as an impediment rather than a servant to the cause of justice.

Analysis:

Note that McNeil (D) was forced in this case to argue a violation of his Sixth Amendment rights because he had made a valid waiver of his Fifth Amendment rights under *Brewer v. Williams*. Had McNeil (D) exercised his right to counsel during the questioning on the Caledonia murders, a separate right from that asserted during the judicial proceedings on the West Allis robbery, McNeil (D) would have been fully protected by both the Fifth and the Sixth Amendments.

Kansas v. Ventris

(*Prosecuting State*) v. (*Criminal Defendant*)

556 U.S. ___, 129 S. Ct. 1841, 173 L. Ed. 2d 801 (2009)

OTHERWISE INADMMISSIBLE EVIDENCE MAY BE ADMISSIBLE FOR PURPOSES OF IMPEACHMENT

I killed him.
Don't rat me out.

■ **INSTANT FACTS** A criminal defendant in jail awaiting trial confessed to an informant planted there by the state, but at trial he blamed the crime on another, and the state sought to introduce the testimony of the informant to impeach the defendant's statements.

■ **BLACK LETTER RULE** An informant's testimony, elicited in violation of the Sixth Amendment, is admissible to challenge the defendant's inconsistent testimony at trial.

■ **PROCEDURAL BASIS**

On certiorari to consider a state court decision reversing the trial court's decision to allow the testimony of an informant.

■ **FACTS**

A sleep-deprived and slightly drug-impaired Ventris (D) agreed with Theel to confront Hicks in his home, purportedly to investigate rumors that Hicks abused his children; in reality, the couple had recently learned that Hicks carried large amounts of cash. One or both of the couple ended up shooting and killing Hicks and then drove off with about $300 of his money and his cell phone. On a tip from friends of the couple, police officers arrested Ventris (D) and Theel and charged them with murder and aggravated robbery. Prior to trial, officers planted an informant in Ventris's (D) holding cell and instructed him to keep his ear open for incriminating statements. The informant suggested to Ventris (D) that Ventris (D) appeared to have something serious weighing on his mind, which caused Ventris (D) to respond that he had shot a man in the head and taken his keys, his wallet, about $350.00, and a vehicle. At trial, however, Ventris (D) blamed the entire incident on Theel. The government sought to call the informant to testify regarding Ventris's (D) prior inconsistent statement. The state conceded there was probably a violation of Ventris's (D) Sixth Amendment right to counsel, but that the testimony should be admitted anyhow, for impeachment purposes, because the defendant should not be allowed to just get up on the stand and lie. The trial court agreed, but instructed the jury to consider the testimony with caution. The jury acquitted Ventris (D) of murder, but found him guilty of aggravated burglary and aggravated robbery. The Kansas Supreme Court reversed, holding that once a criminal prosecution has commenced, the defendant's statements made to an undercover informant surreptitiously acting as the state's agent are not admissible at trial for any reason, including impeachment. The Supreme Court granted the state's petition for certiorari.

■ **ISSUE**

Is a defendant's incriminating statement to a jailhouse informant, concededly elicited in violation of Sixth Amendment strictures, admissible at trial to impeach the defendant's conflicting statement?

■ **DECISION AND RATIONALE**

(Scalia, J.) Yes. An informant's testimony, elicited in violation of the Sixth Amendment, is admissible to challenge the defendant's inconsistent testimony at trial. We have held that the right to have counsel present at various pretrial critical interactions between the defendant and the state includes situations involving the deliberate elicitation by law enforcement officers and their agents of statements pertaining to the charge. The state concedes that Ventris's (D) confession was taken in violation of these dictates and was therefore not admissible in the prosecution's case in chief. We need only consider here whether the state must bear the additional consequence of the inability to counter Ventris's (D) contradictory testimony by placing the informant on the stand. Whether otherwise excluded evidence is admissible for purposes of impeachment depends on the nature of the constitutional guarantee that is violated. The Sixth Amendment is, at its core, a trial right, but we have held that the right covers pretrial interrogations to ensure that police manipulation does not render counsel impotent and deprive the defendant of effective representation at the only stage when legal advice would really help him. But the game of excluding tainted evidence for impeachment purposes is not worth the candle. The interests safeguarded by such exclusion are outweighed by the need to prevent perjury and to assure the integrity of the trial process. We have held in every other context that tainted evidence—evidence whose very introduction does not constitute the constitutional violation, but whose obtaining was constitutionally invalid—is admissible for impeachment. We see no distinction that would alter the balance here. Reversed and remanded.

■ DISSENT

(Stevens, J.) In *Michigan v. Harvey*, the Court held that a statement obtained from a defendant in violation of the Sixth Amendment could be used to impeach his testimony at trial. I dissented in that case, and I dissent here. The Sixth Amendment is violated when the fruits of the state's impermissible encounter with the represented defendant are used for impeachment just as it is when the fruits are used in the prosecutor's case in chief. The Court once again privileges the prosecution at the expense of the Constitution. Although the Court may not be concerned with the use of ill-gotten evidence in derogation of the right to counsel, I am convinced that such shabby tactics are intolerable in all cases.

Analysis:

Consider whether there is a significant practical difference between introducing testimony from an informant as part of the prosecution's case in chief, and introducing the same unconstitutionally obtained evidence for purposes of contradicting the defendant's own original account of the circumstances. The impact on the jury is likely somewhat the same, despite any cautionary advice from the court. Nonetheless, the Court holds here that the interest in obtaining the truth supersedes the constitutional violation, though the dissent vehemently disagrees, admonishing the Court for sanctioning "shabby tactics" that Justice Stevens finds intolerable. Indeed, constitutional implications aside, there are likely even circumstances in which the Court's approach would not result in greater truth, such as when an inmate "boasts" to a cellmate-informant about his or her role in a crime, exaggerating the details in the telling.

■ CASE VOCABULARY

IMPEACH: To discredit the veracity of a witness.

CHAPTER NINE

Entrapment

Sherman v. United States

Instant Facts: Sherman (D), a recovering drug addict, eventually acquiesced to the repeated requests of a government informant to obtain drugs for him.

Black Letter Rule: An entrapment defense must be sustained when the criminal conduct arises from the inducement of law enforcement officers, not the intention of the defendant.

Jacobson v. United States

Instant Facts: Jacobson (D) was convicted of receiving child pornography through the mails after a two-and-a-half-year sting operation by the government.

Black Letter Rule: Predisposition to a broad range of conduct does not demonstrate a predisposition to commit specific acts falling within that range of conduct.

Sherman v. United States

(Recovering Drug User) v. *(Prosecuting Government)*
356 U.S. 369, 78 S. Ct. 819, 2 L. Ed. 2d 848 (1958)

REPEATED REQUESTS TO COMMIT A CRIME AND PLEAS FOR SYMPATHY ESTABLISH ENTRAP-MENT

Am I here for my crimes, or for entraping a recovering addict into scoring me some drugs out of sympathy?

Ooooh! I totally missed the entrapment.

stus.com

■ **INSTANT FACTS** Sherman (D), a recovering drug addict, eventually acquiesced to the repeated requests of a government informant to obtain drugs for him.

■ **BLACK LETTER RULE** An entrapment defense must be sustained when the criminal conduct arises from the inducement of law enforcement officers, not the intention of the defendant.

■ **PROCEDURAL BASIS**

Certiorari to review the criminal defendant's conviction.

■ **FACTS**

Sherman (D) met a government informant while both were seeking treatment for drug addiction from the same doctor. After several encounters, the informant asked Sherman (D) if he knew where he could purchase drugs. Sherman (D) initially declined to obtain drugs for the informant. After repeated requests by the informant and a plea for help because therapy was not effective, Sherman (D) acquiesced and purchased some drugs for the informant. The informant informed federal agents of the activity. After observing Sherman (D) give the informant drugs on three occasions, Sherman (D) was arrested. At trial, the jury was asked to consider whether Sherman (D) was an unwilling party to the transaction or was acting on a predisposition to using drugs. The jury convicted Sherman (D).

■ **ISSUE**

Must a conviction be set aside on the grounds of entrapment when a government informant persuades a reluctant recovering drug addict to obtain drugs?

■ **DECISION AND RATIONALE**

(Warren, C.J.) Yes. A valid entrapment defense exists when the defendant's criminal conduct arises from the inducement of law enforcement officers, not the intention of the defendant. Entrapment occurs when the criminal conduct at issue is a result of the creative activities of law enforcement officials. When the criminal design originates with a law enforcement officer, who plants the idea for a crime in the mind of an otherwise innocent person for the purpose of prosecuting the crime, entrapment exists. Here, the evidence of Sherman's (D) participation in drug addiction therapy, the informant's repeated requests for drugs, and the informant's pleas for sympathy indicate that Sherman (D) did not participate in the crime of his own initiative. Instead, it was the conduct of the informant that induced the crime.

■ **CONCURRENCE**

(Frankfurter, J.) Entrapment ought to be determined not by the specific intentions of the defendant to be charged, but rather by the actions of the law enforcement officer under the circumstances. By asking whether the defendant maintains the specific intent to commit the crime, the inquiry focuses on the past criminal records and predispositions of defendants, leading to different outcomes in different cases depending on the defendant's criminal history. Instead, courts must ask, on a case-by-case basis, whether the police conduct leading up to the crime is likely to induce those not "ready and willing to commit crime." This test sets all defendants, regardless of past criminal history, on equal footing for purposes of an entrapment defense. Here, the same factors viewed by the majority—repeated requests, pleas for sympathy, and the setting in which the conduct occurred—require that the conviction be set aside.

Analysis:

The opinions of Chief Justice Warren and Justice Frankfurter demonstrate the differences between the subjective test and the objective test for entrapment purposes. Under the subjective test, the court views the subjective intentions of the defendant in light of his or her past criminal history and likelihood of committing a crime, as well as the circumstances giving rise to the crime, to determine whether the defendant was induced by a law enforcement officer to commit the crime. Under the objective test, the focus is on the conduct of the officer, not the specific defendant, to determine whether the police conduct would entrap those not ready and willing to commit the crime. The subjective test is applied in the federal courts.

■ CASE VOCABULARY

ENTRAPMENT: A law enforcement officer's or government agent's inducement of a person to commit a crime, by means of fraud or undue persuasion, in an attempt to later bring a criminal prosecution against that person.

Jacobson v. United States

(Pornography Defendant) v. *(Prosecuting Government)*
503 U.S. 540, 112 S. Ct. 1535, 118 L. Ed. 2d 174 (1992)

PRIOR INTEREST IN CHILD PORNOGRAPHY DOES NOT INDICATE A PREDISPOSITION TO RECEIVE CHILD PORNOGRAPHY

The good news is we are setting you free because we agree with your entrapment claim. The bad news is that your neighbors now know you like child pornography.

stus.com

■ **INSTANT FACTS** Jacobson (D) was convicted of receiving child pornography through the mail after a two-and-a-half-year sting operation by the government.

■ **BLACK LETTER RULE** Predisposition to a broad range of conduct does not demonstrate a predisposition to commit specific acts falling within that range of conduct.

■ **PROCEDURAL BASIS**

Certiorari to review the defendant's conviction.

■ **FACTS**

Jacobson (D) ordered and received through the mail two magazines depicting child pornography involving preteen and teenage boys, which was legal under applicable federal law. Three months later, federal child pornography law was amended to criminalize the receipt by mail of sexually explicit materials involving children. That month, postal inspectors located Jacobson's (D) information from the distributor of the pornographic magazines and began to mail him a series of letters and brochures from fictitious organizations advertising child pornography. While the defendant responded to various questionnaires, he received no materials. Two years later, the Customs Service sent additional material through the mail from another fictitious organization advertising similar materials. Again Jacobson (D) received no materials. The Postal Service then sent Jacobson (D) another letter from yet another fictitious organization, questioning the infringement of his rights by the pornography laws and offering a catalog. Jacobson (D) ordered and received a magazine depicting minor boys engaging in sexual activities. He was arrested and convicted under federal child pornography laws, over an entrapment defense.

■ **ISSUE**

Must a conviction be overturned when the government induces the crime and fails to prove beyond a reasonable doubt that the defendant held a predisposition to the crime?

■ **DECISION AND RATIONALE**

(White, J.) Yes. A defendant's predisposition to a broad range of conduct does not demonstrate a predisposition to commit specific acts falling within that range. To rebut an entrapment defense beyond a reasonable doubt, the government must prove that a defendant's predisposition to commit the crime encompasses more than a broad range of conduct, some of which is illegal. Here, the government offered evidence that the defendant had received magazines depicting child pornography in the past. Such receipt, however, occurred prior to the federal law criminalizing such conduct, and there was no proof that defendant had prior knowledge of the content of the magazines before receipt. The government also offered evidence that the defendant expressed an interest in preteen and teen pornography, but failed to prove that the defendant was inclined to violate the law in order to further those interests. The crime was committed after two and a half years of inducement, primarily under the guise of promoting his individual rights through lobbying efforts.

■ DISSENT

(O'Connor, J.) The majority improperly removed the question of predisposition from the jury. Sufficient evidence exists to sustain the jury's conviction, and the majority improperly redefined the meaning of predisposition. Rather than showing a predisposition at the earliest opportunity to commit a crime, the majority requires proof of predisposition at the time a government investigation begins—at the time of its first contact with the defendant. The defendant had no opportunity to commit a crime until the first offer to purchase magazines was extended, at which time he placed an order. He again placed an order when a second offer was extended. Because the defendant had no opportunity to commit the crime until these offers were made, predisposition can be formed only after that time.

Analysis:

The majority's holding in this case demonstrates the difficulties in separating the subjective test from the objective test. While the Court claimed to apply the subjective test to determine the defendant's predisposition toward committing the crime, it placed considerable emphasis on the government's actions in inducing the crime—a reflection of the objective test. "[T]he strong arguable inference is that, by waving the banner of individual rights and disparaging the legitimacy and constitutionality of efforts to restrict the availability of sexually explicit materials, the Government not only excited [Jacobson's] interest in sexually explicit materials banned by law but also exerted substantial pressure on [Jacobson] to obtain and read such material as part of a fight against censorship and the infringement of individual rights."

■ CASE VOCABULARY

PREDISPOSITION: A person's inclination to engage in a particular activity; especially an inclination that vitiates a criminal defendant's claim of entrapment.

CHAPTER TEN

Eyewitness Identification Procedures

United States v. Wade

Instant Facts: Wade (D) was identified before trial in a lineup as a bank robber without notice to counsel with an opportunity to participate.

Black Letter Rule: An in-court identification of a defendant by a witness must be excluded from evidence unless it is offered independent of a pretrial identification obtained without notice to and participation of defense counsel.

Stovall v. Denno

Instant Facts: A stabbing victim identified Stovall (D) as her attacker from her hospital bed when police presented him to her outside the presence of Stovall's (D) attorney.

Black Letter Rule: A showup, rather than a traditional lineup, used for identification of an accused violates the accused's due process rights when it is unnecessarily suggestive under the totality of the circumstances.

Manson v. Brathwaite

Instant Facts: Brathwaite (D) was identified as a drug dealer through a photograph, two days after confrontation with an undercover narcotics agent.

Black Letter Rule: An unnecessarily suggestive pretrial identification of the defendant need not be excluded if, under the totality of the circumstances, it is sufficiently reliable.

United States v. Wade

(Prosecuting Government) v. *(Bank Robber)*
388 U.S. 218, 87 S. Ct. 1926, 18 L. Ed. 2d 1149 (1967)

DEFENSE COUNSEL SHOULD BE PRESENT AT LINEUPS

■ **INSTANT FACTS** Wade (D) was identified before trial in a lineup as a bank robber without notice to counsel with an opportunity to participate.

■ **BLACK LETTER RULE** An in-court identification of a defendant by a witness must be excluded from evidence unless it is offered independent of a pretrial identification obtained without notice to and participation of defense counsel.

■ PROCEDURAL BASIS

Certiorari to review a decision of the court of appeals ordering a new trial.

■ FACTS

Wade (D) and others were indicted for bank robbery and conspiracy to commit bank robbery. Wade (D) was arrested and counsel was appointed to represent him twenty-four days later. Thereafter, without notice to counsel, an FBI agent placed Wade (D) in a lineup in the courtroom, where two bank employees identified the defendant as the robber through visual and voice recognition. At trial, the bank employees again identified the defendant as the robber on direct examination. After a witness testified to the prior lineup identification on cross-examination, the prosecution moved to strike the in-court identification because the lineup violated the Fifth and Sixth Amendments since counsel was not given notice and an opportunity to participate. The motion was denied and Wade (D) was convicted.

■ ISSUE

Must courtroom identifications of a criminal defendant be excluded from evidence when the defendant was presented to the witness before trial at a post-indictment lineup, conducted for identification purposes, without the presence of the defendant's counsel, and no independent basis exists for the identification?

■ DECISION AND RATIONALE

(Brennan, J.) Yes. The presentation of a witness for physical observation, without compulsion to disclose any knowledge or communication, does not violate the Fifth Amendment's prohibition against self-incrimination. Under the Sixth Amendment, however, notice to counsel must be given before exposing a defendant to a lineup to preserve the defendant's rights to assistance of counsel and a fair trial. A pretrial identification is not akin to other pretrial preparatory steps, such as the analysis of a defendant's fingerprints, blood samples, or clothing, which do not require the assistance of counsel at the early stages because adequate challenges are available to such tactics through cross-examination. Instead, the dangers of mistaken identification through suggestive practices by the government, whether by intentional design or the inherent risks of misidentification, threaten a defendant's right to a fair trial. Once a lineup is completed, a defendant is without practical means of recreating the manner in which it was conducted to demonstrate any prejudices against him. Because a jury is left to consider the propriety of the lineup only by weighing the credibility of the police officers who orchestrated the lineup against that of the indicted defendant, a defendant often cannot later demonstrate any improper influence created by the police. A defendant under the observation of a witness or victim often is overcome with stress and emotion and unable to detect any improper influence so as to raise his objections. The assistance of counsel during the pretrial identification, when such influence can be corrected, is essential to relieve any prejudice against the defendant to allow him a fair trial.

The right to counsel at a pretrial identification, however, does not necessarily require exclusion of a subsequent in-court identification by the witness. Where the government proves through clear and convincing evidence that an in-court identification arises independently of the pretrial identification, exclusion is not required. If, from such factors as the prior opportunity to observe the alleged criminal act, the existence of any discrepancy between any pre-lineup description and the defendant's actual description, any identification prior to lineup of another person, the identification by picture of the defendant prior to the lineup, failure to identify the defendant on a prior occasion, and the lapse of time between the alleged act and the lineup identification, it appears to the court that the witness maintains an independent basis for identifying the defendant in court, exclusion is not required. Here, the record is insufficient to determine, on the basis of these factors, whether the in-court identification carried an independent basis and must be left for the trial court's determination. Vacated and remanded.

CONCURRENCE (IN PART), DISSENT (IN PART)

(White, J.) Requiring the government to bear the near-impossible burden of proving that an in-court identification arises independently of an identical pretrial identification threatens the use of relevant and reliable evidence against a defendant merely because counsel was not present at the pretrial identification. The rule excludes an in-court identification regardless of how long the witness has known the defendant, whether others have also identified the defendant, or whether other corroborative evidence identifying the defendant exists. Even when such circumstances demonstrate the reliability of the in-court identification, the majority requires that it be excluded if counsel for the defendant was not present at the lineup. The states maintain a strong governmental interest in utilizing prompt tactics to ensure a proper investigation into the accuracy of the charges brought. Requiring counsel at all stages of pretrial identification threatens to delay an investigation and hinders witness participation, resulting in less reliable evidence. Finally, the Court's holding ignores the government's duty to pursue the truth in every criminal case. While defense counsel must advocate for their clients' interests regardless of guilt or innocence, the government bears the burden of proving the defendant's guilt through accurate, reliable evidence. At a pretrial identification, defense counsel may permissibly obstruct the government's investigative function by instructing their clients to remain silent, refuse requested movements, or even refuse to appear in the lineup. The result will not be more reliable evidence for trial, as sought by the rule set forth by the Court, but rather the complete frustration of the adversary system.

Analysis:

Wade involved the exclusion of an in-court identification based on the absence of counsel at the pretrial identification stage. A companion case, *Gilbert v. California*, involved the exclusion of the pretrial identification itself. Together, the two cases have become known as the *Wade-Gilbert* doctrine, which requires exclusion of all pretrial identifications obtained outside the presence of counsel and those in-court identifications that are reliant upon them.

■ CASE VOCABULARY

LINEUP: A police identification procedure in which a criminal suspect and other physically similar persons are shown to the victim or a witness to determine whether the suspect can be identified as the perpetrator of the crime.

Stovall v. Denno

(Accused Murderer) v. *(Representative of State Government)*
388 U.S. 293, 87 S. Ct. 1967, 18 L. Ed. 2d 1199 (1967)

HOSPITAL–ROOM "SHOWUP" DID NOT VIOLATE THE ACCUSED'S DUE PROCESS RIGHTS

Take a good look at the guy we bring in. You'll need to identify him at trial.

stus.com

■ **INSTANT FACTS** A stabbing victim identified Stovall (D) as her attacker from her hospital bed when police presented him to her outside the presence of Stovall's (D) attorney.

■ **BLACK LETTER RULE** A showup, rather than a traditional lineup, used for identification of an accused violates the accused's due process rights when it is unnecessarily suggestive under the totality of the circumstances.

■ **PROCEDURAL BASIS**

Certiorari to review a decision of the court of appeals affirming the defendant's conviction.

■ **FACTS**

An intruder broke into the home of Dr. and Mrs. Behrendt, killing Dr. Behrendt and stabbing Mrs. Behrendt eleven times. Recovering a shirt and a set of keys from the scene, police traced the evidence to Stovall (D) and arrested him. Arraignment was postponed and Stovall (D) retained counsel. The next day, Stovall (D), who is black, was escorted in handcuffs by five white police officers and two white district attorneys to Mrs. Behrendt's hospital room, where she identified Stovall (D) as her attacker. Stovall (D) had no counsel present. At trial, the officers testified as to Mrs. Behrendt's hospital room identification of the defendant, and Mrs. Behrendt again identified Stovall (D) as her attacker. Stovall (D) was convicted and sentenced to death.

■ **ISSUE**

Does a one-on-one showup violate a defendant's due process rights under these circumstances?

■ **DECISION AND RATIONALE**

(Brennan, J.) No. While the practice of presenting an accused for identification outside of a lineup is disfavored, whether such a practice violates the accused's due process rights must be determined under the totality of the circumstances. Generally, an identification that is "unnecessarily suggestive and conducive to irreparable mistaken identification" violates the accused's due process rights. Here, Mrs. Behrendt was the only person who could exonerate the defendant. Mrs. Behrendt's survival was uncertain and the hospital was not far from the jail so as to substantially burden the defendant. Because a traditional lineup was unavailable in this instance, the totality of the circumstances justifies the conviction.

Analysis:

While the Court recognizes that one-on-one showups for purposes of identification are disfavored, the opinion makes it clear that they do not give rise to due process violations in every case. To constitute a violation, a one-person showup must be (1) suggestive, (2) unnecessary; and (3) supported by a unique need to depart from a lineup. A showup is "suggestive" in virtually every instance. Only when the circumstances, such as the uncertain health of the victim, present a justifiable reason for a one-on-one confrontation will the showup be deemed necessary as a substitute for a lineup.

■ CASE VOCABULARY

LINEUP: A police identification procedure in which a criminal suspect and other physically similar persons are shown to the victim or a witness to determine whether the suspect can be identified as the perpetrator of the crime.

SHOWUP: A pretrial identification procedure in which a suspect is confronted with a witness to or the victim of a crime. Unlike a lineup, a showup is a one-on-one confrontation.

Manson v. Brathwaite

(Representative of State Government) v. *(Suspected Drug Dealer)*

432 U.S. 98, 97 S. Ct. 2243, 53 L. Ed. 2d 140 (1977)

PHOTOGRAPH ID WAS RELIABLE TWO DAYS AFTER A FACE–TO–FACE CONFRONTATION

■ **INSTANT FACTS** Brathwaite (D) was identified as a drug dealer through a photograph, two days after confrontation with an undercover narcotics agent.

■ **BLACK LETTER RULE** An unnecessarily suggestive pretrial identification of the defendant need not be excluded if, under the totality of the circumstances, it is sufficiently reliable.

■ PROCEDURAL BASIS

Certiorari to review a decision of the court of appeals excluding the evidence of a photographic identification.

■ FACTS

Glover, an undercover narcotics agent, and Brown, an informant, approached an apartment believed to be the residence of a known drug dealer to purchase drugs. After knocking on the door, an unknown man answered. Glover and Brown identified themselves and purchased $10 worth of drugs. Glover studied the man's appearance from nearby and described him to a fellow agent. Based on the description, the agent retrieved a file photograph of Brathwaite (D) and left it in Glover's office. When he returned to the office two days later, Glover identified Brathwaite (D) as the man in the apartment. Brathwaite (D) was charged with the possession and sale of illegal drugs. At trial eight months later, Glover testified that Brathwaite (D) was the man who sold him the drugs, providing a positive in-court identification. Brathwaite (D) was convicted.

■ ISSUE

Does the Due Process Clause of the Fourteenth Amendment compel the exclusion, in a state criminal trial of pretrial identification evidence obtained by a police procedure that was suggestive and unnecessary?

■ DECISION AND RATIONALE

(Blackmun, J.) No. It is conceded that the use of one photograph is "suggestive" and that the identification was "unnecessary" because no emergent situation existed. Under such circumstances, two tests have arisen in the courts. The court of appeals below applied a *per se* rule of exclusion because the out-of-court identification was unnecessarily suggestive, without regard to its reliability. This approach has been justified as the elimination of unreliable evidence, deterrence of police conduct, and the fear of misidentification. Other courts rely on the totality of the circumstances to allow such evidence if it appears sufficiently reliable despite any unnecessary suggestion. In determining which approach best makes for sound policy, several state interests must be weighed. First, while both tests alleviate concerns over the dangers of eyewitness identification, the *per se* rule goes too far by automatically excluding relevant and reliable evidence without consideration of alleviating factors. Similarly, both approaches have a deterrent effect on police conduct. Though to a lesser extent than a *per se* exclusion, the totality approach also threatens police with exclusion of evidence obtained through unnecessarily suggestive procedures. Finally, the *per se* rule denies courts of reliable evidence necessary to the administration of justice. Accordingly, the admissibility of pretrial identification testimony must be determined according to various factors supporting its reliability, including the opportunity of the witness to view the criminal at the time of the crime, the witness's degree of attention, the accuracy of his or her prior description of the criminal, the level of certainty demonstrated at the confrontation, and the time between the crime and the confrontation. These factors are to be weighed against the corrupting effect of the suggestive identification. Here, Glover stood several feet away from Brathwaite (D) for two to three minutes with ample light to study his features. Glover was not a passerby catching a glimpse of the defendant, but a police officer trained in the details of eyewitness identification. His description was relayed to agents within minutes of his confrontation and he provided detailed information concerning the defendant's race, height, build, and facial features. Likewise, Glover provided positive assurance that the man in the apartment was the Brathwaite (D). Finally, the photographic identification of the defendant occurred within two days, not weeks or months later. Under the totality of the circumstances, Glover's ability to make a positive identification is not outweighed by any corrupting effect, such as pressure to make an identification under coercion. The identification is sufficiently reliable for admission into evidence despite its unnecessarily suggestive nature. Reversed.

■ CONCURRENCE

(Stevens, J.) In considering the admissibility of identification testimony, the Court's holding appropriately considers only those indicia needed to make that determination without resort to other evidence of guilt.

■ DISSENT

(Marshall, J.) The Court overemphasizes the strength of the three factors to determine the reliability of out-of-court identifications under the totality of the circumstances approach. First, the per *se* rule provides a much stronger deterrent effect against police misconduct, as any unnecessarily suggestive procedure will always result in exclusion. Second, the dangers of mistaken identification present far too great a threat to permit the admission of evidence obtained through an unnecessarily suggestive identification in any case. Finally, the Court fails to credit the impact the *per se* rule has on the administration of justice. An unnecessarily suggestive out-of-court identification is not forever lost to the prosecution because an in-court identification based on a reliable independent basis can be resurrected and offered against the defendant or a second lineup can be arranged under less suggestive circumstances. Also, the purpose of the exclusionary rule at issue is to eliminate evidence that is both unreliable and irrelevant to the issue of guilt. The practice of unnecessarily suggestive identification procedures poses a great societal threat than illegal searches or the denial of counsel, since such identifications may be erroneously used against innocent defendants, and a guilty person may be set free. The *per se* rule better serves the administration of justice. Even applying the totality of the circumstances approach, however, the identification should be excluded. The evidence indicates that Glover's confrontation with Brathwaite (D) occurred not in a matter of minutes, but seconds. During that time, Glover's attention was not exclusively on Brathwaite's (D) features, for he provided details of the door, the interior of the apartment, and the transaction that took place. Further, his training in positive identification does not lead to the conclusion that he is incapable of mistaken identity. Next, while the fact that the identification occurred within two days after the confrontation enhances its reliability, "the greatest memory loss occurs within hours after an event." Finally, Glover's description provided only general details of his physical characteristics, providing immaterial details of the clothing he was wearing and omitting more crucial details. Seen against the corrupting effect of using a single, static photograph for identification, these factors do not justify admission of evidence.

Analysis:

The factors set forth by the Court to consider the reliability of an out-of-court identification also bear directly upon the question of whether a defendant's due process rights have been violated. While a due process challenge places the burden of proof upon the defendant to prove the violation of his rights, courts have tended to place the burden of proof on the government, reasoning that the government gave rise to the issue by implementing an unnecessarily suggestive identification procedure.

CHAPTER ELEVEN

Pretrial Release

Stack v. Boyle

Instant Facts: Twelve defendants indicted for advocating the overthrow of the federal government were denied a request for reduction of bail.

Black Letter Rule: Under the Eighth Amendment, bail must be reasonably fixed to ensure a defendant will appear at trial based on the specific facts of the crime charged and not the character of the crime.

United States v. Salerno

Instant Facts: Organized crime defendants were ordered detained pending trial upon a showing of a threat to the safety of others if released.

Black Letter Rule: Preventative detention of a criminal defendant after indictment does not violate substantive due process under the Fifth Amendment nor constitute excessive bail under the Eighth Amendment when the government has demonstrated through clear and convincing evidence that the defendant presents a threat to the safety of the community.

Stack v. Boyle

(*Communist Party Member*) v. (*Representative of the Federal Government*)

342 U.S. 1, 72 S. Ct. 1, 96 L. Ed. 3 (1951)

UNREASONABLE BAIL VIOLATES THE EIGHTH AMENDMENT

■ **INSTANT FACTS** Twelve defendants indicted for advocating the overthrow of the federal government were denied a request for reduction of bail.

■ **BLACK LETTER RULE** Under the Eighth Amendment, bail must be reasonably fixed to ensure a defendant will appear at trial based on the specific facts of the crime charged and not the character of the crime.

■ **PROCEDURAL BASIS**

Certiorari to review the trial court's denial of the defendants' motion to reduce bail.

■ **FACTS**

Twelve members of the Communist Party, including Stack (D), were arrested in California on charges of violating the Smith Act, a federal statute prohibiting the advocacy of the overthrow of the federal government. Bail was set for the defendants at various amounts, ranging from $250 to $100,000. One defendant, arrested in New York, successfully sought reduction of his bail to $50,000 before removal to California. The government then successfully moved to fix bail at $50,000 for all defendants in California. The defendants subsequently moved for reduction, arguing that in light of their financial means, health, family relationships, and other information, the bail violated the Eighth Amendment as excessive. The government responded with evidence that other defendants charged under the statute have forfeited bail in the past, making defendants a flight risk. The court denied the defendants' motion.

■ **ISSUE**

Is bail fixed at $50,000 based on the character of the offense and forfeiture of bail by other defendants in separate proceedings excessive in light of the crime charged?

■ **DECISION AND RATIONALE**

(Vinson, C.J.). Yes. The right to bail before trial in federal court is required to preserve the presumption of innocence and allow the defendant to prepare a defense against the charges. This right, however, requires adequate assurance that the defendant will appear to stand trial on those charges. Bail set above an amount reasonably likely to further these purposes is excessive in violation of the Eighth Amendment. The amount of bail is to be determined on a case-by-case basis under the specific facts of the case and not by the character of the offense charged. Here, the government failed to show any justification for bail far exceeding the maximum sentence of five years and a $10,000 fine for a Smith Act violation. The fact that other similarly situated defendants have chosen to forfeit lower bail amounts is insufficient justification for the increased bail.

(Jackson, J., writing separately) Federal Rule of Criminal Procedure 46(b) requires each defendant to stand as an individual for purposes of bail according to his individual financial ability, character, and relation to the charges. Each individual's trustworthiness and intention to stand trial must determine the amount of bail set by the court.

Analysis:

While the Eighth Amendment prohibits federal courts from imposing excessive bail, the Supreme Court has not applied that protection to state courts. Most states, however, have similar constitutional or statutory provisions to protect against excessive bail. The calculation of bail in state courts generally follows the same individualized approach discussed by the *Stack* Court.

■ **CASE VOCABULARY**

BAIL: A security such as cash or a bond, especially security required by a court for the release of a prisoner who must appear at a future time.

EXCESSIVE BAIL: Bail that is unreasonably high considering both the offense with which the accused is charged and the risk that the accused will not appear for trial.

United States v. Salerno

(Federal Government) v. *(Mob Boss)*

481 U.S. 739, 107 S. Ct. 2095, 95 L. Ed. 2d 697 (1987)

THE BAIL REFORM ACT IS NOT FACIALLY UNCONSTITUTIONAL

■ **INSTANT FACTS** Organized crime defendants were ordered detained pending trial upon a showing of a threat to the safety of others if released.

■ **BLACK LETTER RULE** Preventative detention of a criminal defendant after indictment does not violate substantive due process under the Fifth Amendment nor constitute excessive bail under the Eighth Amendment when the government has demonstrated through clear and convincing evidence that the defendant presents a threat to the safety of the community.

■ PROCEDURAL BASIS

Certiorari to review a decision of the Second Circuit Court of Appeals declaring a provision of the Bail Reform Act of 1984 unconstitutional.

■ FACTS

Salerno (D) and a co-defendant, Cafaro, were charged with various RICO violations, mail and wire fraud offenses, extortion, and gambling violations. At arraignment, the Government (P) moved for preventative detention of the defendants under the Bail Reform Act of 1984. The Bail Reform Act permits a federal judge to order the pretrial detention of indicted defendants if, after a hearing, the Government proves through clear and convincing evidence that "no condition or combination of conditions will reasonably assure the appearance of the person as required and the safety of any other person and the community." The Government (P) offered evidence showing that Salerno (D) was the boss of a large organized crime family and that Cafaro was a captain. Witnesses testified that Salerno (D) was personally involved in two murder conspiracies. The trial court found that the Government (P) showed through clear and convincing evidence that the defendants' release would jeopardize the safety of the community. On appeal, the defendants argued that the Bail Reform Act is facially unconstitutional because it violates the Due Process Clause of the Fifth Amendment and constitutes excessive bail in violation of the Eighth Amendment. The Second Circuit Court of Appeals reversed the trial court's decision, holding that the Bail Reform Act facially violated substantive due process in that it allowed for the preventative detention of those who may commit future crimes, though not accused of a crime at that time.

■ ISSUE

Does the provision of the Bail Reform Act of 1984 allowing for preventative detention of individuals upon a clear and convincing showing of a threat to the safety of others facially violate substantive due process?

■ DECISION AND RATIONALE

(Rehnquist, C.J.). No. The preventative detention of criminal defendants after indictment does not violate substantive due process under the Fifth Amendment nor constitute excessive bail under the Eighth

Amendment when the government has demonstrated through clear and convincing evidence that the defendants present a threat to the safety of others. The defendants in this case failed to meet their burden of showing that no set of circumstances exists in which the statute could operate constitutionally. First, to establish that the statute violates substantive due process guarantees under the Fifth Amendment, defendants must show that government conduct interferes with a defendant's life, liberty, or property rights. To fall within this category, the Bail Reform Act must serve to punish, rather than regulate, defendants' conduct.

The court must review the legislative history of the statute to determine whether it sets forth a valid regulatory purpose and is rationally related to achieving that purpose. The legislative history of the Bail Reform Act demonstrates that Congress enacted the statute not to punish those who have committed a crime, but to regulate conduct that is likely to endanger the safety of others. The Act carefully sets forth the conduct to which detention is to apply, imposes upon the government a heightened burden of proof, and affords a defendant numerous procedural safeguards through which he or she can contest detention, including a hearing and an opportunity to present witnesses on his or her behalf. The Act is regulatory in nature and is reasonably tailored to achieve its purpose. Congress' interest in regulating the safety of all citizens need not yield to an individual's liberty interests. In times of war and ordinary police activity, for example, legitimate governmental interests in crime prevention can justify the detention of individuals deemed dangerous even before a criminal trial. In light of these legitimate interests, the carefully tailored language of the statute indicates that it may be constitutionally applied to at least some defendants, defeating the facial challenge.

Next, the defendants here argue that the Act facially violates the Eighth Amendment's prohibition against excessive bail, which requires bail to be set solely on the risk of flight in the interest of furthering the integrity of the judicial process. The Eight Amendment does not, however, restrict the government's pursuit of other compelling interests through the regulation of pretrial release. The risk of flight is just one of many factors that may be considered in determining whether the bail set is excessive under the Eighth Amendment. The only limit placed upon the court by the Eighth Amendment is that the bail must not be excessive in light of the governmental interest asserted. If preventative detention sufficiently meets the reasonable objectives sought by the court, the detention is not excessive. The Bail Reform Act of 1984 is not facially unconstitutional under the Fifth or Eighth Amendments.

■ DISSENT

(Marshall, J.). The importance of the Eighth Amendment and the Fifth Amendment cannot be viewed separately to determine that the Bail Reform Act is facially constitutional. There is no meaningful distinction between the imposition of excessive bail and the total denial of bail. Whether bail is excessive or bail is denied, the defendant remains in jail just the same. It is illogical to assume that the Eighth Amendment prohibits one without the other. If such a distinction does exist, the Bail Reform Act serves no purpose, as courts would have unrestricted constitutional power to do that which the statute allows. Similarly, substantive due process under the Fifth Amendment protects much more than a person's right to be free of punishment before conviction. Fundamental to substantive due process is the presumption of innocence every defendant enjoys until proven guilty. This presumption arises at the time of the initial charge and carries through conviction. A defendant acquitted at trial, of course, cannot be detained because his innocence is established. The result should be no different for an indicted defendant enjoying the presumption of innocence. He is as innocent upon indictment as he is upon acquittal. The Bail Reform Act, however, permits the conclusion that one who is presumed innocent may be detained after he has been indicted. The consideration of potential future criminal activity to permit preventative detention transforms an indictment into evidence against the defendant to refute the presumption of innocence. It bears no relation to the governmental function of ensuring that defendants stand trial, as does detention for a risk of flight, but rather presents a governmental interest that exceeds those to be analyzed to determine whether bail is excessive under the Eighth Amendment. The protections of the Eighth Amendment help secure a defendant's substantive due process by prohibiting excessive bail and unjustified detentions because all defendants are presumed innocent until proven otherwise.

■ DISSENT

(Stevens, J.). While pretrial detention may promote a governmental interest in protecting the safety and welfare of the community in some circumstances, the ''future dangerousness'' of a defendant is not one of them. If fear for the safety of others is sufficient to justify such detention, it should be immaterial whether the defendant has been charged, indicted, or convicted of a crime. The appropriateness of preventative detention should be viewed in light of the evidence of the threat to the safety of the community whenever it exists, not merely after an indictment is brought.

Analysis:

Preventative detention, like that addressed in the Bail Reform Act, has received considerable criticism. While the criminal justice system traditionally requires proof of the commission of a crime to justify imprisonment, *Salerno* upholds detentions based not on conduct committed, but on conduct that potentially could be committed if the defendant is given the opportunity. Additionally, while conviction of a crime requires proof beyond a reasonable doubt, preventative detention requires only clear and convincing proof of the potential for future crime.

■ CASE VOCABULARY

PREVENTATIVE DETENTION: Confinement imposed usually on a criminal defendant who has threatened to escape, poses a risk of harm, or has otherwise violated the law while awaiting trial, or on a mentally ill person who may cause harm.

FACIAL CHALLENGE: A claim that a statute is unconstitutional on its face—that is, that it always operates unconstitutionally.

SUBSTANTIVE DUE PROCESS: The doctrine that the Due Process Clauses of the Fifth and Fourteenth Amendments require legislation to be fair and reasonable in content and to further a legitimate governmental objective.

CHAPTER TWELVE

Case Screening

United States v. Armstrong

Instant Facts: Armstrong (D) and others were indicted on several charges involving possession and intent to distribute crack cocaine, as well as using a firearm. Armstrong (D) moved for discovery to show that he was singled out for prosecution because of his race.

Black Letter Rule: To obtain discovery on a claim of selective prosecution based on race, a defendant must produce evidence that similarly situated offenders of a different race could have been prosecuted, but were not.

Blackledge v. Perry

Instant Facts: Perry (D) was convicted of misdemeanor assault with a deadly weapon. After Perry's (D) appeal of this conviction, but before his new trial, the State charged Perry (D) with a felony arising from the same conduct.

Black Letter Rule: A criminal defendant's due process rights are violated if the prosecutor charges the defendant with a more serious crime after the defendant exercises a statutory right to challenge a conviction for a less serious offense arising from the same conduct.

Coleman v. Alabama

Instant Facts: Coleman (D) was convicted of assault with intent to murder in Alabama state court. Coleman (D) was not provided with appointed counsel at the preliminary hearing and argued that he was unconstitutionally denied the assistance of counsel.

Black Letter Rule: Because preliminary hearings are a critical stage of prosecution, defendants are entitled to the assistance of counsel at such hearings.

United States v. Williams

Instant Facts: Williams (D) was indicted by a federal grand jury. The lower courts dismissed the indictment because the prosecutor did not present to the grand jury substantial evidence tending to negate Williams's (D) guilt. The Government argued that the prosecutor was not required to present exculpatory evidence during the grand jury proceedings.

Black Letter Rule: A criminal defendant in federal court is not entitled to a dismissal of the indictment because the prosecutor failed to present to the grand jury substantial exculpatory evidence.

United States v. Armstrong

(Prosecuting Government) v. *(Accused Crack Dealer)*

517 U.S. 456, 116 S. Ct. 1480, 134 L. Ed. 2d 687 (1996)

RACE–BASED PROSECUTION CLAIMS MUST DEMONSTRATE THAT SIMILAR OFFENDERS OF DIFFERENT RACES WERE NOT PROSECUTED

■ **INSTANT FACTS** Armstrong (D) and others were indicted on several charges involving possession and intent to distribute crack cocaine, as well as using a firearm. Armstrong (D) moved for discovery to show that he was singled out for prosecution because of his race.

■ **BLACK LETTER RULE** To obtain discovery on a claim of selective prosecution based on race, a defendant must produce evidence that similarly situated offenders of a different race could have been prosecuted, but were not.

■ **PROCEDURAL BASIS**

Certiorari to review a decision of the court of appeals affirming the district court's grant of the defendants' motion for discovery.

■ **FACTS**

Armstrong (D) and others were indicted on charges involving conspiring to possess crack cocaine with intent to distribute, conspiring to distribute crack cocaine, and federal firearms offenses. Armstrong (D) moved the court for discovery, claiming that he was singled out for prosecution because he is black. The prosecution argued that Armstrong (D) did not produce enough evidence to entitle him to discovery on a claim of selective prosecution.

■ **ISSUE**

In order to obtain discovery on a claim of selective prosecution, must a defendant produce evidence that other similarly situated offenders could have been prosecuted, but were not?

■ **DECISION AND RATIONALE**

(Rehnquist, C.J.) Yes. A defendant claiming, for example, that he was prosecuted because of his race must produce some evidence that similarly situated defendants of other races could have been prosecuted, but were not. A prosecutor's broad discretion in carrying out his or her duty to enforce criminal laws is limited by the equal-protection provisions of the Constitution. However, there is a presumption that prosecutors properly carry out their law enforcement duties. To defeat this presumption, a defendant must meet a very high standard to show that a prosecutor violated the equal-protection provisions of the Constitution in making a decision to prosecute. Because the court of appeals did not require Armstrong (D) to show evidence that non-blacks were not prosecuted for similar crimes, it acted in error. Reversed and remanded.

■ **DISSENT**

(Stevens, J.) The trial judge did not abuse her discretion in ordering the Government to produce evidence relative to Armstrong's (D) claim of selective prosecution. There is a need for heightened judicial vigilance over prosecutions involving crack cocaine because of the severity of penalties for offenses involving crack and because statistics show problematic racial patterns in enforcing these laws.

Analysis:

Note that a claim of selective prosecution is not a defense to the merits of the criminal charge itself, but is an independent claim that a prosecutor exceeded the bounds of his or her discretion by bringing a criminal charge for constitutionally impermissible reasons. Generally, selective-prosecution claims are not likely to succeed because of the heavy burden defendants bear to prove them. Also, federal courts are reluctant to review the decisions of federal prosecutors because federal prosecutors are members of the executive branch of government, whose duty to assist the President in executing federal laws originates in the Constitution.

■ CASE VOCABULARY

DISCOVERY: Compulsory disclosure, at a party's request, of information that relates to the litigation.

Blackledge v. Perry

(*State Official*) v. (*Accused Assailant*)

417 U.S. 21, 94 S. Ct. 2098, 40 L. Ed. 2d 628 (1974)

PROSECUTORS MAY NOT BRING FELONY CHARGES AGAINST DEFENDANTS WHO CHALLENGE MISDEMEANOR CONVICTIONS ARISING FROM THE SAME CONDUCT

"The defendant appealed my misdemeanor conviction. Then, he successfully blocked my attempt to increase it to a felony. I can't wait until he reoffends."

stus.com

■ **INSTANT FACTS** Perry (D) was convicted of misdemeanor assault with a deadly weapon. After Perry's (D) appeal of this conviction, but before his new trial, the State charged Perry (D) with a felony arising from the same conduct.

■ **BLACK LETTER RULE** A criminal defendant's due process rights are violated if the prosecutor charges the defendant with a more serious crime after the defendant exercises a statutory right to challenge a conviction for a less serious offense arising from the same conduct.

■ **PROCEDURAL BASIS**

Certiorari to review a decision of the court of appeals affirming the district court's grant of the defendant's petition for a writ of habeas corpus.

■ **FACTS**

While serving a prison term in North Carolina, Perry (D) was involved in a physical altercation with another inmate. Perry (D) was charged with and convicted of misdemeanor assault with a deadly weapon. Perry (D) appealed his conviction, which, according to North Carolina law, automatically entitled him to a new trial. After Perry's (D) appeal, but before the new trial, the State charged him with felony assault with a deadly weapon with intent to kill and inflict serious bodily injury. Perry (D) pleaded guilty to the felony charges. The State argued that it did not unconstitutionally interfere with Perry's (D) right to appeal his misdemeanor conviction.

■ **ISSUE**

Does the State violate a defendant's constitutional rights when it brings a felony charge against the defendant after the defendant exercises a statutory right to challenge a misdemeanor conviction arising from the same conduct?

■ **DECISION AND RATIONALE**

(Stewart, J.) Yes. A criminal defendant's due process rights are violated if the prosecutor charges that defendant with a more serious crime after the defendant exercises his or her statutory right to challenge a conviction for a less serious offense arising from the same conduct. If, for instance, a criminal defendant has been convicted of a misdemeanor offense arising from particular conduct and later appeals that conviction, the State may not bring felony charges against the defendant arising from the same conduct. A person convicted of an offense should be able to pursue an appeal of a misdemeanor conviction without fearing that the prosecutor will retaliate by bringing a more serious charge against him or her. The fear of a prosecutor's vindictiveness may deter a defendant's challenging a conviction, which is a violation of the defendant's due process rights. Reversed.

Analysis:

The Supreme Court did not require that the defendant produce evidence that the prosecutor actually acted in bad faith or with malice in bringing the felony charges. According to the Court, the mere appearance of vindictiveness would chill the defendant's exercise of the right to appeal. However, the presumption of vindictiveness will not apply in a situation in which the State can show that it could not have brought the more serious charge at the beginning of the proceedings. Also, in *United States v. Goodwin*, 457 U.S. 368 (1982), the Supreme Court rejected the presumption of vindictiveness in a pretrial setting where a defendant challenges an initial charging decision. To prove that the prosecutor made an initial charging decision for vindictive reasons, the defendant must prove that a vindictive motive actually existed.

Coleman v. Alabama

(*Convicted Criminal*) v. (*Prosecuting State*)

399 U.S. 1, 90 S. Ct. 1999, 26 L. Ed. 2d 387 (1970)

DEFENDANTS ARE ENTITLED TO COUNSEL AT PRELIMINARY HEARINGS

■ **INSTANT FACTS** Coleman (D) was convicted of assault with intent to murder in Alabama state court. Coleman (D) was not provided with appointed counsel at the preliminary hearing and argued that he was unconstitutionally denied the assistance of counsel.

■ **BLACK LETTER RULE** Because preliminary hearings are a critical stage of prosecution, defendants are entitled to the assistance of counsel at such hearings.

■ PROCEDURAL BASIS

Certiorari to review a decision by the Alabama Court of Appeals affirming the trial court.

■ FACTS

Coleman (D) was convicted of assault with intent to murder for shooting Reynolds, who had parked his car on the side of the road to change a flat tire. Coleman (D) did not have appointed counsel to represent him at the preliminary hearing. Coleman (D) argued that the failure to provide him with counsel at this stage violated his constitutional right to the assistance of counsel.

■ ISSUE

Is a criminal defendant entitled to counsel at a preliminary hearing?

■ DECISION AND RATIONALE

(Brennan, J.) Yes. Even though it is not necessarily a required step, a preliminary hearing is a "critical stage" of a criminal proceeding that requires the assistance of counsel because there is potential substantial prejudice to the defendant's rights that counsel may help to avoid. Counsel is necessary at the preliminary hearing to protect an indigent accused from an erroneous or improper prosecution by exposing weaknesses in the State's case, developing testimony for impeachment purposes at trial, obtaining discovery vital to preparing a defense, and arguing on issues such as psychiatric examinations and bail. Accordingly, the decision of the court of appeals is vacated and remanded to determine whether the failure to provide counsel was harmless error.

■ CONCURRENCE

(Black, J.) Under Alabama law, the purpose of the preliminary hearing is to determine whether an offense has been committed and whether there is probable cause for charging the defendant with that offense. Because this hearing is a definite part or stage of prosecution, a defendant is entitled to counsel under the Sixth Amendment. Counsel must be present at the preliminary hearing to protect the rights of the accused.

■ DISSENT

(Stewart, J.) If the assistance of counsel is necessary to ensure that the defendant receives a fair trial, then the majority should have vacated the convictions and required a new preliminary hearing to determine whether there was sufficient evidence to take the case to the grand jury. If, as the majority argues, the role of counsel is so crucial, the case should not be remanded for a determination of whether the denial of counsel was harmless error.

Analysis:

The purpose of the preliminary hearing is to allow a magistrate or judge to determine whether there is sufficient evidence to allow the prosecutor to try a criminal defendant on particular charges. However, in 1913, the Supreme Court ruled in *Lem Woon v. Oregon*, 229 U.S. 586 (1913), that a preliminary hearing is not constitutionally required for defendants in state courts. In federal courts, a defendant who is charged with a felony but is not yet indicted is entitled to a preliminary hearing under Fed. R. Crim. P. 5.1. During this hearing, the magistrate or judge may consider hearsay evidence, and the defendant has the right to introduce evidence and cross-examine the Government's witnesses.

■ CASE VOCABULARY

BIND OVER: To hold (a person) for trial; to turn (a defendant) over to a sheriff or warden for imprisonment pending further judicial action.

United States v. Williams

(*Prosecuting Government*) v. (*Indicted Criminal*)

504 U.S. 36, 112 S. Ct. 1735, 118 L. Ed. 2d 352 (1992)

PROSECUTORS ARE NOT REQUIRED TO PRESENT EXCULPATORY EVIDENCE TO THE GRAND JURY

■ **INSTANT FACTS** Williams (D) was indicted by a federal grand jury. The lower courts dismissed the indictment because the prosecutor did not present to the grand jury substantial evidence tending to negate Williams's (D) guilt. The Government argued that the prosecutor was not required to present exculpatory evidence during the grand jury proceedings.

■ **BLACK LETTER RULE** A criminal defendant in federal court is not entitled to a dismissal of the indictment because the prosecutor failed to present to the grand jury substantial exculpatory evidence.

■ **PROCEDURAL BASIS**

Certiorari to review a decision of the Tenth Circuit Court of Appeals affirming the district court's dismissal of an indictment against the defendant.

■ **FACTS**

Williams (D) was indicted by a federal grand jury on seven counts of making false statements or reports for the purpose of misleading banking institutions. Williams (D) brought a motion for disclosure of all exculpatory portions of the grand jury proceedings. After reviewing the transcripts of these portions, Williams (D) asked the court to dismiss the indictment because the Government failed to present to the grand jury substantial exculpatory evidence.

■ **ISSUE**

Is a defendant entitled to dismissal of an indictment if the Government fails to disclose substantial exculpatory evidence during federal grand jury proceedings?

■ **DECISION AND RATIONALE**

(Scalia, J.) No. A federal court criminal defendant is not entitled to the dismissal of an indictment against him or her simply because the prosecutor failed to present exculpatory evidence to the grand jury. The grand jury functions separately and independently from the courts, and thus the courts may not invoke their supervisory powers to prescribe standards for grand jury procedures. Requiring the prosecutor to present exculpatory evidence would alter the historic role of the federal grand jury by transforming it from an accusatory to an adjudicative body. The traditional role of the grand jury is to investigate criminal wrongdoing and to determine if the Government has an adequate basis for bringing criminal charges. It is not for the grand jury to determine the merits of the case; rather, the merits must be determined at trial. Reversed and remanded.

■ **DISSENT**

(Stevens, J.) While the prosecutor should not be required to seek out exculpatory evidence, he or she *should* be required to present such evidence when personally aware of it. Imposing such a requirement on federal prosecutors would protect the fairness of grand jury proceedings by limiting the potential for prosecutors to obtain wrongful indictments. Improperly obtained indictments would have a devastating effect on a suspect's personal and professional life that may not necessarily be negated by a later dismissal. Courts must not tolerate prosecutorial misconduct for the sole reason that such conduct is not prohibited by statute or the Federal Rules of Criminal Procedure.

Analysis:

Note that the holding in *Williams* applies to federal, not state, grand jury proceedings. While some states follow *Williams*, other states require prosecutors to disclose exculpatory evidence to grand juries, although to varying extents. The Supreme Court has held that other evidentiary rules do not apply in federal grand jury proceedings. For example, grand juries may consider evidence that was obtained in violation of the Fourth Amendment. *United States v. Calandra*, 414 U.S. 338 (1974). Likewise, grand juries may consider hearsay testimony. *Costello v. United States*, 350 U.S. 359 (1956).

■ **CASE VOCABULARY**

EXCULPATORY EVIDENCE: Evidence tending to establish a criminal defendant's innocence.

CHAPTER THIRTEEN

Preparing for Adjudication

Hoffman v. United States

Instant Facts: Hoffman (D) was convicted of contempt for invoking the Fifth Amendment privilege against self-incrimination at a federal grand jury proceeding.

Black Letter Rule: The Fifth Amendment privilege against self-incrimination may be invoked if, in view of all the peculiar circumstances of a matter, there is a possibility that the answers sought would have a tendency to incriminate the witness.

People v. Vilardi

Instant Facts: The defendant was convicted of arson involving a laundromat after the prosecution failed to turn over a report finding no evidence of an explosion in the laundromat.

Black Letter Rule: When the prosecution fails to produce exculpatory evidence, the defendant is entitled to a new trial if there is a reasonable possibility that the production of that evidence would have affected the outcome of the case.

Arizona v. Youngblood

Instant Facts: Larry Youngblood (D) was convicted of child molestation, sexual assault, and kidnapping, but the Arizona Court of Appeals reversed on the ground that the State failed to preserve semen samples from the victim's body and clothing.

Black Letter Rule: The failure of the police to preserve potentially useful evidence is not a denial of due process of law unless the defendant can show bad faith on the part of the police.

Williams v. Florida

Instant Facts: Prior to his trial for robbery, Williams (D) objected to the requirement that he provide notice of his intention to claim an alibi and furnish details regarding the alibi, but his objections were overruled and he was convicted as charged.

Black Letter Rule: The Fifth Amendment privilege against self-incrimination is not violated by a requirement that a defendant provide notice of an alibi defense and disclose his alibi witnesses to the prosecution prior to trial.

State v. Reldan

Instant Facts: Reldan (D) was charged with two murders in separate counts of a single indictment. He contended that the joinder was prejudicial and sought separate trials on each count.

Black Letter Rule: No need for severance exists until a defendant makes a convincing showing that he has both important testimony to give concerning one count and a strong need to refrain from testifying on the other.

Barker v. Wingo

Instant Facts: Barker (D) was not brought to trial for murder until more than five years after he had been arrested, during which time the prosecution obtained numerous continuances. He ultimately filed a motion to dismiss the indictment asserting that his right to a speedy trial had been violated.

Black Letter Rule: When addressing speedy trial claims, courts must apply a balancing test, in which the conduct of both the prosecution and the defendant are weighed, including a consideration of the length of delay, the reason for delay, the defendant's assertion of his right, and prejudice to the defendant.

Hoffman v. United States

(*Convicted Contemnor*) v. (*Prosecuting Authority*)

341 U.S. 479, 71 S. Ct. 814, 95 L. Ed. 1118 (1951)

THE FIFTH AMENDMENT APPLIES TO GRAND JURY TESTIMONY

What gives witnesses a right to plead the Fifth, has at least 32 legs, but rarely runs away?

A federal grand jury!

stus.com

■ **INSTANT FACTS** Hoffman (D) was convicted of contempt for invoking the Fifth Amendment privilege against self-incrimination at a federal grand jury proceeding.

■ **BLACK LETTER RULE** The Fifth Amendment privilege against self-incrimination may be invoked if, in view of all the peculiar circumstances of a matter, there is a possibility that the answers sought would have a tendency to incriminate the witness.

■ PROCEDURAL BASIS

Supreme Court review of the affirmance of the defendant's conviction.

■ FACTS

A grand jury convened to investigate certain federal criminal charges, including violations of customs, narcotics, IRS, white slave traffic, perjury, bribery, and conspiracy laws. Hoffman (D) was petitioned to testify before the grand jury, and when questioned about his occupation and contacts with a certain Mr. Weisberg, he refused to answer the questions. Hoffman (D) was found guilty of contempt. On appeal, the reviewing court affirmed his conviction, finding that the answers to the questions could not possibly have incriminated Hoffman (D), so the Fifth Amendment did not apply.

■ ISSUE

Did the Fifth Amendment privilege against self-incrimination apply to Hoffman's (D) testimony at the federal grand jury proceedings?

■ DECISION AND RATIONALE

(Clark, J.) Yes. The Fifth Amendment privilege against self-incrimination may be invoked if, in view of all the peculiar circumstances of a matter, there is a possibility that the answers sought would have a tendency to incriminate the witness. The Court is considering five privilege-against-self-incrimination cases this term, which signals the need to be alert to possible abuses of investigatory powers. The Fifth Amendment must be liberally construed in favor of the right it was intended to protect. Importantly, the self-incrimination at issue is not limited to the crime being investigated, but could also relate to other crimes with which the testifier could be identified. This is not to say that all questions can be refused on Fifth Amendment grounds, no matter how unlikely it is that the answers would be incriminatory. But the witness cannot be forced to explain why he is not responding and thereby, through the explanation itself, reveal incriminatory details. The trial judge must assess whether the circumstances justify application of the privilege, based on all the particular circumstances of the matter before him.

Here, where the grand jury was investigating "rackets" in the area, the court should have recognized that the questions about the defendant's business activities could have elicited incriminatory responses. Further, the additional questions about Weisberg, whom the defendant admitted to knowing for twenty years, could have elicited answers that tied Hoffman (D) to Weisberg, thereby implicating Hoffman (D) in criminal activity. Accordingly, contrary to the courts below, we cannot conclude that there was no possibility that the refused answers would have a tendency to incriminate Hoffman (D). The evils of forced disclosure outweigh any imposition on the prosecution of crime. Reversed.

■ **DISSENT**

(Reed, J.) I agree with the court below.

Analysis:

Although most people are familiar with the aspect of the Fifth Amendment most at issue here, there is another Fifth Amendment protection at work in this case. The Fifth Amendment also provides that a defendant may not be tried for a capital or "infamous" crime unless a grand jury has returned an indictment, finding a sufficient basis on which to prosecute. This provision has been interpreted to apply to all federal felonies. The Supreme Court has held, however, that this part of the Fifth Amendment is not binding on the states.

■ **CASE VOCABULARY**

GRAND JURY: A body of (often 23) people who are chosen to sit permanently for at least a month, and sometimes a year, and who, in ex parte proceedings, decide whether to issue indictments. If the grand jury decides that evidence is strong enough to hold a suspect for trial, it returns a bill of indictment (a *true bill*) charging the suspect with a specific crime.

People v. Vilardi

(Prosecuting Authority) v. *(Convicted Arsonist)*

76 N.Y.2d 67, 555 N.E.2d 915, 556 N.Y.S.2d 518 (1990)

PROSECUTORS MUST TURN OVER EXCULPATORY EVIDENCE

When you say the prosecution "must" turn over exculpatory evidence, is that a hard New York "must", or a squishy Supreme Court "must"?

stus.com

■ **INSTANT FACTS** The defendant was convicted of arson involving a laundromat after the prosecution failed to turn over a report finding no evidence of an explosion in the laundromat.

■ **BLACK LETTER RULE** When the prosecution fails to produce exculpatory evidence, the defendant is entitled to a new trial if there is a reasonable possibility that the production of that evidence would have affected the outcome of the case.

■ PROCEDURAL BASIS

On appeal from the appellate division's granting of a new trial.

■ FACTS

Vilardi (D) was convicted of various counts of arson based on a supposed explosion in a laundromat. His alleged co-conspirators had already been tried and acquitted, despite the fact that they had made inculpatory statements, based in part on an early investigative police report indicating that the investigating officer, a member of the bomb squad, could find no evidence of an explosion in the basement of the laundromat. The same officer had later concluded, however, after reinspecting the premises a year later, that an explosion had occurred.

The earlier report was not produced in response to Vilardi's (D) counsel's discovery request for all reports by explosives experts, and it was therefore not introduced nor referenced at Vilardi's (D) trial; he was convicted of arson. While working on the appeal, however, defense counsel found references to the exculpatory report in the transcript of the co-conspirators' trial, and moved to vacate Vilardi's (D) conviction based on the prosecution's failure to produce the report. The appellate court granted a new trial on the arson charge to which the report related, finding that if there was any chance that the lack of disclosure contributed to the defendant's conviction, his constitutional rights were violated. The People (P) appealed.

■ ISSUE

Did the prosecution's failure to produce the bomb squad investigator's initial exculpatory report result in a violation of the defendant's constitutional rights, such that a new trial was warranted?

■ DECISION AND RATIONALE

(Kaye, J.) Yes. When the prosecution fails to produce exculpatory evidence, the defendant is entitled to a new trial if there is a reasonable possibility that the production of that evidence would have affected the outcome of the case. In *Brady v. Maryland*, the Supreme Court held that the prosecution's failure to produce material, favorable evidence entitles the defendant to a new trial. *Brady* left open the question of whether its holding applied only when a specific request for the evidence had been made before trial. The Court addressed that question in *United States v. Agurs*, developing two different standards based on whether or not a specific request for the exculpatory evidence had been made. Then, in *United*

States v. Bagley, the Court reconsidered this two-tiered approach, adopting a standard like it had just set forth in *Strickland v. Washington* for ineffective assistance of counsel claims. Under that standard, evidence was material, whether specifically requested or not, if there was a reasonable probability that its introduction would have affected the outcome of the trial. But *Bagley* just muddied the waters. Consistent with the mandates of our state constitution, we hold instead that a defendant need only show a reasonable *possibility* that the outcome of his or her trial would have been affected had the prosecution produced the evidence. Under the reasonable possibility standard we adopt today, the prosecution's failure to turn over specifically requested evidence will seldom, if ever, be excused.

Accordingly, as the appellate division found here, the defendant is entitled to a new trial on the arson charge to which the expert's report related, because there was at least a reasonable possibility that the outcome would have been different if that report had been introduced into evidence. Affirmed.

Analysis:

Although the United States Supreme Court is the ultimate judicial authority, here a state court contradicts a recent Supreme Court holding, holding that a possibility—rather than a probability—of a different outcome based on excluded evidence warrants a new trial. Generally speaking, although a state court could not apply lesser constitutional protection to a criminal defendant than that afforded, per the Supreme Court, under the United States Constitution, states are generally free to provide greater protection under their state constitutions, without running afoul of the supremacy doctrine.

■ CASE VOCABULARY

EXCULPATORY EVIDENCE: Evidence tending to establish a criminal defendant's innocence. The prosecution has a duty to disclose exculpatory evidence in its possession or control when the evidence may be material to the outcome of the case.

INCULPATORY EVIDENCE: Evidence showing or tending to show one's involvement in a crime or wrong.

SUPREMACY CLAUSE: The clause in Article VI of the U.S. Constitution declaring that the Constitution, all laws made in furtherance of the Constitution, and all treaties made under the authority of the United States are the "supreme law of the land" and enjoy legal superiority over any conflicting provision of a state constitution or law.

Arizona v. Youngblood

(Prosecuting State) v. *(Convicted Criminal)*
488 U.S. 51, 109 S. Ct. 333, 102 L. Ed. 2d 281 (1988)

SPOLIATION OF EVIDENCE MAY LEAD TO OVERTURNING A CONVICTION

■ **INSTANT FACTS** Larry Youngblood (D) was convicted of child molestation, sexual assault, and kidnapping, but the Arizona Court of Appeals reversed on the ground that the State failed to preserve semen samples from the victim's body and clothing.

■ **BLACK LETTER RULE** The failure of the police to preserve potentially useful evidence is not a denial of due process of law unless the defendant can show bad faith on the part of the police.

■ PROCEDURAL BASIS

Certiorari to review the state supreme court's decision denying review of the Arizona Court of Appeals' reversal of the defendant's conviction.

■ FACTS

A ten-year-old boy was molested and sodomized by a middle-aged man for one and one-half hours. After the assault, the boy was taken to a hospital where a physician used a swab from a "sexual assault kit" to collect semen samples from the boy's rectum. The police also collected the boy's clothing, which they failed to refrigerate. A police criminologist later performed some tests on the rectal swab and the boy's clothing, but he was unable to obtain information about the identity of the boy's assailant. At trial, expert witnesses testified that Youngblood might have been completely exonerated by the timely performance of tests on properly preserved semen samples. Youngblood was convicted of child molestation, sexual assault, and kidnapping. The Arizona Court of Appeals reversed the conviction on the ground that the State had breached a constitutional duty to preserve the semen samples from the victim's body and clothing.

■ ISSUE

Did the failure of the police to preserve potentially useful evidence constitute a denial of due process?

■ DECISION AND RATIONALE

(Rehnquist, J.) No. Youngblood was not denied due process of law by the failure of the police, in investigating the sexual assault of a ten-year-old boy, to refrigerate the boy's clothing and to perform tests on semen samples, thereby preserving potentially useful evidence. No information was concealed and the evidence was made available to the defense expert, who declined to perform any tests on samples. The failure of the police to preserve potentially useful evidence is not a denial of due process of law unless the defendant can show bad faith on the part of the police. Because there was no suggestion of bad faith on the part of the police here, there was no violation of the Due Process Clause. Reversed.

■ CONCURRENCE

(Stevens, J.) The State had a strong incentive to preserve the evidence for its own case. It is unlikely that Youngblood was prejudiced by the State's omission, as defense counsel and the trial court pointed out to the jury that the State failed to preserve the evidence and that they could factor this into their decision. The fact that no juror chose to draw the permissive inference that proper preservation of the evidence would have demonstrated that Youngblood was not the assailant suggests that the lost evidence was immaterial.

■ DISSENT

(Blackmun, J.) The Arizona Court of Appeals was correct in overturning Youngblood's conviction as he was denied the opportunity to present a full defense. The only evidence implicating him was the testimony of the victim. Where no comparable evidence is likely to be available to a defendant, police must preserve physical evidence of a type that they reasonably should know has the potential, if tested, to reveal immutable characteristics of the criminal, and hence to exculpate a defendant charged with the crime.

Analysis:

Youngblood was not denied due process of law because any lost evidence would have been useful to both the State and the defense, and the trial court pointed out to the jury that the failure to preserve evidence was a consideration that they could factor into their decision. Because there was no suggestion of bad faith on the part of the police, however, there was no violation of the Due Process Clause.

■ CASE VOCABULARY

EXCULPATORY EVIDENCE: Evidence that clears or tends to clear an accused person from alleged guilt.

Williams v. Florida

(Convicted Robber) v. *(Prosecuting State)*

399 U.S. 78, 90 S. Ct. 1893, 26 L. Ed. 2d 446 (1970)

THE FIFTH AMENDMENT IS NOT VIOLATED BY REQUIRING THE DEFENDANT GIVE NOTICE OF AN ALIBI DEFENSE

■ **INSTANT FACTS** Prior to his trial for robbery, Williams (D) objected to the requirement that he provide notice of his intention to claim an alibi and furnish details regarding the alibi, but his objections were overruled and he was convicted as charged.

■ **BLACK LETTER RULE** The Fifth Amendment privilege against self-incrimination is not violated by a requirement that a defendant provide notice of an alibi defense and disclose his alibi witnesses to the prosecution prior to trial.

■ **PROCEDURAL BASIS**

Certiorari to review the court of appeals' affirmance of the defendant's conviction.

■ **FACTS**

Prior to his trial for robbery in Florida, Williams filed a motion for a protective order, seeking to be excused from the requirements of Rule 1.200 of the Florida Rules of Criminal Procedure. That rule required a defendant, on written demand from the prosecuting attorney, to give notice in advance of trial of his intention to claim an alibi and to furnish information as to the place he claims to have been and the names and addresses of the alibi witnesses he intends to use. Williams openly declared his intent to claim an alibi, but objected to the further disclosure requirements on the ground that the rule "compels the Defendant in a criminal case to be a witness against himself" in violation of his Fifth and Fourteenth Amendment rights. The motion for a protective order was denied. Williams was convicted as charged and sentenced to life in prison.

■ **ISSUE**

Did application of the Florida notice-of-alibi rule deprive Williams of due process or a fair trial or otherwise compel him to be a witness against himself?

■ **DECISION AND RATIONALE**

(White, J.) No. Florida's notice-of-alibi rule is a requirement that a defendant submit to a limited form of pretrial discovery whenever he or she intends to rely at trial on the defense of alibi. The State in turn is required to notify the defendant of any witnesses it proposes to offer in rebuttal to that defense. Nothing in the Fifth Amendment privilege entitles a defendant to await the end of the State's case before announcing the nature of his defense, any more than it entitles him to await the jury's verdict on the State's case-in-chief before deciding whether or not to take the stand. Affirmed.

CONCURRENCE IN PART, DISSENT IN PART

(Black, J.) The Fifth Amendment clearly states that a criminal defendant cannot be required to give evidence, testimony, or any other assistance to the State to aid it in convicting him or her of a crime.

The Florida notice-of-alibi rule is a patent violation of this constitutional provision because it requires a defendant to disclose information to the State so that the State can use that information to destroy him.

Analysis:

The reciprocal duties of both the State and the defense under the Florida notice-of-alibi rule are key to the Court's conclusion in this case. Disclosure of an alibi defense and evidence relating thereto is not "compelled" testimony within the meaning of the Fifth and Fourteenth Amendments, even when it proves to be testimonial or incriminating.

■ CASE VOCABULARY

PROTECTIVE ORDER: Any order or decree of a court whose purpose is to protect a person from further harassment or abusive service of process or discovery.

State v. Reldan

(Prosecuting Government) v. *(Accused Murderer)*
167 N.J. Super. 595, 401 A.2d 563 (1979)

DEFENDANTS MAY BE TRIED FOR MORE THAN ONE CRIME AT THE SAME TIME

If you wanted separate trials, you probably shouldn't have strangled two Susans.

stus.com

■ **INSTANT FACTS** Reldan (D) was charged with two murders in separate counts of a single indictment. He contended that the joinder was prejudicial and sought separate trials on each count.

■ **BLACK LETTER RULE** No need for severance exists until a defendant makes a convincing showing that he has both important testimony to give concerning one count and a strong need to refrain from testifying on the other.

■ PROCEDURAL BASIS

Motion by the defendant for separate trials on two counts of murder.

■ FACTS

Reldan (D) was charged in Count 1 with the first-degree murder of Susan Heynes and in Count 2 with the first-degree murder of Susan Reeves. Heynes was reported missing from her home on October 6, 1975, and her nude body was found on October 27, 1975. Reeves was reported missing from her home on October 14, 1975, and her nude body was found on October 28, 1975. The medical examiner examined the bodies and found that the cause of death in both cases was strangulation due to a ligature of pantyhose found around the necks of the victims. Reldan (D) was charged with both murders in separate counts of a single indictment on January 20, 1977. The State maintained that the joinder of the two murders was proper as the offenses charged were of the same or similar character. Reldan (D) argued that joinder was prejudicial and sought separate trials on each count.

■ ISSUE

Is joinder of the multiple but related criminal offenses in a single indictment proper?

■ DECISION AND RATIONALE

(Madden, J.) Yes. The manner of the two murders and the disposal of the victims was highly unusual and distinctive. Evidence of the first murder was thus sufficiently probative to justify its admission to prove the identity of the murderer at trial for the other. Admission of the evidence was not so prejudicial as to outweigh its probative value. It was therefore unnecessary to sever on a theory that a jury would be improperly hearing evidence of other crimes in a single trial. Motion denied.

Analysis:

Evidence of other crimes is admissible to prove a relevant fact in issue, such as motive, intent, common scheme or plan, knowledge, absence of mistake, or identity. Here, the facts of the murders demonstrate sufficient similarity to permit evidence of one murder to be introduced into evidence with regard to the other. The state appellate division later affirmed the trial court's decision in this case in *State v. Reldan*, 185 N.J.Super. 494, 449 A.2d 1317 (App.Div.1982). If, however, a defendant makes a convincing

---

showing that he has both important testimony to give concerning one count and a strong need to refrain from testifying on the other, severance should be granted.

■ CASE VOCABULARY

JOINDER OF OFFENSES: Two or more offenses may be charged in the same indictment or information in a separate count for each offense if the offenses charged, whether felonies or misdemeanors or both, are of the same or similar character or are based on the same act or transaction.

SEVERANCE: Separation of cases so that they can be tried separately.

Barker v. Wingo

(*Convicted Murderer*) v. (*Prison Official*)

407 U.S. 514, 92 S. Ct. 2182, 33 L. Ed. 2d 101 (1972)

THE DEFENDANT'S ASSERTION OF OR FAILURE TO ASSERT HIS RIGHT TO A SPEEDY TRIAL IS ONE OF THE FACTORS TO BE CONSIDERED IN AN INQUIRY INTO THE DEPRIVATION OF THAT CONSTITUTIONAL RIGHT

I agreed to thirteen continuances but claimed I was denied a "speedy trial". Unfortunately, judges have no sense of humor.

stus.com

■ **INSTANT FACTS** Barker (D) was not brought to trial for murder until more than five years after he had been arrested, during which time the prosecution obtained numerous continuances. He ultimately filed a motion to dismiss the indictment asserting that his right to a speedy trial had been violated.

■ **BLACK LETTER RULE** When addressing speedy trial claims, courts must apply a balancing test, in which the conduct of both the prosecution and the defendant are weighed, including a consideration of the length of delay, the reason for delay, the defendant's assertion of his right, and prejudice to the defendant.

■ PROCEDURAL BASIS

Certiorari to review the court of appeals' decision affirming the denial of the defendant's petition for a writ of habeas corpus.

■ FACTS

On July 20, 1958, an elderly couple was beaten to death by intruders wielding an iron tire tool. Two suspects, Silas Manning and Willie Barker (D), were indicted. The Commonwealth had a stronger case against Manning and believed that Barker (D) could not be convicted unless Manning testified against him. Manning was unwilling to incriminate himself. By first convicting Manning, the Commonwealth would remove the possible problems of self-incrimination and would be able to assure his testimony against Barker (D). Barker (D) was not brought to trial for murder until more than five years after he had been arrested, during which time the prosecution obtained sixteen continuances. Before Manning was finally convicted, he was tried six times. Barker (D) made no objection to the continuances until three and one-half years after he was arrested. He ultimately filed a motion to dismiss the indictment, asserting that his right to a speedy trial had been violated. The motion was denied and trial commenced with Manning as the chief prosecution witness. Barker (D) was convicted and given a life sentence.

■ ISSUE

Is a defendant deprived of his due process right to a speedy trial when the defendant does not complain about the ensuing delay and is not prejudiced thereby?

■ DECISION AND RATIONALE

(Powell, J.) No. When addressing speedy trial claims, courts must apply a balancing test, in which the conduct of both the prosecution and the defendant are weighed. Four factors to consider include the length of delay, the reason for delay, the defendant's assertion of his right, and prejudice to the defendant. Barker (D) was not seriously prejudiced by the more than five-year delay between his arrest and trial. His Sixth Amendment right to a speedy trial was not violated even though more than four years of the period was attributable to the prosecution's failure or inability to try Manning in order to have Manning's testimony at Barker's (D) trial. The lack of any serious prejudice and the fact, as disclosed by the record, that Barker (D) did not want a speedy trial outweigh opposing considerations and compel the conclusion that Barker was not deprived of his due process right to a speedy trial. Affirmed.

■ CONCURRENCE

(White, J.) Had Barker not so clearly acquiesced in the major delays involved in this case, the result would have been different.

Analysis:

It is impossible to determine with precision when the right to speedy trial has been denied. A defendant's constitutional right to a speedy trial cannot be established by any inflexible rule, and can be determined only on a case-by-case basis, in which the conduct of the prosecution and that of the defendant are weighed.

■ CASE VOCABULARY

HABEAS CORPUS: A form of collateral attack. An independent proceeding initiated to determine whether a defendant is being unlawfully deprived of his or her liberty.

CHAPTER FOURTEEN

The Role of Defense Counsel

Nix v. Whiteside

Instant Facts: Whiteside (D), a convicted felon, argued that he was denied the effective assistance of counsel because his lawyer admonished him not to perjure himself and threatened to disclose any false testimony.

Black Letter Rule: A criminal defendant is not deprived of the effective assistance of counsel when his lawyer admonishes him not to give perjured testimony and threatens to disclose to the court any false testimony the defendant may give.

Gideon v. Wainright

Instant Facts: Gideon (D) was charged with a felony offense in Florida and asked the trial judge to appoint counsel; the judge refused, stating that Florida law only allowed for appointed counsel in capital cases.

Black Letter Rule: Indigent defendants charged with felonies in state court proceedings have the right to have counsel appointed for them.

Scott v. Illinois

Instant Facts: Scott (D) was convicted of theft and fined $50. The State did not appoint counsel to represent him. Scott (D) argues that the State's failure to appoint counsel for him violated his Sixth Amendment right to counsel.

Black Letter Rule: Under the Sixth Amendment, no indigent defendant may be sentenced to imprisonment unless the State has provided him with appointed counsel.

Douglas v. California

Instant Facts: Douglas (D) was convicted in California on thirteen felony charges and appealed as of right, requesting appointed counsel to assist with the appeal. The appellate court denied Douglas's (D) request.

Black Letter Rule: A criminal defendant has a constitutional right to appointed counsel to assist in pursuing a first appeal as of right challenging his or her conviction.

Ross v. Moffitt

Instant Facts: Moffitt (D) was not provided with appointed counsel to assist with his petition for discretionary review in the North Carolina Supreme Court.

Black Letter Rule: A criminal defendant does not have a constitutional right to appointed counsel to assist in pursuing a discretionary appeal in a state court or a petition for certiorari in the Supreme Court of the United States.

Faretta v. California

Instant Facts: Faretta (D) was charged with grand theft and requested permission to represent himself, but the trial court denied his request.

Black Letter Rule: Under the Sixth Amendment, a defendant has the right to represent himself at trial, as long as his decision to do so is voluntary and intelligent.

Strickland v. Washington

Instant Facts: Washington (D) was tried and convicted of several felony charges, including capital murder. In preparation for and during Washington's (D) sentencing hearing, counsel made decisions that Washington (D) later alleged rendered the lawyer's assistance ineffective.

Black Letter Rule: To show entitlement to reversal of a conviction or sentence based on the ineffective assistance of counsel, a defendant must show that counsel's performance was deficient and that this deficiency was prejudicial to the defense.

Nix v. Whiteside

(*State Official*) v. (*Convicted Felon*)

475 U.S. 157, 106 S. Ct. 988, 89 L. Ed. 2d 123 (1986)

COUNSEL'S THREAT TO DISCLOSE CLIENT'S PERJURY IS NOT INEFFECTIVE ASSISTANCE OF COUNSEL

I want to lie in court.

Me, too, but I restrain myself.

stus.com

■ **INSTANT FACTS** Whiteside (D), a convicted felon, argued that he was denied the effective assistance of counsel because his lawyer admonished him not to perjure himself and threatened to disclose any false testimony.

■ **BLACK LETTER RULE** A criminal defendant is not deprived of the effective assistance of counsel when his lawyer admonishes him not to give perjured testimony and threatens to disclose to the court any false testimony the defendant may give.

■ PROCEDURAL BASIS

Certiorari to review the court of appeals' decision to grant Whiteside's (D) petition for a writ of habeas corpus.

■ FACTS

Whiteside (D) went to Love's apartment to purchase marijuana. Whiteside (D) and Love argued over the marijuana. According to Whiteside (D), Love started to reach under his pillow and move towards Whiteside (D), at which point Whiteside (D) stabbed and killed Love. In discussions with his appointed counsel, Whiteside (D) said that, although he had never actually seen a gun, he was convinced that Love had a gun. Just before trial, Whiteside (D) told his lawyer that he had seen "something metallic" in Love's hand. Whiteside's (D) lawyer advised him that testifying to this would be perjury and that he would withdraw from the representation if Whiteside (D) insisted on perjuring himself at trial. The lawyer also indicated that, if Whiteside (D) actually gave the false testimony, the lawyer would have to inform the court of the perjury. Whiteside (D) ultimately testified at trial, did not perjure himself, and was convicted.

■ ISSUE

Is a criminal defendant who threatens to give false testimony denied the effective assistance of counsel when his lawyer seeks to dissuade him from giving this testimony by threatening to disclose the perjury to the court?

■ DECISION AND RATIONALE

(Burger, C.J.) No. A lawyer who indicates his intent to inform the court if his client gives perjured testimony does not fail to adhere to reasonable professional standards and thus does not deprive his client of his Sixth Amendment right to counsel. Although lawyers are ethically bound to preserve their clients' confidences, they are also ethically bound to disclose the falsity of evidence, as well as a client's stated intent to commit a crime, including perjury. Lawyers may not advocate or passively tolerate a client's giving false testimony. In this case, Whiteside's (D) lawyer successfully dissuaded him from committing perjury and did not disclose client communications until Whiteside (D) challenged the representation. Reversed.

■ CONCURRENCE

(Brennan, J.) The Supreme Court has no authority to establish rules of ethical conduct for attorneys practicing in state courts. Thus, the majority opinion's discussion of what amounts to a lawyer's appropriate response to a client's statement of intent to commit perjury has no binding effect.

■ CONCURRENCE

(Stevens, J.) In this particular case, Whiteside (D) intended to commit perjury and his lawyer successfully dissuaded him from doing so. As a result, Whiteside (D) was not prejudiced by his attorney's conduct. However, the majority opinion leaves open the question of what constitutes appropriate action on the part of an attorney whose client actually gives perjured testimony.

Analysis:

In *Whiteside*, the Supreme Court states that a lawyer's duties to his client are "limited by" his duty to "comply with the law" and with standards of professional conduct, which include disclosing a client's criminal or fraudulent act. After *Whiteside*, the ABA Ethics Committee issued Formal Opinion 87–353 to address the situation of a criminal defendant giving perjured testimony. The Opinion specifically rejects the narrative approach outlined in footnote 6 of the opinion in *Whiteside*.

■ CASE VOCABULARY

PERJURY: The act or an instance of a person's deliberately making material false or misleading statements while under oath.

Gideon v. Wainwright

(Accused Criminal) v. *(State Official)*

372 U.S. 335, 83 S. Ct. 792, 9 L. Ed. 2d 799 (1963)

STATE COURT DEFENDANTS CHARGED WITH FELONIES ARE ENTITLED TO APPOINTED COUNSEL

■ **INSTANT FACTS** Gideon (D) was charged with a felony offense in Florida and asked the trial judge to appoint counsel; the judge refused, stating that Florida law only allowed for appointed counsel in capital cases.

■ **BLACK LETTER RULE** Indigent defendants charged with felonies in state court proceedings have the right to have counsel appointed for them.

■ **PROCEDURAL BASIS**

Certiorari to review lower courts' decisions denying Gideon's petition for a writ of habeas corpus.

■ **FACTS**

Gideon (D) was charged with breaking and entering with intent to commit a misdemeanor, which is a felony offense in Florida. Gideon (D) asked the trial judge to appoint counsel for him. The trial judge refused, stating that Florida law allows for appointed counsel only in capital cases. Gideon's (D) case went to trial before a jury, during which Gideon conducted his own defense as best he could. Gideon (D) was convicted and sentenced to five years in prison.

■ **ISSUE**

Does an indigent criminal defendant charged with a felony in state court have a Sixth Amendment right to have counsel appointed to represent him?

■ **DECISION AND RATIONALE**

(Black, J.) Yes. Indigent criminal defendants charged with felonies in state courts have the right to have counsel appointed for them because the Sixth Amendment to the Constitution applies to the states via the Fourteenth Amendment. A provision in the Bill of Rights that is essential to a fair trial is made applicable to the states by the due process provisions of the Fourteenth Amendment. The appointment of counsel is a fundamental right because lawyers in criminal courts are "necessities, not luxuries." Because the government is able to hire a lawyer to prosecute a case, a criminal defendant who cannot afford to do the same is at a disadvantage. Thus, to ensure that all criminal defendants receive a fair trial, indigent defendants must be entitled to have counsel appointed to represent them. The Supreme Court's earlier ruling in *Betts v. Brady*, 316 U.S. 455 (1942), which held that the failure to appoint counsel did not necessarily violate a defendant's due process rights, is overruled. Reversed.

■ **CONCURRENCE**

(Harlan, J.) Although *Betts v. Brady* should be overruled, its holding was not as aberrational as the majority opinion suggests. The holding in *Betts* simply extended to non-capital cases the decision in *Powell v. Alabama*, 287 U.S. 45 (1932), which held that defendants in capital cases were entitled to appointed counsel. Moreover, it has long been recognized that the Sixth Amendment right to appointed counsel is broader in federal prosecutions; at the time *Betts* was decided, it would have been a break in precedent to extend this broad right to the states.

Analysis:

A defendant's right to the assistance of counsel and to have counsel appointed has been incorporated into Fed. R. Crim. P. 44. Earlier, attorneys who were appointed to represent indigent defendants were not paid for their services. Congress recognized the unfairness in this situation and adopted the Criminal Justice Act of 1964, which required federal courts to adopt plans that included limited compensation for appointed attorneys.

Scott v. Illinois

(Convicted Misdemeanant) v. *(Prosecuting State)*
440 U.S. 367, 99 S. Ct. 1158, 59 L. Ed. 2d 383 (1979)

INDIGENT DEFENDANTS MAY NOT BE INCARCERATED FOR MISDEMEANORS UNLESS THEY WERE PROVIDED COUNSEL

■ **INSTANT FACTS** Scott (D) was convicted of theft and fined $50. The State did not appoint counsel to represent him. Scott (D) argues that the State's failure to appoint counsel for him violated his Sixth Amendment right to counsel.

■ **BLACK LETTER RULE** Under the Sixth Amendment, no indigent defendant may be sentenced to imprisonment unless the State has provided him with appointed counsel.

■ **PROCEDURAL BASIS**

Certiorari to review a decision of the Illinois Supreme Court affirming the lower courts' decisions to uphold Scott's (D) conviction.

■ **FACTS**

Scott (D) was accused of shoplifting merchandise worth less than $150. Under Illinois law, the maximum penalty for this offense was a $500 fine, one year in jail, or both. After a bench trial, Scott (D) was convicted of theft and fined $50. The Illinois court did not appoint counsel to represent Scott (D) at his trial.

■ **ISSUE**

Does the Sixth Amendment require a state to appoint counsel for an indigent defendant accused of a crime for which imprisonment is merely an authorized penalty?

■ **DECISION AND RATIONALE**

(Rehnquist, J.) No. In *Argersinger v. Hamlin*, 407 U.S. 25 (1972), the Supreme Court held that, under the Sixth Amendment, indigent defendants may not be sentenced to imprisonment unless the state has appointed counsel to represent them. Actual imprisonment is a more severe penalty than fines or the mere threat of imprisonment. Thus, because imprisonment is such a severe sanction, it cannot be imposed unless the defendant was offered appointed counsel to represent him. Extending the right to appointed counsel to cases in which imprisonment is a possible penalty would create confusion and would impose unpredictable and substantial costs on the states. Thus, the "actual imprisonment" standard from *Argersinger* remains intact. Affirmed.

■ **CONCURRENCE**

(Powell, J.) The problem with the *Argersinger* rule is that it impedes the operation of criminal courts by requiring trial judges to forego the possibility of sentencing a defendant to imprisonment prior to knowing anything about the case or hearing evidence. Despite this problem, the *Argersinger* rule was reaffirmed by the majority, and it is important for the Supreme Court to provide clear guidance to lower courts.

■ **DISSENT**

(Brennan, J.) The "actual imprisonment" standard is a misinterpretation of *Argersinger* and creates an unworkable test for determining whether a defendant is entitled to appointed counsel. The majority opinion creates a situation in which a criminal defendant who is entitled to a jury trial may not be entitled to appointed counsel. A rule requiring appointed counsel in any case in which imprisonment is an authorized offense would be better because it would more faithfully adhere to the principles of the Sixth Amendment. The "authorized imprisonment" rule would also be easier to administer and would not impede the trial court's sentencing discretion.

■ **DISSENT**

(Blackmun, J.) The right to counsel under the Sixth Amendment should extend at least as far as the right to a jury trial. Such a rule would create a "bright line" test on which defendants, prosecutors, and courts may rely.

Analysis:

Note that, even where the Constitution does not require the states to appoint counsel, the states are free to do so. In fact, despite *Argersinger* and *Scott*, the states have adopted varied approaches to appointing counsel for defendants accused of misdemeanors. In a recent case, the Supreme Court held that a state may not impose a suspended sentence that may result in later incarceration unless the state provided the defendant with counsel. *See Alabama v. Shelton*, 535 U.S. 654 (2002).

Douglas v. California

(Convicted Felon) v. *(Prosecution)*

372 U.S. 353, 83 S. Ct. 814, 9 L. Ed. 2d 811 (1963)

INDIGENT DEFENDANTS ARE ENTITLED TO APPOINTED COUNSEL FOR THE FIRST APPEAL AS OF RIGHT

■ **INSTANT FACTS** Douglas (D) was convicted in California on thirteen felony charges and appealed as of right, requesting appointed counsel to assist with the appeal. The appellate court denied Douglas's (D) request.

■ **BLACK LETTER RULE** A criminal defendant has a constitutional right to appointed counsel to assist in pursuing a first appeal as of right challenging his or her conviction.

■ **PROCEDURAL BASIS**

Certiorari to review the California Supreme Court's decision affirming the lower courts' decisions to uphold Douglas's (D) convictions.

■ **FACTS**

Douglas (D) and Bennie Will Meyes were charged with thirteen felonies. A public defender was appointed to represent them. Douglas (D) and Meyes were ultimately tried and convicted of all thirteen felonies, including robbery, assault with a deadly weapon, and assault with intent to commit murder. Douglas (D) and Meyes appealed as of right to the California District Court of Appeal. Douglas (D) and Meyes requested, but were denied, appointed appellate counsel. Pursuant to California law, the California District Court of Appeal reviewed the record and determined that appointing counsel would assist neither Douglas (D) nor the court.

■ **ISSUE**

Does an indigent defendant have a constitutional right to appointed counsel for purposes of pursuing a first appeal as of right?

■ **DECISION AND RATIONALE**

(Douglas, J.) Yes. Indigent defendants are entitled to appointed counsel for their first appeal as of right because the denial of counsel amounts to discrimination against those who cannot afford to retain appellate counsel. The kind of appeal a defendant pursues should not depend on whether he or she can pay for counsel. Under California's procedure, if a defendant can pay for counsel, the court of appeals passes on the merits of the case with the benefit of written briefs and oral argument. If a defendant cannot afford counsel, then the court of appeals prejudges the merits of the case without the benefit of briefs or argument. This is unfair because rich defendants can require the court to listen to argument before deciding the merits, but a poor defendant cannot. Poor defendants who are denied counsel and opt to pursue an appeal are further burdened with a preliminary determination that their cases lack merit. Reversed.

■ **DISSENT**

(Harlan, J.) The majority improperly decided the case using an equal-protection analysis; rather, the majority should have focused solely on whether California's procedure is consistent with due process.

The California procedure is not unconstitutional because it does not actually deny indigent defendants the right to an appeal. Although the majority characterizes California's procedure as discriminating in favor of the rich, there is nothing in the Constitution that requires the states to equalize economic imbalances that inevitably result from certain uniform laws. California's procedure does not violate due process because, even if counsel is not appointed, a defendant receives an appraisal of the merits of his case based on the trial record, as well as full consideration of his appeal.

Analysis:

While nothing in the Constitution requires convicted defendants to be given the right to appeal in state or federal prosecutions, if a jurisdiction provides an appellate procedure, it must be equally accessible to all. Although a defendant may pursue an appeal without the benefit of counsel, having counsel is beneficial for both the defendant and the courts. Lawyers can distinguish good claims from bad, prepare concise pleadings that focus only on promising claims, and dissuade prisoners from bogging down the court system with voluminous pleadings containing frivolous arguments.

■ CASE VOCABULARY

APPEAL AS OF RIGHT: An appeal to a higher court from which permission need not be first obtained. Also termed "appeal by right."

EX PARTE: Done or made at the instance and for the benefit of one party only, and without notice to, or argument by, any person adversely interested.

Ross v. Moffitt

(*State Official*) v. (*Convicted Felon*)
417 U.S. 600, 94 S. Ct. 2437, 41 L. Ed. 2d 341 (1974)

INDIGENT DEFENDANTS ARE NOT ENTITLED TO APPOINTED COUNSEL FOR DISCRETIONARY APPEALS

■ **INSTANT FACTS** Moffitt (D) was not provided with appointed counsel to assist with his petition for discretionary review in the North Carolina Supreme Court.

■ **BLACK LETTER RULE** A criminal defendant does not have a constitutional right to appointed counsel to assist in pursuing a discretionary appeal in a state court or a petition for certiorari in the Supreme Court of the United States.

■ PROCEDURAL BASIS

Certiorari to review lower courts' decisions overturning Moffitt's (D) conviction.

■ FACTS

Moffitt (D) was tried and convicted in Mecklenberg County, North Carolina. The State provided Moffitt (D) with counsel for his trial and for his first appeal as of right. However, Moffitt (D) was denied counsel for purposes of pursuing a discretionary appeal in the North Carolina Supreme Court.

■ ISSUE

Does an indigent defendant have a constitutional right to appointed counsel for purposes of pursuing a discretionary appeal in state court or an application for review by the Supreme Court of the United States?

■ DECISION AND RATIONALE

(Rehnquist, J.) No. The decision in *Douglas v. California*, 372 U.S. 353 (1963), should not be extended because neither the Due Process Clause nor the Equal Protection Clause requires that a defendant be provided with counsel for discretionary appeals. Denying a defendant counsel is not manifestly unfair because, in appellate proceedings, a defendant does not need an attorney as a shield as in trial proceedings, but rather seeks to use counsel as a sword to overturn a conviction. Failing to provide counsel for discretionary appeals does not discriminate against indigent defendants on the basis of their poverty. Although poor defendants do not have the same advantages as rich defendants, the relative disparity in this context is far less than in the context of a first appeal as of right. The materials prepared by appointed counsel on the first appeal, along with a defendant's own filings, are enough to give a state supreme court an adequate basis for deciding whether to grant review. In addition, the purpose of discretionary review, unlike an appeal as of right, is not to decide whether the finding of guilt was correct. In fact, a court may deny discretionary review even when it believes that the conviction appears to be incorrect. Reversed.

■ DISSENT

(Douglas, J.) The majority should have affirmed the lower courts' decisions because, as the appellate judge found, there is no logical basis for differentiating between appeals as of right and discretionary appeals. The decision in *Douglas* should be extended to the discretionary review context because that decision was grounded on fairness and equality. These same concepts of fairness and equality require counsel in subsequent discretionary appeals.

Analysis:

The opinion in *Ross* does not address whether a defendant is entitled to appointed counsel if discretionary review is granted and the defendant is required to present a brief and oral argument. However, as a matter of practice, state high courts and the United States Supreme Court routinely appoint counsel once review has been granted. In addition, the decisions in *Douglas* and *Ross* left open the question of whether a defendant is entitled to appointed counsel for a second appeal as of right.

■ CASE VOCABULARY

DISCRETIONARY REVIEW: The form of appellate review that is not a matter of right but that occurs only with the appellate court's permission.

Faretta v. California

(Convicted Felon) v. *(Prosecuting State)*

422 U.S. 806, 95 S. Ct. 2525, 45 L. Ed. 2d 562 (1975)

CRIMINAL DEFENDANTS HAVE A CONSTITUTIONAL RIGHT TO REPRESENT THEMSELVES AT TRIAL

■ **INSTANT FACTS** Faretta (D) was charged with grand theft and requested permission to represent himself, but the trial court denied his request.

■ **BLACK LETTER RULE** Under the Sixth Amendment, a defendant has the right to represent himself at trial, as long as his decision to do so is voluntary and intelligent.

■ **PROCEDURAL BASIS**

Certiorari to review the lower courts' decisions affirming Faretta's conviction.

■ **FACTS**

Faretta (D) was charged with grand theft under California law. A public defender was assigned to represent him. Faretta (D) requested that he be permitted to represent himself. The trial judge advised Faretta (D) that he thought he was making a mistake, but initially allowed him to proceed *pro se*. Later, however, after questioning Faretta about the extent of his legal research, the trial judge ruled that Faretta had not knowingly and intelligently waived his right to counsel and that he had no constitutional right to represent himself. The judge re-appointed the public defender to represent Faretta (D) and required that Faretta's (D) defense be conducted only through the lawyer. The jury convicted Faretta (D) and he was sentenced to imprisonment.

■ **ISSUE**

Does a defendant have a constitutional right to represent himself in a criminal prosecution?

■ **DECISION AND RATIONALE**

(Stewart, J.) Yes. The Sixth Amendment requires that a criminal defendant be permitted to represent himself or herself, as long as the waiver of counsel is voluntary and intelligent. The right of self-representation is implied in the language and spirit of the Sixth Amendment, the provisions of which accord the accused the right to make a defense. This right is personal to the defendant because it is he or she who suffers the consequences if the defense fails. The implied right to self-representation is well supported in history. Self-representation was required practice in felony prosecutions in England, and was guaranteed in various colonial charters and declarations of rights. Historically, the right to counsel was considered supplemental to the right of self-representation. In addition, where a defendant does not want representation, a lawyer's skill and experience is less valuable to the process. However, before waiving the right to counsel, a defendant must be advised of the dangers and disadvantages of doing so. The record must establish that the defendant's electing to represent himself or herself is made with full understanding and free will. Reversed.

■ **DISSENT**

(Burger, C.J.) The right to self-representation is not included in either the express language or history of the Sixth Amendment. The Sixth Amendment guarantees that defendants receive the fullest possible

---

defense, which is usually realized through the express guarantee of the right to counsel. The majority also improperly relies on history to support its decision by taking English and early American history out of context. Moreover, because the Sixth Amendment was proposed and adopted after Congress signed legislation guaranteeing the right to self-representation, the omission of this right from the Sixth Amendment must be construed as intentional. Thus, the issue of whether to allow defendants to proceed *pro se* must be left to the decision of legislatures.

■ **DISSENT**

(Blackmun, J.) The majority's holding presents a host of procedural problems for trial courts. For example, it is not clear whether or when a defendant must be advised of the right to proceed *pro se*. Likewise, the standards for measuring whether the defendant's waiver of counsel is "voluntary" and "intelligent" are not clear. If a defendant proceeds *pro se*, is he or she constitutionally entitled to "standby" counsel or to be treated differently at trial?

Analysis:

In *Martinez v. Court of Appeal of California*, 528 U.S. 152 (2000), the Supreme Court declined to extend the holding in *Faretta* to appellate proceedings. The Court found that neither history nor constitutional structure require that a defendant be guaranteed the right of self-representation in pursuing an appeal. The decision in *Martinez* deals only with constitutional requirements; a state may nonetheless legislate a defendant's right of self-representation in appellate proceedings.

■ **CASE VOCABULARY**

PRO SE: For oneself; on one's own behalf; without a lawyer.

Strickland v. Washington

(*State Official*) v. (*Convicted Felon*)

466 U.S. 668, 104 S. Ct. 2052, 80 L. Ed. 2d 674 (1984)

OBJECTIVELY UNREASONABLE AND PREJUDICIAL REPRESENTATION CONSTITUTES INEFFECTIVE ASSISTANCE OF COUNSEL

I lost my "ineffective assistance of counsel" case because the standard for attorneys is so low. Apparently, the Supreme Court doesn't want every conviction followed by a case against the defense attorney.

stus.com

■ **INSTANT FACTS** Washington (D) was tried and convicted of several felony charges, including capital murder. In preparation for and during Washington's (D) sentencing hearing, counsel made decisions that Washington (D) later alleged rendered the lawyer's assistance ineffective.

■ **BLACK LETTER RULE** To show entitlement to reversal of a conviction or sentence based on the ineffective assistance of counsel, a defendant must show that counsel's performance was deficient and that this deficiency was prejudicial to the defense.

■ **PROCEDURAL BASIS**

Certiorari to review the appellate court's decision to reverse the trial court's upholding of Washington's (D) sentence.

■ **FACTS**

Washington (D) was indicted in Florida for kidnapping and murder, and was appointed counsel to represent him. Against the advice of his counsel, Washington (D) confessed to two murders, waived his right to a jury trial, and pleaded guilty to capital murder. Washington (D) stated that he was under extreme stress when he committed the crimes. In preparation for the sentencing hearing, counsel did not seek out character witnesses or request a psychiatric examination. He also did not request a pre-sentence report, believing that the report would be more detrimental than beneficial. After a hearing, Washington (D) was sentenced to death. Washington (D) challenged his sentence on the ground that he was provided ineffective assistance of counsel. Washington (D) claimed his counsel's representation was ineffective because he failed to request a continuance to prepare for sentencing, request a psychiatric evaluation, investigate and present character witnesses, seek a pre-sentence report, present meaningful arguments to the sentencing judge, investigate the medical examiner's reports and cross-examine the prosecution's medical experts.

■ **ISSUE**

In order to obtain a reversal of a conviction or sentence based on ineffective assistance of counsel, must a defendant show that his counsel's performance was deficient and that this deficiency actually prejudiced his defense?

■ **DECISION AND RATIONALE**

(O'Connor, J.) Yes. The Sixth Amendment right to counsel encompasses the right to the effective assistance of counsel; when counsel's representation is ineffective, the defendant's constitutional rights are violated. The crux of assessing whether counsel's performance was ineffective is determining whether his or her conduct so undermined the functioning of the adversarial process that the trial did not yield a fair result. A defendant must show that counsel's performance was not objectively reasonable. In assessing counsel's performance, courts must be highly deferential and adhere to a strong presumption that counsel's conduct falls within the range of reasonable professional assistance. Likewise, courts must view the conduct not from a hindsight perspective, but from counsel's perspective at the time of the conduct. Even if counsel's performance was professionally unreasonable, a conviction or sentence will not be set aside unless this conduct actually prejudiced the defense. While there is a presumption of prejudice in cases involving conflicts of interest, in most cases, the defendant must affirmatively demonstrate prejudice. To demonstrate actual prejudice, the defendant must show, based on the totality of the evidence, that there is a reasonable probability that, but for counsel's deficient professional conduct, the result of the proceeding would have been different. "Reasonable probability" is a probability sufficient to undermine confidence in the outcome. In this case, Washington's (D) counsel's performance was neither professionally deficient, nor prejudicial to Washington (D). Reversed.

CONCURRENCE IN PART, DISSENT IN PART

(Brennan, J.) While the majority correctly sets forth the appropriate standards for claims of ineffective assistance of counsel, Washington's (D) death sentence should be vacated because the death penalty amounts to cruel and unusual punishment prohibited by the Eighth Amendment.

■ DISSENT

(Marshall, J.) The majority's standards for adjudicating claims of ineffective assistance of counsel are meaningless and will not provide appropriate guidance for lower courts. Although defense attorneys' decision-making should be accorded a certain amount of deference in assessing the reasonableness of their performance, there are certain aspects of a criminal attorney's job that are more conducive to judicial oversight and thus more precise standards. The majority's standard for prejudice is also problematic because it is difficult to tell, from a cold record, whether a better result would have been achieved by competent counsel. Moreover, there is the possibility that evidence of prejudice may be missing from the record because of the incompetence of counsel.

Analysis:

In the vast majority of cases in which a defendant claims ineffective assistance of counsel, courts have concluded that counsel's performance fell within the range of reasonable professional conduct. Counsel's performance is not deficient simply because a different attorney may have made different tactical or strategic decisions. In addition, even though certain conduct has been found to be deficient in one case, it does not mean that the same conduct would be found deficient in another case.

■ CASE VOCABULARY

AGGRAVATING CIRCUMSTANCE: A fact or situation that relates to a criminal offense or defendant and that is considered by the court in imposing punishment (especially a death sentence).

MITIGATING CIRCUMSTANCE: A fact or situation that does not bear on the question of a defendant's guilt but that is considered by the court in imposing punishment and especially in lessening the severity of a sentence.

CHAPTER FIFTEEN

Plea Bargaining and Guilty Pleas

Brady v. United States

Instant Facts: Brady (D) pleaded guilty to a charge of kidnapping, which carried a maximum penalty to death, in exchange for a lesser sentence after learning that his co-defendant had confessed to the crime and was available to testify against him.

Black Letter Rule: A guilty plea is not involuntary merely because it was entered into to avoid the possibility of the death penalty.

North Carolina v. Alford

Instant Facts: Alford (D) maintained that he was innocent of the murder for which he had been charged but, after considering the evidence against him, pleaded guilty to second-degree murder to avoid being sentenced to death if he was found guilty of the charge.

Black Letter Rule: A court may not enter a judgment upon a plea of guilty unless it is satisfied that there is a factual basis for the plea.

Bordenkircher v. Hayes

Instant Facts: A state prosecutor carried out a threat to reindict Hayes (D) under the state's Habitual Criminal Act if Hayes (D) did not plead guilty to the offense with which he was originally charged.

Black Letter Rule: It is not a vindictive exercise of a prosecutor's discretion, and therefore not a violation of due process, to carry out a threat to reindict a defendant on more serious charges if the defendant does not plead guilty to the original offense charged.

Santobello v. New York

Instant Facts: After Santobello (D) pleaded guilty to a lesser-included offense as part of a plea agreement whereby a prosecutor agreed to dismiss the more serious charge and would not make a recommendation as to the sentence, a different prosecutor appeared at the sentencing hearing and recommended that Santobello (D) receive the maximum prison sentence.

Black Letter Rule: When a plea of guilty has been entered in consideration of a promise made by a prosecutor, the prosecutor must fulfill that promise.

United States v. Brechner

Instant Facts: Although it had initially agreed to do so, the U.S. Attorney's Office declined move for a downward departure in Brechner's (D) sentence because he did not comply with the "truthfulness" terms of the written cooperation agreement.

Black Letter Rule: A prosecutor is not bound by promises made pursuant to a cooperation agreement if the defendant does not fulfill his agreed promises.

McMann v. Richardson

Instant Facts: A petition for certiorari sought reversal of three separate judgments of the federal appeals courts ordering hearings on petitions for habeas corpus that alleged that the defendants' guilty pleas were triggered by coerced confessions.

Black Letter Rule: If a defendant's plea of guilty is based on reasonably competent advice, it is an intelligent plea not open to attack on the ground that the defendant's counsel may have misjudged the admissibility of the defendant's confession.

Brady v. United States

(Convicted Kidnapper) v. *(Prosecuting Government)*
397 U.S. 742, 90 S. Ct. 1463, 25 L. Ed. 2d 747 (1970)

GUILTY PLEAS ENTERED INTO TO AVOID THE DEATH PENALTY ARE VALID

No, plea bargaining to avoid the death penalty is self-serving, not "involuntary".

stus.com

■ **INSTANT FACTS** Brady (D) pleaded guilty to a charge of kidnapping, which carried a maximum penalty to death, in exchange for a lesser sentence after learning that his co-defendant had confessed to the crime and was available to testify against him.

■ **BLACK LETTER RULE** A guilty plea is not involuntary merely because it was entered into to avoid the possibility of the death penalty.

■ PROCEDURAL BASIS

Appeal from a court of appeals decision affirming the district court's finding that the defendant's guilty plea was voluntary.

■ FACTS

Brady (D), along with his co-defendant, was charged with kidnapping and faced a maximum penalty of death. After initially pleading not guilty, Brady (D) changed his plea to guilty upon learning that his co-defendant had confessed to the crime and would be available to testify against him. Brady (D) later appealed, claiming that his fear of the death penalty was the reason that he pleaded guilty and that the subsequent decision in *United States v. Jackson,* 390 U.S. 570 (1968), required the invalidation of every plea of guilty entered into when the fear of death was shown to be a factor in making the plea.

■ ISSUE

Must a plea of guilty be invalidated because a fear of the death penalty factored into the defendant's decision to plead guilty?

■ DECISION AND RATIONALE

(White, J.) No. A plea is only invalid if it was (1) not voluntarily made and (2) not knowingly and intelligently made with sufficient awareness of the relevant circumstances and the likely consequences. Applying the standard of voluntariness of guilty pleas articulated in *Shelton v. United States*, 246 F.2d 571 (1957), Brady's (D) plea of guilty was voluntarily made because it was made merely to avoid the possibility of the death penalty and it was not induced by threats, misrepresentation or promises that were improper as having no proper relationship to the prosecutor's business. Brady's (D) plea was knowingly and intelligently made because competent counsel advised him, he was made aware of the charge against him, and there was no evidence that he was mentally incompetent. Although Brady (D) was informed that the jury could impose the death penalty, and the Court determined several years later in *U.S. v. Jackson* that the jury had no such power when a judge could impose only a lesser sentence if the trial were to the court or there was a plea of guilty, Brady's (D) plea of guilty was intelligently made in the light of the then-applicable law and did not become vulnerable to being withdrawn because a later judicial decision indicated that the plea rested on a faulty premise. Affirmed.

Analysis:

In *U.S. v. Jackson*, the U.S. Supreme Court held that the federal law that allowed a jury to recommend the death penalty was invalid because it discouraged assertion of the Fifth Amendment right not to plead guilty and could deter exercise of the Sixth Amendment right to demand a jury trial. In *Brady*, the Court made it clear that, although *Jackson* prohibited the imposition of the death penalty by a jury, *Jackson* did not hold that the federal law was inherently coercive or that a plea of guilty under that statute was invalid, even though a fear of the death penalty may have been a factor in the plea.

■ CASE VOCABULARY

VOLUNTARY: Unconstrained by interference, not impelled by another's influence; done by design or intention; proceeding from the free and unrestrained will of the person.

KNOWINGLY: With knowledge; consciously, intelligently; willfully; intentionally.

COERCED: Compelled to compliance.

North Carolina v. Alford

(Prosecuting State) v. *(Confessed Murderer)*

400 U.S. 25, 91 S. Ct. 160, 27 L. Ed. 2d 162 (1970)

A GUILTY PLEA MAY BE UPHELD EVEN WHEN THE DEFENDANT MAINTAINS HIS INNOCENCE

I am as pure as the driven snow, but I'm pleading guilty anyway to reduce my sentence.

stus.com

■ **INSTANT FACTS** Alford (D) maintained that he was innocent of the murder for which he had been charged but, after considering the evidence against him, pleaded guilty to second-degree murder to avoid being sentenced to death if he was found guilty of the charge.

■ **BLACK LETTER RULE** A court may not enter a judgment upon a plea of guilty unless it is satisfied that there is a factual basis for the plea.

■ PROCEDURAL BASIS

Appeal from order of the United States District Court for the Middle District of North Carolina summarily denying the defendant's petition for writ of habeas corpus; the court of appeals reversed and remanded, and the Supreme Court noted probable jurisdiction.

■ FACTS

The State presented substantial evidence that supported the charge that Alford (D) had committed first-degree murder. Alford (D), after hearing the evidence against him, decided to plead guilty to a lesser charge of second-degree murder. At the time Alford (D) entered his plea of guilty, he maintained to the court that he was innocent of the charge. The judge accepted Alford's plea and sentenced him to prison. Alford (D) later argued that, because he continued to maintain that he did not commit the murder, the judge should not have accepted his guilty plea.

■ ISSUE

Should the court accept a plea of guilty even when the defendant continues to profess innocence at the time the plea is entered?

■ DECISION AND RATIONALE

(White, J.) Yes. Even when a defendant professes innocence, a guilty plea may be accepted when there is a factual basis supporting the charge against the defendant. A court may not enter a judgment upon a plea of guilty, however, unless it is satisfied that there is a factual basis for the plea. Here, even though Alford's (D) plea was accompanied his statement that he did not commit the murder, a sufficient factual basis did exist because the State presented testimony that (1) Alford (D) took a gun from his house, (2) he stated his intention to kill the victim, and (3) he returned home declaring that he had killed the victim. An express admission of guilt is not a constitutional prerequisite to the imposition of a criminal penalty, and an individual accused of a crime may voluntarily, knowingly, and understandingly consent to the imposition of a prison sentence even if he is unwilling (or unable) to admit participation in the crime. There is also no material difference between a plea that refuses to admit the commission of a crime and a plea containing a protestation of innocence, provided that the defendant intelligently concludes that his or her interests are best served by pleading guilty and that the record before the judge contains strong evidence of actual guilty. Vacating the decision of the court of appeals and remanding.

Analysis:

Ordinarily, a judgment of conviction based on a plea of guilty is justified by (1) the admission that the defendant committed the crime and (2) the consent that judgment be entered without a trial. When a guilty plea does not include an admission of guilt but rests on a protestation of innocence, state and lower courts are divided as to whether the plea can be accepted. The Court here noted that there was no constitutional distinction between neither admitting nor denying charges in plea of *nolo contendere* and expressly denying the charges. Thus, a plea of guilty does not need to include an express admission of guilt in order for the plea to be accepted and a criminal penalty be imposed, as long as there is a factual basis for the charge.

■ CASE VOCABULARY

NOLO CONTENDERE: "I will not contest it"; a plea in a criminal case that has a similar legal effect to pleading guilty; a type of plea that may be entered with leave of court to a criminal complaint or indictment by which the defendant neither admits nor denies the charges, though a fine or sentence may be imposed pursuant to it.

Bordenkircher v. Hayes

(Prison Superintendent) v. *(Repeat Offender)*

434 U.S. 357, 98 S. Ct. 663, 54 L. Ed. 2d 604 (1978)

REINDICTING A DEFENDANT ON MORE SERIOUS CHARGES WHEN THE DEFENDANT REFUSES TO PLEAD GUILTY TO A LESSER OFFENSE DOES NOT VIOLATE DUE PROCESS

■ **INSTANT FACTS** A state prosecutor carried out a threat to reindict Hayes (D) under the state's Habitual Criminal Act if Hayes (D) did not plead guilty to the offense with which he was originally charged.

■ **BLACK LETTER RULE** It is not a vindictive exercise of a prosecutor's discretion, and therefore not a violation of due process, to carry out a threat to reindict a defendant on more serious charges if the defendant does not plead guilty to the original offense charged.

■ PROCEDURAL BASIS

Certiorari to review the court of appeals' reversal of the district court's dismissal of the defendant's habeas corpus petition.

■ FACTS

After being indicted on a charge of uttering a false instrument, Hayes (D) was told by the prosecutor that if he didn't plead guilty to that charge the prosecutor would reindict Hayes (D) under the state's Habitual Criminal Act and, if convicted, he would be sentenced to life in prison. Hayes (D) did not plead guilty and the prosecutor reindicted him on the more serious charge. Hayes (D) was found guilty and, as required by the Act, was sentenced to life in prison.

■ ISSUE

Is it a vindictive exercise of the prosecutor's discretion and a violation of the Due Process Clause to carry out a threat made during plea negotiations to reindict a criminal defendant on more serious charges if the defendant does not plead guilty to the offense with which he or she was originally charged?

■ DECISION AND RATIONALE

(Stewart, J.) No. A prosecutor does not vindictively exercise his or her discretion, and therefore does not violate due process, by carrying out a threat to reindict a defendant on more serious charges if the defendant does not plead guilty to the originally charged offense. Hayes (D) was fully informed of terms of the plea offer and understood that he risked being reindicted under the Habitual Criminal Act if he did not plead guilty. As a practical matter, the case was no different than if Hayes (D) had initially been indicted as a recidivist and the prosecutor had offered to drop that charge as part of a plea agreement. While it is a violation of the Due Process Clause to punish a person for legally attacking a conviction, there is no such element of punishment or retaliation in plea bargaining so long as the defendant is free to accept or reject the prosecution's offer. Reversed.

■ DISSENT

(Blackmun, J.) It was a vindictive exercise of the prosecutor's discretion, and, therefore, violative of the Due Process Clause, to reindict Hayes (D) under the Habitual Criminal Act because the sole reason for the new indictment was to discourage Hayes (D) from exercising his right to a trial.

■ DISSENT

(Powell, J.) Given that Hayes's (D) two prior felony convictions did not result in any imprisonment and the third charge involved less than $100, the prosecutor was not justified in seeking a reindictment under the Habitual Criminal Act where a conviction would result in Hayes (D) receiving a mandatory sentence of life in prison. The prosecutor's actions denied Hayes (D) due process because the admitted purpose was to discourage Hayes from exercising his constitutional rights by threatening him with a potential penalty that was extreme considering Hayes's (D) criminal history.

Analysis:

There is a distinction between reindicting a convicted misdemeanant on a felony charge after the defendant invoked an appellate remedy and carrying out a threat to reindict a defendant on more serious charges if the defendant does not plead guilty to the original charge. The former action violates due process because it is retaliation against the defendant for legally attacking a conviction while the latter does not violate due process because there is no such element of punishment or retaliation so long as the defendant is free to accept or reject the prosecution's offer.

■ CASE VOCABULARY

RECIDIVIST: Habitual criminal; a criminal repeater.

DUE PROCESS: The constitutional guarantee of notice and the opportunity to be heard and to defend in an orderly proceeding adapted to the nature of case; the guarantee of due process requires that every person have the protection of a day in court and the benefit of general law.

Santobello v. New York

(Criminal Defendant) v. *(Prosecuting State)*

404 U.S. 257, 92 S. Ct. 495, 30 L. Ed. 2d 427 (1971)

PROSECUTORS MUST KEEP THEIR PROMISES WHEN THE DEFENDANT PLEADS GUILTY IN RELIANCE THEREON

■ **INSTANT FACTS** After Santobello (D) pleaded guilty to a lesser-included offense as part of a plea agreement whereby a prosecutor agreed to dismiss the more serious charge and would not make a recommendation as to the sentence, a different prosecutor appeared at the sentencing hearing and recommended that Santobello (D) receive the maximum prison sentence.

■ **BLACK LETTER RULE** When a plea of guilty has been entered in consideration of a promise made by a prosecutor, the prosecutor must fulfill that promise.

■ PROCEDURAL BASIS

Certiorari to review a state appellate court's affirmance of the trial court's conviction of the criminal defendant.

■ FACTS

Santobello (D) agreed to plead guilty to a lesser-included offense in exchange for the prosecutor's promises that he would dismiss the more serious charge and that he would not make a recommendation at the sentencing hearing. At the sentencing hearing, the original prosecutor was replaced by a new prosecutor who recommended that Santobello (D) receive the maximum prison sentence. Santobello (D) objected on the ground that the plea agreement prevented the prosecution from making a recommendation.

■ ISSUE

Is the prosecutor's office bound by a promise not to make a sentencing recommendation when that promise was the consideration for a plea of guilty?

■ DECISION AND RATIONALE

(Burger, J.) Yes. Plea agreements presuppose a fairness in securing the agreement between the defendant and the prosecutor. When a promise or agreement of the prosecutor is the inducement for the defendant to plead guilty, that promise must be fulfilled. Here, the state failed to keep a commitment concerning a sentencing recommendation on the defendant's guilty plea, so the case must be remanded to the state court to decide whether the circumstances require only that there be specific performance of the agreement on the guilty plea, or whether the circumstance require that the petitioner be granted the opportunity to withdraw his plea of guilty. Judgment vacated and the case remanded.

■ CONCURRENCE

(Douglas, J.) A constitutional rule should apply in state cases whereby if a plea bargain is not kept by the prosecutor, the sentence must be vacated and the state court must decide, in light of the circumstances of each case, whether due process requires (1) that there be specific performance of the plea bargain or (2) that the defendant be given the option to go to trial on the original charges.

■ **DISSENT**

(Marshall, J.) A defendant who has entered a plea of guilty should be able to replead to the original charges even if the plea of guilty was conditioned on a promise by the prosecutor that the prosecutor did not keep.

Analysis:

The disposition of charges pursuant to plea agreements plays an essential part in the efficiency of judicial administration. However, the value of plea agreements presupposes fairness in the securing the agreement. Consequently, if a defendant enters a plea of guilty in reliance on a promise or agreement by the prosecutor, the prosecutor must fulfill that promise or agreement.

■ **CASE VOCABULARY**

DUE PROCESS: The constitutional guarantee of notice and the opportunity to be heard and to defend in an orderly proceeding adapted to the nature of case; the guarantee of due process requires that every person have the protection of a day in court and the benefit of general law.

United States v. Brechner

(Plaintiff) v. *(Defendant)*
99 F.3d 96 (1996)

A BREACH BY THE DEFENDANT RELEASES THE GOVERNMENT FROM ITS OBLIGATIONS UNDER A COOPERATION AGREEMENT

■ **INSTANT FACTS** Although it had initially agreed to do so, the U.S. Attorney's Office declined move for a downward departure in Brechner's (D) sentence because he did not comply with the "truthfulness" terms of the written cooperation agreement.

■ **BLACK LETTER RULE** A prosecutor is not bound by promises made to a cooperation agreement if the defendant does not fulfill his agreement.

■ **PROCEDURAL BASIS**

Appeal from a U.S. District Court order for specific performance of a cooperation agreement.

■ **FACTS**

Brechner (D) and the U.S. Attorney's Office entered into a cooperation agreement whereby the U.S. Attorney's Office promised to recommend a downward departure from the sentencing guidelines if Brechner (D) assisted in the government's bribery investigation of a bank officer. The cooperation agreement also required Brechner (D) to provide complete, truthful, and accurate information and testimony. During a subsequent debriefing session, Brechner (D) initially denied receiving certain kickbacks but, upon the advice of his attorney, acknowledged that he had received the kickbacks. The U.S. Attorney's office later declined to move for a downward sentencing departure on behalf of Brechner (D) because of Brechner's (D) misrepresentations and the difficulty in prosecuting the bank officer with Brechner (D) as the sole witness.

■ **ISSUE**

Is the U.S. Attorney's office bound by its promises pursuant to a cooperation agreement even when the defendant does not completely comply with the agreement?

■ **DECISION AND RATIONALE**

(Leval, J.) No. The government's purpose in entering into the cooperation agreement in this case was to conduct a bribery investigation of a bank officer. The fact that Brechner (D) was not truthful, even though he later corrected his misstatements, undermined the purpose of that investigation because Brechner (D) was the government's sole witness, and his failure to be truthful undermined his credibility as a witness. Therefore, Brechner's (D) misstatements were material and not, as the district court found, "trivial defects" that did not prejudice the government. Reversed.

Analysis:

A defendant has the same obligations as a prosecutor to comply with the terms of an agreement. Consequently, a prosecutor is not bound by the terms of a cooperation agreement if the defendant breaches the agreement. The breach in this case was particularly noteworthy because the defendant's lack of honesty was determined to be material to the underlying purpose of the agreement.

■ CASE VOCABULARY

MISREPRESENTATION: Any manifestation by words or other conduct by one person to another that, under the circumstances, amounts to an assertion not in accordance with the facts.

McMann v. Richardson

(Warden) v. *(Prisoner)*

397 U.S. 759, 90 S. Ct. 1441, 25 L. Ed. 2d 763 (1970)

GUILTY PLEAS ARE VALID WHEN BASED ON REASONABLY COMPETENT ADVICE

■ **INSTANT FACTS** A petition for certiorari sought reversal of three separate judgments of the federal appeals courts ordering hearings on petitions for habeas corpus that alleged that the defendants' guilty pleas were triggered by coerced confessions.

■ **BLACK LETTER RULE** If a defendant's plea of guilty is based on reasonably competent advice, it is an intelligent plea not open to attack on the ground that the defendant's counsel may have misjudged the admissibility of the defendant's confession.

■ PROCEDURAL BASIS

Certiorari to review the appellate court's reversal of the trial courts' denial of the defendants' petitions for writs of habeas corpus.

■ FACTS

Three state court prisoners alleged that their pleas of guilty should be set aside because the pleas were triggered by coerced confessions. A U.S. Court of Appeals ordered hearings for the defendants on their petitions for habeas corpus.

■ ISSUE

Does a defendant's assertion that his guilty plea was motivated by a coerced confession entitle him to have the plea impeached in a collateral proceeding?

■ DECISION AND RATIONALE

(White, J.) No. If the defendants here had considered that their confessions were coerced and, therefore, unusable at trial, they probably would not have entered a guilty plea. If there was a question as to whether their confessions were admissible, each of the defendants had the benefit of counsel to help determine whether it would be in his or her best interest to enter a guilty plea. If the defendants' pleas of guilty were based on reasonably competent advice from their counsel, their pleas are intelligent and not open to attack on the ground that their counsel may have misjudged the admissibility of their confessions. Accordingly, the court of appeals erred in reversing the trial courts' denials of the defendants' habeas corpus petitions. Vacated and remanded.

Analysis:

Whether a guilty plea is unintelligent and improperly motivated by a confession erroneously thought admissible depends on whether the advice to plead guilty was within the range of competence required of criminal law attorneys. The range of competence required of an attorney includes determining (1) how the facts, as they are understood, would be viewed by a court; (2) whether those facts, if proved, would convince a judge or jury of the defendant's guilt; (3) whether, on those facts, evidence seized without a warrant would be admissible; and (3), based on those facts, whether the trier of fact would find a confession voluntary and admissible.

■ **CASE VOCABULARY**

CERTIORARI: Most commonly used to refer to the Supreme Court of the United States, which uses the writ of certiorari as a discretionary device to choose the cases it wishes to hear.

COERCED: Compelled to compliance.

COLLATERAL PROCEEDING: One in which a particular question may arise or be involved incidentally, but that is not instituted for the very of purpose of deciding such question.

HABEAS CORPUS: The name given to a variety of writs having as their objective bringing a party before a judge. Initially, the writ only permitted a prisoner to challenge a state conviction on constitutional grounds that related to the jurisdiction of the state court, but the scope of inquiry has gradually expanded and the writ now extends to all constitutional challenges.

CHAPTER SIXTEEN

The Trial Process

Duncan v. Louisiana

Instant Facts: Duncan (D) was denied his request for jury trial on an assault charge because the Louisiana Constitution provided a right to jury trial only in felony cases.

Black Letter Rule: Under the Fourteenth Amendment, all criminal defendants have a constitutional right to trial by jury on a non-petty offense.

Taylor v. Louisiana

Instant Facts: Taylor (D) was tried and convicted by an all-male jury because Louisiana law systematically excluded women from jury service.

Black Letter Rule: A petit jury must represent a fair cross section of the community to ensure a defendant's right to trial by an impartial jury under the Sixth Amendment.

Ham v. South Carolina

Instant Facts: The judge declined Ham's (D) request to ask specific questions relating to prospective juror bias against him based on his race and personal appearance.

Black Letter Rule: The Fourteenth Amendment requires a state trial judge to explore racial prejudices of prospective jurors to ensure a fair, impartial jury.

People v. Newton

Instant Facts: Newton (D) was charged with the murder of a white police officer in California.

Black Letter Rule: When a prospective juror harbors preconceived notions of a defendant's guilt that cannot be set aside by consideration of the evidence, the juror must be dismissed for cause to ensure an impartial jury.

United States v. Salamone

Instant Facts: Salamone (D) was convicted of firearms violations by a jury consisting of many jurors who owned firearms, despite the dismissal of potential jurors who were members of the National Rifle Association.

Black Letter Rule: A juror may be challenged for cause based on membership or affiliation in a particular group only upon a factual determination that such affiliation impacts or impairs the juror's ability to be impartial.

Batson v. Kentucky

Instant Facts: Batson (D), a black man, was convicted of burglary by an all-white jury after the government used its peremptory challenges to remove all black persons from the jury.

Black Letter Rule: The exercise of a peremptory challenge by the State to strike black jurors from a black defendant's jury violates the Equal Protection Clause of the Fourteenth Amendment absent a race-neutral explanation for the challenge.

United States v. Thomas

Instant Facts: An eleven-member jury convicted Thomas (D), a black defendant, on drug charges after the only black juror was disqualified during deliberations.

Black Letter Rule: When the evidence discloses any possibility that a juror's views arise from the sufficiency of the government's evidence, disqualification must be denied.

Olden v. Kentucky

Instant Facts: Olden (D) was denied an opportunity to impeach a witness against him on cross-examination to establish his defense theory.

Black Letter Rule: Under the Sixth Amendment, a defendant is entitled to confront witnesses against him, which includes the right of cross-examination.

Maryland v. Craig

Instant Facts: Craig (D) was convicted on the basis of a child abuse victim's one-way closed-circuit testimony.

Black Letter Rule: When necessary to protect a child witness from trauma that would be caused by testifying in the physical presence of the defendant, impairing the child's ability to communicate, the Confrontation Clause does not prohibit use of a procedure that, despite the absence of a face-to-face confrontation, ensures the reliability of the evidence by subjecting it to rigorous adversarial testing and thereby preserves the essence of effective confrontation.

Crawford v. Washington

Instant Facts: The state sought to introduce a statement Crawford's (D) wife gave to investigating officers, though she refused to testify at trial on marital privilege grounds; Crawford (D) argued that admitting the statement would violate the Confrontation Clause.

Black Letter Rule: The Sixth Amendment guarantee that the accused in a criminal prosecution shall enjoy the right to be confronted with the witnesses against him extends beyond in-court testimony and includes statements resulting from police interrogations.

Cruz v. New York

Instant Facts: Eulogio Cruz (D) was convicted of felony murder after the introduction of the confession of his nontestifying co-defendant, which corroborated Eulogio's (D) earlier pretrial confession.

Black Letter Rule: When a non-testifying codefendant's confession incriminating the defendant is not directly admissible against the defendant, the Confrontation Clause bars its admission at their joint trial, even if the jury is instructed not to consider it against the defendant, and even if the defendant's own confession is admitted against him.

Gray v. Maryland

Instant Facts: Gray (D) was convicted after a redacted confession of a co-defendant was offered at their joint trial with a limiting instruction.

Black Letter Rule: The use of blanks or "deleted" references in a redacted confession of a co-defendant may not be offered against a defendant at a joint trial, even with a limiting instruction.

United States v. Burr

Instant Facts: Burr (D) subpoenaed documents from the President of the United States.

Black Letter Rule: The Sixth Amendment right to compel witnesses includes the right to compel production of documents within the witness' possession.

Taylor v. Illinois

Instant Facts: Taylor (D) was convicted of attempted murder after the testimony of a favorable witness was excluded because of discovery violations.

Black Letter Rule: The *per se* exclusion of evidence knowingly disclosed in violation of discovery rules does not violate the Compulsory Process Clause.

Griffin v. California

Instant Facts: Griffin (D) was convicted of murder after the prosecutor commented on his failure to testify on his own behalf.

Black Letter Rule: The Fifth Amendment, in its direct application to the federal government and in its bearing on the states by the Fourteenth Amendment, forbids a prosecutor from commenting on a defendant's decision not to testify at his trial and court instructions that the defendant's silence is evidence of his guilt.

United States v. Thomas

Instant Facts: An eleven-member jury convicted Thomas (D), a black defendant, on drug charges after the only black juror was disqualified during deliberations.

Black Letter Rule: When the evidence discloses any possibility that a juror's views arise from the sufficiency of the government's evidence, disqualification must be denied.

Duncan v. Louisiana

(Convicted Assailant) v. *(Prosecuting State)*

391 U.S. 145, 88 S. Ct. 1444, 20 L. Ed. 2d 491 (1968)

CRIMINAL DEFENDANTS ARE ENTITLED TO A JURY TRIAL ON ASSAULT CHARGES

■ **INSTANT FACTS** Duncan (D) was denied his request for jury trial on an assault charge because the Louisiana Constitution provided a right to jury trial only in felony cases.

■ **BLACK LETTER RULE** Under the Fourteenth Amendment, all criminal defendants have a constitutional right to trial by jury on a non-petty offense.

■ **PROCEDURAL BASIS**

Certiorari to review the defendant's conviction.

■ **FACTS**

Duncan (D) was charged with simple assault in state court, a misdemeanor under Louisiana law carrying a maximum sentence of two years in prison and a $300 fine. Duncan (D) requested a jury trial, which was denied because the Louisiana Constitution provided for jury trials only in felony cases. Duncan (D) was convicted and sentenced to sixty days in a local prison and a $150 fine.

■ **ISSUE**

Does the Fourteenth Amendment Due Process Clause confer a right to trial by jury in trials of all non-petty criminal offenses in the states?

■ **DECISION AND RATIONALE**

(White, J.) Yes. The right to a trial by jury is granted as a protection against oppression by the government. Fear of the unchecked power of the judiciary found expression in the criminal law by the participation of the community in determining a defendant's guilt or innocence. Because of the importance of this right, the Fourteenth Amendment requires its enforcement in the states in order to preserve due process of law for all criminal defendants. A jury trial is not required, however, for crimes in which the maximum sentence constitutes a petty offense. In England and under the Sixth Amendment, it has been long recognized that crimes imposing minimal sentences need not be tried by a jury because the threat of harm to the defendant is insufficient to outweigh the benefits of efficient law enforcement and simplified judicial administration. The same interests apply under the Fourteenth Amendment. The focus must be on the maximum sentence available for the crime charged, not on the actual sentence imposed by the court. Federal law defines a petty offense as one in which the maximum imprisonment exceeds six months and the fine is no greater than $500. While the Court need not define the exact line between petty and serious crimes in this case, the maximum penalty of two years and a fine of $300 for the crime charged here renders the crime a serious offense to which trial by jury must be afforded under the Fourteenth Amendment. Reversed.

■ **DISSENT**

(Harlan, J.) The role of the jury is to reflect the public's views of the criminal laws, choosing to enforce harsher penalties than that which a court may impose or relieving a defendant of crimes viewed as less serious to justify a penalty. The jury may, however, be unable to comprehend the detailed intricacies of the law, leading to inaccurate conclusions and considerable delay in judicial administration. While the right to trial by jury is self-evident for serious crimes, the Court's attempt to draw a line between those offenses in which the consequences outweigh the interest in efficient law enforcement and those that do not provides no justification for requiring a state to honor the federal system without regard to the state of their judicial dockets and prevailing local views.

Analysis:

You may recall from Chapter 1 that the justices of the *Duncan* Court debated the appropriateness of total incorporation as opposed to selective incorporation of the Bill of Rights into the Fourteenth Amendment. While the majority here chose to selectively incorporate the Sixth Amendment based on the fundamental rights implicated, you may wish to revisit the separate opinions in Chapter 1 to understand the opposing views of the justices.

■ CASE VOCABULARY

DUE PROCESS: The conduct of legal proceedings according to established rules and principles for the protection of private rights, including notice and the right to a fair hearing before a tribunal with the power to decide the case.

PETTY OFFENSE: A minor or insignificant crime.

SERIOUS OFFENSE: An offense not classified as a petty offense and usually carrying at least a six-month sentence.

INCORPORATION: The process of applying the provisions of the Bill of Rights to the states by interpreting the Fourteenth Amendment's Due Process Clause as encompassing those provisions.

Taylor v. Louisiana

(Convicted Kidnapper) v. *(Prosecuting State)*

419 U.S. 522, 95 S. Ct. 692, 42 L. Ed. 2d 690 (1975)

SYSTEMATIC EXCLUSION OF WOMEN FROM PETIT JURIES UNDER STATE LAW VIOLATES THE SIXTH AMENDMENT

■ **INSTANT FACTS** Taylor (D) was tried and convicted by an all-male jury because Louisiana law systematically excluded women from jury service.

■ **BLACK LETTER RULE** A petit jury must represent a fair cross section of the community to ensure a defendant's right to trial by an impartial jury under the Sixth Amendment.

■ PROCEDURAL BASIS

Certiorari to review the defendant's conviction.

■ FACTS

Taylor (D), a male, was indicted of aggravated kidnapping in Louisiana state court. The Louisiana Constitution and the Code of Criminal Procedure excluded women from jury service unless they previously declared their desire to participate. Within the judicial district, fifty-three percent of the population eligible for jury duty was female, but no more than ten percent of those in the jury wheel were women. Taylor (D) moved to quash the petit jury venire because women were systematically excluded, depriving him of his constitutional right to a fair trial by a representative segment of the community. The motion was denied and the defendant was later tried and convicted by an all-male jury.

■ ISSUE

Does the system of excluding women from jury service unless they previously file a written declaration of their desire to participate in jury service violate the Sixth and Fourteenth Amendments by denying defendants a jury consisting of a fair cross section of the community?

■ DECISION AND RATIONALE

(White, J.) Yes. While the state jury-selection system impacts the rights of women, Taylor (D) does not lack standing to challenge a violation of his constitutional rights though he is not a member of the excluded class. In *Duncan v. Louisiana*, the Court held that the right to a jury trial afforded by the Sixth Amendment is binding on the states through the Fourteenth Amendment. The selection of a petit jury from a representative cross section of the community is an essential element of the right to a trial by an impartial jury. The purpose of a jury is to expose the arbitrary power of the courts to the common-sense judgment of the community as a whole, which is destroyed if large segments of the population are systematically excluded from the jury pool. A jury selection procedure that systematically excludes women, who actually constitute a majority in the jurisdiction, violates the fair-cross-section rule essential to the Sixth Amendment. While the Court has held that a system excluding women from jury selection does not violate women's due process or equal protection rights because a rational basis for their exclusion was demonstrated, that issue is quite different from whether such a system violates the defendant's Sixth Amendment rights. A state may exempt individuals from jury duty on the basis of special hardship or incapacity, but it is untenable to conclude that all women, as a class, would suffer such hardship. A system that presumes that women fall under this exemption, without a case-by-case evaluation, does not result in a fair cross section of the community. While the states are free to fashion the qualifications and exemptions applicable to jury selection in their courts, those requirements must be designed to ensure that jury panels represent a fair cross section. The rule established by the Court, however, does not require that every jury be composed of any particular composition. A jury resulting from a state procedure that does not systematically favor one section of the population over another meets the requirements of the Sixth Amendment. Reversed and remanded.

■ DISSENT

(Rehnquist, J.) The Court's decision provides no reason why the purpose of the jury system is undermined by the exclusion of one sex over the other. While women may offer perspectives distinct from those of their male counterparts, so too do doctors, lawyers, and other groups, whose exclusion has been endorsed by the majority. The Court offers no reason why the prophylactic purpose of the jury system is destroyed absent the female perspective.

Analysis:

The Court's decision does not go so far as to guarantee that a defendant's jury, or even the venire from which it is chosen, constitutes a fair cross section of the community. Instead, the Court merely condemns the systematic exclusion of large, distinct groups, such as women, from the venire. While fifty-three percent of the jurisdiction's population eligible for jury service was female, the actual female representation on the venire may be much less. Indeed, the jury may continue to be predominantly male without violating the Sixth Amendment.

■ CASE VOCABULARY

FAIR–CROSS–SECTION REQUIREMENT: The principle that a person's right to an impartial jury, guaranteed by the Sixth Amendment, includes a requirement that the pool of potential jurors fairly represent the composition of the jurisdiction's population.

JURY: A group of persons selected according to the law and given the power to decide questions of fact and return a verdict in the case submitted to them.

PETIT JURY: A jury, usually consisting of six or twelve persons, summoned and empanelled in the trial of a specific case.

VENIRE: A panel of persons selected for jury duty and from among whom the jurors are to be chosen.

JURY WHEEL: A physical device or electronic system used for storing and randomly selecting names of potential jurors.

Ham v. South Carolina

(Black Civil Rights Activist) v. *(Prosecuting State)*
409 U.S. 524, 93 S. Ct. 848, 35 L. Ed. 2d 46 (1973)

PROSPECTIVE JURORS' RACIAL BIAS MAY BE QUESTIONED DURING VOIR DIRE

Raise your hand if you're a racist.

stus.com

■ **INSTANT FACTS** The judge declined Ham's (D) request to ask specific questions relating to prospective juror bias against him based on his race and personal appearance.

■ **BLACK LETTER RULE** The Fourteenth Amendment requires a state trial judge to explore racial prejudices of prospective jurors to ensure a fair, impartial jury.

■ PROCEDURAL BASIS

Certiorari to review a decision of the Supreme Court of South Carolina affirming the conviction.

■ FACTS

Ham (D) was a well-known black activist in the South who was charged with possession of marijuana. Ham (D) claimed he was framed by local law enforcement officers in retaliation for his role in the civil rights movement. Prior to the judge's voir dire of prospective jurors, defense counsel requested that the judge ask three questions relating to possible prejudice against Ham (D) because he was black and wore a beard. The judge declined to honor counsel's request, instead asking questions on prejudice and bias specified by South Carolina statutes, though unrelated to race. A jury was selected and the defendant was convicted. The Supreme Court of South Carolina ultimately affirmed the conviction.

■ ISSUE

Does the trial judge's refusal to examine jurors on voir dire as to possible prejudice against the defendant violate his constitutional rights?

■ DECISION AND RATIONALE

(Rehnquist, J.) Yes. The Due Process Clause of the Fourteenth Amendment was adopted to insure the essential demands of fairness and to prohibit states from engaging in invidious discrimination on the basis of race. While a trial court need not present questions to a jury in any specific form or in a certain quantity merely by request of the defendant, voir dire must be conducted to determine a prospective juror's racial prejudice when race is a potential factor in the case. Prejudice on the basis of physical appearance, such as the wearing of a beard, however, is not a fundamental right secured by the Fourteenth Amendment and need not be explored by a trial judge during voir dire. Because the judge failed to properly inquire of the jurors' potential racial prejudice, the court denied Ham (D) his due process rights under the Fourteenth Amendment. Reversed.

■ CONCURRENCE IN PART, DISSENT IN PART

(Douglas, J.) While the Court's decision with respect to exploring racial prejudice during voir dire is correct, the Fourteenth Amendment similarly requires the trial judge to explore bias on the basis of the defendant's facial hair. The defendant's due process rights allow him a trial by an impartial jury, and prejudices toward his facial hair or outward appearance are serious enough to question their holders' neutrality. Over fifty reported cases demonstrate the importance that the public places on socially accepted hair growth in educational, employment, and military settings. Denial of the defendant's opportunity to explore these deep-rooted prejudices violates his due process rights.

Analysis:

Although the Court held that Ham (D) was entitled to question prospective jurors' racial bias, the Court has since held that this right is not triggered merely because the defendant and an alleged victim are of different races. To require racial questioning, special circumstances must exist to warrant it. Here, Ham's (D) defense that he was framed based on his role in the black civil rights movement provided such circumstances.

■ **CASE VOCABULARY**

VOIR DIRE: A preliminary examination of a prospective juror by a judge or lawyer to decide whether the prospect is qualified and suitable to serve on a jury.

People v. Newton

(*Prosecuting State*) v. (*Co–Founder of the Black Panther Party*)

Case No. 41266 (Cal. Super. Ct. 1968)

JURORS MUST BE OPEN TO THE POSSIBILITY OF THE DEFENDANT'S INNOCENCE

Apparently, leaking pre-trial propaganda about a defendant's guilt only works if your jurors know to fake impartiality.

stus.com

■ **INSTANT FACTS** Newton (D) was charged with the murder of a white police officer in California.

■ **BLACK LETTER RULE** When a prospective juror harbors preconceived notions of a defendant's guilt that cannot be set aside by consideration of the evidence, the juror must be dismissed for cause to ensure an impartial jury.

■ PROCEDURAL BASIS

Voir dire of a prospective juror by defense counsel.

■ FACTS

Newton (D) was the co-founder and Minister of Defense of the Black Panther Party. He was charged with the 1967 murder of a white police officer in Oakland, California. Because of the significant pretrial publicity in the case, the judge allowed extensive voir dire by defense counsel to ensure the jury was impartial. After the jury was impaneled, the defendant was convicted of murder.

■ ISSUE

Must a prospective juror who believes a defendant is guilty and is unable to objectively review the evidence be dismissed for cause?

■ DECISION AND RATIONALE

(Judge undisclosed; from the voir dire transcript.) Yes. Defense counsel questioned a prospective juror, Mr. Strauss, about his ability to enter the trial without preconceived notions of Newton's (D) guilt. After establishing that the juror understood that Newton (D) was presumed innocent until proven guilty under the law, the juror stated that he could not accept that Newton was innocent of the charges. Although the district attorney established that without further evidence the juror would vote not guilty as to the charges, the juror testified under examination of defense counsel that he would do so only because the law requires it, but that he believed Newton (D) was guilty. Under such circumstances, the juror must be dismissed for cause to ensure a fair, impartial jury.

Analysis:

A prospective juror who comes before the court with prior knowledge of a case need not be dismissed in every instance. Only when the court is satisfied that the juror is unable to consider the evidence at trial to reach a fair verdict must the juror be stricken for cause.

■ CASE VOCABULARY

VOIR DIRE: A preliminary examination of a prospective juror by a judge or lawyer to decide whether the prospect is qualified and suitable to serve on a jury.

United States v. Salamone

(*Prosecuting Government*) v. (*Convicted Firearms Violator*)
800 F.2d 1216 (3d Cir. 1986)

STRIKING JURORS FOR CAUSE ON THE BASIS OF THEIR NRA MEMBERSHIP WAS AN ABUSE OF DISCRETION

■ **INSTANT FACTS** Salamone (D) was convicted of firearms violations by a jury consisting of many jurors who owned firearms, despite the dismissal of potential jurors who were members of the National Rifle Association.

■ **BLACK LETTER RULE** A juror may be challenged for cause based on membership or affiliation in a particular group only upon a factual determination that such affiliation impacts or impairs the juror's ability to be impartial.

■ PROCEDURAL BASIS

Appeal from the defendant's conviction.

■ FACTS

Salamone (D) was charged with seven firearms offenses. During pretrial voir dire, the trial court excused one potential juror and five potential alternates for cause because of their membership in the National Rifle Association. The impaneled jury consisted of ten jurors who possessed firearms at their home and five alternates also possessed firearms. Two of those alternates ultimately served on the jury. Defendant was convicted of six of the counts against him and sentenced to twenty years in prison and a $35,000 fine.

■ ISSUE

Did the trial court abuse its discretion in dismissing potential jurors in a weapons violation case solely on the basis of their membership in the National Rifle Association?

■ DECISION AND RATIONALE

(Higginbotham, Cir. J.) Yes. The National Rifle Association is a national organization that advocates the rights of all citizens to own firearms and oppose gun control measures by the government. Association with a group, however, does not mean that a prospective juror shares all its views or that he or she is unable to correctly apply the law to reach a verdict. A challenge for cause permits the disqualification of a juror on narrowly specified grounds that demonstrate a bias that affects the outcome of the trial. While a trial judge is afforded considerable deference in ordering the dismissal of a potential juror, he or she must do so on the basis of the juror's particular beliefs, not affiliation with any organization. Here, the court asked the stricken jurors no question that would enable the court to determine whether they would be able to faithfully and correctly apply the law in the case. Without such a factual determination, there is no nexus between each juror's affiliation with the National Rifle Association and his or her individual views on the issues to be considered at trial. Reversed.

Analysis:

A challenge for cause can be justified in two ways: (1) the potential juror is unqualified to serve by statute, or (2) he or she is biased. A juror may be statutorily disqualified if, for example, he is under the age of eighteen, he is not a U.S. citizen, he is unable to understand or speak English, he is mentally infirm, or he is currently charged or has been convicted of a felony without having his civil rights restored. Bias can be actual, as demonstrated through voir dire, or implied, such as by blood relation to a party or counsel to the case.

■ **CASE VOCABULARY**

CHALLENGE FOR CAUSE: A party's challenge supported by a specified reason, such as bias or prejudice, that would disqualify a potential juror.

Batson v. Kentucky

(*Convicted Burglar*) v. (*Prosecuting State*)

476 U.S. 79, 106 S. Ct. 1712, 90 L. Ed. 2d 69 (1986)

THE USE OF PEREMPTORY CHALLENGES TO STRIKE ALL BLACK JURORS IS *PRIMA FACIE* DISCRIMINATORY

■ **INSTANT FACTS** Batson (D), a black man, was convicted of burglary by an all-white jury after the government used its peremptory challenges to remove all black persons from the jury.

■ **BLACK LETTER RULE** The exercise of a peremptory challenge by the State to strike black jurors from a black defendant's jury violates the Equal Protection Clause of the Fourteenth Amendment absent a race-neutral explanation for the challenge.

■ PROCEDURAL BASIS

Certiorari to review the defendant's conviction.

■ FACTS

Batson (D), a black man, was indicted in Kentucky state court for second-degree burglary and receipt of stolen goods. During jury selection, the prosecutor used his peremptory challenges to strike all four black persons on the venire, resulting in an all-white jury. Defense counsel moved to discharge the jury because the striking of the black potential jurors violated the fair-cross-section requirements of the Sixth Amendment and the Equal Protection Clause of the Fourteenth Amendment. The judge denied the motion, ruling that the parties were free to exercise their peremptory challenges for any reason they chose and that the fair-cross-section requirement applied only to the selection of the venire, not selection of the jury. Batson (D) was convicted.

■ ISSUE

Does race-based exercise of peremptory challenges violate the Equal Protection Clause of the Fourteenth Amendment?

■ DECISION AND RATIONALE

(Powell, J.) Yes. Although a peremptory challenge generally may be exercised for any reason, the Equal Protection Clause prohibits a prosecutor from excluding a black juror based on a presumption that he will be unable to impartially serve on the jury on account of his race. Although the Court's jurisprudence has held that a peremptory challenge is subject to the constraints of the Equal Protection Clause, many courts have construed this directive as requiring a defendant to prove that the prosecutor has engaged in the systematic exclusion of black jurors over an extended period of time. The result of this near impossible burden has left prosecutors' peremptory challenges virtually immune from constitutional scrutiny. To establish a prima facie constitutional violation, however, a defendant need not look at the past conduct of the prosecutor, but only demonstrate the systematic use of peremptory challenges on the basis of race in the defendant's trial. The defendant must establish that he is a member of a cognizable racial group, that the prosecutor has used peremptory challenges to exclude members of his racial group from the venire, and that the facts and other circumstances create an inference that the prosecutor has used peremptory challenges on the basis of race. The trial judge supervising voir dire must consider the circumstances presented, including any pattern of striking black jurors and any statements or questions posed by the prosecution, to determine whether a prima facie case of purposeful discrimination is established. The burden then shifts to the State to establish a race-neutral explanation for each peremptory challenge. While the prosecutor's explanation need not rise to the level of a challenge for cause, it must not rest on the assumption that blacks as a group will be partial because they share the same race as the defendant. The court must determine whether the proffered explanation sufficiently rebuts the presumption of discrimination. While the peremptory challenge serves an important function in our system of justice, the limitations placed upon them are necessary to further equal protection and the interests of justice. Here, the defendant made a timely objection to the prosecutor's peremptory challenges and the court failed to require a race-neutral explanation for the challenges. The matter is remanded for such a determination and, if no proper explanation is offered, the conviction must be reversed. Remanded.

■ CONCURRENCE

(Marshall, J.) The Court's decision takes a giant leap toward eliminating racial discrimination through the use of peremptory challenges, but the only certain cure is the elimination of peremptory challenges completely. The Court's holding addresses only those flagrant demonstrations of racial discrimination that rise to a prima facie case, allowing more subtle discrimination to survive. Even for those flagrant violations, a prosecutor can easily fashion a race-neutral explanation for the challenge, such as the juror's demeanor during voir dire, without the court's exacting scrutiny. The inherent dangers of race-based peremptory challenges can only be eradicated through the abolition of the peremptory challenge.

■ DISSENT

(Burger, J.) The peremptory challenge is essential to ensuring that an impartial jury is selected. The Court's opinion ignores the fact that individuals develop predispositions through common human experiences, including one's race, and that peremptory challenges account for these experiences without the necessity of expressing the truth prevalent in most common stereotypes. Further, while the Court does not require the prosecution's neutral explanation in response to a prima facie showing of discrimination to rise to the level of a challenge for cause, any such explanation may well be seen as arbitrary and capricious, insufficient to rebut the prima facie discrimination.

■ DISSENT

(Rehnquist, J.) The use of a peremptory challenge to exclude a black juror from the jury of a black defendant does not violate the Equal Protection Clause so long as a peremptory challenge can be used to exclude a white juror from a white defendant's jury, Hispanics from a Hispanic defendant's jury, and Asians from an Asian defendant's jury. The peremptory challenge is race neutral, not singling out a specific race for discriminatory treatment. While it may be exercised based on stereotype in a given case, it does not violate the Equal Protection Clause if applied to all races.

Analysis:

While *Batson* marks an important development in criminal procedure, its holding is limited. Notice that in order to challenge race-based peremptory challenges, the Court requires the jury to share the same race as the defendant. If the State uses peremptory challenges to strike black jurors in a murder trial of a white defendant accused of killing a white man, because he had beaten and tortured blacks, the literal language of *Batson* would not apply. The Court has since relaxed the standing requirement to permit a challenge in this circumstance, though a prima facie showing of purposeful discrimination becomes more difficult.

■ CASE VOCABULARY

PEREMPTORY CHALLENGE: One of a party's limited number of challenges that need not be supported by any reason, although a party may not use such a challenge in a way that discriminates on the basis of race, ethnicity, or gender.

BATSON CHALLENGE: A defendant's objection that the prosecution has used peremptory challenges to exclude potential jurors on the basis of race, ethnicity, or gender.

STRIKE: The removal of a prospective juror from the jury panel.

United States v. Thomas

(Prosecuting Government) v. (Convicted Drug Dealer)

116 F.3d 606 (2d Cir. 1997)

A JUROR WHOSE VIEWS ARE BASED, IN PART, ON THE SUFFICIENCY OF THE EVIDENCE SHOULD NOT BE DISQUALIFIED

■ **INSTANT FACTS** An eleven-member jury convicted Thomas (D), a black defendant, on drug charges after the only black juror was disqualified during deliberations.

■ **BLACK LETTER RULE** When the evidence discloses any possibility that a juror's views arise from the sufficiency of the government's evidence, disqualification must be denied.

■ **PROCEDURAL BASIS**

Appeal from a guilty verdict rendered by an eleven-member jury.

■ **FACTS**

During jury selection in Thomas's (D) drug trial, the prosecution sought to exercise a peremptory challenge to exclude the only black person remaining as a potential juror. Because Thomas (D) is black, the defense objected to the peremptory challenge as racially motivated. The court sustained the objection because, while the government's challenge was not racially motivated, the government's reason—that the juror failed to make eye contact with the prosecuting attorney—was an insufficient basis for the strike. The court later explained that the strike was disallowed because the juror was the only remaining black juror in a case involving the black defendant. The juror was later impaneled as "Juror No. 5." After several weeks of trial, a group of jurors informed the court clerk that Juror No. 5 was distracting them during defense counsel's summation by making disruptive noises and indicating agreement with defense counsel's arguments before deliberations. After meeting with counsel, the court ordered each witness interviewed *in camera* to determine the extent of Juror No. 5's disruption and to consider his dismissal from the jury. After questioning each witness about the distractions, seven jurors indicated that Juror No. 5 presented some distraction, but all but one indicated it would not affect their ability to deliberate. Nonetheless, the judge dismissed Juror No. 5 because he feared his actions would create an adversarial environment for deliberations. After objection by defense counsel, however, the judge reconsidered and permitted Juror No. 5 to remain.

After more than a day of deliberation, two jurors separately informed the court clerk that deliberations were prolonged because "an unnamed juror" and "Juror No. 5" were causing problems. After discussion with counsel, the court chose to give the jury more time to deliberate before any action was taken. A day later, a third juror passed a note to the court clerk indicating the jury was unable to reach a verdict because Juror No. 5 held a "predisposed disposition." After additional *in camera* interviews, several jurors specifically identified Juror No. 5 as the cause of the disruption, while others indicated a general tension among the jurors. At least five jurors indicated that Juror No. 5 insisted on acquittal for such reasons as racial unity, a belief that drug dealing was commonplace, a belief that defendants acted out of economic necessity, and a conviction that the prosecution had not met its burden. Juror No. 5 himself informed the judge that he believed the prosecution had not presented sufficient evidence of guilt beyond a reasonable doubt. After hearing argument from counsel, the court disqualified Juror No. 5 because he was unwilling to consider the evidence due to his own preconceived cultural, economic, or social ideas about the case. After dismissing Juror No. 5, the remaining eleven jurors returned a guilty verdict.

■ ISSUE

Did the trial judge err in disqualifying a black juror in a black defendant's drug trial when some evidence suggested his views were based on the sufficiency of the government's evidence?

■ DECISION AND RATIONALE

(Cabranes, J.) Yes. Under Federal Rule of Criminal Procedure 23(b), a trial judge has unilateral authority to order the disqualification of jurors for just cause during the course of deliberations and to proceed with the case using the remaining eleven jurors. Just cause has been previously shown not only when a juror suffers illness or unavailability, but also when he is found unable to fulfill his duty to render an impartial verdict such as when a juror feels threatened by a party to the case or when life circumstances change during the course of deliberations so as to impair his ability to impartially render a verdict. Here, the exposed bias arises from neither physical inability nor change in circumstances, but from a general opposition to the enforcement of criminal drug laws. Just as when a juror disregards the court's instructions due to an event or relationship that renders him impartial, a court is empowered to disqualify a jury who intends to engage in jury nullification. Jury nullification is a power of the jury, not a right to be condoned and preserved by the court. When a court is not successful in preventing jury nullification through instruction and admonition, disqualification is the appropriate remedy. Investigating jury misconduct during deliberation, however, is not an easy task.

The duty to ensure a fair trial must be balanced by the equally important goal of maintaining secrecy over the jury deliberations, which is fundamental to the proper operation of the jury system. To protect juror secrecy, the trial judge must limit his or her inquiries into the mental processes of the jury during deliberations so as to avoid the compulsion of revealing the reasoning underlying a jury's verdict. When just cause can be obtained from evidence not pertaining to the specific deliberations of the jury, the judge must rely on that evidence alone in deciding whether to disqualify a juror. When, however, the juror's bias arises not from an identifiable event or relationship, but from reports of conduct occurring in the jury room outside the view of the court and others, the judge must use carefully tailored inquiries to collect sufficient evidence to determine whether a juror is intent on disregarding the applicable law and court instructions or is simply unpersuaded by the proof presented at trial. When the evidence discloses any possibility that a juror's view arises from the sufficiency of the government's evidence, disqualification must be denied. This low evidentiary standard protects against both the wrongful disqualification of a juror and an intrusion upon the secrecy of jury deliberations. Here, Juror No. 5 should not have been disqualified as there was some evidence provided from Juror No. 5 and other jurors to indicate that at least part of Juror No. 5's views were based on his belief that the government had not met its burden of proof.

Analysis:

The threat of jury nullification underscores the importance of proper, thorough voir dire before trial. Through voir dire, the court can dismiss those jurors most likely to disagree with the enforcement of the law, who are unable to objectively consider the evidence supporting guilt or innocence, and who are likely to impose their own subjective view on the way the law ought to be enforced. A jury must be properly impaneled to further the legislature's interest in regulating and enforcing the law.

■ CASE VOCABULARY

PEREMPTORY CHALLENGE: One of a party's limited number of challenges that need not be supported by any reason, although a party may not use such a challenge in a way that discriminates on the basis of race, ethnicity, or gender.

BATSON CHALLENGE: A defendant's objection that the prosecution has used peremptory challenges to exclude potential jurors on the basis of race, ethnicity, or gender.

STRIKE: The removal of a prospective juror from the jury panel.

IN CAMERA: In the judge's private chambers.

Olden v. Kentucky

(*Convicted Sodomizer*) v. (*Prosecuting State*)

488 U.S. 227, 109 S. Ct. 480, 102 L. Ed. 2d 513 (1988)

DEFENDANTS HAVE A RIGHT TO CROSS-EXAMINE WITNESSES TO ESTABLISH THEIR MOTIVES

■ **INSTANT FACTS** Olden (D) was denied an opportunity to impeach a witness against him on cross-examination to establish his defense theory.

■ **BLACK LETTER RULE** Under the Sixth Amendment, a defendant is entitled to confront witnesses against him, which includes the right of cross-examination.

■ PROCEDURAL BASIS

Certiorari to review a decision of the Kentucky Court of Appeals affirming the defendant's conviction.

■ FACTS

Matthews, a young white woman, was traveling in Kentucky with a friend, Patton, to exchange Christmas gifts with Olden's (D) half brother, Russell, with whom Matthews was having an extramarital affair. According to Matthews, after exchanging gifts, she and Patton went to a local tavern that served predominantly black patrons. After drinking several beers, Matthews became uncomfortable when the bar grew crowded and demanded to Patton that they leave. After Patton refused, Matthews went alone to a nearby table in anger. After a while, Matthews lost track of Patton and was approached by Olden (D), who told her Patton had been involved in a car accident. Olden (D) and a friend, Harris, offered to take Matthews to Patton. After leaving the bar in Harris' car, Olden (D) raped and sodomized Matthews at knifepoint while Harris held her arms. Matthews was then driven to a dump, where two other men joined the group, again raping Matthews. Matthews was then dropped off near Russell's house. Olden (D) and Harris were indicted for kidnapping, rape, and forcible sodomy. The defendants raised the defense of consent, claiming that Matthews had propositioned Olden (D) and left in the car looking for cocaine. By the time of the trial, Matthews and Russell had separated from their spouses and began living together. Olden's (D) theory was that Matthews had fabricated the events to protect her relationship with Russell, who would have grown suspicious upon seeing her leave in Harris's car. At trial, Olden (D) argued that his defense required that he be allowed to introduce evidence of Matthews' and Russell's cohabitation. The court granted the prosecution's motion *in limine* to exclude reference to the cohabitation and denied Olden's (D) attempt at impeachment after Matthews testified under direct examination that she was then living with her mother. Olden (D) was acquitted by a jury of kidnapping and rape, but convicted of forcible sodomy. Olden (D) appealed, arguing that the court's refusal to allow him to impeach Matthews violated his Sixth Amendment right to confront witnesses against him. The Kentucky Court of Appeals upheld the conviction, holding that the evidence, while relevant, was outweighed by its prejudicial effect in light of its probative value, because it would expose Matthews' interracial relationship with Russell.

■ ISSUE

Did the court deny the defendant's Sixth Amendment right to confront witnesses against him by refusing to allow impeachment evidence on cross-examination?

■ DECISION AND RATIONALE

(Per curiam.) Yes. The Sixth Amendment right to confront a witness, applicable to the states through the Fourteenth Amendment, includes the right to cross-examine that witness at trial in order to impeach or otherwise discredit her testimony. Here, Olden's (D) consent defense required evidence of Matthews' alleged motive to lie about the rape in order to protect her relationship with Russell. Given an opportunity to hear the defendant's theory of the case on cross-examination, a reasonable juror could have questioned Matthews' credibility and reached a different verdict. Any prejudice caused by revealing Matthews' interracial relationship was speculative and does not outweigh the strong potential to establish her motive to lie. Matthews' testimony was corroborated only by Russell's, whose impartiality must be questioned in light of his relationship with Matthews. Additionally, the guilty verdict against Olden (D) on only the sodomy charge and not on rape and kidnapping demonstrates that the evidence supporting conviction was far from overwhelming. Reversed and remanded.

Analysis:

Commentators suggest that the Supreme Court agreed to hear this case not to establish new Sixth Amendment law, but to reverse the conviction based on a troublesome jury verdict. Deciding the case *per curiam,* the Court questions Matthews' inconsistent statements, acknowledges the jury's unusual verdict (convicting Olden (D) of sodomy but not of rape or kidnapping), and notes the weakness of the State's case.

■ CASE VOCABULARY

CONFRONTATION CLAUSE: The Sixth Amendment provision guaranteeing a criminal defendant's right to directly confront an accusing witness and to cross-examine that witness.

CROSS–EXAMINATION: The questioning of a witness at a trial or hearing by a party opposed to the party who called the witness to testify.

PER CURIAM: By the court as a whole.

Maryland v. Craig

(Prosecuting State) v. *(Convicted Child Abuser)*

497 U.S. 836, 110 S. Ct. 3157, 111 L. Ed. 2d 666 (1990)

CHILD WITNESSES MAY BE QUESTIONED WITHOUT THE DEFENDANT "PRESENT"

Bring the hamster out here. I demand to meet my accuser whiskers-to-whiskers.

stus.com

■ **INSTANT FACTS** Craig (D) was convicted on the basis of a child abuse victim's one-way closed-circuit testimony.

■ **BLACK LETTER RULE** When necessary to protect a child witness from trauma that would be caused by testifying in the physical presence of the defendant, impairing the child's ability to communicate, the Confrontation Clause does not prohibit use of a procedure that, despite the absence of a face-to-face confrontation, ensures the reliability of the evidence by subjecting it to rigorous adversarial testing and thereby preserves the essence of effective confrontation.

■ **PROCEDURAL BASIS**

Certiorari to review a decision of the Maryland Court of Special Appeals affirming the defendant's conviction.

■ **FACTS**

Craig (D) was charged with child abuse of a six-year-old girl attending her kindergarten center. Before the case went to trial, the State sought to introduce the testimony of the girl through a one-way closed-circuit television under a Maryland state procedure. To invoke the procedure, the judge must find that the child victim's in-court testimony will cause the child serious emotional distress, preventing her from reasonably communicating. If allowed, the child witness, the prosecutor, and defense counsel retire to a separate room, where the child is questioned. The questioning is displayed on a monitor in the courtroom for the judge and jury to view. The defendant is entitled to electronically communicate with her attorney, but the witness is unable to see or hear the defendant. The State offered expert testimony indicating the in-court testimony would likely cause the child serious emotional distress. Over the defendant's Confrontation Clause objection, the court allowed the procedure as the child was competent to testify, and the essence of the Confrontation Clause is maintained through cross-examination, the right to view the witness, and the right to have the jury view the child's demeanor. Craig (D) was convicted and the Maryland Court of Special Appeals affirmed.

■ **ISSUE**

Does the Sixth Amendment's Confrontation Clause allow a child witness in a child abuse case to testify against a defendant at trial, outside the defendant's physical presence, by one-way closed-circuit television?

■ **DECISION AND RATIONALE**

(O'Connor, J.) Yes. The Confrontation Clause does not afford a defendant the absolute right to a face-to-face encounter with witnesses against her. The essence of the Confrontation Clause is to "ensure the reliability of the evidence against a criminal defendant by subjecting it to rigorous testing in the context of an adversary proceeding before the trier of fact." While this is typically accomplished through a face-to-face meeting with the witness in the courtroom, the Confrontation Clause is not without exceptions when the court makes an individualized finding that a child witness requires special protections from the emotional trauma of face-to-face testimony. A "confrontation" need not be face-to-face as long as the witness is subjected to examination under oath and the jury is permitted to view the demeanor of the witness to judge her credibility. The admission of presumptively reliable hearsay statements, for example, demonstrates circumstances in which a face-to-face confrontation is not required because adequate proof of their reliability outweighs any burden on Confrontation Clause rights. While the Confrontation Clause expresses a preference for face-to-face meetings, they are not required in every instance. The Maryland procedure includes all the procedural protections required to dispense with a face-to-face confrontation. It requires the judge to ensure the child is competent to testify under oath, affords the defendant the full opportunity to cross-examine the child, and allows the jury to witness the questioning to determine the child's demeanor as she testifies. The State's interest in protecting the physical and psychological well-being of child abuse victims is sufficiently important to outweigh the defendant's right to a face-to-face encounter.

■ DISSENT

(Scalia, J.) The unmistakable language of the Sixth Amendment allows a defendant a face-to-face encounter with witnesses against him that cannot yield to the public policy concerns expressed by the Court. The Court reaches the implausible conclusion that face-to-face confrontation is merely one "element" of confrontation. It identifies the right by the purposes it achieves, and then eliminates the right itself. Using dicta from prior decisions and claiming to follow Supreme Court precedent, the Court seeks to assure reliable evidence at trial when the Confrontation Clause's plain language provides only a specific means for achieving such a goal. The Court is not permitted to engage in a cost-benefit analysis of the plain language of the Sixth Amendment and then alter its meaning to meet its desired findings. If the Sixth Amendment is better served by dispensing with face-to-face confrontation, it must be done through further amendment, not judicial intervention.

Analysis:

he key to the Court's decision here was an individualized finding that the child abuse victim would suffer serious emotional trauma that would impair her ability to communicate. Earlier, in *Coy v. Iowa*, the Court held that the use of an in-court screen to obstruct the witness's view of the defendant violated the Confrontation Clause because it relied on a statute that presumed trauma would result from a face-to-face encounter. Such a presumption does not provide a strong enough governmental interest to outweigh a defendant's Sixth Amendment rights.

■ CASE VOCABULARY

CONFRONTATION CLAUSE: The Sixth Amendment provision guaranteeing a criminal defendant's right to directly confront an accusing witness and to cross-examine that witness.

CROSS–EXAMINATION: The questioning of a witness at a trial or hearing by a party opposed to the party who called the witness to testify.

Crawford v. Washington

(Convicted Assailant) v. *(Prosecuting Authority)*

541 U.S. 36, 124 S. Ct. 1354, 158 L. Ed. 2d 177 (2004)

THE CONFRONTATION CLAUSE APPLIES TO STATEMENTS GIVEN TO POLICE

■ **INSTANT FACTS** The state sought to introduce a statement Crawford's (D) wife gave to investigating officers, though she refused to testify at trial on marital privilege grounds; Crawford (D) argued that admitting the statement would violate the Confrontation Clause.

■ **BLACK LETTER RULE** The Sixth Amendment guarantee that the accused in a criminal prosecution shall enjoy the right to be confronted with the witnesses against him extends beyond in-court testimony and includes statements resulting from police interrogations.

■ **PROCEDURAL BASIS**

Supreme Court review of the defendant's conviction.

■ **FACTS**

Crawford (D) and his wife, Sylvia, went together to the home of Lee, who had allegedly tried to rape Sylvia earlier. Crawford (D) and Sylvia were arrested that night and provided with *Miranda* warnings. Both gave tape-recorded statements that were in substantial agreement, but Sylvia's statement differed from Crawford's (D) with respect to whether Lee had drawn a weapon before Crawford (D) assaulted him. Crawford (D) was charged with assault and attempted murder, and pleaded self-defense. Sylvia asserted her marital privilege and refused to testify at Crawford's (D) trial, but the state sought to introduce her recorded statement into evidence, arguing that it was admissible under the exception to the rule against hearsay for a statement against penal interest, since in providing the statement Sylvia had implicated herself in the crime.

Crawford (D) argued that the admission of Sylvia's statement would violate his Sixth Amendment right to confront witnesses against him. The trial court concluded, however, that the right, described in *Ohio v. Roberts*, does not bar admission of unavailable witnesses' statements if such statements bear sufficient indicia of reliability. To satisfy that test, the evidence must either fall within a firmly rooted hearsay exception or bear particularized guarantees of trustworthiness. The court admitted Sylvia's statement based on its trustworthiness, and the jury convicted Crawford (D) of assault. The court of appeals reversed, but the state supreme court reinstated Crawford's (D) conviction, holding that an unavailable witness's statement is sufficiently reliable when it is substantially identical to a co-defendant's confession.

■ **ISSUE**

Was Crawford's (D) wife's recorded statement admissible against him, where she refused to testify on the ground of marital privilege and he therefore had no opportunity to cross-examine her?

■ **DECISION AND RATIONALE**

(Scalia, J.) No. The Sixth Amendment guarantee that the accused in a criminal prosecution shall enjoy the right to be confronted with the witnesses against him extends beyond in-court testimony and includes statements resulting from police interrogations. Because the constitutional text itself does not clarify exactly what the Sixth Amendment guarantee includes, we must turn to the historical underpinnings of the Confrontation Clause to fully understand its meaning. The Clause has its roots in Roman law, and the issue arose many times throughout the history of the English common law and in the Colonies as well. Cases such as the famous treason trial of Sir Walter Raleigh gave rise to the principle that justice cannot be served if out-of-court statements are used against a defendant without availing him the opportunity to confront his accusers face to face.

The expansive history of the Confrontation Clause supports two inferences. First, the Sixth Amendment is not solely concerned with in-court testimony; rather, its primary concern is "testimonial hearsay," and police interrogations, like that involved here, fall within that class. Second, the Framers of the Constitution would not have allowed admission of testimonial statements from witnesses who did not appear at trial unless they were unavailable *and* the defendant had a prior opportunity for cross-examination. As this body of law developed, the cross-examination requirement became dispositive. Supreme Court precedent is in accord with this history. Testimonial statements of witnesses absent from trial have been held admissible only when the declarant was unavailable and the defendant had a prior opportunity to cross-examine.

The *Roberts* test for admissibility, which requires a firmly established hearsay exception or sufficient indicia of trustworthiness, is both too broad and too narrow, and it departs from historical principles. Accordingly, we reject those standards. The Framers would not have wanted the application of constitutional guarantees to hinge on the vagaries of evidence rules, much less on amorphous notions of "reliability." Dispensing with the confrontation requirement because the evidence is obviously reliable is like dispensing with a jury trial because the defendant is obviously guilty. This is not what the Sixth Amendment prescribes.

We could resolve the present case simply by applying the *Roberts* factors and concluding that Sylvia's statement was unreliable, but that would be a failure to interpret the Constitution in a way that secures its intended restraint on judicial discretion. Judges cannot always be relied upon to safeguard the rights of the people. Vague standards, as applied in *Roberts*, are manipulable. Where testimonial statements are at issue, the only true indicium of reliability sufficient to satisfy Constitutional demands is the right to confrontation.

■ CONCURRENCE IN PART, DISSENT IN PART

(Rehnquist, C.J.) I concur in the judgment, but I dissent from the majority's decision to overrule *Roberts*. The court's rationale is not any better rooted in history than current doctrine.

Analysis:

Crawford v. Washington marked a significant change in the Supreme Court's interpretation of the Confrontation Clause after nearly a quarter-century of tinkering. *Crawford* left prosecutors, defense attorneys, and courts throughout the country scrambling to figure out the resulting constitutional contours of evidence law. The Court followed *Crawford* with *Davis v. Washington*, in which it refined its definition of what constitutes a testimonial statement in the context of 911 calls and statements to the police at the scene of a crime. Still, *Crawford* and *Davis* leave many questions unanswered, one of the most intriguing of which involves the application of *Crawford* to the testimony of experts. Lower court opinions have yielded conflicting decisions.

■ CASE VOCABULARY

HEARSAY: Traditionally, testimony that is given by a witness who relates not what he or she knows personally, but what others have said, and that is therefore dependent on the credibility of someone other than the witness. Such testimony is generally inadmissible under the rules of evidence. In federal law, a statement (either a verbal assertion or nonverbal assertive conduct), other than one made by the declarant while testifying at the trial or hearing, offered in evidence to prove the truth of the matter asserted.

Cruz v. New York

(Convicted Murderer) v. *(Prosecuting State)*

481 U.S. 186, 107 S. Ct. 1714, 95 L. Ed. 2d 162 (1987)

A LIMITING JURY INSTRUCTION DOES NOT UNDO THE DAMAGE OF A WRONGFULLY ADMITTED CONFESSION

I'm instructing you to ignore the co-defendant's confession, even though I know you won't.

stus.com

■ **INSTANT FACTS** Eulogio Cruz (D) was convicted of felony murder after the introduction of the confession of his nontestifying co-defendant, which corroborated Eulogio's (D) earlier pretrial confession.

■ **BLACK LETTER RULE** When a non-testifying codefendant's confession incriminating the defendant is not directly admissible against the defendant, the Confrontation Clause bars its admission at their joint trial, even if the jury is instructed not to consider it against the defendant, and even if the defendant's own confession is admitted against him.

■ **PROCEDURAL BASIS**

Certiorari to review a decision of the New York Court of Appeals affirming the defendants' convictions.

■ **FACTS**

In March 1982, Jerry Cruz was murdered in New York (although this is not the murder for which the defendants here were convicted). After questioning Jerry's brother, Norberto, the police learned that Benjamin (D) and Eulogio Cruz (D), two brothers unrelated to Jerry and Norberto, had appeared at Norberto's apartment in November 1981, where Eulogio (D) admitted that Benjamin (D) had killed a gas station attendant after he shot Eulogio (D) while they attempted to rob the gas station the night before. In May 1982, the police questioned Benjamin (D) about Jerry's murder. Denying any involvement and growing frustrated with the unwillingness of the police to believe him, Benjamin (D) spontaneously confessed to murdering the gas station attendant to prove that he would tell the truth about Jerry's murder if he had committed it. That evening, he gave a detailed videotaped confession to the Assistant District Attorney implicating Eulogio (D) in the murder of the gas station attendant. Benjamin (D) and Eulogio (D) were indicted for felony murder. Tried jointly over Eulogio's (D) objection, the prosecutor was permitted to introduce Benjamin's (D) videotaped confession to the jury with an instruction that it was not to be considered against Eulogio (D). Norberto was called to testify about Eulogio's (D) November 1981 confession to his role in the gas station attendant's murder, which was the only admissible evidence linking him to the crime. Benjamin (D) did not testify at trial. Eulogio (D) claimed that Norberto fabricated the November 1981 encounter because he suspected that Eulogio (D) and Benjamin (D) had killed Jerry. The jury convicted both defendants. The New York Court of Appeals affirmed, holding that Eulogio's (D) earlier confession was "interlocked" with Benjamin's (D) videotaped confession.

■ **ISSUE**

Does the introduction into evidence of a nontestifying co-defendant's interlocking confession, corroborating that of the defendant, violate the Sixth Amendment's Confrontation Clause?

■ DECISION AND RATIONALE

(Scalia, J.) Yes. A defendant's Sixth Amendment right to confront witnesses against him affords the defendant the right to cross-examine those witnesses. When two or more defendants are tried jointly, a pretrial confession of one defendant that implicates another is admissible only against the confessing defendant unless the confessing defendant waives his Fifth Amendment right against self-incrimination. A witness is generally a witness against a defendant only if his testimony is admissible to the jury.

In *Bruton v. United States*, the Court held that the admission of a confession of a co-defendant with a limiting instruction that it not be used against the defendant at trial violates the Confrontation Clause when the co-defendant chooses to exercise his Fifth Amendment right and not testify at trial and introduction of the confession would confuse the jury. Thereafter, in *Parker v. Randolph*, the Court revisited the issue and held that when each defendant tried jointly individually confesses to the crime charged, the Confrontation Clause is not violated by introduction of a co-defendant's confession because the evidence will result in no "devastating effect" upon the defendant as the defendant has already devastated his case by his own confession. The right of confrontation will be of little benefit to the defendant at trial in such circumstances. The devastating effect of the confession, however, is but one factor to consider in assessing a Confrontation Clause violation. Each confession stands on its own, leaving open the questions of whether a confession was truly made and the extent of that confessing defendant's culpability for the crime, even when the defendants' confessions "interlock."

The fact that the defendant's confession interlocks here with that of the co-defendant demonstrates the devastating effect of its introduction. If the two confessions do not interlock, the co-defendant's confession will be relatively harmless since they provide two different accounts of the crime, helping to support the defendant's case. Only when the confessions do interlock does devastation occur. As a practical matter, a defendant at trial is seeking to avoid his earlier confession as inaccurately reported or not truly made. If the defendant stands by his confession, there is no need to introduce the confession of his co-defendant at all. An interlocking confession by a non-testifying co-defendant must be considered under the same factors set forth in *Bruton*—the likelihood that the limiting instruction will be disregarded by the jury, the probability that such disregard will have a devastating effect, and the determinability of those facts in advance of trial. The interlocking nature of a co-defendant's confession concerns not the harmfulness of the confession, but its reliability in terms of whether it should be admitted into evidence; its reliability is irrelevant, however, to whether a jury would be likely to disregard a limiting instruction. Because Benjamin (D) did not testify at trial, his confession incriminating Eulogio (D) is not directly admissible against Eulogio (D) even if the jury is instructed not to consider it against him.

■ DISSENT

(White, J.) While in *Bruton* the defendant did not himself confess, Eulogio (D) did make such a confession and his confession was properly admitted into evidence. It makes little sense to require the exclusion of Benjamin's (D) interlocking confession under such circumstances. A defendant's own confession is the most reliable evidence of his guilt and a jury is unlikely to disregard it even if instructed to do so. This is no less true when a co-defendant's confession interlocks with the defendant's confession. The consideration of the co-defendant's confession is not remotely likely to create a devastating effect on the defendant's case. The rule established by the Court threatens to eliminate the practice of joint trials, wasting state funds, inconveniencing witnesses and public authorities, and risking inconsistent verdicts. There is no Sixth Amendment violation when the defendant himself confesses to the crime.

Analysis:

The right-to-confrontation problem is relieved when the confessing co-defendant testifies at trial and subjects himself to cross-examination. Prosecutors may offer a plea bargain to reduce the charges brought against the co-defendant in exchange for the co-defendant's willingness to testify against the defendant. *See* Chapter 15, *infra*. Additionally, the co-defendant's confession may be redacted so as to remove any "interlocking" references, though a limiting instruction must still be given to the jury.

■ CASE VOCABULARY

CONFRONTATION CLAUSE: The Sixth Amendment provision guaranteeing a criminal defendant's right to directly confront an accusing witness and to cross-examine that witness.

CROSS–EXAMINATION: The questioning of a witness at a trial or hearing by a party opposed to the party who called the witness to testify.

FELONY MURDER: Murder that occurs during the commission of a dangerous felony (often limited to rape, kidnapping, robbery, burglary, and arson).

Gray v. Maryland

(Convicted Murderer) v. *(Prosecuting State)*

523 U.S. 185, 118 S. Ct. 1151, 140 L. Ed. 2d 294 (1998)

A REDACTED CONFESSION OF A CO–DEFENDANT IS INADMISSIBLE IN A JOINT TRIAL

■ **INSTANT FACTS** Gray (D) was convicted after a redacted confession of a co-defendant was offered at their joint trial with a limiting instruction.

■ **BLACK LETTER RULE** The use of blanks or "deleted" references in a redacted confession of a co-defendant may not be offered against a defendant at a joint trial, even with a limiting instruction.

■ **PROCEDURAL BASIS**

Certiorari to review the defendant's conviction.

■ **FACTS**

Anthony Bell confessed to Baltimore police that he, Gray (D), and another man had beaten a young woman, resulting in her death. Bell and Gray (D) were indicted for murder and were tried jointly. At trial, the court permitted the introduction into evidence of a redacted version of Bell's confession, with a limiting instruction to the jury. The officer who read the redacted confession used the term "deleted" whenever reference was made to Gray's (D) name. Immediately after reading the redacted confession, the officer testified that on the basis of that confession, he arrested Gray (D). The written confession was offered to the jury with Gray's (D) name stricken to leave a white space where reference to his involvement was made. Bell did not testify at the trial, but Gray (D) denied his participation in the murder. The jury convicted both Bell and Gray (D) of murder.

■ **ISSUE**

Does the redaction of a co-defendant's confession to exclude specific reference to the defendant, but leaving blank spaces where defendant's name had appeared, violate the Sixth Amendment's Confrontation Clause when offered at a joint trial with a limiting instruction to the jury to consider it only against the confessing co-defendant?

■ **DECISION AND RATIONALE**

(Breyer, J.) Yes. In *Bruton v. United States*, the Court held that the admission of a co-defendant's confession with a limiting instruction that it not be used against the defendant at trial violates the Confrontation Clause when the co-defendant chooses to exercise his Fifth Amendment right and not testify at trial and introduction of the confession would confuse the jury. That rule was limited by *Richardson v. Marsh*, in which the Court held that the admission of a confession that is not incriminating on its face and requires additional evidence to link the defendant to the crime does not violate the Confrontation Clause. The obvious deletion of a name and insertion of the term "deleted," however, presents the same prejudice to the defendant as a confession that directly implicates him by name, which must be excluded under the Confrontation Clause. Jurors are intelligent enough to realize that the omitted name is that of the defendant and, if the jurors' intelligence is discounted, human curiosity will lead them to wonder to whom the blank references relate. With the defendant in the courtroom and the

---

judge's limiting instruction not to consider the confession against him, jurors will logically make the link between the blank confession and the defendant. All the while, the attention given to the redaction overemphasizes the defendant's role in the crime. While redactions may be used to relieve the confession's devastating effects upon the defendant, redactions that insert blank spaces or the term "deleted," as a class, violate the Sixth Amendment's Confrontation Clause. These redactions, though dependent on inference to link them to the defendant, refer directly to someone, often the defendant, and facially incriminate the defendant. Only when the inference to be drawn requires additional evidence to link the defendant to the crime is a redacted confession admissible.

■ DISSENT

(Scalia, J.) The Court, on the one hand, concedes that inference is required to link the redacted confession to the defendant, and on the other hand, holds that it facially incriminates him. The two cannot co-exist. The confession is facially incriminating only if it does so independent of other evidence. While some redactions may facially link the confession to the defendant, the use of blanks or the term "deleted" does not. Though the jury may speculate, these generic terms do not directly refer to the defendant nor allow a permissible link to him without additional evidence. The Confrontation Clause should exclude only those confessions that, unlike here, facially identify the defendant without resort to inference or speculation. To permit introduction of a redacted confession by eliminating all reference to the defendant would render the confession nonsensical and untrue. If a co-defendant implicates another person, a court must not restructure his words in order to make his confession appropriate for introduction in a joint trial. The use of blanks or "deleted" maintains the integrity of the confession and, requiring a reasonable inference to connect it to the defendant, does not violate the Confrontation Clause.

Analysis:

Gray demonstrates the difficulty in redacting a co-defendant's confession for use in a joint trial. While redactions can be used to relieve Confrontation Clause concerns over the admission of a co-defendant's confession at a joint trial, they must remain true to their content to secure conviction of the confessing co-defendant while at the same time protecting the other defendant from incrimination without a right of cross-examination. Of course, if the co-defendant himself chooses to testify, Confrontation Clause concerns are relieved.

■ CASE VOCABULARY

REDACTION: The careful editing of a document, especially to remove confidential references or offensive material.

United States v. Burr

(Prosecuting Government) v. *(Defendant Charged with Treason)*
25 Fed. Cas. 30 (D. Va. 1807) (No. 14,692D)

THE SIXTH AMENDMENT REQUIRES EVEN THE PRESIDENT TO TURN OVER DOCUMENTS

■ **INSTANT FACTS** Burr (D) subpoenaed documents from the President of the United States.

■ **BLACK LETTER RULE** The Sixth Amendment right to compel witnesses includes the right to compel production of documents within the witness' possession.

■ PROCEDURAL BASIS

Trial court ruling on a motion for a subpoena duces tecum.

■ FACTS

Burr (D) moved the court for a subpoena duces tecum requiring President Jefferson to produce a letter from General Wilkinson to the President relating to Burr (D) and the President's response to the letter. Burr (D) claimed the letters were material to his defense against the treason charges against him.

■ ISSUE

Does the Sixth Amendment right to compel the attendance of witnesses at trial permit a defendant to direct a subpoena duces tecum to the President of the United States?

■ DECISION AND RATIONALE

(Marshall, C.J.) Yes. The Sixth Amendment provides a defendant with a compulsory process for obtaining witnesses in his or her favor. This right extends beyond compulsory attendance at trial and requires the production of documents from those compulsory witnesses as well. No exception is stated for the President of the United States. As long as the documents requested are relevant to the defense and the Government offers no strong justification, such as national security, to withhold them, the Sixth Amendment requires their production.

Analysis:

Interestingly, Chief Justice Marshall, sitting as trial judge because of the political significance of this case, enforced the Sixth Amendment against President Jefferson because there is no exception for the President in the language of the Sixth Amendment. Yet he construes the defendant's right to "obtain witnesses in his favor" to include the right to obtain documents within the witness's possession, though the language fails to so provide. Few cases have challenged the right to compulsory process because most defendants are afforded full subpoena powers in a criminal trial.

■ CASE VOCABULARY

SUBPOENA DUCES TECUM: A subpoena ordering the witness to appear and to bring specified documents or records.

Taylor v. Illinois

(Attempted Murderer) v. *(Prosecuting State)*

484 U.S. 400, 108 S. Ct. 646, 98 L. Ed. 2d 798 (1988)

LATE–DISCLOSED WITNESSES CANNOT TESTIFY

■ **INSTANT FACTS** Taylor (D) was convicted of attempted murder after the testimony of a favorable witness was excluded because of discovery violations.

■ **BLACK LETTER RULE** The *per se* exclusion of evidence knowingly disclosed in violation of discovery rules does not violate the Compulsory Process Clause.

■ **PROCEDURAL BASIS**

Certiorari to review a decision of the Illinois Appellate Court affirming the conviction.

■ **FACTS**

Bridges was involved in an argument with Travis on a Chicago street. About an hour later, Taylor (D), Travis, and others confronted Bridges and beat him. Prosecution witnesses testified that as Bridges attempted to flee, Taylor (D) drew a gun and shot him in the back. After Bridges fell, Taylor (D) pointed the gun at Bridges' head, but the gun misfired. Two friends of Taylor testified for the defense that Bridges' brother was the shooter and that he had fired the gun into the group and shot Bridges. Prior to trial, the prosecutor filed a discovery motion seeking the identification of all defense witnesses. The defense originally identified the two friends and two other witnesses who did not testify. On the day of the trial, the court allowed defense counsel to amend his response to include Travis and a Chicago police officer, though neither testified at trial. On the second day of trial and after the prosecution had offered witness testimony, defense counsel again moved to amend his discovery response to include two more witnesses, including Wormley, who had witnessed the entire incident, or so defense counsel claimed to have just recently discovered. Defense counsel represented that he had informed the prosecution about Wormley, but that Wormley was not named in discovery because he could not locate him. Concerned with the failure to disclose Wormley earlier, the court required Wormley to appear as an offer of proof. Wormley testified outside the presence of the jury that he had not seen the incident but that he had witnessed Bridges and his brother with guns wrapped in a blanket and that they were looking for Taylor (D) prior to the shooting. On cross-examination, Wormley admitted he had met Taylor (D) only four months prior to the trial and acknowledged that defense counsel had met with him in his home a week earlier. Finding that the testimony contradicted defense counsel's representations to the court, Wormley was not allowed to testify. Defendant was later convicted of attempted murder, and the Illinois Appellate Court affirmed.

■ **ISSUE**

Does the court's refusal to allow testimony of a witness who the defendant willfully failed to identify during pretrial discovery violate the defendant's right to obtain the testimony of favorable witnesses?

■ **DECISION AND RATIONALE**

(Stevens, J.) No. While the Sixth Amendment's Compulsory Process Clause allows a defendant the right to use the subpoena power to compel the testimony of favorable witnesses, it does not permit the admission of incompetent, privileged, or otherwise inadmissible testimony. The State's interest in enforcing firm rules of evidence to govern an orderly criminal trial must be considered together with the defendant's right to compel his witness's testimony to establish competent evidence of the facts in his favor. Discovery rules, like cross-examination, are a necessary tool in balancing these interests to ensure that the evidence at trial is complete and trustworthy. The exclusion of evidence for blatant violations of the rules of discovery is an appropriate sanction. While a continuance, an order for mistrial, or disciplinary sanctions are less burdensome on the defendant's right to compulsory process, they are less effective sanctions and threaten the integrity of the adversary system. A defendant facing potential imprisonment will not likely be deterred from fabricating evidence merely under the threat of potential disciplinary sanctions. Just as evidence that is not discovered until the end of the trial is presumed not to have affected the outcome, evidence that is produced at the eleventh hour must be considered suspect. The trial judge may request an explanation for such late production and, if the reasons indicate a willful violation of the discovery rules, exclusion of the witness is the proper sanction. Exclusion is required not because the prosecution has been prejudiced, but because of the detrimental effect willful discovery violations have on the judicial process. Even when the prosecution can minimize the prejudice through voir dire, the blatant abuse of the discovery process mandates the harsh sanction. Here, defense counsel had interviewed Wormley in his home one week prior to trial. Despite amending his discovery responses on the day trial began, he did not list Wormley as a potential witness. The only inference that can be drawn from this conduct is that the defendant, accountable for the actions of his attorney, sought to gain a tactical advantage by fabricating the witness's testimony and depriving the prosecution a meaningful opportunity to rebut it.

■ DISSENT

(Brennan, J.) While discovery violations must be sanctioned to ensure the full truth-seeking function of the court, the sanction imposed by the court does not further that objective. Depriving a defendant the opportunity to present favorable witnesses because of discovery violations committed by his attorney excludes material evidence that may establish his innocence. When the defendant has no personal involvement in the violation and less restrictive sanctions are available, exclusion of the testimony should not be the *per se* sanction. Sanctions serve to remedy the negative effects of discovery violations and deter them for recurring. Less restrictive sanctions, when adequate to serve these purposes, effectively strike the balance between the State's interests in fully preparing its case and the defendant's Sixth Amendment rights.

Analysis:

The decisions of counsel, such as the knowing violation of the rules of discovery, generally bind the client because of the attorney-client relationship. Some decisions, however, are considered personal to the client, requiring the attorney to honor the client's wishes in deciding a course of action. Such decisions as whether to enter a guilty plea, waive a jury trial, and testify at trial must be honored by counsel. Failure to abide by the client's wishes in these circumstances constitutes ineffective assistance of counsel.

■ CASE VOCABULARY

COMPULSORY PROCESS CLAUSE: The clause of the Sixth Amendment to the U.S. Constitution giving criminal defendants the subpoena power for obtaining witnesses in their favor.

SUBPOENA: A writ commanding a person to appear before a court or other tribunal, subject to a penalty for failing to comply.

OFFER OF PROOF: A presentation of evidence for the record (but outside the jury's presence), usually made after the judge has sustained an objection to the admissibility of that evidence, so that the evidence can be preserved on the record for an appeal of the judge's ruling.

Griffin v. California

(Convicted Murderer) v. *(Prosecuting State)*

380 U.S. 609, 85 S. Ct. 1229, 14 L. Ed. 2d 106 (1965)

COMMENTS ON A DEFENDANT'S REFUSAL TO TESTIFY ARE NOT ALLOWED

■ **INSTANT FACTS** Griffin (D) was convicted of murder after the prosecutor commented on his failure to testify on his own behalf.

■ **BLACK LETTER RULE** The Fifth Amendment, in its direct application to the federal government and in its bearing on the states by the Fourteenth Amendment, forbids a prosecutor from commenting on a defendant's decision not to testify at his trial and court instructions that the defendant's silence is evidence of his guilt.

■ PROCEDURAL BASIS

Certiorari to review the decision of the California Supreme Court affirming the defendant's conviction.

■ FACTS

Griffin's (D) California murder trial was bifurcated on the issues of guilt and penalty. While the defendant did not testify during the trial of his guilt, the judge instructed the jury, in accordance with the California Constitution, that the failure of the defendant to explain or deny facts or evidence against him of which the defendant can be reasonably assumed to have knowledge justifies an inference of the truth of those facts. The court warned, however, that no such inference can be drawn if it is determined that the defendant had no knowledge of the facts. The evidence at trial indicated that on the night of the murder, Griffin (D) was with the victim in the alley where her body was found. As permitted by the state constitution, the Government made numerous comments to the jury regarding Griffin's (D) failure to testify and rebut the evidence against him. The jury convicted the defendant of murder and the death penalty was imposed. The California Supreme Court affirmed the conviction.

■ ISSUE

Does comment on a defendant's failure to testify on his own behalf to rebut evidence offered against him violate the Fifth Amendment right against self-incrimination as applied to the states?

■ DECISION AND RATIONALE

(Douglas, J.) Yes. In federal court, it is well established that a prosecutor's comment on a defendant's failure to testify constitutes reversible error as a violation of a federal statute. The same reasoning underlying the federal statute applies to the Fifth Amendment. Both preserve the presumption of innocence and recognize that the reasons for a defendant's refusal to take the stand may vary, including nervousness, timidity, and the desire to avoid impeachment on cross-examination. An evidentiary rule, such as that within the California Constitution, that penalizes a defendant for asserting his constitutional rights cannot be applied by the courts. Even if a jury reaches an inference of guilt from the defendant's silence, the court must not solemnize such an inference by highlighting the defendant's refusal to testify. The Fifth Amendment, as applied to the federal courts directly and to the state courts by the Fourteenth Amendment, forbids comment on the accused's silence or instructions from the court that the accused's silence is evidence of his guilt.

■ CONCURRENCE

(Harlan, J.) Because the Court has previously held that the Fifth Amendment applies to the States through the Fourteenth Amendment, a state prosecutor may not comment on the refusal of the defendant to take the stand. However, the Court's conclusion, while correct under prior precedent, demonstrates the continuing expansion of the incorporation doctrine, which constitutes a significant departure from historical constitutional jurisprudence.

■ DISSENT

(Stewart, J.) At issue is whether prosecutorial comments concerning a defendant's failure to testify on his own behalf compel him to be a witness against himself in violation of the Fifth and Fourteenth Amendments. The compulsion that gave rise to the Fifth Amendment concerned the necessity that one tried with a crime answer questions favorable to the Government for fear of incarceration, banishment, or mutilation. The state practice of allowing comment on the failure to testify and permitting an inference of the truth of uncontested evidence stretches the limits of the meaning of compulsion. A comment concerning a defendant's refusal to provide rebutting testimony does not compel his testimony, as the comment does nothing more than demonstrate the obvious fact that the defendant has not testified and, therefore, has offered no evidence to rebut that which the State has offered against him. A jury instruction warning the jury that the defendant's failure to testify does not constitute his guilt creates no more impermissible inference than if the jury were set free to weigh this fact on its own. States must be free to establish the rules governing their courts. The California procedure does nothing more than bring forward a fact obvious from the proceedings with instructions to the jury to limit any impermissible inferences it may draw from it. The procedure does not compel the defendant to testify, as he did not in fact testify at his trial, and there is no Fifth Amendment violation.

Analysis:

While comment by the court on the defendant's failure to testify violates the Fifth Amendment, the Court here reserved the question of whether the defendant can request the court to comment and instruct the jury of the reasonable inferences they may draw from his refusal to testify. Later, in *Carter v. Kentucky*, the Court addressed this issue, concluding that a defendant has a right to request an instruction that the jury may draw no inference from the defendant's refusal to testify. The Court has also held that a judge's decision to provide a "no-inference" instruction, as opposed to the "negative-inference" instruction given in *Griffin*, does not violate the Fifth Amendment.

■ CASE VOCABULARY

SELF–INCRIMINATION CLAUSE: The clause of the Fifth Amendment to the U.S. Constitution barring the government from compelling criminal defendants to testify against themselves.

BIFURCATED TRIAL: A trial that is divided into two stages, such as for guilt and punishment or for liability and damages.

United States v. Thomas

(Prosecuting Government) v. *(Convicted Drug Dealer)*
116 F.3d 606 (2d Cir. 1997)

A JUROR WHOSE VIEWS ARE BASED, IN PART, ON THE SUFFICIENCY OF THE EVIDENCE SHOULD NOT BE DISQUALIFIED

I got a unanimous verdict by kicking the dissenter.

I smell an appeal coming.

stus.com

■ **INSTANT FACTS** An eleven-member jury convicted Thomas (D), a black defendant, on drug charges after the only black juror was disqualified during deliberations.

■ **BLACK LETTER RULE** When the evidence discloses any possibility that a juror's views arise from the sufficiency of the government's evidence, disqualification must be denied.

■ **PROCEDURAL BASIS**

Appeal from a guilty verdict rendered by an eleven-member jury.

■ **FACTS**

During jury selection in Thomas's (D) drug trial, the prosecution sought to exercise a peremptory challenge to exclude the only black person remaining as a potential juror. Because Thomas (D) is black, the defense objected to the peremptory challenge as racially motivated. The court sustained the objection because, while the government's challenge was not racially motivated, the government's reason—that the juror failed to make eye contact with the prosecuting attorney—was an insufficient basis for the strike. The court later explained that the strike was disallowed because the juror was the only remaining black juror in a case involving the black defendant. The juror was later impaneled as "Juror No. 5." After several weeks of trial, a group of jurors informed the court clerk that Juror No. 5 was distracting them during defense counsel's summation by making disruptive noises and indicating agreement with defense counsel's arguments before deliberations. After meeting with counsel, the court ordered each witness interviewed *in camera* to determine the extent of Juror No. 5's disruption and to consider his dismissal from the jury. After questioning each witness about the distractions, seven jurors indicated that Juror No. 5 presented some distraction, but all but one indicated it would not affect their ability to deliberate. Nonetheless, the judge dismissed Juror No. 5 because he feared his actions would create an adversarial environment for deliberations. After objection by defense counsel, however, the judge reconsidered and permitted Juror No. 5 to remain.

After more than a day of deliberation, two jurors separately informed the court clerk that deliberations were prolonged because "an unnamed juror" and "Juror No. 5" were causing problems. After discussion with counsel, the court chose to give the jury more time to deliberate before any action was taken. A day later, a third juror passed a note to the court clerk indicating the jury was unable to reach a verdict because Juror No. 5 held a "predisposed disposition." After additional *in camera* interviews, several jurors specifically identified Juror No. 5 as the cause of the disruption, while others indicated a general tension among the jurors. At least five jurors indicated that Juror No. 5 insisted on acquittal for such reasons as racial unity, a belief that drug dealing was commonplace, the belief that defendants acted out of economic necessity, and because the prosecution had not met its burden. Juror No. 5 himself informed the judge that he believed the prosecution had not presented sufficient evidence of guilt beyond a reasonable doubt. After hearing argument from counsel, the court disqualified Juror No. 5 because he was unwilling to consider the evidence due to his own preconceived cultural, economic, or social ideas about the case. After dismissing Juror No. 5, the remaining eleven jurors returned a guilty verdict.

■ ISSUE

Did the trial judge err in disqualifying a black juror in a black defendant's drug trial when some evidence suggested his views were based on the sufficiency of the government's evidence?

■ DECISION AND RATIONALE

(Cabranes, J.) Yes. Under Federal Rule of Criminal Procedure 23(b), a trial judge has unilateral authority to order the disqualification of jurors for just cause during the course of deliberations and to proceed with the case using the remaining eleven jurors. Just cause has been previously shown not only when a juror suffers illness or unavailability, but also when he is found unable to fulfill his duty to render an impartial verdict such as when a juror feels threatened by a party to the case or when life circumstances change during the course of deliberations so as to impair his ability to impartially render a verdict. Here, the exposed bias arises from neither physical inability nor change in circumstances, but from a general opposition to the enforcement of criminal drug laws. Just as when a juror disregards the court's instructions due to an event or relationship that renders him impartial, a court is empowered to disqualify a jury who intends to engage in jury nullification. Jury nullification is a power of the jury, not a right to be condoned and preserved by the court. When a court is not successful in preventing jury nullification through instruction and admonition, disqualification is the appropriate remedy. Investigating jury misconduct during deliberation, however, is not an easy task.

The duty to ensure a fair trial must be balanced by the equally important goal of maintaining secrecy over the jury deliberations, which is fundamental to the proper operation of the jury system. To protect juror secrecy, the trial judge must limit his or her inquiries into the mental processes of the jury during deliberations so as to avoid the compulsion of revealing the reasoning underlying a jury's verdict. When just cause can be obtained from evidence not pertaining to the specific deliberations of the jury, the judge must rely on that evidence alone in deciding whether to disqualify a juror. When, however, the juror's bias arises not from an identifiable event or relationship, but from reports of conduct occurring in the jury room outside the view of the court and others, the judge must use carefully tailored inquiries to collect sufficient evidence to determine whether a juror is intent on disregarding the applicable law and court instructions or is simply unpersuaded by the proof presented at trial. When the evidence discloses any possibility that a juror's view arises from the sufficiency of the government's evidence, disqualification must be denied. This low evidentiary standard protects against both the wrongful disqualification of a juror and an intrusion upon the secrecy of jury deliberations. Here, Juror No. 5 should not have been disqualified as there was some evidence provided from Juror No. 5 and other jurors to indicate that at least part of Juror No. 5's views were based on his belief that the government had not met its burden of proof.

Analysis:

The threat of jury nullification underscores the importance of proper, thorough voir dire before trial. Through voir dire, the court can dismiss those jurors most likely to disagree with the enforcement of the law, who are unable to objectively consider the evidence supporting guilt or innocence, and who are likely to impose their own subjective view on the way the law ought to be enforced. A jury must be properly impaneled to further the legislature's interest in regulating and enforcing the law.

■ CASE VOCABULARY

PEREMPTORY CHALLENGE: One of a party's limited number of challenges that need not be supported by any reason, although a party may not use such a challenge in a way that discriminates on the basis of race, ethnicity, or gender.

BATSON CHALLENGE: A defendant's objection that the prosecution has used peremptory challenges to exclude potential jurors on the basis of race, ethnicity, or gender.

STRIKE: The removal of a prospective juror from the jury panel.

IN CAMERA: In the judge's private chambers.

CHAPTER SEVENTEEN

Sentencing

Mistretta v. United States

Instant Facts: Prisoners challenged the constitutionality of the Sentencing Commission guidelines.

Black Letter Rule: Sentencing guidelines are constitutional, amounting to neither an excessive delegation of legislative power nor a violation of the separation of powers principle.

Williams v. New York

Instant Facts: The jury found Williams (D) guilty of first-degree murder and recommended life imprisonment, but the trial judge imposed the death sentence based on the evidence presented at trial and additional information obtained through a pre-sentence investigation prepared by the probation department.

Black Letter Rule: The imposition of a death sentence for murder in the first degree is not void under the Due Process Clause solely by reason of the fact that the trial court, before imposing sentence, considered additional information obtained through the court's probation department and other sources.

McMillan v. Pennsylvania

Instant Facts: McMillan (D) was convicted by a jury of aggravated assault and the trial judge imposed a lesser sentence than that required under Pennsylvania's Mandatory Minimum Sentencing Act, which provides that anyone convicted of certain enumerated felonies is subject to a mandatory minimum sentence of five years' imprisonment if the sentencing judge finds, by a preponderance of the evidence, that the person "visibly possessed a firearm" during the commission of the offense.

Black Letter Rule: The right to a jury trial is not violated by Pennsylvania's Mandatory Minimum Sentencing Act, which requires a five-year minimum sentence on a finding by the court, by a preponderance of the evidence, that a defendant possessed a firearm during the commission of certain enumerated offenses.

Apprendi v. New Jersey

Instant Facts: Apprendi (D) was convicted pursuant to a guilty plea of possession of a firearm for an unlawful purpose and unlawful possession of a prohibited weapon. The trial judge found by a preponderance of the evidence that Apprendi's (D) actions fell within the New Jersey hate crime statute and he sentenced him to an extended term.

Black Letter Rule: The Constitution requires that any fact that increases the penalty for a crime beyond the prescribed statutory maximum, other than the fact of a prior conviction, must be submitted to a jury and proved beyond a reasonable doubt.

Blakely v. Washington

Instant Facts: The judge increased Blakely's (D) sentence well beyond the statutory range based on facts that were never admitted by Blakely (D) nor found by a jury, and Blakely (D) appealed.

Black Letter Rule: The imposition of a sentence outside the statutory range based on facts that were never admitted nor put before a jury deprives a criminal defendant of his Sixth Amendment rights.

North Carolina v. Pearce

Instant Facts: Pearce (D) was convicted of assault with intent to commit rape and sentenced to prison for a term of twelve to fifteen years. His conviction was later reversed but he was retried, convicted again, and sentenced by the trial judge to an eight-year prison term, which, when added to the time he had already spent in prison, amounted to a longer total sentence than that originally imposed.

Black Letter Rule: In imposing a new sentence upon a defendant whose original sentence has been set aside, a trial judge may consider events subsequent to the first trial and may impose a sentence that is greater or less than the original sentence.

Mistretta v. United States

(Prisoners) v. *(Prosecuting Government)*
488 U.S. 361, 109 S. Ct. 647, 102 L. Ed. 2d 714

SENTENCING GUIDELINES ARE CONSTITUTIONAL

NEWS 9

Today the Supreme Court upheld the Judical Branch's power to promulgate self-governing rules for sentencing. Not exactly a surprise.

stus.com

■ **INSTANT FACTS** Prisoners challenged the constitutionality of the Sentencing Commission guidelines.

■ **BLACK LETTER RULE** Sentencing guidelines are constitutional, amounting to neither an excessive delegation of legislative power nor a violation of the separation of powers principle.

■ PROCEDURAL BASIS

Certiorari to review the decision of the United States District Court for the Western District of Missouri finding that the sentencing guidelines were constitutional.

■ FACTS

Mistretta (D) was under indictment on three counts centering on a cocaine sale. He pleaded guilty to a conspiracy-to-distribute count and was sentenced under the sentencing guidelines to 18 months' imprisonment and other penalties. Because the earlier indeterminate sentencing system had resulted in serious disparities among the sentences imposed by federal judges upon similarly situated offenders, and in uncertainty as to an offender's actual date of release by Executive Branch parole officials, Congress passed the Sentencing Reform Act of 1984. The Act created the United States Sentencing Commission as an independent body in the Judicial Branch with power to promulgate binding sentencing guidelines establishing a range of determinate sentences for all categories of federal offenses and defendants, according to specific and detailed factors. Mistretta (D) claimed that the guidelines were unconstitutional, but the district court upheld their constitutionality. Mistretta (D) appealed, arguing that the Commission's acts violated the separation-of-powers doctrine and that Congress had delegated excessive authority to the Commission to structure the guidelines.

■ ISSUE

Are the sentencing guidelines constitutional?

■ DECISION AND RATIONALE

(Blackmun, J.) Yes. The Sentencing Guidelines are constitutional, since Congress neither delegated excessive legislative power to the Commission nor violated the separation-of-powers principle by placing the Commission in the Judicial Branch, by requiring federal judges to serve on the Commission and to share their authority with nonjudges, or by empowering the President to appoint Commission members and to remove them for cause. The decision of the United States District Court for the Western District of Missouri, which determined that the sentencing guidelines were constitutional, is affirmed.

Analysis:

The Constitution's structural protections do not prohibit Congress from delegating to an expert body within the Judicial Branch the intricate task of formulating sentencing guidelines consistent with such

---

significant statutory direction as is present, nor from calling upon the accumulated wisdom and experience of the Judicial Branch in creating policy on a matter uniquely within the understanding of judges.

■ **CASE VOCABULARY**

INDETERMINATE SENTENCE: A sentence to incarceration with a spread of time between a minimum date of parole eligibility and a maximum discharge date. A completely indeterminate sentence has a minimum of one day and a maximum of natural life.

SENTENCING GUIDELINES: Guidelines established by the U.S. Sentencing Commission to be followed by federal courts in the sentencing of those convicted of federal offenses. The guidelines prescribe a range of sentences for each class of convicted persons as determined by categories of offense behavior and offender characteristics.

Williams v. New York

(Convicted Murderer) v. *(Prosecuting State)*
337 U.S. 241, 69 S. Ct. 1079, 93 L. Ed. 1337 (1949)

OTHER ACTS MAY BE CONSIDERED WHEN IMPOSING DEATH SENTENCE

■ **INSTANT FACTS** The jury found Williams (D) guilty of first-degree murder and recommended life imprisonment, but the trial judge imposed the death sentence based on the evidence presented at trial and additional information obtained through a pre-sentence investigation prepared by the probation department.

■ **BLACK LETTER RULE** The imposition of a death sentence for murder in the first degree is not void under the Due Process Clause solely by reason of the fact that the trial court, before imposing sentence, considered additional information obtained through the court's probation department and other sources.

■ PROCEDURAL BASIS

Certiorari to review the decision of the court of appeals affirming the defendant's conviction.

■ FACTS

A jury in a New York state court found Williams guilty of murder in the first degree and recommended life in prison. About five weeks after the verdict, and after a statutory pre-sentence investigation report was provided to the judge, the defendant was sentenced to death. In giving his reasons for imposing the death sentence, the judge narrated the shocking details of the crime as shown by the trial evidence, expressed his own belief in guilt, and stated that the pre-sentence investigation revealed many material facts concerning Williams' background that, though relevant to the question of punishment, could not have been brought to the attention of the jury in its consideration of the question of guilt. The judge specifically referred to thirty uncharged burglaries committed in the same vicinity as the murder. The pre-sentence report also indicated that Williams possessed "a morbid sexuality" and classified him as a "menace to society."

■ ISSUE

May a judge properly consider information contained in a pre-sentence report when sentencing a convicted criminal to death?

■ DECISION AND RATIONALE

(Black, J.) Yes. A judge, who is charged with the responsibility of imposing sentences, is not restricted by the Due Process Clause to the consideration of only information received in open court. A sentencing judge is not confined to the narrow issue of guilt. His or her task, within statutory or constitutional limits, is to determine the type and extent of punishment after the issue of guilt has been determined. When pronouncing sentence, a judge must have the most complete information possible regarding the defendant, and is not limited by rigid adherence to the restrictive rules of evidence applicable at trial. The death sentence imposed here was not void under the Due Process Clause solely by reason of the fact that the court had considered additional information contained in the pre-sentence investigation and through other sources. The defendant was not denied due process of law by the judge's consideration of this evidence and the decision of the lower court affirming his sentence was correct. Affirmed.

■ DISSENT

(Murphy, J.) The jury unanimously recommended life imprisonment as a suitable punishment for the defendant. Though vested with the statutory authority to do so, a judge should hesitate to increase the severity of such a community expression. The "high commands of due process were not obeyed" in this case.

Analysis:

Permitting a sentencing judge to avail himself of out-of-court information secures a broad discretionary power that is susceptible of abuse, but nevertheless that power may be exercised even when the death sentence is imposed. The Supreme Court reiterated the principle of *Williams* in *United States v. Watts*, 519 U.S. 148, 117 S. Ct. 633, 136 L. Ed. 2d 554 (1997), in which it reaffirmed that "a sentencing judge may take into account facts introduced at trial relating to other charges, even ones of which the defendant has been acquitted."

■ CASE VOCABULARY

PRE–SENTENCE INVESTIGATION: Investigation of the relevant background of a convicted offender, usually conducted by a probation officer attached to a court, designed to act as a sentencing guide for the sentencing judge.

McMillan v. Pennsylvania

(Convicted Felon) v. *(Prosecuting State)*

477 U.S. 79, 106 S. Ct. 2411, 91 L. Ed. 2d 67 (1986)

PENNSYLVANIA'S MANDATORY MINIMUM SENTENCING ACT IS CONSTITUTIONAL

I love mandatory minimum sentencing guidelines-- They both reduce the burden of proof AND annoy judges.

stus.com

■ **INSTANT FACTS** McMillan (D) was convicted by a jury of aggravated assault and the trial judge imposed a lesser sentence than that required under Pennsylvania's Mandatory Minimum Sentencing Act, which provides that anyone convicted of certain enumerated felonies is subject to a mandatory minimum sentence of five years' imprisonment if the sentencing judge finds, by a preponderance of the evidence, that the person "visibly possessed a firearm" during the commission of the offense.

■ **BLACK LETTER RULE** The right to a jury trial is not violated by Pennsylvania's Mandatory Minimum Sentencing Act, which requires a five-year minimum sentence on a finding by the court, by a preponderance of the evidence, that a defendant possessed a firearm during the commission of certain enumerated offenses.

■ PROCEDURAL BASIS

Certiorari to review the decision of the Supreme Court of Pennsylvania upholding the Constitutionality of Pennsylvania's Mandatory Minimum Sentencing Act.

■ FACTS

Pennsylvania's Mandatory Minimum Sentencing Act was adopted in 1982. It provides that anyone convicted of certain enumerated felonies is subject to a mandatory minimum sentence of five years' imprisonment if the sentencing judge finds, by a preponderance of the evidence, that the person "visibly possessed a firearm" during the commission of the offense. At the sentencing hearing, the judge is directed to consider the evidence introduced at trial and any additional evidence offered by either the defendant or the Commonwealth. The Act operates to divest the judge of discretion to impose any sentence of less than five years for the underlying felony; it does not authorize a sentence in excess of that otherwise allowed for that offense. Each defendant in this case, including McMillan (D), was convicted of, among other things, one of the Act's enumerated felonies. In each case the Commonwealth gave notice that at sentencing it would seek to proceed under the Act. No hearing was held, however, because each of the sentencing judges before whom the defendants appeared found the Act unconstitutional and imposed a lesser sentence than that required by the Act.

■ ISSUE

Does Pennsylvania's Minimum Sentencing Act violate due process by reallocating or reducing the burdens of proof in criminal cases?

■ DECISION AND RATIONALE

(Rehnquist, J.) No. A state may properly treat visible possession of a firearm as a sentencing consideration that must be proved by a preponderance of the evidence rather than as an element of a particular offense that must be proved beyond a reasonable doubt. While there are constitutional limits beyond which states may not go in this regard, the applicability of the reasonable-doubt standard is usually dependent on how a state defines the underlying offense. Here, the Pennsylvania legislature has made visible possession of a firearm a sentencing factor that comes into play only after the defendant has been found guilty of a specific crime. The constitutional limits on a state's power are not exceeded by the Act, which only raises the minimum sentence that may be imposed and neither alters the maximum sentence nor creates a separate offense calling for a separate penalty. The Pennsylvania Supreme Court properly concluded that Pennsylvania's Mandatory Minimum Sentencing Act is constitutional. Affirmed.

■ DISSENT

(Stevens, J.) The legislature may not dispense with the requirement of proof beyond a reasonable doubt for conduct that it targets for severe criminal behavior. Because Pennsylvania's Minimum Sentencing Act describes conduct that the Pennsylvania Legislature intended to prohibit, and because it mandates lengthy incarceration for the same, visible possession of a firearm is an element of the underlying criminal offense to which the proof beyond a reasonable doubt requirement applies.

Analysis:

This case is controlled by *Patterson v. New York,* 432 U.S. 197, 97 S. Ct. 2319, 53 L. Ed. 2d 281, in which the Court rejected a claim that whenever a state links the "severity of punishment" to the "presence or absence of an identified fact," the state must prove that fact beyond a reasonable doubt. All nine justices cited *Patterson*. Note that in *Almendarez-Torres v. United States,* 523 U.S. 224, 118 S. Ct. 1219, 140 L. Ed. 2d 350 (1998), however, the Court upheld Congress's right to treat recidivism as a sentencing factor to be determined by the judge by a preponderance of the evidence.

■ CASE VOCABULARY

MANDATORY STATUTES: Generic term describing statutes that require and not merely permit a course of action. They are characterized by such directives as "shall" and not "may."

Apprendi v. New Jersey

(Convicted Weapons Violator) v. *(Prosecuting State)*

530 U.S. 466, 120 S. Ct. 2348, 147 L. Ed. 2d 435 (2000)

NEW JERSEY'S HATE CRIME STATUTE IS UNCONSTITUTIONAL

■ **INSTANT FACTS** Apprendi (D) was convicted pursuant to a guilty plea of possession of a firearm for an unlawful purpose and unlawful possession of a prohibited weapon. The trial judge found by a preponderance of the evidence that Apprendi's (D) actions fell within the New Jersey hate crime statute and he sentenced him to an extended term.

■ **BLACK LETTER RULE** The Constitution requires that any fact that increases the penalty for a crime beyond the prescribed statutory maximum, other than the fact of a prior conviction, must be submitted to a jury and proved beyond a reasonable doubt.

■ PROCEDURAL BASIS

Certiorari to review the decision of the New Jersey Supreme Court affirming the defendant's conviction.

■ FACTS

Apprendi (D) fired several .22–caliber bullets into the home of an African–American family that had recently moved into a previously all-white neighborhood in New Jersey. Apprendi (D) was arrested and admitted that he was the shooter. After further questioning he made a statement—which he later retracted—that even though he did not know the occupants of the house personally, "because they are black in color he does not want them in the neighborhood." A New Jersey grand jury returned a twenty-three-count indictment charging Apprendi (D) with four first-degree, eight second-degree, six third-degree, and five fourth-degree offenses. The charges alleged shootings on four different dates, as well as the unlawful possession of various weapons. None of the counts referred to the hate crime statute, and none alleged that Apprendi (D) acted with a racially biased purpose. Pursuant to a plea agreement, Apprendi (D) pleaded guilty to two counts of second-degree possession of a firearm for an unlawful purpose and one count of the third-degree offense of unlawful possession of an antipersonnel bomb. The prosecutor dismissed the other 20 counts. Under state law, a second-degree offense carries a penalty range of five to ten years; a third-degree offense carries a penalty range of between three and five years. As part of the plea agreement, the State reserved the right to request that the court impose a higher "enhanced" sentence on the ground that that offense was committed with a biased purpose. Apprendi (D) reserved the right to challenge the hate crime sentence enhancement on the ground that it violated the United States Constitution. The trial judge held an evidentiary hearing on the issue of Apprendi's "purpose" for the shooting and concluded that the evidence supported a finding "that the crime was motivated by racial bias." Having found "by a preponderance of the evidence" that Apprendi's (D) actions were taken "with a purpose to intimidate" as provided by the statute, the trial judge held that the hate crime enhancement applied. Rejecting Apprendi's (D) constitutional challenge to the statute, the judge sentenced him to a twelve-year term of imprisonment on Count 18 and to shorter concurrent sentences on the other two counts.

■ ISSUE

Does the Due Process Clause of the Fourteenth Amendment require that the jury determine, based on proof beyond a reasonable doubt, that that the defendant should be sentenced to a term in excess of the maximum prison sentence?

■ DECISION AND RATIONALE

(Stevens, J.) Yes. The Constitution requires that any fact that increases the penalty for a crime beyond the prescribed statutory maximum, other than the fact of a prior conviction, must be submitted to a jury and proved beyond a reasonable doubt. The New Jersey hate crime statute, which allowed the judge to make factual determinations based on a preponderance of evidence that would increase the maximum sentence of the defendant convicted of the second-degree offense of unlawful possession of prohibited weapons from ten to twenty years, thereby imposing punishment identical to that imposed for a first-degree crime, violated due process. The Due Process Clause requires such factual determinations to be made by the jury on the basis of proof beyond a reasonable doubt. The fact that the state legislature placed its hate crime sentence enhancer within the sentencing provisions of the criminal code did not mean that a finding of biased purpose to intimidate, which is required for hate crime sentence enhancement, is not an essential element of the offense that must be decided by the jury beyond a reasonable doubt. The decision of the New Jersey Supreme Court affirming the sentence imposed under the New Jersey hate crime statute was therefore in error. Reversed and remanded.

■ CONCURRENCE

(Scalia, J.) The Constitution means what it says. The guarantee that "in all criminal prosecutions, the accused shall enjoy the right to . . . trial, by an impartial jury," means that all the facts that must exist in order to subject the defendant to a legally prescribed punishment must be found by the jury.

■ CONCURRENCE

(Thomas, J.) The Constitution requires a broader rule than the Court adopts. This decision marks nothing more than a return to the *status quo* that reflected the original meaning of the Fifth and Sixth Amendments.

■ DISSENT

(O'Connor, J.) The Court improperly embraces a universal and seemingly bright-line rule limiting the power of Congress and state legislatures to define criminal offenses and the sentences that follow from convictions. If the Court's opinion is accurate, it will have the effect of invalidating significant sentencing reform accomplished at the federal and state levels over the past three decades.

■ DISSENT

(Breyer, J.) Judges, rather than juries, have traditionally determined the presence or absence of sentence-affecting facts in a given case. The Court's new rule will likely impede legislative attempts to provide authoritative guidance as to how courts should respond to the presence of traditional sentencing factors. The factor at issue here—motive—is such a factor. The State of New Jersey has determined that one motive—racial hatred—is particularly bad and ought to make a difference in respect to punishment for a crime. That determination is reasonable.

Analysis:

Apprendi has been subject to much debate. The decision placed in doubt the continued vitality of *McMillan v. Pennsylvania*, as the justices in *Apprendi* acknowledged. If the Constitution requires a jury, not a judge, to determine, beyond a reasonable doubt, any fact that increases the maximum punishment of a defendant, why should the rule be different in regard to facts that increase the minimum punishment as in *McMillan*? In *Harris v. United States,* the Court ruled, 5–4, that *McMillan* remains good law.

■ CASE VOCABULARY

DETERMINATE SENTENCE: A sentence for a fixed period of time.

SENTENCING ENHANCEMENT: Such a fact increases a defendant's punishment but is not subject to the constitutional protections to which elements are subject.

SENTENCING FACTOR: A fact that was not found by a jury but that could affect the sentence imposed by the judge.

Blakely v. Washington

(Convicted Kidnapper) v. *(Prosecuting Authority)*
542 U.S. 296, 124 S. Ct. 2531, 159 L. Ed. 2d 403 (2004)

SENTENCE–ENHANCING FACTS MUST BE FOUND BY THE JURY

■ **INSTANT FACTS** The judge increased Blakely's (D) sentence well beyond the statutory range based on facts that were never admitted by Blakely (D) nor found by a jury, and Blakely (D) appealed.

■ **BLACK LETTER RULE** The imposition of a sentence outside the statutory range based on facts that were never admitted nor put before a jury deprives a criminal defendant of his Sixth Amendment rights.

■ **PROCEDURAL BASIS**

Certiorari to review the defendant's sentence for kidnapping.

■ **FACTS**

Blakely (D) was charged with first-degree kidnapping of his estranged wife but pleaded down to second-degree kidnapping involving domestic violence and use of a firearm. No trial was held, and the defendant admitted to no facts other than the guilty plea itself. Second-degree kidnapping is a class B felony, which has a maximum sentence of ten years. The Washington sentencing reform act, however, provided a range of forty-nine to fifty-three months, unless there were substantial and compelling reasons justifying a longer sentence. The state recommended a sentence within the recommended range, but the sentencing judge imposed a longer sentence based on what he found to be "deliberate cruelty" in Blakely's (D) wife's description of the incident. Blakely (D) objected to a sentence that was more than three years longer than he expected, so the judge held a hearing, taking testimony from various witnesses, including Blakely's (D) wife and son. The judge stuck to the original ninety-month enhanced sentence, based on thirty-two findings of fact. Blakely appealed, arguing that this sentencing procedure deprived him of his right to have a jury determine beyond a reasonable doubt all facts essential to his sentence. The Supreme Court granted certiorari.

■ **ISSUE**

Does the imposition of a sentence outside the statutory range based on facts found by a judge that were never put before a jury or admitted by the defendant deprive the defendant of his constitutional rights?

■ **DECISION AND RATIONALE**

(Scalia, J.) Yes. The imposition of a sentence outside the statutory range based on facts that were never admitted nor put before a jury deprives a criminal defendant of his Sixth Amendment rights. In *Apprendi v. New* Jersey, we held that the Sixth Amendment requires that any fact that increases a criminal penalty beyond the statutory maximum must be submitted to the jury and proved beyond a reasonable doubt. For purposes of *Apprendi* analysis, the maximum sentence is the one the judge may impose based solely on the facts as found by the jury or admitted by the defendant. Because the state's sentencing procedure did not comply with *Apprendi* or the Sixth Amendment in this case, Blakely's (D) sentence is invalid.

Leaving too much sentencing discretion to the judge or the legislature is counter to the Framers' intent. The very reason the Framers put a jury-trial guarantee in the Constitution was that they were unwilling to trust government to mark out the role of the jury. *Apprendi*'s bright-line rule removes this unconstitutional discretion from sentencing decisions. We do not find all determinate sentencing schemes unconstitutional, but only hold that they must be implemented in a manner that respects the Sixth Amendment.

A defendant may still waive his *Apprendi* rights and allow the judge to impose a sentence at his or her discretion. A defendant who pleads guilty may either stipulate to the relevant facts or consent to judicial fact-finding. Although the *Apprendi* approach may have its limitations, it is certainly better than the methodology it replaced, under which a defendant could see his sentence balloon post-trial based on facts never put before the jury. Reversed.

■ DISSENT

(O'Connor, J.) Although the Court says it is not finding all determinate sentencing schemes unconstitutional, that is, in essence, the effect of today's decision. As a result of the Court's holding, legislatures will scramble to eliminate their sentencing guidelines, thereby obliterating twenty years of effort. The majority requires, basically, that any fact that could increase a defendant's sentence become an element of the offense, which carries with it many associated costs. What I have feared most has come to pass: over twenty years' of sentencing reform are lost, and tens of thousands of criminal judgments are in jeopardy.

■ DISSENT

(Breyer, J.) I agree with the majority's analysis, but not its conclusion, because the majority ignores the adverse consequences inherent therein. Sentencing must now, as a result of today's decision, take one of three forms. First, legislators could create a determinate sentencing system under which everyone charged with the same crime receives the same sentence, but this uniformity would come at an intolerable cost. Second, legislators could return to indeterminate sentencing schemes, leaving the defendant's sentence within the discretion of the judge or parole board. But this system would diminish the jury's role—an outcome the majority says it wants to avoid. Third, the approach that the majority seems to think legislators will take is to retain structured schemes, modified to meet *Apprendi* requirements.

The real question here is, "[w]hy does the Sixth Amendment permit a jury trial right (in respect to a particular fact) to depend upon a legislative labeling decision, namely, the legislative decision to label the fact a *sentencing fact*, instead of an *element of the crime*?" And the answer to that question is, because the fairness and effectiveness of a sentencing system and the criminal justice system itself depends on the legislature's constitutional authority, within the limits of due process, to make that labeling decision. The majority's restriction of the legislature's power prevents the legislature from seeking the Constitution's fairness goals. Whatever the faults of the present system—and there are some—they are better addressed by the legislature than in one unchangeable decision of the Court.

Analysis:

Blakely called into question the constitutionality of the federal sentencing guidelines and many state sentencing guidelines schemes. Immediately after the decision, state prosecutors' offices and the United States Department of Justice scrambled to determine how best to respond. The DOJ took the position that the rule announced in *Blakely* did not apply to the federal guidelines, which could continue to be constitutionally applied through fact-finding by a judge at sentencing, using the preponderance of the evidence standard. The government's argument was that the lower federal courts were not free to invalidate the federal guidelines given the prior Supreme Court decisions upholding their constitutionality, and that, moreover, the federal guidelines were distinguishable from the system invalidated in *Blakely*.

■ CASE VOCABULARY

INDETERMINATE SENTENCING: The practice of not imposing a definite term of confinement, but instead prescribing a range for the minimum and maximum term, leaving the precise term to be fixed in some other way.

SENTENCING GUIDELINES: A set of standards for determining the punishment that a convicted criminal should receive, based on the nature of the crime and the offender's criminal history.

North Carolina v. Pearce

(Prosecuting State) v. *(Convicted Criminal)*

395 U.S. 711, 89 S. Ct. 2072, 23 L. Ed. 2d 656 (1969)

THE DUE PROCESS CLAUSE IMPOSES CERTAIN LIMITS ON HARSHER SENTENCES AFTER RETRIAL

■ **INSTANT FACTS** Pearce (D) was convicted of assault with intent to commit rape and sentenced to prison for a term of twelve to fifteen years. His conviction was later reversed but he was retried, convicted again, and sentenced by the trial judge to an eight-year prison term, which, when added to the time he had already spent in prison, amounted to a longer total sentence than that originally imposed.

■ **BLACK LETTER RULE** In imposing a new sentence upon a defendant whose original sentence has been set aside, a trial judge may consider events subsequent to the first trial and may impose a sentence that is greater or less than the original sentence.

■ PROCEDURAL BASIS

Certiorari to review the decision of the United States Court of Appeals for the Fourth Circuit, granting habeas corpus relief.

■ FACTS

Pearce (D) was convicted in a North Carolina court of assault with intent to commit rape. The trial judge sentenced him to prison for a term of twelve to fifteen years. Several years later, he initiated a state post-conviction proceeding that culminated in the reversal of his conviction by the North Carolina Supreme Court on the ground that an involuntary confession was unconstitutionally admitted in evidence against him. Pearce (D) was retried, convicted, and sentenced by the trial judge to an eight-year prison term, which, when added to the time Pearce (D) had already spent in prison, amounted to a longer total sentence than that originally imposed. The conviction and sentence were affirmed on appeal. Pearce (D) then began this habeas corpus proceeding in the United States District Court for the Eastern District of North Carolina. That court held that the longer sentence imposed upon retrial was unconstitutional and void. Upon the failure of the state court to resentence Pearce within sixty days, the federal court ordered his release. That order was affirmed by the United States Court of Appeals for the Fourth Circuit and the United States Supreme Court granted certiorari.

■ ISSUE

Does the guarantee against double jeopardy restrict the general power of a judge to impose upon reconviction a longer sentence than the defendant originally received after his or her original conviction?

■ DECISION AND RATIONALE

(Stewart, J.) No. Neither the double jeopardy provision nor the equal protection clause bars imposition of a more severe sentence upon reconviction of a defendant who has had original the conviction set aside at his own behest. However, whenever a judge imposes a more severe sentence upon retrial, the judge's reasons for doing so must affirmatively appear and must be based upon objective information concerning identifiable conduct on the part of the defendant occurring after the time of original sentencing, and factual data upon which the increased sentence is based must be made a part of the record so that the constitutional legitimacy of the increased sentence may be fully reviewed on appeal. Because the record here failed to show any reason or justification for increased punishment, the Due Process Clause justified setting the sentence aside and the decision granting habeas corpus relief was correct. Affirmed.

■ CONCURRENCE

(White, J.) The Court should authorize an increased sentence on retrial based on any objective, identifiable data not known to the trial judge at the time of the original sentence.

Analysis:

The rule announced in *Pearce* creates a rebuttable presumption of vindictiveness. Due process does not forbid enhanced sentences or charges, but only enhancement motivated by actual vindictiveness toward the defendant for having exercised guaranteed rights. Where the presumption applies, the sentencing court must rebut the presumption that an increased sentence resulted from vindictiveness. Where the presumption does not apply, the defendant must affirmatively prove actual vindictiveness.

■ CASE VOCABULARY

HABEAS CORPUS: The name given to a variety of writs having as their objective bringing a party before a judge. Initially, the writ only permitted a prisoner to challenge a state conviction on constitutional grounds that related to jurisdiction of the state court, but the scope of inquiry has gradually expanded and the writ now extends to all constitutional challenges.

POST–CONVICTION REMEDIES: Almost every state has one or more post-conviction procedures that permit prisoners to challenge at least some constitutional violations.

CHAPTER EIGHTEEN

Double Jeopardy

Blockburger v. United States

Instant Facts: Blockburger (D) was found guilty and sentenced on three counts arising from two illegal narcotic sales to the same purchaser within a short interval of time.

Black Letter Rule: Two sales of narcotics to the same purchaser, but at different times, do not qualify as a continuing offense because the Narcotics Act penalizes each individual sale.

Brown v. Ohio

Instant Facts: Brown (D), who had pleaded guilty in one community to joyriding in a vehicle that he had stolen a few days earlier in another community, was subsequently prosecuted and convicted for auto theft in the community where he had stolen the car.

Black Letter Rule: A conviction of a lesser-included offense precludes a subsequent prosecution for the greater offense even though the two actions occurred several days apart.

Missouri v. Hunter

Instant Facts: Hunter (D) was convicted in a single trial of both armed criminal action and first-degree robbery and received a prison sentence on both charges.

Black Letter Rule: When a cumulative punishment is authorized under two state statutes, regardless of whether those two statutes proscribe the same conduct, a cumulative punishment may be imposed under the statutes in a single trial.

Fong Foo v. United States

Instant Facts: After a federal district court judge had, part way through the trial, directed the jury to return verdicts of acquittal as to all the defendants and then ordered a formal judgment of acquittal, the government filed a writ of mandamus in a federal court of appeals to vacate the judgment and reassign the case for trial.

Black Letter Rule: A judgment of acquittal, even if based on error, is a final judgment that cannot be appealed.

Ashe v. Swenson

Instant Facts: Ashe (D), who was found not guilty of armed robbery of a poker player at a poker game, was subsequently tried again for the armed robbery of another poker player at that same poker game and was found guilty.

Black Letter Rule: After a jury determines that a defendant had no involvement in the offense charged, the defendant cannot be retried for that offense.

Downum v. United States

Instant Facts: After the jury was discharged on the motion of the prosecutor because his key witness was not present, the case was retried before another jury and the defendant was found guilty.

Black Letter Rule: If an impaneled jury is discharged because the prosecution's witness is unavailable, double jeopardy applies to bar the impaneling of a second jury and a new trial.

Bartkus v. Illinois

Instant Facts: After Bartkus (D) was tried in federal court for robbery and was acquitted, a state grand jury indicted him on the same charges and he was found guilty and sentenced to life in prison.

Black Letter Rule: Successive federal and state prosecutions do not violate the Fifth Amendment's Double Jeopardy Clause.

Blockburger v. United States

(*Convicted Drug Seller*) v. (*Prosecuting Government*)
284 U.S. 299, 52 S. Ct. 180, 76 L. Ed. 306 (1932)

SEPARATE AND DISTINCT OFFENSES, EVEN IF OF THE SAME NATURE, DO NOT CONSTITUTE A CONTINUING OFFENSE

■ **INSTANT FACTS** Blockburger (D) was found guilty and sentenced on three counts arising from two illegal narcotic sales to the same purchaser within a short interval of time.

■ **BLACK LETTER RULE** Two sales of narcotics to the same purchaser, but at different times, do not qualify as a continuing offense because the Narcotics Act penalizes each individual sale.

■ PROCEDURAL BASIS

Appeal from the trial court's decision finding Blockburger (D) guilty of multiple counts involving illegal narcotics sales.

■ FACTS

Blockburger (D) was charged with violating two provisions of the Harrison Narcotics Act and subsequently was found guilty on two counts of selling drugs not in their original stamped package and one count of selling drugs not pursuant to a written order of the person purchasing the drugs. Blockburger (D) received a separate fine and a separate sentence for each of the counts. The terms of imprisonment as to each count were to run consecutively.

■ ISSUE

Did Blockburger's (D) two illegal narcotic sales to the same purchaser over a short period of time constitute a continuing offense for which only one single penalty could be imposed?

■ DECISION AND RATIONALE

(Sutherland, J.) No. The Narcotics Act did not create the offense of engaging in the business of selling drugs. If it did, Blockburger's (D) multiple narcotics sales would be a continuing offense. What the Narcotics Act did was to penalize any sale made in absence of the Act's qualifying requirements. Since each sale that Blockburger (D) made violated the Act, each sale could be punished separately. Additionally, the Act created a separate offense for selling narcotics not pursuant to a written order. Since that offense required a different proof element than selling narcotics in the absence of the Act's qualifying requirements, it constituted a separate offense that could be punished separately. Affirmed.

Analysis:

Although a defendant may engage in a single criminal act, the commission of that act may subject him to more than one penalty. Multiple commissions of the same act, even if they involve the same party, are treated as multiple offenses. If a single criminal act violates multiple related laws, separate offenses can be charged if each of the multiple related laws requires different elements of proof.

■ CASE VOCABULARY

CONTINUING OFFENSE: Type of crime that is committed over a span of time, as for example, a conspiracy. A continuing offense may consist of separate acts or a course of conduct that arises from that singleness of thought, purpose, or action that may be deemed a single impulse.

Brown v. Ohio

(*Convicted Car Thief*) v. (*Prosecuting State Government*)
432 U.S. 161, 97 S. Ct. 2221, 53 L. Ed. 2d 187 (1977)

DOUBLE JEOPARDY MAY BAR TRIAL FOR THE GREATER OFFENSE AFTER CONVICTION OF A LESSER–INCLUDED OFFENSE

Joyriding in the car I stole was the smartest thing I ever did!

stus.com

■ **INSTANT FACTS** Brown (D), who had pleaded guilty in one community to joyriding in a vehicle that he had stolen a few days earlier in another community, was subsequently prosecuted and convicted for auto theft in the community where he had stolen the car.

■ **BLACK LETTER RULE** A conviction of a lesser-included offense precludes a subsequent prosecution for the greater offense even though the two actions occurred several days apart.

■ PROCEDURAL BASIS

Certiorari to review the state appellate court's affirmance of the defendant's conviction for auto theft.

■ FACTS

Brown (D) stole a car in one community and several days later was charged with joyriding in another community. Brown (D) pleaded guilty to the charge, paid a fine, and served a thirty-day jail sentence. Upon his release, Brown (D) returned to the community where he stole the car and, despite his double-jeopardy objection, was convicted of auto theft. The appellate court found that under state law, joyriding was a lesser-included offense of auto theft. However, it affirmed the trial court decision because the time lapse between the theft of the car and when Brown (D) was picked up for joyriding was sufficient to establish that they were separate acts and therefore could be separately prosecuted.

■ ISSUE

Does a conviction for joyriding preclude a subsequent prosecution for auto theft if joyriding is a lesser-included offense of auto theft and the joyriding conviction occurred several days after the theft of the car?

■ DECISION AND RATIONALE

(Powell, J.) Yes. Under the state law, joyriding was a lesser-included offense of auto theft. As such, neither offense required proof of an additional fact that the other did not, and the only difference between the two offenses was whether there was an intent to permanently or temporarily deprive the owner of possession of the vehicle. The fact that that the two offenses occurred several days apart did not make them separate offenses because the Double Jeopardy Clause cannot be avoided by dividing a crime into a series of crimes based on the time of occurrence. Reversed.

■ CONCURRENCE

(Brennan, J.) All charges growing out of conduct that constitutes a single criminal act must be tried in a single proceeding. The appellate court's decision should be reversed because Brown was prosecuted in two separate proceedings.

■ **DISSENT**

(Blackmun, J.) The fact that several days elapsed between the time Brown (D) stole the car and when he was picked up for joyriding creates an issue of whether the two offenses were separate acts, and the state court could properly find that the acts were sufficiently distinctive to justify a second prosecution.

Analysis:

Brown reiterates the test in *Blockburger v. United States*, 284 U.S. 299, that when the same act or transaction constitutes a violation of two distinct statutory provisions, the necessary determination is whether each provision requires a proof of a fact that the other does not. Here, the elements overlapped, but that is not always the case with lesser-included offenses; the greater offense may include additional elements. *Brown* also points out that the passage of time is not enough to divide a single crime into a series of crimes that may be prosecuted separately.

■ **CASE VOCABULARY**

LESSER–INCLUDED OFFENSE: An offense composed of some, but not all, of the elements of the greater crime, and that does not have any element not included in the greater offense. A principal sometimes included in criminal statutes providing that an accused charged with one of the offenses enumerated in a criminal accusation cannot be convicted or sentenced for one of the less serious offenses that were necessarily included in the criminal activity.

Missouri v. Hunter

(Prosecuting State Government) v. *(Convicted Robber)*
459 U.S. 359, 103 S. Ct. 673, 74 L. Ed. 2d 535 (1983)

DEFENDANTS MAY BE SENTENCED IN A SINGLE TRIAL UNDER MULTIPLE STATUTES PROSCRIBING THE SAME CONDUCT

■ **INSTANT FACTS** Hunter (D) was convicted in a single trial of both armed criminal action and first-degree robbery and received a prison sentence on both charges.

■ **BLACK LETTER RULE** When a cumulative punishment is authorized under two state statutes, regardless of whether those two statutes proscribe the same conduct, a cumulative punishment may be imposed under the statutes in a single trial.

■ **PROCEDURAL BASIS**

Certiorari to review the appellate court's decision vacating the defendant's sentence.

■ **FACTS**

Hunter (D) was convicted in a single trial of both armed criminal action and the underlying felony offense, first-degree robbery. The state statute provided for prescribed punishments for both offenses. Hunter (D) subsequently received prison sentences on both charges. The state supreme court concluded that armed criminal action and the underlying offense were the same offense under the Double Jeopardy Clause and set aside Hunter's (D) conviction for armed criminal action.

■ **ISSUE**

When a cumulative punishment is authorized under two state statutes, regardless of whether those two statutes proscribe the same conduct, may a cumulative punishment be imposed under those statutes in a single trial?

■ **DECISION AND RATIONALE**

(Burger, J.) Yes. The state supreme court construed the two statutes under which Hunter (D) was charged, one proscribing armed criminal action and the other proscribing robbery in the first degree, as defining the same crime. It also, however, recognized that the state legislature intended that the punishment for violations of the statutes be cumulative. The Court is bound to accept the state supreme court's construction of the state's statutes, but not its legal conclusion that these two statutes violated the Double Jeopardy Clause. When the legislature makes its intent clear to specifically authorize cumulative punishments under two statutes, regardless of whether those statutes proscribe the same conduct, a court's task of statutory construction is at an end and cumulative punishment may be imposed under both statutes in a single trial. Vacated and remanded.

■ **DISSENT**

(Marshall, J.) Although a state has wide latitude to define crimes and to prescribe punishment, the Constitution does not permit a state to punish as two crimes conduct that constitutes only one offense within the meaning of the Double Jeopardy Clause.

Analysis:

Under *Hunter*, the Double Jeopardy Clause does not apply to protect a defendant from multiple punishments when the legislature specifically authorizes cumulative punishment under two criminal statutes that proscribe the same conduct. However, *Hunter* does not address whether the result would be the same in the event of multiple trials. As pointed out in the dissent, a concern with the ruling in *Hunter* is that if the Double Jeopardy Clause imposes no restrictions on a legislature's power to authorize multiple punishments, there may be no limit to the number of convictions a state could obtain on the basis of the same act, state of mind, and result.

■ CASE VOCABULARY

CONCURRENT SENTENCE: A sentence imposed that is to be served at the same time as another sentence imposed earlier or at the same proceeding.

CUMULATIVE SENTENCE: Separate sentences (each additional to the others) imposed upon a defendant who has been convicted on an indictment containing several counts, each of such counts charging a distinct offense, or who is under conviction at the same time for several distinct offenses.

SAME OFFENSE: For double-jeopardy purposes, the same criminal act, omission, or transaction for which the person has already stood trial. For sentencing and enhancement-of-punishment purposes, an offense that is quite similar to a previous one.

Fong Foo v. United States

(*Alleged Conspirators*) v. (*Prosecuting Government*)

369 U.S. 141, 82 S. Ct. 671, 7 L. Ed. 2d 629 (1962)

ENTRY OF JUDGMENT OF ACQUITTAL BARS RETRIAL

It's unfair! He always gets to appeal my guilty verdicts. Just once I should get to appeal his acquittal.

stus.com

■ **INSTANT FACTS** After a federal district court judge had, part way through the trial, directed the jury to return verdicts of acquittal as to all the defendants and then ordered a formal judgment of acquittal, the government filed a writ of mandamus in a federal court of appeals to vacate the judgment and reassign the case for trial.

■ **BLACK LETTER RULE** A judgment of acquittal, even if based on error, is a final judgment that cannot be appealed.

■ PROCEDURAL BASIS

Certiorari to review the court of appeals' decision to grant the government's petition for a writ of mandamus to vacate the judgment of acquittal and reassign the case for trial.

■ FACTS

During the course of a trial, a federal district court judge directed the jury to return verdicts of acquittal as to all the defendants and a formal judgment of acquittal was entered. According to the record, the basis for the judge's action was the supposed improper conduct on the part of the Assistant U.S. Attorney and/or the supposed lack of credibility in the testimony of the prosecution's witnesses. The prosecution filed a petition for a writ of mandamus to have the judgment vacated and the case reassigned for trial. The court of appeals granted the petition on the ground that, under the circumstances revealed by the record, the trial court was without power to direct the judgment of acquittal.

■ ISSUE

If a judgment of acquittal is based on an egregiously erroneous foundation, can the judgment be set aside?

■ DECISION AND RATIONALE

(Per curiam.) No. The defendants were tried under a valid indictment in a federal court that had jurisdiction over both them and the subject matter. The trial terminated with the entry of a final judgment of acquittal. Regardless of whether there was an egregiously erroneous basis for the judgment, the verdict of acquittal was final and could not be reviewed without putting the defendants in jeopardy twice. Reversed.

■ CONCURRENCE

(Harlan, J.) Unless the basis for the district court's decision to direct a judgment of acquittal was based solely on prosecutor misconduct, the Double Jeopardy Clause prevents a retrial of the defendants.

■ DISSENT

(Clark, J.) The District Court had no power to direct a judgment of acquittal without either hearing or canvassing the testimony presented by the government. Therefore, the judgment is based on a nullity.

Analysis:

In *Fong,* the Court essentially set out a bright line rule whereby under the double jeopardy rule, any judgment of acquittal is a bar to a new indictment. Both the concurring opinion and the dissenting opinion in *Fong* agreed that a retrial would not be prevented if the judgment of acquittal was based solely on the alleged misconduct of the prosecutor. Arguments have been made that an acquittal obtained by fraud should not bar a retrial, and the Appellate Court of Illinois has held that double jeopardy does not forbid a second trial when the judge was bribed to return an acquittal in the first trial.

■ CASE VOCABULARY

WRIT OF MANDAMUS: A writ that issues from a court of superior jurisdiction and is directed to an inferior court commanding the performance of a particular act. The writ of mandamus has been abolished under rules practice in favor of a complaint in the nature of mandamus, which accomplishes the same thing.

DOUBLE JEOPARDY: Common-law and constitutional (Fifth Amendment) prohibition against a second prosecution after a first trial for the same offense.

Ashe v. Swenson

(Convicted Armed Robber) v. *(Warden)*

397 U.S. 436, 90 S. Ct. 1189, 25 L. Ed. 2d 469 (1970)

THE STATE MAY BE COLLATERALLY ESTOPPED FROM RETRYING A DEFENDANT

■ **INSTANT FACTS** Ashe (D), who was found not guilty of armed robbery of a poker player at a poker game, was subsequently tried again for the armed robbery of another poker player at that same poker game and was found guilty.

■ **BLACK LETTER RULE** After a jury determines that a defendant had no involvement in the offense charged, the defendant cannot be retried for that offense.

■ PROCEDURAL BASIS

Certiorari to review the court of appeals' decision affirming the denial of the defendant's petition for a writ of habeas corpus.

■ FACTS

Ashe (D) was charged with separate offenses of armed robbery for each of six poker players at a poker game. Ashe (D) initially went to trial on the charge of robbing one of the players in the game. The jury found Ashe (D) not guilty. Ashe (D) was later brought to trial for the robbery of another player at the poker game. This time the jury found him guilty and sentenced him to prison. Ashe (D) appealed the judgment, claiming that after he had been found not guilty of robbing one of the players at the poker game, the double jeopardy rule prevented him from being tried for robbing another player at that same game. The federal court of appeals affirmed the state court decision.

■ ISSUE

After a jury has determined that a defendant was not guilty of the offense charged, can he be brought before a new jury to litigate the issue again?

■ DECISION AND RATIONALE

(Stewart, J.) No. Once a defendant has been determined by a jury to be not guilty of an offense charged, collateral estoppel applies to bar a retrial of the same issue involving the same parties. There was no indication in the record of the first trial that the jury found that an armed robbery did not occur at the poker game, or that the named victim in that trial was not robbed. Therefore, the issue before the jury in the first case was whether Ashe (D) was one of the robbers. Once the first jury had determined that he was not one of those robbers, Ashe (D) could not be brought to trial again in the robbery of another poker player at the same game, because the issue at the second trial—was Ashe (D) one of the robbers—was the same issue as that decided at the first trial. Reversed and remanded.

■ CONCURRENCE

(Harlan, J.) In *Benton v. Maryland*, 395 U.S. 784, the Court held that the Fourteenth Amendment imposes the Double Jeopardy Clause on the states. Ashe's (D) acquittal in the first trial thus brought double jeopardy standards into play.

■ DISSENT

(Burger, J.) Collateral estoppel is more appropriate in a civil proceeding because issues of finality and conservation of resources—the justifications for applying collateral estoppel to civil cases—are more important in a civil case than a criminal case. The application of the collateral estoppel rule to Ashe (D) expanded the rule beyond its rational and legitimate objectives

Analysis:

In *Ashe*, the Court established collateral estoppel as an element of the Fifth Amendment guarantee against double jeopardy, thereby expanding the scope of double jeopardy protection for a defendant. As a practical matter, this decision could discourage prosecutors from trying offenses separately with regard to each individual victim in hopes of honing their trial strategy.

■ CASE VOCABULARY

COLLATERAL ESTOPPEL: When an issue of ultimate fact has been determined by a valid judgment, the issue cannot be again litigated between the same parties in future litigation.

DOUBLE JEOPARDY: Common-law and constitutional (Fifth Amendment) prohibition against a second prosecution after a first trial for the same offense.

Downnum v. United States

(*Convicted Forger*) v. (*Prosecuting Government*)
372 U.S. 734, 83 S. Ct. 1033, 10 L. Ed. 2d 100 (1963)

ONCE THE JURY IS DISCHARGED, THE DEFENDANT USUALLY CANNOT BE RETRIED

■ **INSTANT FACTS** After the jury was discharged on the motion of the prosecutor because his key witness was not present, the case was retried before another jury and the defendant was found guilty.

■ **BLACK LETTER RULE** If an impaneled jury is discharged because the prosecution's witness is unavailable, double jeopardy applies to bar the impaneling of a second jury and a new trial.

■ **PROCEDURAL BASIS**

Certiorari to review the court of appeals' decision affirming the defendant's conviction.

■ **FACTS**

Downnum (D) was brought to trial and a jury was selected, sworn in, and asked to return at an appointed time. When the jury appeared at the appointed time, the prosecution asked that the jury be discharged because a key witness on two of the counts against Downnum (D) was not present. Downnum (D) moved to dismiss for want of prosecution and asked that trial continue on the other four counts. The motion was denied and the jury was discharged. The case was called again two days later, a second jury was impaneled, the trial proceeded, and Downnum (D) was found guilty of the offenses charged.

■ **ISSUE**

If an impaneled jury is discharged because the prosecution's witness is unavailable, does double jeopardy apply to bar the impaneling of a second jury and a new trial?

■ **DECISION AND RATIONALE**

(Douglas, J.) Yes. The prohibition of the Double Jeopardy Clause is not against being punished twice; it is against being put in jeopardy twice. Therefore, the decision to discharge a jury before it has reached a verdict should be exercised only in very extraordinary and striking circumstances. When a prosecutor impanels a jury without first ascertaining whether or not a key witness is, or will be, available, the situation is no different than proceeding into a trial with insufficient evidence. Allowing a prosecutor to discharge a jury and retry the case when he or she has more evidence clearly would subject the defendant to double jeopardy. Reversed.

■ **DISSENT**

(Clark, J.) The issue here is whether the action of the prosecutor in failing to check on the presence of his witness before allowing a jury to be sworn in deprived Downnum (D) of his rights and entitled him to a verdict of acquittal on the merits. The answer was no, because Downnum (D) was never formally arraigned in the presence of the jury, no evidence was presented or heard, and he was not required to put up any defense. In addition, because the second jury was impaneled two days later, Downnum (D) was not subject to any continued or prolonged anxiety, caused any additional expense or embarrassment, or prejudiced in any way.

Analysis:

Although this decision applied the double jeopardy rule when a selected and sworn jury was discharged on the motion of the prosecutor, it stopped short of saying that double jeopardy would apply in all circumstances in which a jury was discharged without the defendant's consent before it reached a verdict. The Court further noted instances (such as the inability of the jury to agree or jury bias) in which the discharge of the jury would be warranted and a new trial could be held without invoking double jeopardy.

■ CASE VOCABULARY

IMPANEL: The act of the clerk of the court in making up a list of the jurors who have been selected for the trial of a particular cause. All the steps of ascertaining who shall be the proper jurors to sit in the trial of a particular case up to the final formation.

DOUBLE JEOPARDY: Common-law and constitutional (Fifth Amendment) prohibition against a second prosecution after a first trial for the same offense.

Bartkus v. Illinois

(Convicted Robber) v. *(Prosecuting State Government)*

359 U.S. 121, 79 S. Ct. 676, 3 L. Ed. 2d 684 (1959)

ACQUITTAL IN FEDERAL COURT DOES NOT BAR TRIAL AND CONVICTION IN STATE COURT ON THE SAME CHARGES

Yes, they can make you jump through both hoops. Double Jeopardy loses to dual citizenship.

STATE CHARGES

FEDERAL CHARGES

stus.com

■ **INSTANT FACTS** After Bartkus (D) was tried in federal court for robbery and was acquitted, a state grand jury indicted him on the same charges and he was found guilty and sentenced to life in prison.

■ **BLACK LETTER RULE** Successive federal and state prosecutions do not violate the Fifth Amendment's Double Jeopardy Clause.

■ **PROCEDURAL BASIS**

Certiorari to review the state appellate court's decision affirming the defendant's state-court conviction.

■ **FACTS**

Bartkus (D) was tried in federal court for robbery and was acquitted of the charge. He was later indicted on substantially the same charges in a state court. Although the federal government turned over all of its evidence against Bartkus (D) to the state prosecutors, there was no evidence that the state prosecution was a sham and a cover for another federal prosecution. Bartkus (D) was found guilty and was sentenced to life in prison under the state's habitual criminal statute. The state court considered and rejected Bartkus's (D) plea of *autrefois acquit*.

■ **ISSUE**

Does the Fifth Amendment's Double Jeopardy Clause bar the prosecution of a defendant in a state court after the defendant has been acquitted of the same charges in federal court?

■ **DECISION AND RATIONALE**

(Frankfurter, J.) No. Every U.S. citizen is also a citizen of a state or territory. By virtue of this dual citizenship, an allegiance is owed to both the federal government and the state or territory. The dual citizenship also creates a liability for punishment for an infraction of the laws of either. There may be instances when the same act violates both a federal law and a state law. In these cases, the long-standing position of the Court has been that successive state and federal prosecutions are not in violation of the Double Jeopardy Clause. Affirmed.

■ **DISSENT**

(Black, J.) The holding of the Court weakens the constitutional guarantees against double prosecution. Bartkus's (D) acquittal in federal court would have barred a second trial in any court of the United States. Just because a second trial is held in state court does not change the fact that the defendant is put in jeopardy twice for the same conduct.

■ **DISSENT**

(Brennan, J.) The extent of participation of the federal authorities in the state prosecution of Bartkus (D) constituted a second federal prosecution of Bartkus.

Analysis:

The Court noted that a number of states have statutes that bar a second prosecution if the defendant has been tried by another government for the same offense. However, the Court also noted that the determination of when a federal and a state statute are so much alike that a prosecution under one bars prosecution of the other often depends on consideration of the nature of the state statute, as well as an understanding of the scope of the bar that has been historically raised to prevent successive state prosecutions. As such, the state is in a better position to determine when successive federal and state prosecutions violate the Double Jeopardy Clause.

■ CASE VOCABULARY

AUTREFOIS ACQUIT: Formerly acquitted. The name of a plea in bar to a criminal action, stating that the defendant has been once already indicted and tried for the same alleged offense and has been acquitted.

SOVEREIGNTY: The supreme, absolute, and uncontrollable power by which any independent state is governed; supreme political authority.

CHAPTER NINETEEN

Post-Trial Process: Correcting Erroneous Verdicts

Jackson v. Virginia

Instant Facts: Jackson (D), who was convicted of first-degree murder after a state court bench trial, appealed the conviction on the ground that there was insufficient evidence of premeditation.

Black Letter Rule: A review of the sufficiency of the evidence to support a criminal conviction requires a determination as to whether the record evidence could reasonably support a finding of guilt beyond a "reasonable doubt."

Arizona v. Fulminante

Instant Facts: Fulminante (D), while serving a prison sentence for a federal crime unrelated to the murder of his stepdaughter, admitted to a prison inmate, in exchange for protection, that he committed the murder.

Black Letter Rule: The harmless-error rule should be applied in cases involving the admission of a coerced confession.

Teague v. Lane

Instant Facts: Teague (D), who was African–American, was convicted by an all-white jury of attempted murder, armed robbery, and aggravated battery.

Black Letter Rule: Unless they fall within an exception to the general rule, new constitutional rules of criminal procedure will not be applicable to those cases that have become final before the new rules are announced.

Wainwright v. Sykes

Instant Facts: Sykes (D), during his trial for murder, did not object to inculpatory statements made by him to the police and he was found guilty of murder.

Black Letter Rule: Absent a showing of "cause" and "prejudice" attendant to a state procedural waiver, a federal habeas corpus review of a waived objection to the admission of a confession at trial is barred.

Smith v. Murray

Instant Facts: After failing to raise an issue as to the admissibility of a psychiatrist's testimony in a sentencing hearing, after which Smith (D) was sentenced to death, Smith's (D) attorney raised the admissibility issue for the first time in a habeas corpus petition.

Black Letter Rule: A habeas corpus petition should be dismissed if, in the absence of any "cause" or "prejudice," the underlying constitutional claim was not first raised in a state proceeding on direct appeal.

Jackson v. Virginia

(Convicted Murderer) v. *(Prosecuting State Government)*
443 U.S. 307, 99 S. Ct. 2781, 61 L. Ed. 2d 560 (1979)

THE SUFFICIENCY OF EVIDENCE IS ANALYZED BASED ON THE REASONABLE–DOUBT STANDARD

■ **INSTANT FACTS** Jackson (D), who was convicted of first-degree murder after a state court bench trial, appealed the conviction on the ground that there was insufficient evidence of premeditation.

■ **BLACK LETTER RULE** A review of the sufficiency of the evidence to support a criminal conviction requires a determination as to whether the record evidence could reasonably support a finding of guilt beyond a "reasonable doubt."

■ PROCEDURAL BASIS

Certiorari to review the court of appeals' decision reversing the trial court's grant of the defendant's petition for a writ of habeas corpus.

■ FACTS

Jackson (D) was convicted of first-degree murder after a bench trial in state court. The judge applied the "reasonable doubt" standard in his appraisal of the state's evidence with respect to establishing premeditation. In a habeas corpus proceeding, the federal district court, based on its application of the "no evidence" standard, found no evidence of premeditation on the trial court record. Applying the same "no evidence" standard, the federal court of appeals found that there was some evidence of premeditation on the record and reversed the district court's decision.

■ ISSUE

Is the "no evidence" standard the proper standard to be applied in a federal habeas corpus proceeding when the claim is made that a person has been convicted in a state court upon insufficient evidence?

■ DECISION AND RATIONALE

(Stewart, J.) No. The federal courts of appeals have generally assumed that, so long as the "reasonable doubt" instruction is given at trial, the "no-evidence" doctrine of *Thompson v. Louisville*, 362 U.S. 199, remains the appropriate guide for assessing a conviction on the ground of insufficient evidence. However, the right to be proven guilty beyond a reasonable doubt, articulated in *In re Winship*, 397 U.S. 358, requires application of that standard when reviewing whether there was sufficient evidence for the conviction. Even when a jury is properly instructed as to the application of the reasonable doubt standard, it might still convict the defendant when a rational trier of fact would not find guilt beyond a reasonable doubt. The same may be said of a trial judge presiding over a bench trial. Therefore, the reviewing court has the responsibility to review the record evidence to determine whether it could reasonably support a finding of guilty. The inquiry does not require the court to determine whether it believes the evidence establishes guilt beyond a reasonable doubt, but whether, in a light most favorable to the prosecution, any rational trier of fact could have found the essential elements of the crime beyond a reasonable doubt. Applying the reasonable doubt standard here, there was sufficient evidence of premeditation to support Jackson's (D) conviction for first-degree murder. Affirmed.

■ **CONCURRENCE**

(Stevens, J.) Although the "reasonable doubt" standard has the desirable effect of significantly reducing the risk of an inaccurate factfinding and erroneous conviction, there is no appreciable risk when the facTFBinding has been originally made under the reasonable doubt standard, reviewed at the trial court level, and reviewed at the appellate court level under the "no evidence" standard. The presumption should be that trial judges and juries will rationally and honestly apply the reasonable doubt standard, so long as the trial is free of procedural error and the record contains evidence tending to prove each of the elements of the offense.

Analysis:

Jackson determined that the "no evidence" rule was inadequate to protect against the misapplication of the "reasonable doubt" standard because only some evidence was required to meet that standard. The concern is that, if a reviewing judge is required to apply the reasonable doubt standard, the judge will become the factfinder because he or she would be required to determine whether the evidence at trial established guilt beyond a reasonable doubt.

■ **CASE VOCABULARY**

REASONABLE DOUBT: Reasonable doubt that will justify acquittal is doubt based on reason and arising from evidence or lack of evidence, and it is doubt that a reasonable man or woman might entertain.

HABEAS CORPUS: The name given to a variety of writs having as their objective bringing a party before a judge. Initially, the writ only permitted a prisoner to challenge a state conviction on constitutional grounds that related to jurisdiction of the state court, but the scope of inquiry has gradually expanded and the writ now extends to all constitutional challenges.

NO EVIDENCE: Under the rule that the court may render judgment non obstante if a directed verdict would have been proper, the term "no evidence" does not mean literally no evidence at all; "no evidence" comprehends those situations wherein by the application of established principals of law the evidence is deemed legally insufficient to establish an asserted proposition of fact.

Arizona v. Fulminante

(Prosecuting State Government) v. *(Convicted Murderer)*

499 U.S. 279, 111 S. Ct. 1246, 113 L. Ed. 2d 302 (1991)

A CONVICTION BASED ON A COERCED CONFESSION MAY WARRANT RE-TRIAL

I'd like to argue that admission of a coerced confession is mere "harmless error".

You're welcome to try.

stus.com

■ **INSTANT FACTS** Fulminante (D), while serving a prison sentence for a federal crime unrelated to the murder of his stepdaughter, admitted to a prison inmate, in exchange for protection, that he committed the murder.

■ **BLACK LETTER RULE** The harmless-error rule should be applied in cases involving the admission of a coerced confession.

■ **PROCEDURAL BASIS**

Certiorari to review the state appellate court's reversal of the defendant's murder conviction.

■ **FACTS**

After Fulminante's (D) stepdaughter was murdered, he left the state and was later convicted of a federal crime unrelated to his stepdaughter's murder. While he was in prison, Fulminante (D) began receiving tough treatment because of rumors that had circulated that he was a child murderer. In exchange for protection, he confessed to the murder to a fellow inmate who was a paid informant for the FBI masquerading as an organized crime figure. After Fulminante (D) was released from prison, he confessed again to the inmate/informant's wife, whom he had never met before. Fulminante (D) was subsequently indicted on a charge of first-degree murder in Arizona. The trial court denied his motion to suppress the confession on the ground that it was coerced. Fulminante (D) was found guilty of the murder and sentenced to death. The state supreme court determined that the confession was coerced and that U.S. Supreme Court precedent precluded the use of a harmless-error analysis. The case was remanded for a trial without the use of the coerced confession. The state appealed.

■ **ISSUE**

Should the harmless-error analysis be applied in cases involving the admission of a coerced confession?

■ **DECISION AND RATIONALE**

(White, J.) Yes. The harmless-error rule of *Chapman v. California*, 386 U.S. 18 (before an error can be held harmless, the court must be able to declare a belief that it was harmless beyond a reasonable doubt) has been applied to "trial errors" (errors that occurred during the presentation of the case to the jury), and there is no reason not to extend the rule to involuntary or coerced confessions. Applying the harmless error rule to the record here, the state failed to meet is burden of establishing, beyond a reasonable doubt, that the admission of Fulminante's (D) confession to the informant was harmless because (1) the transcript disclosed that both the state and the trial court recognized that a successful prosecution depended on believing that confession and the confession to the inmate/informant's wife; (2) the jury's assessment of the confession to the inmate/informant's wife could have rested in large part on the existence of the confession to the inmate/informant; and (3) the admission of the confession to the inmate/informant led to the admission of other evidence prejudicial to Fulminante (D). Affirmed.

■ CONCURRENCE

(Kennedy, J.) The harmless-error rule should apply in the case of a coerced confession. However, a court conducting a "harmless-error" inquiry must appreciate the indelible impact a confession may have on the trier of fact and the possibility that, unlike with an isolated statement that incriminates the defendant only when connected with other evidence, the trier of fact may rest its decision solely on the basis of that confession.

■ DISSENT

(Rehnquist, J.) The state supreme court decision should be affirmed but on the ground that the harmless-error rule is inapplicable to erroneously admitted coerced confessions. The harmless-error rule should not be applied to coerced confessions because a coerced confession is fundamentally different from other types of erroneously admitted evidence to which the rule has applied. A defendant's confession is probably the most probative and damaging evidence that can be admitted against him. It is so damaging because a jury should not be expected to ignore it even if told to do so, and because it is impossible to know what weight or credit the jury gave to the confession. The consistent line of authority has recognized that a basic tenet of the criminal justice system is the prohibition against using a defendant's coerced statement against him at a criminal trial.

Analysis:

Fulminante illustrates the disagreement in the Court regarding the admission of a coerced confession. From the majority perspective, *Fulminate* created an opportunity to make coerced confessions subject to the harmless-error test. The dissent, on the other hand, saw the majority opinion as an unwarranted departure from *Chapman,* which specifically noted that the use of a coerced confession against a defendant in a criminal trial could not be categorized as harmless error.

■ CASE VOCABULARY

HARMLESS ERROR: An error that is trivial or formal or merely academic and was not prejudicial to the substantive rights of the party assigning it, and in no way affected the final outcome of the case. Harmless error is not a ground for granting a new trial or for setting aside a verdict or for vacating, modifying, or otherwise disturbing a judgment or order, unless such refusal appears to the court inconsistent with substantial justice.

COERCED: Compelled to compliance.

STARE DECISIS: Doctrine that, when a court has once laid down a principal of law as applicable to a certain state of facts, it will adhere to that principle, and apply it to all future cases, where the facts are substantially the same, regardless of whether the parties and the property are the same.

Teague v. Lane

(Convicted Armed Robber) v. *(Prison Warden)*

489 U.S. 288, 109 S. Ct. 1060, 103 L. Ed. 2d 334 (1989)

PROCEDURAL RULES USUALLY DO NOT APPLY RETROACTIVELY

These new constitutional rules won't help us, but think how much harder it will be to convict our kids!

stus.com

■ **INSTANT FACTS** Teague (D), who was African–American, was convicted by an all-white jury of attempted murder, armed robbery, and aggravated battery.

■ **BLACK LETTER RULE** Unless they fall within an exception to the general rule, new constitutional rules of criminal procedure will not be applicable to those cases that have become final before the new rules are announced.

■ PROCEDURAL BASIS

Certiorari to review the court of appeals' decision affirming the federal district court's denial of the defendant's petition for a writ of habeas corpus.

■ FACTS

Teague (D), who was African–American, was convicted by an all-white jury of attempted murder, armed robbery, and aggravated battery. During jury selection, the prosecutor used all ten of his peremptory challenges to exclude African–Americans. After losing his state appeals, Teague (D) filed a habeas corpus petition in federal district court alleging that the prosecutor's use of peremptory challenges denied him the right to be tried by a jury that was representative of his community. After the district court denied relief, a U.S. court of appeals agreed to hear the case after the Court's decision in *Batson v. Kentucky*, 476 U.S. 79, which held that a defendant could make out a prima facie case of discrimination by meeting a three-part test. The court of appeals subsequently held that Teague (D) could not benefit from *Batson* because of the U.S. Supreme Court's decision in *Allen v. Hardy*, 478 U.S. 255, held that *Batson* could not be applied retroactively to cases on collateral review. Teague (D) petitioned the U.S. Supreme Court that the fair cross section requirement in *Taylor v. Louisiana*, 419 U.S. 522, should apply to a petit jury, as well as a jury venire.

■ ISSUE

Should new constitutional rules of criminal procedure be applied in cases that have become final before the new rules are announced?

■ DECISION AND RATIONALE

(O'Connor, J.) No. A new rule should not be applied retroactively to cases on collateral review because it affects the finality of a judgment. However, there are two exceptions where a new constitutional rule of criminal procedure will become applicable to cases that have become final before the new rules are announced: (1) if the rule provides constitutional protection to any primary, private individual conduct; and (2) if the rule requires the observance of those procedures that are implicit in the concept of liberty. Since Teague's (D) conviction had occurred several years earlier, and his case was up on collateral review, the rule urged by Teague (D), that the fair cross section requirement be extended to petit juries, would not apply to Teague (D) unless his case fell within an exception. The new rule urged by Teague (D) did not fall within the first exception, because the application of the fair cross section requirement would not accord constitutional protection to any primary activity. The second exception also did not apply, because the absence of a fair cross section does not undermine the fundamental fairness that must underlie a conviction or seriously diminish the likelihood of obtaining an accurate conviction. If the new rule were applied to Teague (D), there would be an inequitable result because the rule would not be applied retroactively to others similarly situated.

■ DISSENT

(Brennan, J.) The Court's exaggerated concern for treating similarly situated petitioners the same precludes the federal courts from considering on collateral review a vast range of important constitutional challenges. Sometimes a claim that, if successful, would create a new rule not appropriate for collateral review is better presented by a habeas case than by one on direct review. In any case, permitting federal courts to decide novel habeas claims not substantially related to guilt or innocence profits society.

Analysis:

The retroactivity approach that the Court adopted led to a holding that habeas corpus cannot be used as a vehicle to create new constitutional rules of criminal procedures unless those rules would be applied retroactively to all defendants on collateral review through one of two exceptions. The concern with this position is that the two exceptions are narrowly drawn and, as a result, opportunities for development of the rules of criminal procedure will be limited.

■ CASE VOCABULARY

PEREMPTORY CHALLENGE: The right to challenge a juror without assigning a reason for the challenge.

HABEAS CORPUS: The name given to a variety of writs having as their objective bringing a party before a judge. Initially, the writ only permitted a prisoner to challenge a state conviction on constitutional grounds that related to jurisdiction of the state court, but the scope of inquiry has gradually expanded and the writ now extends to all constitutional challenges.

COLLATERAL: Related to; complimentary.

VENIRE: Sometimes used as the name of the writ for summoning a jury, more commonly called a "*venire facias.*" The list of jurors summoned to serve as jurors for a particular term.

PETIT JURY: The ordinary jury for the trial of civil or criminal action; so called to distinguish it from the grand jury.

RATIO DECIDENDI: The ground or reason of a decision. The point in a case that determines the judgment.

Wainwright v. Sykes

(*Prison Warden*) v. (*Convicted Murderer*)

433 U.S. 72, 97 S. Ct. 2497, 53 L. Ed. 2d 594 (1977)

THE FAILURE TO COMPLY WITH THE CONTEMPORANEOUS–OBJECTION RULE FORECLOSED FEDERAL HABEAS CORPUS REVIEW

■ **INSTANT FACTS** Sykes (D), during his trial for murder, did not object to inculpatory statements made by him to the police and he was found guilty of murder.

■ **BLACK LETTER RULE** Absent a showing of "cause" and "prejudice" attendant to a state procedural waiver, a federal habeas corpus review of a waived objection to the admission of a confession at trial is barred.

■ PROCEDURAL BASIS

Certiorari to review the federal court of appeals' affirmance of the district court's decision ordering a hearing in state court on the voluntariness of the defendant's statement, which had been admitted without objection.

■ FACTS

Sykes (D) was tried for murder. During the trial, statements made by Sykes (D) to the police admitting to the murder were admitted into evidence. At no time during the trial did Sykes (D) question the admissibility of the inculpatory statements. Sykes (D) appealed the conviction but did not challenge the admissibility of the inculpatory statements. Sykes (D) later filed habeas corpus petitions in both the state courts of appeal and the state supreme court to vacate the conviction on the ground that the inculpatory statements were involuntarily made. After these challenges were unsuccessful, Sykes (D) filed a habeas corpus petition in U.S. district court, asserting the inadmissibility of the statements by reason of his lack of understanding of the *Miranda* warnings. The district court determined that Sykes (D) had a right to a hearing on the voluntariness of the statements. The court of appeals affirmed and the warden appealed.

■ ISSUE

Absent a showing of "cause" and "prejudice" attendant to a state procedural waiver, is a federal habeas corpus review of a waived objection to the admission of a confession at trial barred?

■ DECISION AND RATIONALE

(Rehnquist, J.) Yes. A federal habeas corpus review of a waived objection to the admission of a confession at trial is barred, absent a showing of "cause" and "prejudice," because a contemporaneous objection (1) enables the record to be made with respect to the constitutional claim when the recollections of the witnesses are the freshest; (2) enables the judge, who observed the demeanor of the witnesses, to make the factual determinations necessary for properly deciding the federal constitutional question; and (3) may lead to the exclusion of the evidence objected to, thereby making a major contribution to the finality of the litigation. On the other hand, allowing a review could encourage defense attorneys to hold back constitutional claims during the initial trial with the intent to raise those claims in a federal habeas court if they are not successful at the trial court level. Reversed and remanded.

■ DISSENT

(Brennan, J.) Any realistic system of federal habeas corpus jurisdiction must be premised on the reality that the ordinary procedural default is born of the inadvertence, negligence, inexperience, or incompetence of the trial counsel. Punishing a lawyer's unintentional errors by closing the federal courthouse door to his client is both senseless and a misdirected method of deterring the slighting of state rules.

Analysis:

The Court noted the well established principal of federalism that a state decision resting on an adequate foundation of state substantive law is immune from review in federal court, while the adequacy of an independent state procedural ground is not entitled to the same deference. However, the decision in *Sykes* points out the severity of the consequences if a procedural default cannot be shown to be the result of "cause" and "prejudice."

■ CASE VOCABULARY

HABEAS CORPUS: The name given to a variety of writs having as their objective bringing a party before a judge. Initially, the writ only permitted a prisoner to challenge a state conviction on constitutional grounds that related to jurisdiction of the state court, but the scope of inquiry has gradually expanded and the writ now extends to all constitutional challenges.

INCULPATORY: In the law of evidence, going or tending to establish guilt; intended to establish guilt.

CORAM NOBIS: In our presence; before us. The office of "writ of *coram nobis*" is to bring attention of the court to, and obtain relief from, errors of fact either through duress or fraud or excusable mistake, where facts did not appear on the face of the record, and were such known, would have prevented rendition of the judgment questioned. The essence of *coram nobis* is that it is addressed to the very court that renders the injustice that is alleged to have been done. Abolished and superceded by Fed. R. Civ. P. 60(b).

Smith v. Murray

(*Convicted Murderer*) v. (*Prison Warden*)

477 U.S. 527, 106 S. Ct. 2661, 91 L. Ed. 2d 434 (1986)

CLAIMS SHOULD BE MADE ON APPEAL AND NOT RAISED FOR THE FIRST TIME IN A HABEAS CORPUS HEARING

■ **INSTANT FACTS** After failing to raise an issue as to the admissibility of a psychiatrist's testimony in a sentencing hearing, after which Smith (D) was sentenced to death, Smith's (D) attorney raised the admissibility issue for the first time in a habeas corpus petition.

■ **BLACK LETTER RULE** A habeas corpus petition should be dismissed if, in the absence of any "cause" or "prejudice," the underlying constitutional claim was not first raised in a state proceeding on direct appeal.

■ **PROCEDURAL BASIS**

Certiorari to review the court of appeals' decision affirming the denial of habeas corpus relief.

■ **FACTS**

Smith (D) was sentenced to death after a psychiatrist who had examined him at the time of the trial testified as to Smith's admission of an earlier incident of sexual assault. Smith's (D) attorney objected to the testimony but made a conscious decision not to raise the issue when he filed his brief raising several other separate claims. Smith's (D) conviction was confirmed. Smith's (D) attorney later sought a writ of habeas corpus in state court and, at that time, raised the issue of the admissibility of the psychiatrist's testimony. The petition was denied and a writ of habeas corpus was then sought in U.S. District Court. The District Court denied the petition and the court of appeals affirmed.

■ **ISSUE**

Should a habeas corpus petition be dismissed when the underlying constitutional claim was not first raised in a state proceeding on direct appeal?

■ **DECISION AND RATIONALE**

(O'Connor, J.) Yes. A habeas corpus petition should be dismissed if the underlying constitutional claim was not first raised in a direct appeal in state court unless there is "cause" for the failure to do so or "prejudice" as a result. In the case of *Smith*, neither is present. Smith's (D) attorney was aware of the issue (he had raised the objection to the admission of the psychiatrist's testimony at trial but made a conscious decision not to purse the objection on appeal). Smith claimed that the default should be excused because his attorney's decision, although deliberately made, was made in ignorance. However, the mere fact that an attorney fails to recognize the factual or legal basis for a claim, or fails to raise the claim despite recognizing it, does not constitute procedural default. Furthermore, there was no evidence that the failure to make the claim on appeal was an error of such magnitude that it rendered Smith's (D) attorney's performance deficient. Affirmed.

■ DISSENT

(Stevens, J.) To the extent there has been a procedural default, it is exceedingly minor because Smith's (D) counsel raised a timely objection to the admissibility of the psychiatrist's testimony. Furthermore, the issue was raised in both the state and federal habeas corpus proceedings and the Court of Appeals decided the case on the merits. Finally, it should not be surprising that the issue was not raised in an original appeal to the state supreme court because of the well-established principle that appellate arguments should be carefully winnowed, and state supreme court precedent at that time would have decisively barred that claim.

Analysis:

The Court noted that a federal habeas corpus writ may be granted, even in the absence of showing cause for the procedural default, if the constitutional violation has probably resulted in the conviction of an innocent person. To determine whether such injustice has occurred, the record should be reviewed to determine, by application of the "cause" and "prejudice" test, whether a "fundamental miscarriage of justice" has occurred.

■ CASE VOCABULARY

HABEAS CORPUS: The name given to a variety of writs having as their objective bringing a party before a judge. Initially, the writ only permitted a prisoner to challenge a state conviction on constitutional grounds that related to jurisdiction of the state court, but the scope of inquiry has gradually expanded and the writ now extends to all constitutional challenges.

AMICUS CURIAE: A person with strong interest or views on the subject matter of an action may petition the court for permission to file a brief, ostensibly on behalf of a party but actually to suggest a rationale consistent with its own views.